LITTLE,
BROWN

LB

LARGE
PRINT

ALSO BY ALAN WEISMAN

The World Without Us

An Echo in My Blood

Gaviotas: A Village to Reinvent the World

La Frontera: The United States Border with Mexico

PHOTOGRAPH BY ROBERTO NEUMILLER

COUNTDOWN

OUR LAST, BEST HOPE FOR A FUTURE ON EARTH?

ALAN WEISMAN

Ⓛ Ⓑ

LITTLE, BROWN AND COMPANY

LARGE PRINT EDITION

Little, Brown and Company
Hachette Book Group
237 Park Avenue, New York, NY 10017
littlebrown.com

First Edition: September 2013

Little, Brown and Company is a division of Hachette Book Group, Inc.
The Little, Brown name and logo are trademarks of Hachette Book Group, Inc.

The publisher is not responsible for websites (or their content) that are not owned by the publisher.

Unless otherwise noted, all photographs are by the author.

Library of Congress Cataloging-in-Publication Data
Weisman, Alan.
    Countdown : our last, best hope for a future on earth? / Alan Weisman.
      pages cm
    Summary: A powerful investigation into the chances for humanity's future.
    ISBN 978-0-316-09775-8 (hc) / 978-0-316-23981-3 (large print) /
978-0-316-27743-3 (int'l)
    1. Nature—Effect of human beings on.   2. Overpopulation.
3. Population ecology.   I. Title.
    GF75.W454 2013
    304.2—dc23   2013017113

10 9 8 7 6 5 4 3 2 1

RRD-C

Printed in the United States of America

for Beckie,
for seeing it through.

Contents

CONTENTS

This calls for wisdom. If anyone has insight,
let him calculate the number of the beast,
for it is man's number.

— REVELATION 13:18
NEW TESTAMENT,
NEW INTERNATIONAL VERSION

When wisdom dictates that you do not need more
children, a vasectomy is permissible.

— THE AYATOLLAH ALI KHAMENEI,
CA. 1989

Author's Note

Many readers may recall my last book, *The World Without Us,* as a thought experiment that imagined what would happen if people vanished from our planet.

The idea of theoretically wiping us off the face of the Earth was to show that, despite colossal damage we've wreaked, nature has remarkable resilience and healing powers. When relieved of the pressures we humans daily heap upon it, restoration and renewal commence with surprising swiftness. Eventually, even new plants, creatures, fungi, et al., evolve to fill empty niches.

My hope was that readers, seduced by the gorgeous prospect of a refreshed, healthy Earth, might then ask themselves how we could add *Homo sapiens* back into the picture—only in harmony, not mortal combat, with the rest of Earthly life.

In other words, how might we continue to have a world *with* us?

Welcome to another thought experiment, on exactly that subject. Only this time, there's no imagining: the scenarios here are real. And in addition to the people I describe, locals and informed experts, there's everyone else—including you and me. As it turns out, we're all part of the response to what basically came down to four questions I went around the world asking—questions that several of the aforementioned experts called the most important on Earth.

"But probably," one of them added, "they're impossible to answer."

When he made that remark, we were lunching at one of the world's oldest, most hallowed institutions of higher learning, where he was distinguished faculty. In that moment, I was glad not to be an expert. Journalists rarely claim depth in any field: our job is to seek people who dedicate their careers to study—or who actually live—whatever it is we're investigating, and to ask them enough common-sense questions so the rest of us might understand.

If such questions are arguably the most important in the world, whether or not the experts deem their answers impossible is irrelevant: we'd damned well better find them. Or keep asking until we do.

So I did, in more than twenty countries over two years. Now, you get to ask them for yourselves, as you follow my travels and inquiry.

If by the end you think that we're onto the answers—well, I'm pretty sure you'll figure out what we ought to do next.

A.W.

PART ONE

CHAPTER 1

A Weary Land of Four Questions

i. Battle of the Babies

A cold January afternoon in Jerusalem, late Friday before the Jewish Sabbath. The winter sun, nearing the horizon, turns the gilded Dome of the Rock atop the Temple Mount to blood-orange. From the east, where the muezzin's afternoon call to Muslim prayer has just ended on the Mount of Olives, the golden Dome is suffused in a smudged pinkish corona of dust and traffic fumes.

At this hour, the Temple Mount itself, the holiest site in Judaism, is one of the quieter spots in this ancient city, empty but for a few scholars in overcoats, hurrying with their books across a chilly, cypress-shaded plaza. Once, King Solomon's original tabernacle stood here. It held the Ark of the

Covenant, containing stone tablets on which Moses was believed to have incised the Ten Commandments. In 586 BCE, invading Babylonians destroyed it all and took the Jewish people captive. A half-century later, Cyrus the Great, emperor of Persia, liberated them to return and rebuild their temple.

Around 19 CE, the Temple Mount was renovated and fortified with a surrounding wall by King Herod, only to be demolished again by the Romans within ninety years. Although exile from the Holy Land occurred both before and after, this Roman destruction of Jerusalem's Second Temple most famously symbolizes the Diaspora that scattered Jews across Europe, northern Africa, and the Middle East.

Today, a remaining fragment of the Second Temple's sixty-foot-high perimeter in Jerusalem's Old City, known as the Western (or "Wailing") Wall, is an obligatory pilgrimage for Jews visiting Israel. Yet, lest they inadvertently tread where the Holy of Holies once stood, an official rabbinical decree prohibits Jews from ascending to the Temple Mount itself. Although it is at times defied, and exceptions can be arranged, this explains why the Temple Mount is administered by Muslims, who also hold it sacred. From here, the Prophet Muhammad is said to have journeyed one night upon a winged steed all the way to Seventh Heaven and back. Only Mecca and Medina, Muhammad's birthplace and burial site, are considered holier. In a rare agreement between Israel and Islam, Muslims alone may pray on this hallowed ground, which they call al-Haram al-Sharif.

But not as many Muslims come here as they once did. Before September 2000, they flocked by the thousands, lining up at a fountain ringed by stone benches to perform purification ablutions before entering the crimson-carpeted, marbled al-Aqsa Mosque across the plaza from the Dome of the Rock. Especially, they came on Friday at noon for the imam's weekly sermon, a discourse on current events as well as the Qur'an.

One frequent topic back then, recalls Khalil Toufakji, people jokingly called "Yasser Arafat's biology bomb." Except it was no joke. As Toufakji, today a Palestinian demographer with Jerusalem's Arab Studies Society, remembers: "We were taught in the mosque, in school, and at home to have lots of children, for lots of reasons. In America or Europe, if there's a problem, you can call the police. In a place with no laws to safeguard you, you rely on your family."

He sighs, stroking his neat gray moustache; his own father was a policeman. "Here, you need a big family to feel protected." It's even worse in Gaza, he adds. One Hamas leader there had fourteen children and four wives. "Our mentality goes back to the Bedouins. If you have a big enough tribe, everyone's afraid of you."

Another reason for the large families, Toufakji agrees, is definitely no joke to Israelis. The Palestine Liberation Organization's best weapon, its leader Arafat liked to say, was the Palestinian womb.

During Ramadan, Toufakji and some of his own thirteen siblings would be among the half-million worshippers overflowing al-Aqsa Mosque, spilling onto al-Haram al-Sharif's stone plaza. That was before the day in September 2000 when former Israeli defense minister Ariel Sharon paid a visit to the Temple Mount, escorted by a thousand Israeli riot police. At the time, Sharon was a candidate for prime minister. He had once been found willfully negligent by an Israeli commission for not protecting more than a thousand Palestinian civilian refugees massacred by Christian Phalangists during Lebanon's 1982 civil war, while his occupying Israeli forces stood by. Sharon's trip to the Temple Mount, intended to assert Israelis' historical right to it, ignited demonstrations and rock throwing, which were met by tear gas and rubber bullets. When stones from the Temple Mount were hurled at Jews worshipping at the Western Wall below, the ammunition turned live.

The mayhem soon spiraled into hundreds of deaths

in Jerusalem and beyond, in what became known as the Second Intifada. Eventually came suicide bombings—and then, especially after Sharon was elected prime minister, years of mutual retaliation for shootings, massacres, rocket attacks, and more suicide bombs, until Israel began walling itself in.

A barrier of towering concrete and wire more than two hundred kilometers long now nearly encircles the West Bank—except for where it thrusts deeply across the Green Line that delineates captured territories Israel has occupied since the 1967 Six-Day War with its surrounding Arab adversaries. In places it zigzags through cities like Bethlehem and Greater Jerusalem, curling back on itself to isolate individual neighborhoods, cutting Palestinians off not just from Israel but from each other and from their fields and orchards, and prompting charges that its purpose is to annex territory and seize wells as much as to guarantee security.

It also stops most Palestinians from reaching the al-Aqsa Mosque, except if they live in Israel or the parts of East Jerusalem within the security barrier. Yet of those, often only Palestinian men over age forty-five are allowed by Israeli police past the metal detectors at Temple Mount gates. Officially, this is to forestall any Arab youths tempted again to stone worshipping Jews—especially foreign Jewish tourists, as they tuck written prayers into crevices between the Western Wall's massive blocks of pale limestone rising above the adjacent plaza.

That custom is particularly popular as Sabbath begins, but in recent years, getting anywhere near the Western Wall on Friday at sundown has become a challenge even for Jews. Unless you're a *haredi,* and a male.

The Hebrew word *haredi* means, literally, "fear and trembling." In today's Israel, it refers to ultra-Orthodox Jews, whose dour dress and fervid quaking before God hearken to bygone centuries and distant lands where their ancestors lived during two millennia of Diaspora. To the alarm of non-*haredi* Jews, the Western Wall has been effectively usurped and converted into a *haredi* synagogue. On *Shabbat,* tens of thousands of bowing, trembling, rejoicing, chanting, praising, praying black-frocked men in broad-rimmed hats and ritual fringes engulf it, save for a small fenced section reserved for women — that is, for women who dare approach it. Females who insist on a Jewish woman's right to don prayer shawls and phylacteries — or the ultimate *haredi* horror: to actually touch and read from a Torah scroll — may be spat upon by *haredi* men, who have flung chairs at the brazen blasphemers, and be called whores by screaming rabbis who try to drown out their Sabbath songs.

Women, extremist *haredim* believe, should be home

readying the *Shabbat* meal for their pious men and their burgeoning families. Although still a minority, Israel's *haredim* are relentlessly bent on changing that status. Their simple tactic: procreation. *Haredi* families average nearly seven children, and frequently hit double digits. Their multiplying offspring are considered both the solution to modern Jews, who defile their religion, and as the best defense against Palestinians, who threaten to outproliferate Jews in their historic homeland.

The Jerusalem daily *Haaretz* reports a *haredi* man who boasts 450 descendents. Their soaring numbers force Israeli politicians to include *haredi* parties in coalitions that rule Israeli governments. Such clout has won the ultra-Orthodox privileges that elicit howls from other Israelis: exemption from military service (supposedly, they defend Judaism by incessant study of Torah) and a government allowance for each Israeli child brought into the world. Until 2009, this subsidy actually rose for each new birth, until the cost of the escalating demographics shocked even conservative Prime Minister Benyamin Netanyahu, who modified it to a flat rate. Any dampening effect on *haredi* reproduction is not yet evident at the Western Wall, where thousands of young boys with black yarmulkes and bouncing sidelocks swirl around their dancing, bearded fathers.

COUNTDOWN

A waxing moon, yellow as Jerusalem limestone, climbs high above the walled Old City, and *haredim* begin to stream homeward—on foot; no motorized conveyance allowed on *Shabbat*—to their pregnant wives and their daughters. Most head into Mea She'arim, one of Jerusalem's biggest neighborhoods, which is visibly deteriorating under the pressure of so many people. Torah scholarship pays little or nothing; *haredi* wives mostly work at whatever jobs they can sandwich between child-rearing, and more than one-third of the families are below the poverty line. Vestibules and staircases of shabby high-rises are jammed with baby strollers. The air whiffs of overflowing garbage, overstressed sewers, and—surprising for a place where no vehicles can circulate on *Shabbat*—diesel exhaust. Because many *haredim* insist that the Israel Electric Corporation's nonstop coal-fired plants commit a sacrilege by working through Sabbath, before sundown they crank up hundreds of portable generators in Mea She'arim basements to keep the lights on. The traditional *z'mirot* heard around Sabbath tables are sung over their dull roar.

Four kilometers north of Mea She'arim, the land rises into limestone ridges. A hill just across the Green Line, Ramat Shlomo, is the site of an ancient quarry

that provided the nearly thirty-foot foundation slabs
Herod used to build the Second Temple's wall. In
1970, not long after the area was captured, Israel
planted a forest there. Unlike the early Jewish National
Fund forests — regimental rows of Australian eucalyptus or monocultured Aleppo pines, financed with
coins saved by Jewish children worldwide in blue JNF
collection tins — this was a mixed woodland that
included some native oaks, conifers, and terebinths.
The young forest was declared a nature preserve, a
designation that Palestinians protested, claiming the
real intention was to prevent a nearby Arab village,
Shuafat, from growing. Their suspicion was confirmed
when, in 1990, the forest was bulldozed to make way
for a new *haredi* Jerusalem neighborhood — or new
West Bank settlement, depending on who's describing it.

"Shaved the whole hill," admits Ramat Shlomo
settler and Hasidic rabbi Dudi Zilbershlag. A founder
of *Haredim* for the Environment, a nonprofit organization whose name also translates as *Fear for the
Environment,* he regrets that. "But then," he adds,
brightening, "we replanted."

In his living room, Zilbershlag sips rose hip tea,
surrounded by glass-fronted hardwood bookshelves
that hold rows of leather-bound Kabbalah and Talmudic literature. One case is devoted to silver menorahs,

Shabbat candlesticks, and *kiddush* cups. A robust man in his fifties with a wide smile, thick gray *payos* curling out from either side of his black skullcap, and a gray beard reaching the black vest he wears over his white shirt and ritual fringes, he is also the founder of Israel's largest charity: Meir Panim, a soup kitchen network. His ultra-Orthodox environmental group mainly focuses on urban issues: noise, air pollution, congested roads, open burning of trash, and ubiquitous junk food wrappers strewn through packed *haredi* neighborhoods. But his own interest goes beyond, to the preservation of nature.

"According to Gematria," he explains — Kabbalist numerology — "the words *God* and *nature* are equivalents. So nature is the same as God."

You don't need miracles, he says, to know that God exists. "I see God in nature's details: trees, valleys, sky, and sun." Yet in a mystery that perhaps only a Kabbalist can resolve, he notes that Jewish survival has depended on miracles involving God's dominion over, and even suspension of, natural law. "A classic example is when Israel left Egypt, He made the seas part."

That act was preceded by other unnatural miracles: water turning to blood, swarms of frogs in the desert, night that lasted for three days, hail that selectively battered Egyptian crops, and death that slaughtered only Egyptian livestock and Egyptian firstborn children. All these divine interventions are commemorated in the Passover seder, which begins with Jewish children asking four traditional questions about the evening's symbolism. The answers, given over the course of the meal, recount Israel's miraculous deliverance from slavery.

In each corner of Dudi Zilbershlag's home is a reminder — a stroller, a playpen, a crib — of children who have asked these questions: he and his wife, Rivka, had eleven themselves, and they expect to be grandparents many times over. Yet nothing is ever certain in this mythic land, where tension between two peoples who claim it crackles the atmosphere. As pressures and stakes rise daily — and sheer numbers, with each trying to outpopulate the other — so does a reality that has begun to dawn on Jews and Arabs alike, spanning both sides' political and religious spectra:

In historic Palestine — that is, between the Mediterranean Sea and the Jordan River in the disputed lands of Israel and Palestine, a distance of barely fifty miles — there are now nearly 12 million people.

In the aftermath of World War I, the British, who governed Palestine under an international mandate, believed that this land, much of it desert, could sustain 2.5 million at most. During the 1930s, to persuade a doubtful Crown that it should be a homeland for Jews, Zionist David Ben-Gurion argued that Jewish determination and ingenuity to transform what the British considered a backwater should not be discounted.

"No square inch of land shall we neglect; not one source of water shall we fail to tap; not a swamp that we shall not drain; not a sand dune that we shall not fructify; not a barren hill that we shall not cover with trees; nothing shall we leave untouched," wrote Israel's future first prime minister. Ben-Gurion was referring to the carrying capacity of Palestine's soil and water resources to support human beings—both Jew and Arab, who in early writings he imagined coexisting.

He was convinced that the land could support 6 million people. Later, as prime minister, Ben-Gurion would offer prizes to Israeli "heroines" who had ten or more children (an offer eventually discontinued because so many winners were Arab women). Today, Israel's *haredi* population doubles every seventeen years. At the same time, with half of all Palestinians just entering or nearing their reproductive years, the Arab population of historic Palestine—Israel, the West Bank, and the Gaza Strip—could surpass that of Israeli Jews by 2016.

At that point, projections of which side will win

this demographic derby—or lose, depending on point of view—get hazy. Historically, much of Israel's growth has depended on immigration of Jews from elsewhere. More than a million Russians arrived after the collapse of the Soviet Union. Yet the trend of Jews making *aliyah* to Israel has slowed dramatically. Far more Jews now move from Israel to the United States than vice versa. Nevertheless, as the birthrate of *haredim* increases exponentially, Jews may retake the majority in the 2020s. At least for a while.

Even more important than who's leading is something neither Jewish nor Arab demographers deny: If things continue as they're headed, by the middle of this century the number of humans jammed between the sea and the Jordan will nearly double, to at least 21 million.

Even Jesus's miracle with loaves and fishes might not come close to slaking their needs. Such relentless arithmetic begs a new set of four questions:

The First Question

How many people can their land really hold? For that matter, since the influence of this Holy Land extends far beyond its disputed borders, how many people can our planet hold?

It is a question that, anywhere on Earth, requires panoramic knowledge, expertise, and imagination to attempt an answer. Which people? What do they eat? How do they shelter themselves, and move about? Where do they get their water—and how much water is there for them to get? And their fuel: how much is available, and how dangerous is its exhaust? And— getting back to food—do they grow it themselves? If so, how much can they harvest, meaning: how much does it rain, how many rivers flow through the land, how good and plentiful are the soils, how much fertilizer and other forms of chemistry are involved, and what's the downside of using them?

The list continues: What kinds of houses, and how big? And made from what? If of local material, how much is on hand? (Although half of Israel is a desert, it is already worried about running out of construction-grade sand—let alone water to mix cement.) How about suitable building sites—and all the roads, sewer pipes, gas lines, and power lines that must connect to them? And the infrastructure for all the schools, hospitals, and businesses to serve and employ...how many people??

Any complete answers to such questions demand input from ecologists, geographers, hydrologists, and agronomists, not just engineers and economists. But in Israel and Palestine—like everywhere else—most decisions are made by none of them. Politics, which includes military strategy along with business and culture, has been the ultimate arbiter here since civilization began, and still is.

A business-savvy and politically astute nonprofit director, for a Hasidic rabbi Dudi Zilbershlag is also a cultural realist, at least to a point. He accepts that Israel needs secular as well as religious Jews—who else will support all the Talmudists?—and even, he adds, that ultimately his children and Arabs will have to live together. "We must find a common language and let peace prevail."

What he cannot do, however, is ever imagine restricting the numbers of children his people bring into the world.

"God brings children into the world. He'll find a place for them," says *haredi* environmental educator Rachel Ladani.

If the phrase *population control* evokes Malthusian shudders or nightmares of Chinese totalitarian rule for some, to Hasidic Jews like Ladani and Dudi Zilbershlag, it's plain unthinkable. Ladani lives in ultra-Orthodox Bnei Brak, Israel's most densely populated city, just inland from coastal Tel Aviv. She finds no conflict between teaching environmental awareness and being the mother of eight. Her family's Hasidic lifestyle means walking to stores, school, and the synagogue, rarely venturing beyond their neighborhood. None, including Rachel, has ever been on an airplane. "My two daughters and six sons produce less carbon dioxide in one year," she enjoys saying, "than someone from America visiting Israel does in one flight."

Perhaps: But they all eat food and need shelter, which in turn require building materials and all the connecting infrastructure — as will their own myriad offspring. And despite the proximity of services — within two blocks are grocers, kosher butchers, falafel outlets, and many shops selling baby goods and wigs (acceptably modest head covering for Orthodox women; Rachel's is auburn, cut in a pageboy) — it's clear that austere *haredim* aren't immune to modern, energy-hungry temptations. In Bnei Brak, parked cars are everywhere: on road dividers, wheels halfway up sidewalks. Motorcycles swarm through streets crammed with houses encrusted with satellite dish antennae.

This is the thickest concentration of humans in Israel's northern, nondesert half, which, at 740 people per square kilometer, has higher population density than any country in the Western world. (Holland, Europe's densest, has 403 people per square kilometer.) So what does Rachel Ladani think will happen when her country's population doubles by 2050? Or to our world, which, according to the United Nations, by mid-century may host nearly 10 billion of us?

"I don't have to think about it. God made the problem, and He will solve it."

There was once a pine forest nearby, where Rachel's Russian immigrant mother taught her the names of flowers and birds. When she was only ten, she met a female landscape architect—a double revelation: she had known neither that anything like landscape architecture existed, nor that women worked. When she married at nineteen, she didn't tell the *rebbe* who officiated that she was also enrolling in Technion, the Israel Institute of Technology. It took her five years to get her degree, as during that time she also had three children.

She and her husband, Eliezer, principal of a school for learning disabilities, managed to have five more even as Rachel worked to keep their bursting city beautiful. When she was forty, she discovered Israel's premier environmental think tank, the Heschel Center for Environmental Learning and Leadership in Tel Aviv. Like Technion, it wasn't Orthodox, but it opened her eyes and changed her life without changing her faith.

"The environment is like Torah. It's a part of you," she tells the girls she teaches in religious schools. In a country where schoolchildren once sang patriotic songs about Zionists transforming the land by covering it in concrete, she teaches them to open their own eyes by watching seeds sprout, and by gazing at nature until they begin to really see. She quotes an ancient midrash, a rabbinical commentary on the Torah, in which God shows Adam the trees of Eden, saying "See my works, how lovely they are. All I have created I have created for you."

Yet as Heschel Center founder Jeremy Benstein noted in a 2006 book, *The Way Into Judaism and the Environment,* in the same midrash God goes on to warn Adam: "Take care not to corrupt and destroy My world, because if you ruin it there is no one to come after you to put it right."

When he cited that, Benstein was replying to the theological optimism of the deeply devout that somehow God will not let us down if we're doing the right things in His eyes. "We are bidden," he reminded in his book, "not to depend on miracles to solve our problems. God makes it clear that there will be no one to clean up after us."

Benstein grew up in Ohio and attended Harvard before coming to Israel. He earned a doctorate in environmental anthropology from Jerusalem's Hebrew University. With other emigrants from America, he founded Heschel and taught at the Arava Institute, a sustainability research center at a southern Israeli kibbutz. The Intifadas made two things about population clear to him: it had a huge impact on the joint Israeli-Palestinian environment, but discussing it was nearly taboo.

"Because, we're still recovering from the massacre of a third of the world's Jews," he says, straddling a chair in the Heschel Center's library. The Holocaust, which led the United Nations to cleave Palestine in two to create a Jewish homeland, is eternally fresh here. "The meaning of six billion," he wrote in his 2006 book, "should rightfully take a backseat to the six million." Especially, he adds, since a million of the slaughtered Jews were children.

"There are fewer Jews in the world now than in 1939. We see ourselves like any indigenous population decimated by Western culture. We have the right to replenish ourselves."

Yet Benstein, himself the father of twins, knows it took only twelve years for the world to go from 6 to 7 billion. Researching Torah and biblical tractates for environmental guidance, such as the edict in Exodus 23:11 to let the land lie fallow every seventh year, he has also looked for clues to what exactly God meant when He directed humans to be fruitful and multiply.

"It seems to imply that there is a limit. Because it doesn't say, be fruitful and multiply ad infinitum, or as much as you can. It says, 'Be fruitful and multiply and fill up the Earth.'"

Benstein, whose Harvard degree is in linguistics, has probed the nuanced language of Genesis. "If we take that seriously, then there will be a time when we will have fulfilled that commandment, and we can stop. The question becomes: When? Have we gotten there yet? And rabbis can't answer the question of what does it mean for the Earth to be full. That's a question for ecologists."

In Genesis, however, he finds an interesting hint. It occurs after forty chapters of men taking wives and subsequent lists of begats and generations of sons. Old Testament people had no problem obeying the commandment to multiply, which they did with vigor and frequently with lust. But then comes Joseph, one of thirteen offspring of the patriarch Jacob.

Joseph has two sons before he interprets the Egyptian pharaoh's dream. At that point, Benstein writes: "He stopped procreating before the famine he knew lay ahead. The Talmud uses this example to state: 'It is forbidden to engage in marital relations in the time of famine.'"

A parallel Talmudic passage, he adds, "sees the prohibition as a call to population control, stating bluntly: 'When you see great deprivation entering the world, keep your wife childless.'"

But a mere head count, Benstein says, doesn't fully explain the hunger and thirst afflicting much of humanity, predicted to worsen gravely during this century. While human population quadrupled over the past hundred years, he calculates that our consumption of resources, as measured by combined gross domestic products worldwide, increased by a factor of seventeen. This gorging at the planetary buffet has been enjoyed by a comparative few, and at the expense of many. An unequal distribution of goods, which caused woes and wars even in biblical times, has never been so skewed as today.

Yet consumption and population are two faces of the same coin, he acknowledges. As it spins ever faster, it raises questions that transcend his divided nation, because the entire world is growing dizzy from forces whirling out of control.

ii. The Water

The Second Question

If, in order to have an ecosystem robust enough to insure human survival, we have to avoid growing past 10 billion—or even reduce our numbers from the 7 billion we're already at—is there an acceptable, nonviolent way to convince people of all the cultures, religions, nationalities, tribes, and political systems of the world that it's in their best interest to do so? Is there anything in their liturgies, histories, or belief systems—or any other reason—that potentially embraces the seemingly unnatural idea of limiting what comes most naturally to us, and to all other species: making copies of ourselves?

Ayat Um-Said knows one. "Not religion. Reality." With wide eyes lined with blue eye shadow that complements her lavender hijab and purple wool coat, she glances over at her mother. Ruwaidah Um-Said, bundled in a green velvet dress and a black wool head scarf against the January chill, leans on the arm of her white plastic chair and ticks off the ages of her children: "Twenty-five, twenty-four, twenty-three, twenty-two, twenty, nineteen, sixteen, fourteen, thirteen, and ten." Six boys, four girls. Her youngest leans against her knee, bundled in a black zip-collared sweatshirt over a turtleneck and a fleece-lined nylon jacket over that. The only heat in their home—three rooms on the ground floor of a five-story concrete box in Al-Amari, a refugee camp that's now a permanent neighborhood in the West Bank city of

Ramallah—emanates from the bodies of the people living here, which are always plenty.

Ruwaidah was born here in 1958, ten years after her family was expelled from Lydda—Lod, in biblical times—when Israel was created. Back there, her father had an orchard of pomegranate, orange, and lemon trees, and also grew onions, radishes, spinach, green beans, wheat, and barley. "He always assumed we would be going back, so he refused to buy property around here." She looks around at the dank blue walls she's seen all her life, bare except for darker blue wainscoting. "The United Nations owns this land." She spits. "We own the house."

As several thousand Al-Amari refugees gradually realized that they weren't returning to their villages anytime soon, over a decade concrete and mortar replaced the UN's tents. After another decade and a Six-Day War, when there were no longer borders because everything had become Israel's, her father took them to see their land. He still had a deed, but it didn't matter. He finally gave up when their trees disappeared under a runway of what is now Ben-Gurion International Airport.

Something else gradually changed. "Every Palestinian family had someone in jail, or wounded, or killed. So families that used to have five or six children started having more." Ruwaidah points at a school photo of her thirteen-year-old, Yassim. "When a relative gets killed, you have another child to bear his name. And we're going to need a lot more," she adds, turning to her daughter Ayat, "to liberate the whole land."

Ayat smiles sweetly but shakes her head. "Just two," she says.

Ruwaidah shrugs helplessly. All her daughters only want two, hoping for one of each.

"Everyone my age," says Ayat, "is sick of living six to a room. And who can afford so many kids? Life's so expensive."

There's no place to grow their own food—and even if there were, with water often flowing from West Bank taps just twice a week, they couldn't irrigate. The UN used to allot them sugar, rice, flour, cooking oil, and milk, but that budget ended. "The only chance to earn a living," says Ayat, her arms around her son, Zacariah, and her daughter, Rheem, "is education. Which costs money."

Two of her brothers made it to university. Another, miraculously, gets paid to play football in Norway. For the rest, jobs are rare and usually pay miserably. "And now, with most of Israel closed, finding work is even harder."

The walls that tower over Ramallah and the interminable waits at ubiquitous Israeli military checkpoints make it all but impossible to go where there might be work — or go anywhere. Women in labor give birth waiting to get through; one even named her baby Checkpoint. Security walls are visible practically everywhere on the West Bank, in many places separating farmers from their olive groves. Like the Israeli settlements — towns, really, with high-rises, shopping malls, industrial parks, and expanding fringes of mobile homes — they crowd Palestinians into ever closer quarters.

With housing so scarce and everyone so cramped, there's no more preaching in the mosques about babies. "It's not the imam's business anyhow," snaps Ayat.

"That's exactly what Israelis want you to think," says a neighbor woman who's entered, wrapped in a fringed brown hijab.

"So let the politicians liberate Palestine already, not ask us to do it by having a lot of kids. How come Arafat had only one daughter himself?" On TV, Ayat sees that Israeli politicians pay *haredim* to have more babies. "Here, the more babies you have, the more *you* pay."

At least the UN clinic still dispenses free IUDs.

In Bethlehem, Abeer Safar studies a wall map of the kidney-bean-shaped West Bank. Where the bean bends is Jerusalem. Bethlehem, her hometown, is just a few kilometers below.

Abeer trained as a chemical engineer at Jordan's

University of Science and Technology. Here she's a water specialist with ARIJ, a Palestinian research institute. She wears jeans, a black sweater over a lime turtleneck, a gold pendant chain, and her long brown hair uncovered. She and her husband live in his family's home, which, like most houses here, is growing taller. With the birthplace of Jesus hemmed in by Israel's security walls — segregation walls, as Palestinians call them — there's no choice.

It makes no sense to her. If Israel keeps carving Palestine into shards, no viable Palestinian state can ever form. But if it stays a single state, Jews risk ending up the outnumbered minority. The only way a minority could stay in power would be by apartheid, not democracy. Then again, Abeer, in her late thirties, is only now expecting her first child. Other professional Palestinian women have also deferred their childbearing, and girls today now want schooling and jobs before babies.

Even so, it will take time before the sheer pressure of numbers drops, and meanwhile there are more immediate concerns. "We share the West Bank aquifers with Israel," says Abeer, "but there's no basin-wide management."

Meaning that Israel manages it alone, and Palestine is not allowed to tap new wells. The main recharge areas of the region's principal Western Mountain Aquifer now fall inside the undulating security wall.

Nevertheless, three-fourths of the groundwater originating in the West Bank highlands goes to Israel. "And," says Abeer, "the settlements take whatever they want"—including for keeping swimming pools full. Per capita, Palestinians claim, Israelis get 280 liters per day while they get just 60. World Health Organization guidelines recommend at least 100.

Israeli environmentalists agree that it's madness that half their country's allotment of precious water goes to agriculture, which produces only 1 percent of Israel's income. Although Israel has pioneered techniques like drip irrigation and recycling wastewater for crops, they argue that to raise thirsty plants like cotton and flowers to sell to Europe, or potatoes for Poland, which can surely grow its own, means exporting its most vital resource. ("The good news," notes the *Jerusalem Post,* "is that by 2020, all Israelis will be drinking recycled sewage. The bad news: There may not be enough.")

The Jordan River is now a fetid ditch trickling from a lake whose very name evokes conflict, because it has three of them: Lake Kinneret to the Jews, Lake Tiberius to the Palestinians, the Sea of Galilee to Christians. Since it forms part of Israel's international border with a country named for it, the Jordan's riparian basin is a restricted military area, so Palestine has no access to it. Jordan gets a share, as does Syria, which controls some of its headwaters. (Others are in the Golan Heights, which Israel seized from Syria in 1967 and won't give back. Israeli air attacks on Arab League projects to divert those waters helped spark the Six-Day War.)

Today, all but 2 percent of the Jordan is already allotted by the time it leaves the lake. What dribbles to the Dead Sea is runoff from fields or fish farms, sour with pesticides, fertilizer, hormones, fish wastes, and untreated sewage. Pilgrims trying to bathe at the spot where tradition says Jesus was baptized and Joshua crossed into the Holy Land would contract a rash — or vomit, should they swallow some of the once-pure holy water.

Over 90 percent of wastewater in the West Bank flows untreated into the environment. Until 2013, there was only one sanitary landfill, near Lake Kinneret-Tiberius; another finally opened for Bethlehem and Hebron. Most solid wastes, however, are burned or just left to blow into the desert. But it's not just Palestinian waste.

"Settlements discharge untreated wastewater freely onto Palestinian farmlands," says Abeer. "Many have factories that don't apply Israeli environmental laws." Her field teams, traveling back roads after main routes were closed to Palestinians after the last intifada, try to track effluent from pesticide and fertilizer plants that moved to the West Bank after they were closed in Israel by court order.

"All this flows into the aquifer that Israel drinks from, too. We argue that they're poisoning themselves." But Israel won't issue the Palestinians permits to build more sewage treatment plants unless they agree to also treat sewage from Jewish settlements. "Which we won't, because they're illegal." She fingers her pendant chain. "It's a standoff."

It would also exhaust their beleaguered budget: a third of a million Jews now live in West Bank settlements. Then there's the Gaza Strip—1.5 million people on a piece of land twenty-five miles long and four to seven miles deep, its population doubling every twelve to fifteen years. It's suspected that Israel unilaterally withdrew in 2005 because its Coastal Aquifer is now so depleted that 90 percent of Gazan wells are pumping wastes from septic fields, or seawater. Although Israel's National Water Carrier pipeline passes right by, delivering Lake Kinneret water to the southern Negev desert that it intends to develop next, the portion it sells to the Palestinians covers only 5 percent of Gaza's needs.

Two peoples, genetically nearly identical, by some accounts locked in enmity since Abraham-Ibrahim's two jealous wives, Sarah and Hagar, bore, respectively, the Jews and the Arabs, fighting over a parched sliver of land—albeit one with an outsized influence on the world, historically, religiously, and politically.

Yet by one more measure—ecologically—how much does their tiny sandbox on the edge of the sea, and their combined 12 million or so—barely 1/584th of humanity's current population—mean in a world headed to 10 billion?

Much more than that world realizes, believes Yossi Leshem. Unless, that is, you look up.

iii. The Heavens

The Third Question

How much ecosystem is required to maintain human life? Or, what species or ecological processes are essential to our survival?

Or, at what point does our overwhelming presence displace so many other species that eventually we push something off the planet that we didn't realize our own existence depended on, until it's too late? What can't we absolutely live without?

Yossi Leshem actually started by looking down, from a cliff in the Judean Mountains. He should have

been in a Tel Aviv University ornithology lab, corre-
lating the lengths of warbler bills to their diets for his
master's degree in biology. Instead, desperate to be
out in nature, he had volunteered to help another
scientist observe long-legged buzzards. The first time
he rappelled his burly body down to their nest to
band three buzzard chicks, he was hooked on raptors.

He switched from warblers to studying Bonelli's
eagle, a large Afro-Asian–southern European bird of
prey. In Israel, at least seventy pairs had been recorded,
but by 1982, only sixteen remained. Leshem decided
to find out why, and to see if anything could save
them. It didn't take long to find the cause.

In the 1960s, Israel had released fifty thousand
strychnine-laced chickens to quell a rabies outbreak
blamed on a surge in the jackal population—due, it
turned out, to a surge in the human population. The
jackals were feasting on dead turkeys, hens, calves,
and cows in burgeoning garbage dumps of farm
wastes. The success of the chicken operation—which
also killed countless wildlife, and probably caused
the extinction of Galilee leopards—greatly reinforced
officials' belief in the merits of poison. As the numbers of people grew and agriculture intensified, planes
spraying DDT and organophosphates increasingly
filled Israeli skies. Bonelli's eagles, feeding on poisoned chukars and pigeons, began dropping. Although

DDT is now banned, Israel's pesticide use per area under cultivation is still the highest in the developed world. In 2011, just eight eagle pairs remained.

Leshem's biggest discovery, however, came in the early 1980s while researching another endangered raptor for his doctorate: a powerful carrion eater named the lappet-faced vulture. For a better sense of their numbers, he hired a pilot to fly him over Israel's southern Negev desert during autumn migration. Aloft, what he saw amazed him. Flocks of big birds, tiny birds, and everything in between. Millions of them.

An encounter near Hebron with a honey buzzard, his pilot mentioned, had recently destroyed a five-million-dollar Israeli Air Force jet. Suddenly Yossi Leshem knew what he should be studying. He was soon at IAF headquarters, scouring records of bird strikes with military aircraft. On average, three serious collisions occurred every year. Between 1972 and 1982, he saw that more planes had been lost and more pilots killed in encounters with birds than with enemy sorties.

"Different migrating birds come at different times, at different elevations," Leshem, a veteran of four wars and a reserve officer, told the IAF. "Wouldn't you like to know exactly when and where?"

The air force provided him a motorized glider. Over the next two years he spent 272 days following swirling clouds of songbirds, V's of geese, and flocks of cranes, storks, and pelicans soaring over Negev sands, Galilee farmlands, and JNF pine forests. He reported back to headquarters that this was no mere avian migration route: it was *the* route. Each year, a billion birds flew through Israeli airspace. Because there are no thermals to ride over open water, many birds that seasonally migrate between Africa and Europe or western Asia avoid the Mediterranean. Some cross at the Strait of Gibraltar or hop from Tunisia to Italy via Sicily, but the most—280 different species—come right over Israel and Palestine, the crossroads between three continents, where there's always warm air rising off the land.

Per area, Leshem wrote in his PhD thesis, Israel held the world record for migrating birds, and also for military planes aloft at any given moment. To avoid more fatal collisions required two things, he told the air force. The first was a radar station. Fortunately, at that time the dissolving Soviet Union was holding a garage sale of military hardware, and they found a weather tracking station from Moldova, valued at $1.6 million, selling for $20,000. And the Jewish former USSR general who ran it agreed to come along and adapt it for bird research.

The other thing they needed was cooperation with Israel's neighbors, so that bird-spotters in other countries could warn them when migrations were heading their direction. Leshem convinced the IAF to let him contact the Turkish and Jordanian air forces, and to get Palestinian and Jordanian ornithologists to share data with their Israeli counterparts. He already knew ornithologists in Lebanon, Egypt, and even Iran. Information from Syria he could get indirectly, via a Birdlife International office in Amman.

These relationships, and the camouflaged radar station they installed off the Jerusalem–Tel Aviv Highway, reduced collisions 76 percent and saved an estimated $750 million in lost or damaged aircraft, not to mention pilot lives—and the lives of birds. And perhaps much more. Should anything ever threaten the viability of this narrow air corridor, or the ecosystem below it that feeds and shelters migrating birds as they stop over, it will affect far more than Israel and Palestine. Birds aren't merely colorful and musical; they're pollinators, seed spreaders, and insect eaters. The ecosystems of much of Africa and Europe would be unimaginable, and possibly in collapse, without this bottleneck.

Not only fighter jets threaten it. The lappet-faced vultures that Yossi Leshem studied have vanished from the Negev, as have the huge bearded vultures that used to nest above the Dead Sea at Masada. Before more species fall, he has mobilized a national campaign against pesticides, using birds themselves as the alternatives. Realizing that barn owls that once sheltered in wooden farm buildings have no decent roosts in modern metal structures, Leshem, his colleagues, and hundreds of Israeli, Palestinian, and Jordanian schoolchildren have placed nearly 2,000 nesting boxes in agricultural fields.

"One pair of owls eat about five thousand rodents a year. Multiply that by two thousand," says Leshem. "So farmers quit using heavy pesticides. Maybe we can't stop them all, but of 826 pesticides used in Israel, we can reduce the worst ones." He readjusts the knit yarmulke riding his bushy gray curls. "Our sperm counts are now down 40 percent. Our cancer rates are up that much. All from hormones and pesticides. In the Huleh Valley, they've used so many chemicals it's affected cognitive ability. We know, because they've been testing children for twenty years. Now they're now testing the grandchildren."

The Huleh Valley, just north of Lake Kinneret, is where common cranes winter. In the 1950s, the Huleh Swamp—the biologically richest spot in the Near East—was drained to convert the land for agriculture. Too late, Israel realized that the wetland had been the lake's filter. Nitrogen and phosphorus nutrients it once absorbed now flowed unimpeded into Kinneret, along with so much exposed peat that

Israel's most important water source was in danger of turning into oxygen-poor green muck.

Three thousand hectares of the Huleh had to be reflooded to save Lake Kinneret from dying. But that was less than one-tenth of the former wetland that once provided for migrating waterfowl. Farmers were threatening to poison all the cranes raiding their peanut fields, along with seventy thousand pelicans and one hundred thousand white storks plundering carp and tilapia farms, until Leshem and his colleagues found grants to spread thousands of pounds of corn and chickpeas for the cranes, and to raise mosquito fish in Huleh Lake for storks and pelicans.

In what is now a daily winter tourist attraction, thirty thousand screeching cranes are led away from Huleh peanut fields by a tractor expelling corn kernels on the spongy ground, with the snowy Golan Heights as a backdrop. It's a surreal spectacle in this arid corridor, where so few wet places are left for birds that fly a third of the way around the world to replenish themselves. Were Huleh to vanish entirely, a cascade of ecological disaster from Russia to South Africa could result.

From a rocky hillside banding station he established on the grounds of the Israeli Knesset, Yossi Leshem looks east across Jerusalem toward Jordan and imagines

Cranes, Huleh Valley, Israel

what the prophet Jeremiah must have seen here when he noted, "The stork in the heavens knows her appointed times; and the turtledove and the crane and the swallow observe the time of their coming."[1]

"He didn't need radar. He was looking at a sky filled with at least three times the birds we see today. More."

Jerusalem's population then was less than two thousand. The desert below would have been filled with sage, pink sorrel, and thistle flowers. A green overstory of oaks, pistacias, and olive trees buzzed with warblers, tits, chaffinches, bee-eaters, sparrows, and sunbirds. From the Judean Hills would come cheetahs, lions, wolves, and leopards to hunt red deer, gazelles, oryx, wild ass, and ibex. Today, some birds remain. Most of the others are gone.

"Our nature reserves are mere fragments of that ancient ecosystem," says Leshem. "We're a country the size of New Jersey, our upper half totally overpopulated. We're full of roads and security walls that cut gazelle and ibex herds into populations that can't reach each other. A male gazelle needs to dominate a group of females. Suddenly there's this wall and he can't get to them. The same with mongoose and wolves—they roam seventy kilometers in one night

---

1. Jeremiah 8:7.

to find prey. Birds can fly. But mammals and reptiles: they have a problem."

He gestures toward the Judean Hills at the city's edge, where there's a remnant herd of twenty gazelles. "Feral dogs chase after their calves. Their future is doubtful."

And people's, too, he adds. "Palestinians are so fragmented. Like the wildlife."

iv. The Desert

Deep in the Negev, in the sands of the Arava Rift Valley just above Israel's southern tip, is a fenced nature preserve for its remaining mammals. Among them is the white oryx, which the Crusaders mistook for unicorns. Extinct save for a few zoo specimens on other continents, they have been bred here in hopes of reintroducing them to their native ecosystems. The Arabian leopards, caracals, wolves, and hyenas here are caged, but the oryx, ibex, and other ungulates roam along a five-kilometer loop that can be driven by tourists. There are even ostrich, though these are Somali stand-ins for the original local subspecies: the Arabian ostrich, last seen wild here in 1966.

Ten minutes away is Ketura, the kibbutz home to the Arava Institute, a graduate environmental studies program for Arabs and Jews. Its faculty members, who teach renewable energy, transboundary water management, and sustainable agriculture, are Israeli and Palestinian; many students are also from Jordan, just a few kilometers to the east. Arava's guiding creed is that the environment is a shared birthright and a shared crisis, one whose urgency trumps all political, cultural, and economic differences that divide people.

The communal dining hall for students and kibbutzniks serves milk from their own dairy and abundant fresh cucumber, tomatoes, and greens. Eating salad three meals a day, a habit shared by Israelis and Palestinians, dates back to pioneer years when meat was a luxury, and may account for both peoples having among the world's highest life expectancies — nearly eighty years — despite all the ambient pesticides. Some of those are used even here: Kibbutz Ketura's income derives mainly from groves of nonnative date palms, a species vulnerable to a beetle whose female lays eggs inside date pits, producing offspring that attack the trees. The chemical vigilance to protect them is work that Israelis don't want and that Palestinians, their mobility and work permits deeply checked by military occupation, couldn't get even if they chose. As a result, the Holy Land's population is further strained by thousands of Thai agricultural guest workers, including a contingent at Kibbutz Ketura to handle such toxic jobs.

The low-wage Thai workers, hunters back home, supplement their diets in Israel with traps and slingshots to take gazelles, badgers, jackals, foxes, rabbits, wild boar—even cows and dogs. Using glue traps, they catch rodents, birds, frogs, salamanders, snakes, and lizards. Because kosher dietary laws permit only the slaughter of domestic animals, few Israelis hunt. But already scarce wildlife, as Arava Institute founder Alon Tal wrote in his book *Pollution in a Promised Land*, have been critically depleted by thirty thousand Thai trappers. In the Golan Heights alone, he estimates, they've exterminated 90 percent of the gazelle population.

A trim man in his early fifties with a gray goatee, Tal is among the few Israeli environmentalists who has dared broach a loaded subject in a nation founded to rescue a culture targeted for annihilation. "Our land is *full*. Future historians may identify the present deadlock as one of Israel's greatest tragedies." The population issue became deadlocked, says Tal, deputy chair of Israel's Green Party, by subsidies that reward ultra-Orthodox families for having more children. "An average Orthodox Jew who dies leaves a hundred progeny. Think of the diapers alone!"

The pressures that those diapers embody become lethal not just to the environment, but to people, when Jews and Palestinians claim the same piece of real estate. The blessing of their mutual longevity further adds to their competing numbers. As an ecology professor at Ben-Gurion University, Tal has designed many environmental projects with Palestinian counterparts, especially for joint water management. "But population underlies everything. If we don't deal with it soon, it will be too late. We'll be ecologically barren and socially untenable. I'd drop everything else to get it on the table. But it's very hard."

Alon Tal drives a half-hour south from Ketura to Israel's southernmost city, Eilat. Across the border, at a Days Inn in Aqaba, Jordan, he'll address a gathering of Arava Institute alumni: young Jordanians, Jews, and Palestinians, now working for government and nonprofit agencies as environmental planners and scientists. En route, he passes Israeli desalination plants on the Gulf of Aqaba, transmuting salt water into drinking water. A reason why people deny, or defy, the threat of overpopulation, says Tal, is his country's technological optimism. Faith that Israel could make a desert bloom inspired donations from Jews worldwide, resulting in inventions like drip irrigation. When David Ben-Gurion realized that the

Promised Land of milk and honey lacked a critical contemporary Middle Eastern ingredient — oil — his challenge to international Jewish physicists to harness his nation's one plentiful resource, sunlight, produced the modern rooftop solar collector.

The conviction here that humans can find endless ways to stretch the carrying capacity of this land is not a Jewish exclusive. Tareq Abu Hamed, a Palestinian who runs Arava's Center for Renewable Energy and Energy Conservation, is filling the campus with photovoltaic panels. His goal is to perfect solar-driven electricity to split water molecules into their components, oxygen and hydrogen, then store the hydrogen in a boron-based medium for release on demand as carbon-free fuel.

"This region has the highest solar radiation in the world. We can reduce pollution and make ourselves energy independent," he says.

Yet techno-fixes for what limits Israel and Palestine's existence crash into certain realities. Eilat's desalination plants are now surrounded by giant mounds of salt. Some gets sold as Red Sea salt for aquariums, some as kosher table salt. But markets can absorb only so much, and dumping the excess back into the Gulf is a hypersaline hazard to marine life. It also takes formidable energy to push seawater through reverse-osmosis filters. In Israel, bereft not only of oil but of rivers to dam for hydroelectric power, energy comes from coal-fired plants that shroud its Mediterranean coast. In 2011, water shortages became so severe that by emergency decree, Israel's desalination plants began operating around the clock, burning even more coal.

More solar energy would seem an obvious remedy, but the Middle East's sunlight advantage is compromised by the fact that at 113°F, a temperature reached frequently at Arava, the efficiency of solar panels drops. "We're working on solving that," says Tareq Abu Hamed, mopping his shaved head.

Yet temperatures keep rising. If the patriarch Jacob were to return—he passed nearby four thousand years ago, en route to reuniting with his son Joseph, who was warning Egyptians of coming shortages—except for far less wildlife, the landscape would still look familiar. The primary vegetation, now as then, is a drought-resistant acacia tree, the food source for gazelles, ibex, insects, and birds. "All Arava Valley agriculture is based on them," says Abu Hamed's Arava colleague, ecologist Elli Groner. "They hold the soil in place, and its water."

The problem is that the acacias are dying, due to reduced precipitation.

"If they go, there will be a total ecosystem collapse—what ecologists call a stage shift, from one state to a new one. We don't know what that new one is. Nobody can predict."

Israel's Nature Protection Authority has suggested watering them. Groner, who directs long-term ecological research here, removes his wire-rimmed glasses and gestures at the dry valley. "With water from Lake Kinneret? From the desalination plants?"

Israel's forestry agency, he adds, "did the only thing they know to do. They started planting new acacias. Donors to the Jewish National Fund can now adopt an acacia tree in Israel, to replace a dead one."

Population ecologists often speak of the Netherlands Fallacy: The fact that so many densely packed Dutch have such a high standard of living is not proof that humans can thrive in essentially an unnatural, artificial environment. Like everyone else, the Dutch need things that only an ecosystem can provide; fortunately, they can afford to purchase those things from elsewhere. Israel likewise survives on the surplus (and largess) of others.

Suppose, though, that the cost of shipping fuel to bring bananas, blueberries, or grain from across oceans becomes prohibitively high—due either to scarcity, or to what burning fuel adds to the atmosphere. Should Israel, Palestine, or any place on Earth ever be forced to depend on its own self-sufficiency, it will have to contend with numerous human dependents—and with the fact that humans depend on other living things, which require sufficient soil and water to flourish.

Not just Israelis and Palestinians: In the Holy Land, they aren't even the most fecund. Bedouin families, Alon Tal guesses, once may have averaged as many as fourteen children, which would be the world's highest. Because they've always been roving desert nomads, no one was ever sure. But there are a lot of them.

With only the Negev left for more cities and military bases, Israel is claiming lands where Bedouins traditionally have grazed their flocks. With little choice, they're moving into cities that Israel is building for them, too.

In the new Bedouin city of Rahat, Ahmad Amrani, a schoolteacher and one of Alon Tal's Green comrades, stands atop the flat roof of the four-story home he now shares with various members of his family. Actually, the Amranis inhabit the entire street. "Every street down there," he says, indicating his raw city, where thirteen mosques rise amid windblown dust and plastic scraps, "is another family."

His house, faced in polished Jerusalem limestone, is mostly empty. Behind it is a Bedouin tent where his relatives spend most of their time, seated on carpets and drinking sweetened tea. Unlike his father and grandfather, Ahmad doesn't dress in a caftan and keffiyeh; he wears jeans and a leather jacket. He also attended university, the first in his family.

"Ten years ago, when I went to Ben-Gurion University, I was one of four Bedouin students. Today there are 400." He pauses. "And 350 of them are women."

Making the transition to the confines of urbanity after a life spent on camelback, driving goats across an open desert, has not been easy for Bedouin men, he says. Nobody gets to be a sheik anymore. With most men not working or providing, women are taking on that role. Very quickly, the young women see that the more education they have, the better that goes.

The big question now is who these educated women are going to marry. "It's sensitive," Amrani says. "Because they have higher self-esteem, they have a hard time finding suitable mates. More are staying single. And nobody's having fourteen children anymore." He heads down to the tent, for tea and almond cookies. His schoolteacher wife and their one child, a son, will be home shortly.

———

Before leaving Israel and Palestine, one more question remains to be posed. Its answer, however, will emerge more clearly beyond this incandescent Middle Eastern flash point, where human passions, both spiritual and fierce, resist being reduced to mere demography. Still, it bears recalling that, in the time of Genesis, when only a few thousand were here, battles over precious wells were already under way among growing tribes.

The Fourth Question

If a sustainable population for the Earth turns out to be less than the 10+ billion we're headed to, or even less than the 7 billion we already number, how do we design an economy for a shrinking population, and then for a stable one—meaning, an economy that can prosper without depending on constant growth?

CHAPTER 2

A World Bursting Its Seams

Cape Canaveral, June 1994: Six hundred scientists and engineers are touring the John F. Kennedy Space Center in a caravan of blue-and-white air-conditioned buses. They've gathered from thirty-four countries for the World Hydrogen Energy Conference, united in a dream to switch the planet from an economy fueled with dirty coal and petroleum to one run on clean hydrogen. They've come bearing designs for cars, appliances, aircraft, heating, cooling, and entire industries—all pollution-free.

For them, this is an inspirational pilgrimage. The white spherical tank on the pad, where the shuttle *Columbia* will presently lift spaceward, is filled with pure hydrogen. Since even before the moon shots, the power for NASA astronauts in space has come from hydrogen fuel cells, refillable devices that, like batteries, chemically convert fuel directly to electricity. Although the hydrogen that NASA uses was derived from natural gas in a process that also produces carbon dioxide, the conference participants are hopeful that the efficiency of solar technology will soon improve so much that water molecules, not hydrocarbons, will be the feedstock.

Nearly two decades later, they and a new generation of researchers, such as Arava Institute's Tareq Abu Hamed, would still be hoping for an economical way of producing clean hydrogen energy. It's frustrating, because there's more hydrogen in the universe than all the other elements combined. Whether burned by internal combustion or injected into a fuel cell, its exhaust is simply water vapor. Theoretically, that exhaust could be captured, condensed, and tapped again for hydrogen, ad infinitum. A perfect, closed system — except for one annoying detail: In this universe, usable amounts of pure hydrogen gas occur naturally only in places like the Sun. On Earth, all hydrogen is tightly bound with other elements, such as oxygen, carbon, nitrogen, and sulfur. Breaking the bonds to free it — pulling the H out of H_2O — requires more energy than hydrogen produces. The number of solar panels needed to milk enough hydrogen from water to run our civilization isn't remotely practical. After years of trying, the most efficient way to extract hydrogen is still using superheated steam to strip it from natural gas, a process that also releases that pesky pollutant CO_2.

That's especially unfortunate, since during a lunch address at the 1994 hydrogen conference, NASA director Daniel Goldin imparted some disturbing news. Over the previous decade, he said, satellite data revealed that the world's sea levels had risen nearly an inch. Goldin didn't have to connect the dots for this particular audience: They knew the connection between the rise in seas, global temperatures, and the carbon dioxide expelled using man-made energy. Worldwide, four-fifths of our energy comes from ancient organic waste that nature didn't need to run the planet, so it was buried safely away. Over eons, the buried organic matter compressed into highly concentrated coal and petroleum. Then, in less than three centuries, humans dug up hundreds of millions of years' worth of the stuff and burned it. Its exhaust loaded the atmosphere with more carbon dioxide than the Earth has seen in at least 3 million years—a time when the world was rather balmy, and its oceans one hundred feet higher.

That was one of two reasons the hydrogen researchers were intent on an alternative to fossil fuel. The other was addressed that afternoon, by a physicist named Albert Bartlett. A University of Colorado emeritus professor, Bartlett professed to know little about hydrogen but something about basic arithmetic. He was particularly fascinated by what happens when things start to double.

"Imagine," he said, "a species of bacteria that reproduces by dividing in two. Those two become four, the four become eight, and so forth. Let's say we place one bacterium in a bottle at 11:00 a.m., and at noon we observe the bottle to be full. At what point was it half full?"

The answer, it turned out, is 11:59 a.m.

As awareness penetrated his audience, Bartlett nodded in return, his bald pate encircled by a few remaining gray tufts. "Now," he continued, "if you were a bacterium in that bottle, at what point would you realize you were running out of space? At 11:55 a.m., when the bottle is only 1/32 full, and 97 percent is open space, yearning for development?"

Everyone giggled. "Now suppose that with a minute to spare, the bacteria discover three new bottles to inhabit. They sigh with relief: They have three times more bottles than had ever been known, quadrupling their space resource. Surely this makes them self-sufficient in space. Right?"

Except, of course, it doesn't. Bartlett's point was that in exactly two more minutes, all four bottles will be full.

Exponential doubling, he noted, doesn't only gobble space. In 1977, U.S. President Jimmy Carter observed in a speech to the nation that, "During the 1950s, people used twice as much oil as during the 1940s. During the 1960s, we used twice as much as during the 1950s. And in each of those decades, more oil was consumed than in all of mankind's previous history." But as the century drew to a close, that rate inevitably had slowed.

"We've picked the low-hanging fruit," said Bartlett. "Finding more gets progressively harder."

Albert Bartlett didn't know back then about twenty-first-century technologies for fracturing bedrock to release trapped natural gas, or squeezing the petroleum out of tar sands — or rather, he did, but at the time, when the price of oil was around sixteen dollars per barrel, their cost seemed prohibitively high, as in higher-hanging fruit. But even so, they were just the equivalent of finding a couple of new bottles: As demand keeps increasing exponentially with countries like China and India zooming past the United States, they at best give us a few more decades — and a lot more CO_2.

Albert Bartlett, now in his late eighties, has told his bacteria-bottle story more than fifteen hundred times, to students, scientists, policy makers, and any group who will listen. "They still don't seem to get it," he laments, deploring what seems to have devolved into a race to see how much damage fossil fuels will wreak before they're exhausted, as humans scrape ever deeper for the dirtiest ones.

He's amazed that people find the concept of exponential doubling so slippery, even when he spices it up with more examples. In one, a Chinese emperor is enamored with a new game that one of his subjects has invented, called chess. He summons the inventor. "Choose your reward," he commands. "Whatever you wish."

"All I want is rice to feed my family," he said.

"Done," the emperor replied. "How much do you need?"

"Just a bit. In fact, Your Highness can measure it out on the chessboard. Put one rice grain on the first square. Put two on the next, and double the amount on each square thereafter. That will be sufficient."

The emperor neglected to consider that anyone who could dream up chess must be a shrewd mathematician. At the end of the first row on the chessboard, the eighth square, the inventor had 128 grains of rice—barely a mouthful. But by the sixteenth, he was up to 32,768. After three rows, the tally was 8,388,608 rice grains, enough to empty the palace's storerooms. By half the chessboard, he would be owed all the rice in China—and by the final square, 18 quintillion grains of rice: more than the entire planet had ever produced. Things never got that far, of course; long before, the emperor had him beheaded.

There are others, all forehead slappers: If you fold a sheet of paper in half, and could keep folding (seven folds is the usual physical limit), after forty-two times its thickness would reach the moon. But the entertainment value of exponential doubling begins to wane when it dawns on you that you've been one of the doublers. Albert Bartlett, who lives in Boulder, Colorado, began giving his talk in the 1960s when he saw a chamber of commerce brochure that boasted, "Doubling its population in ten years, Boulder is indeed a stable and prosperous community."

Quick math showed Bartlett that if the doubling continued at that rate, by 2000 Boulder would be bigger than New York City. Some stability. Fortunately, the doubling slowed, as Boulder residents resisted developing all the empty bottles of open space that surrounded their city, lest the scenic reason for living there in the first place vanish—along with the city's water supply.

In recent years, Bartlett has raised some controversy by proposing an end to immigration before the United States is engulfed with humanity. But even critics who challenge the ethical, practical, social, and environmental complexity of such a measure don't argue with his math — especially when the scale gets so big that we lose sight of what's happening to us. The planetary scale, for instance. In 1900, there were 1.6 billion people on Earth. Then, during the twentieth century, the world's population doubled, and then doubled again. How much space did that leave in our bottle? How can we tell if, in fact, we've already filled it up?

The shuttles have stopped flying from Cape Canaveral. Something else has stopped in Florida, too, at least for now: the biggest single-dwelling housing boom in history. In 1999, the *Tampa Tribune* reported, land-use plans for the state's 470 cities and counties would allow for 101 million residents, amounting to "stuffing the populations of California, Texas, New York and Pennsylvania into Florida's borders." That figure may have accurately reflected Florida planners' chronic disregard for orchards, farms, woodlands, wildlife, lakes, rivers, and aquifers.

Ten years later, the ghost suburbs infringing one of Earth's rarest ecosystems, the Everglades, attested that they disregarded more than that. A wasteland of empty Spanish-tiled condos, foreclosed shopping centers, and unfinished hospitals was succumbing to advancing mold atop what, a decade earlier, were marshlands filled with wood storks and endangered Cape Sable sparrows, edged by tomato fields.

This is one of several ground zeros in America's Sun Belt of the 2008 subprime mortgage bust. Having run out of qualified home buyers as U.S. middle-class jobs were outsourced, banks invented mortgages based on a fantasy that someone who couldn't afford monthly payments on 6 percent loans would magically be able to pay ballooned rates seven or ten years later. Concealing thousands of these dubious loans in packages impressively named derivatives, they then sold them to duped investors around the world. (For good measure, they purchased short positions on those packages that allowed them a tidy profit when they proved worthless.)

Presumably, the world now knows better—except, despite the economic carnage that left Florida with three hundred thousand vacant housing units, its local governments have since approved zoning for five hundred fifty thousand more. Such an apparent disconnect from reality reveals what psychologists might call a dysfunctional codependence between our population and our economy. If we measure economic health, as we commonly do, by the number of monthly housing starts, somebody has to live in those houses we then build, and furnish and decorate them, and buy whatever it takes to run and maintain them. That's a lot of products, each representing jobs for whoever made and sold them. The more jobs, the more workers—wherever they live—needed to fill them. The more products, the more customers needed to buy them. That sounds nicely circular, and it might be—except for the *more* part.

At some point, something finally runs out. In the housing market collapse, the shortage was of people with enough money to pay their mortgages, leading to millions of foreclosures. But in the United States as in the world, people's numbers keep growing nonetheless, and as they do, so must the planet's economy to feed, clothe, shelter them—and beyond those basics, serve and entertain them in as many ways as they need or desire, and in as many ways as marketers can persuade them that there's something new and exciting that they also need. So instead of a circle, it's a spiral. Numbers spiral upward, cities spiral outward, housing adds up, and then suddenly there's sprawl. Which, except for developers, is too much of a good thing.

In 1950, two-thirds of humans still lived rurally. Today, more than half live in cities. Urban dwellers, needing fewer farm hands, tend to have fewer children. In fact, humanity's doubling rate has finally slowed. But slowing doesn't mean not growing. To say that urbanization has solved overpopulation overlooks the fact that, in much of the world, the barn door was closed only after the horses had already bolted.

Even if today's breeding generation is having fewer children per family, because their grandparents and parents had so many, every four-and-a-half days there are a million more people on the planet. Even to a schoolchild, that does not sound very sustainable.

There are now nearly five hundred cities with a million or more people. Twenty-seven cities have more than 10 million, and twelve of those have more than 20 million. (Greater Tokyo, the biggest urban area, has 35 million.) By the middle of this century, at our present decelerating pace, we'll still add nearly half again as many people as we already have, increasing to between 9 and 10 billion,[1] maybe more, all eliminating wastes and emitting carbon dioxide, all requiring food, fuel, living space, multiple services — and for those who've recently moved to town from the hinterlands, considerably more electricity to charge their mobile phones and plug in their inevitable TVs.

All that CO_2 adds up, and keeps adding: A 2008 study by Oregon State University scientists Paul Murtaugh and Michael Schlax estimated that, predicting

---

1. This estimate, widely accepted, comes from the United Nations Population Division.

eventual emissions by a mother's descendants, under current conditions in the United States, "each child adds about 9441 metric tons of carbon dioxide to the carbon legacy of an average female, which is 5.7 times her lifetime emissions." It doesn't take the math skills of a physicist to calculate that something is askew when five-hundred-year floods or storms start hitting twice or more in the same decade. In recent years, on every inhabited continent and archipelago, students have watched their schools drown.

As we struggle already with sustaining 7 billion, awakening to surprises like dust storms from China big enough to span oceans, or the forests of western North America, Siberia, and Australia exploding in flames, the prospect of 10+ billion not only defies our imagination, but like subprime lending, it might also defy reality. In the entire history of biology, every species that outgrows its resource base suffers a population crash—a crash sometimes fatal to the entire species. The issue may be not just whether we need to stop growing, but whether, for our own survival, we must humanely bring our numbers down from where they are now to a figure we can, literally, all live with.

———

Whether we accept it or not, this will likely be the century that determines what the optimal human population is for our planet. It will come about in one of two ways:

Either we decide to manage our own numbers, to avoid a collision of every line on civilization's graph — or nature will do it for us, in the form of famines, thirst, climate chaos, crashing ecosystems, opportunistic disease, and wars over dwindling resources that finally cut us down to size. Managing population, as China has attempted, conjures frightening images of coercive governments invading our bedrooms and even our nurseries. Yet a surprising assortment of cultures have found nonintrusive ways to encourage people that smaller families might be in their own self-interest, as well as their society's.

And the best interest of their planet?

"The idea that growing human numbers will destroy the planet is nonsense. But over-consumption will," read a 2010 *Prospect Magazine* article titled "The Overpopulation Myth." Many would agree: Reduce the amount of stuff in our lives, and shrink our footprint so that we're not stomping the hell out of everything else. And learn to share: If we equitably distributed all the food we grow, there'd be plenty for everybody.

These are worthy goals. But the notion that everybody's consumptive urge could be stifled anytime soon is probably wishful hoping. If saving the planet depends on changing acquisitive human nature—meaning, among other things, bucking the vast budgets of commercial advertising—the Earth will likely be thoroughly sacked long before that's ever accomplished.

As for equal distribution of food: Does that mean among all living species, or just our own? Ever since God informed Noah that in order to start the human race anew, he had to save not just his family but all the animals, it should be understood that we can't have a world without them. But with food production for humans currently occupying some 40 percent of the Earth's nonfrozen terrestrial surface, plus all our roads, cities, and towns, we've claimed nearly half the planet for just one species—us. How are all the others going to make a living?

If everyone were vegetarian, herbivores argue, we'd only need a quarter of that land, since all the rest presently goes either to grazing livestock or to growing feed for them. (And producing a kilogram of beef emits as much carbon dioxide as an average car driving 160 miles, and uses ten times the water as a kilo of wheat.) All very true—but again, not so easy, as it's also true that world meat demand is still rising, not falling. Most people, when they finally can afford it, tend to crave it. Healthier or not, vegans may not prevail anytime soon.

Since population is mainly growing in the poorest countries, and since poor women have the babies, to expect the weakest to rescue the world from the damage the most powerful have done to it seems grossly unjust. "Blaming environmental degradation on overpopulation lets the real culprits off the hook," reads "10 Reasons to Rethink 'Overpopulation,'" a 2006 issues paper on PopDev, a website run by Hampshire College's Population and Development Program director and women's health activist Betsy Hartmann. "In terms of resource consumption alone," it continues, "the richest fifth of the world's people consume 66 times as much as the poorest fifth. The U.S. is the largest emitter of greenhouse gases responsible for global warming—and the least willing to do anything about it."

Except for China's carbon emissions having now surpassed the USA's, and the odds favoring the wealthy now being even more lopsided, these arguments are still persuasive. However, fair or not, in today's global ecosystem everyone's presence matters. Our numbers have reached a point where we've essentially redefined the concept of original sin. From the instant we're born, even the humblest among us compounds the world's mounting problems by needing food, firewood, and a roof, for starters. Literally and figuratively, we're all exhaling CO_2 and pushing other species over the edge. And not only is the United States an egregious polluter, it's also still growing, faster than any other developed nation. Any discussion of population reduction that doesn't include the USA would be pointless, let alone racist.

Then, there's the rosy opinion that necessity has always given birth to invention when we need it, and that our creative knack for technology will surely solve the future — Israel's technological optimism. "We learn how to dig deeper, pump faster. And we invent new sources of energy," wrote University of Maryland economist Julian Simon in his 1996 book, *The Ultimate Resource 2*. The ultimate resource he referred to was human ingenuity, and he advocated population growth, so we'd have more of it.

Yet technological leaps have yet to solve anything without causing other unforeseen problems. Plus, as the hydrogen community knows, they're hard problems. That includes the other form of hydrogen-based energy, cold fusion — basically, a controlled H-bomb — whose projected arrival seems perpetually forty years away. So far, our best alternative energy sources are solar and wind. Although there are multiple ways to apply them far more widely than we do, we've barely begun, and the world's biggest business, intent on squeezing the last drop of petroleum out of the Earth's crust, isn't helping matters much. Even if we vastly improved our energy efficiency, to ramp solar and wind up to meet the demands of all our transport and industries, and of our Chinas and Indias, would be far beyond their capacity to deliver at this point.

And even if we somehow conjured up a truly limitless, emissions-free energy source, it wouldn't cure traffic, or sprawl, or noise pollution. Inevitably, it would only stimulate hunger for more resources. However, the one technology that in fact could make a dent in our collective impact is one we already have: the one that lets us curb the number of consumers.

Family planning—a less onerous term for birth control—can't solve everything: we still should try to convert everyone possible, especially the coming generation, from energy-addicted carnivores into sharing, environmentally astute, low-carbon sustainers. It's also not without its perils: like anything else humans do, it can be, and has been, misused for evil, such as eugenics. And if population reduction implies a shrinking economy, we're already plenty scared of that one. Yet when numbers come down, as Japan, whose aging population is already on the verge of shrinking, is discovering, there may be new opportunities for prosperity that we missed in the mad rush to grow and grow more, until we smash into reality.

Among them is the chance to equalize things far better than we have. So let's define *optimum population* as the number of humans who can enjoy a standard of living that the majority of us would find acceptable. A standard of living, say, roughly equivalent to a European level, pre-euro-crisis[2]: far less energy-intensive than the United States or China, far more hospitable than much of Africa or Southeast Asia, and with the highest possible percentage of educated, enabled women — which may be the most effective contraceptive of all.

So how many is that? And how do we get there?

Since it took nearly two hundred thousand years since *Homo sapiens* first appeared for our population to reach 1 billion, around 1815, and now we suddenly have seven times that many — how the hell did that happen? How did we get *here?*

---

2. The result of the same housing debacle.

CHAPTER 3

Body Counts and the Paradox of Food

i. Bodies

Genetic evidence suggests that at some point between fifty thousand to one hundred thousand years ago, our *Homo sapiens* ancestors possibly numbered as few as ten thousand. Then they began to wander out of Africa, following the species corridor north through present-day Israel and Palestine and branching into Europe, Asia, and beyond. Discovering more sustenance as they spread, they began to increase, but almost imperceptibly. As the Worldwatch Institute's Robert Engelman notes in his book *More,* had they multiplied at modern growth rates (currently 1.1 percent annually worldwide, which means doubling every sixty-three years), within a few millennia, not just

Earth but the entire solar system couldn't have contained us.

The simple reason population remained low until recent human history was that people died about as fast as people were born. For tens of thousands of years, most of them likely didn't see their first birthday. Birth rates might be high, but so were infant mortality rates. A woman would give birth to seven, and two might live.

Two people, one man and one woman who produce two children, essentially replace themselves.[1] Any more than two, population grows. The fact that population grew so slowly until about two centuries ago means that the average number of children who lasted long enough to have children themselves was barely more than two. For every family with more than two who survived to adulthood, others had only one or none who made it — at any number below two, population contracts.

Occasionally, it contracted dramatically, such as during the Black Plague, which killed off an estimated one-fourth of humanity in the mid-fourteenth

---

1. Demographers today put replacement rate at slightly higher than two (an average of 2.1 children per female in the developed world) because some child mortality is inevitable. For developing nations, where children are more vulnerable, the number is higher. The world's average replacement rate is 2.33.

century. But even without unusual epidemics, the general pall of death that hung over every family didn't began to dissolve until 1796. That year, British surgeon Edward Jenner discovered a vaccine for smallpox, a disease that used to knock back our numbers each year by the millions. Jenner's cure was also the first vaccine for anything. It inspired nineteenth-century French chemist Louis Pasteur to develop others, against rabies and anthrax. Pasteur made two other key contributions to human survival. One was the familiar process our dairies still use. Pasteurization extended the shelf life of milk, which improved nutrition and reduced infections from pathogens such as salmonella and those causing scarlet fever, diphtheria, and tuberculosis.

Pasteur was also instrumental in convincing humanity that disease did not occur through some mysterious spontaneous generation, but was spread by germs. In the nineteenth century, hand soap became common for the first time, both in homes and in hospitals. Before, patients died as often from infections picked up from a surgeon's unsterilized hands and scalpel as from the ailment he was trying to fix. One of the first uses of surgical disinfectant was in a maternity ward in Vienna, where doctors washing their hands in a chlorine solution lowered both infant and maternal mortality by a factor of

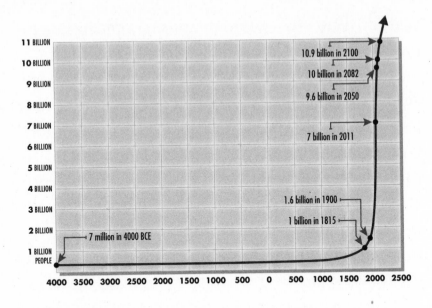

ten—an innovation with a direct impact on the number of living humans.

In the twentieth century, medical advances kept coming, each saving—and extending—more human lives. After Cuban microbiologist Carlos Finlay pinpointed the carrier of the yellow fever virus, American doctors William Gorgas and Walter Reed implemented the world's first massive mosquito control program, without which the Panama Canal would never have been completed. More vaccines for diphtheria, tetanus, and finally polio, and the crucial invention of antibiotics, all lowered mortality and increased longevity—which meant that more total people, young and old, were alive. In 1800, average life expectancy at birth for most humans was forty years. Today, in much of the world, it's nearly double.

More people not dying early and living longer: Who could object to that? "The humane goals of lowering the death rate are very important to me," admits Albert Bartlett cheerfully, "if it's my death they're lowering."

No disagreement from anyone over forty, who might well not be alive without these medical victories. Probably nobody else will protest, either. So any discussion of an optimum population for the human race must assume optimal health care. The idea of lowering medical standards to limit our numbers is no more acceptable than thinning ourselves by selective culling.

That doesn't dismiss, however, an ethical argument raised by the implications of further medical advances. If any of the current greatest challenges—say, finding cures for malaria or HIV—were successfully met, it would spur a significant uptick in humanity's census. Malaria alone kills a child every thirty seconds. If children stop dying from it, they'll survive to reproduce more children who also won't die of malaria. As it would be unconscionable to oppose malaria eradication just to keep human numbers in check, the question becomes whether funders of malaria and HIV research have a moral obligation to also fund family planning—lest our numerical impact threaten the very ecological underpinnings of human life.

Thus far, there's no vaccine against extinction.

ii. Brave New Cornucopia

The other reason that humanity ballooned so suddenly in the last century was an unprecedented increase of the food supply. To be able to nourish everyone on Earth sounds like another moral no-brainer. Yet this one's a little trickier. It raises a paradox that, at first, seems as counterintuitive as the unexpected results of exponential doubling.

The growing number of people was crucial to the success of the labor-intensive European Industrial Revolution. But it also meant that Europe had to produce more food than ever before to feed them. A German chemist, Justus von Liebig, is credited with two contributions to that cause—one huge, the other monumental. The huge one was developing the world's first infant formula. Whether his creation was, as he claimed, nutritionally equivalent to mother's milk is still hotly contested. Nevertheless, it freed many mothers from the exhausting business of breast-feeding indefinitely, and it allowed their babies to survive early weaning. And since lactation releases hormones that tend to suppress ovulation, less breast-feeding resulted in even more pregnancies.

Justus von Liebig's second, monumental discovery was that nitrogen, along with phosphorus and potassium, is one of the essential nutrients for plants. Although he is considered the inventor of fertilizer, he was not responsible for the artificial nitrogen fertilizer used today, an innovation that probably changed the course of human events more than any other in modern history, cars and computers included. That would come later. In von Liebig's day, commercial nitrogen fertilizers came chiefly from the excrement of seabirds and bats. Particularly prized was guano from islands off the coast of Peru, where cormorants, pelicans, and gannets that fed on enormous schools of nutrient-rich anchovetas had deposited layers of white poop 150 feet thick. In the nineteenth century, galleons and steamships carried more than 20 million tons of it around Cape Horn to Europe.

Having neglected to patent his discoveries, von Liebig profited little from them. Later, chagrined at the riches accrued by Nestlé and other competitors, he did secure the rights to one last invention that arguably contributed to human nutrition: the beef bouillon cube.

*   *   *

The essential nutrient nitrogen is a gas so relatively inert that, unlike hydrogen, there's plenty of it floating around in its free state. In fact, over three-fourths of the air we breathe is pure nitrogen. Nothing in our lungs chemically combines with it, so we harmlessly exhale it away. In all nature, only one family of enzymes can fix airborne nitrogen — that is, absorb and chemically convert it into a nongaseous form, such as the plant food ammonium. And just a few plants host bacteria bearing these enzymes, which, in return, get fed by nodules on their roots.

They are mainly legumes, such as lentils, beans, clover, soy, peas, alfalfa, gum acacia, and peanuts. Until synthetic fertilizer, such symbiotic plant-bacteria pairs were the main source of nitrogen in soil, limiting the amount of plant life the planet could produce. Virtually anything green that grew was benefiting from nitrogen that leguminous plants had fixed. For that reason, farmers traditionally would rotate legumes with grains, or grow them together (such as corn and beans in Latin America), or plow cover crops like nitrogen-rich clover into their fields to replenish them.

Justus von Liebig was now bringing extra nitrogen into the mix from halfway around the world, but since his fertilizers came from natural sources, they, too, were limited by the biological food chain. By the beginning of the twentieth century, the easy pickings on Peruvian islands were already exhausted, and new guano wasn't being produced as fast as new human babies. The next nitrogen source to be exploited was saltpeter: sodium nitrate crystals that occur in abundance only in very dry environments such as Death Valley, California, and Chile's Atacama Desert. Then, in 1913, agricultural technology broke through nature's ceiling. Fritz Haber and Carl Bosch, who figured out how to grab nitrogen out of the air and feed it to plants in quantities far beyond what von Liebig had ever imagined, were also Germans. Each would be awarded a Nobel Prize for his separate contribution to what became known as the Haber-Bosch process, which has transformed the world like no other. And each would be undone by his German nationality.

Fritz Haber was born to a Prussian Hasidic Jewish merchant family in 1868. He studied chemistry under Robert Bunsen, whose eponymous burner considerably enhanced laboratory research. In 1905, while teaching at the University of Karlsruhe and researching thermodynamics, Haber discovered that by passing nitrogen and hydrogen over an iron catalyst at $1,000°C$, he could produce small amounts of ammonia. Later, adding high pressure, he accomplished this at half the temperature.

After he published his findings, his process was acquired by the German dye manufacturer BASF. They assigned a young engineer, Carl Bosch, to scale Haber's ammonia lab experiment up to industrial levels. Bosch spent four years designing double-chambered pipes that wouldn't explode under pressure, a purified iron catalyst, and blast furnaces that could handle both high pressures and temperatures.

In 1913, BASF opened its first synthetic ammonia plant. Ammonia was the feedstock for ammonium sulfate—nitrogen fertilizer. The dye manufacturer was now in a completely new business: agro-industry. Within a few years their new artificial nutrient was already making history, as an Allied blockade cut Germany's access to Chilean saltpeter during World War I. Not only could Germany now keep feeding itself, but ammonium sulfate could be converted into synthetic saltpeter, from which BASF was soon manufacturing gunpowder and explosives. Without the Haber-Bosch process, World War I would have been far shorter.

Fritz Haber's discovery of how to synthesize fertilizer was so enormous that a Nobel Prize in chemistry should have been no surprise. But coming in 1918 just as the war ended, it was controversial. During the war, Haber achieved the rank of captain for first proposing, and then directing, Germany's use of chemical weapons against enemy trenches. When his wife, also a chemist, learned he was responsible for chlorine and mustard gas attacks, she committed suicide. (Later, their chemist son would also take his life, for the same reason.)

Haber's knack for developing agricultural chemistry that could be turned to darker purposes didn't end there. A pesticide fumigant he created to use in grain storage, cyanide-based Zyklon A, was later refined by Nazi chemists into the more potent Zyklon B gas used in extermination camps. Although born Jewish, Haber was not a direct victim of his own invention. For converting to Lutheranism as a student and for his substantial military contribution, he was assured in 1933 that orders from the new Nazi government that cost a dozen Jews in his laboratory their jobs didn't apply to him. When he quit in protest over their firing, he was shocked to find that his only choice was exile. A patriot who'd had no qualms about applying his genius to chemical warfare, outside of Germany he became a broken man. Within a year he died—en route to Palestine, where Zionist and future Israeli president Chaim Weizmann had invited him to head the research institute that today bears Weizmann's name.

Carl Bosch, named director of I. G. Farben, the conglomerate that bought BASF, became one of the most powerful industrialists in Germany. His own Nobel Prize, in 1931, was for his high-pressure chemistry achievements, which also included inventing steam reformation of natural gas to produce hydrogen. Alarmed by the Third Reich, at one point he met with Hitler to try to discourage him from leading their country into another war. The Fürher wasn't swayed, except to arrange for Bosch's dismissal from I. G. Farben, which later produced Zyklon B. Despondent and alcoholic, Bosch died in 1940.

Between the two wars that their work helped to prolong so horribly, Haber and Bosch's synthetic fertilizer process spread around the world, eventually revolutionizing agriculture. Creating artificial fertilizers requires high temperature and pressure, meaning intense energy inputs (now 1 percent of the world's total). Because fertilizers also need natural gas for their hydrogen component, they are doubly dependent on fossil fuels. Our supply of artificial nitrogen, therefore, will last only as long as they do. But as long as we have it, artificial nitrogen practically doubles the amount of that plant nutrient that nature can provide, and nearly half of us could not be here without it.

Before artificial nitrogen fertilizer became widely available, the world's population was around 2 billion. When we no longer have it — or if we ever decide to stop using it — that may be a number to which our own naturally gravitates.

iii. Hunger

In August 1954, twenty-nine-year-old Bill Wasson was reassured that God existed. Raised in a devout, charitable Catholic family in Phoenix, Arizona, he'd never had cause to doubt — until, while preparing to be a missionary, the Benedictines expelled him during his final year of seminary. Emergency surgery to remove half of his thyroid, they ruled, had left him too weak for the priesthood.

Crushed, he'd returned home. His family convinced their sorely depressed son to enter graduate school. He earned a master's degree in law and sociology, but remained underweight and moody. A Mexican vacation almost turned disastrous when he relapsed, until a Mexico City doctor determined that he'd been unwittingly overdosing himself with his daily thyroid medication. Suddenly Wasson felt better than he had in years. Grateful to have found a physician he trusted, he stayed and took a position teaching psychology and criminology at the University of the Americas.

Still, he mourned his lost dream to be a priest to the needy. He finally went to a psychoanalyst, who was also a Catholic priest. "You're not crazy," he told Wasson. Instead of psychotherapy, he prescribed a meeting with the new bishop of Cuernavaca, an hour south of Mexico City. In his first year, 1953, Bishop Sergio Méndez Arceo had already scandalized wealthy parishioners, and endeared himself to the poor, by adding street mariachis to the cathedral's Sunday Mass. After two hours of grilling the gangly, fair-haired American, he told Wasson to get ready. "In four months, I'm ordaining you."

He gave him Tepetates, the Cuernavaca market-place church. Wasson loved it. He turned half his quarters into a free clinic and soup kitchen. When a thief who'd been pilfering the poor box turned out to be a homeless orphan, he refused to let the police jail him. "He's not a criminal," Wasson said. "He's just hungry."

Instead, he took the boy in. The next day came a knock on his door. It was the police, with eight more orphans from their lockup. "Since you think they're just innocent waifs, you can have these, too."

Wasson scrambled fast. By that night, he'd found a vacant beer warehouse they could all sleep in. The word soon got around: a gringo priest was taking in abandoned boys. Within a month, he had thirty.

Within three months, eighty-three. He was amazed that there were so many out there. He wanted to find them all.

In 1954, Mexico's population had just passed 25 million. Surging twice as fast as the planet's population, it would more than quadruple in just the next half-century. Many of his boys, Wasson soon learned, had more than ten siblings. Some even had more than twenty, if they counted half-siblings in *casas chicas*—the families their fathers kept on the side. When women died—all too often from the exhaustion of raising so many, mainly by themselves—men frequently disappeared.

One night he returned to find the boys huddled around his radio, listening to reports of a hurricane in Veracruz. Orphaned children were reported wandering the flooded streets. "Padre, you have to go save them," they insisted.

They were living on donated food, and on blankets on the floor. "We barely have enough beans and tortillas and blankets for ourselves—" he started to protest.

But they'd already decided. "We'll share."

He came back with thirty more. Fortunately, people who'd learned what he was doing, and who kept telling him he couldn't keep taking them all, also kept helping him find food and money when he ignored them. When he realized that several new boys from the ravaged Gulf Coast were worrying about brothers they'd left behind, he returned to find them. His family numbered nearly two hundred when the bishop's secretary quit her job to help him, because the boys had sisters, too.

By 1975, Nuestros Pequeños Hermanos, Our Little Brothers and Sisters, population twelve hundred, was the biggest orphanage in the world. Mexico City was the biggest city in the world, and Mexico itself, population 60 million, was the planet's fastest-growing country—so fast that the government that year defied the Catholic Church and began a national family-planning program. Mule-back riders were soon climbing mountains and descending canyons, their polystyrene saddlebags bearing condoms and birth control pills—and also polio and diphtheria-pertussis-tetanus vaccines. Women, it turned out, were willing to hike to a village clinic for pills to avoid pregnancy as long as their living children would be vaccinated against diseases that might otherwise kill them.

Within a decade, Mexico's doubling rate slowed from every fifteen years to every twenty-four years. Had it not continued to lower, theoretically by the twenty-second century there might have been a billion Mexicans—a physical impossibility that long before would have overwhelmed both its environment and whatever fence its neighbor to the north might have built to keep them out. Today, Mexico's average family is just 2.2 children: almost replacement rate. Even so, the sheer momentum of population growth means Mexico will keep growing in coming decades, as the ones already born add children of their own.

Father Bill Wasson already had more than he could feed. More than half the time he was off raising funds to keep them alive, clothed, and schooled. In the late 1970s, he moved his huge family south of Cuernavaca to a donated former sugarcane hacienda that Emiliano Zapata's troops had sacked during the 1910 Mexican Revolution. The plan was to grow enough corn, beans, and vegetables to feed all the children. To assist came Dr. Edwin Wellhausen, recently retired from the International Maize and Wheat Improvement Center, known by its Spanish acronym, CIMMYT.[2] Founded by the Rockefeller Foundation near the famous Teotihuacán pyramids northeast of Mexico City, CIMMYT is considered today the birthplace of the so-called Green Revolution. Its late director, Dr. Norman Borlaug, was awarded the Nobel Peace Prize for developing a disease-resistant, high-yield strain of dwarf wheat (dwarf, because normal wheat plants would fall over from the weight of the

---

2. Centro Internacional de Mejoramiento de Maíz y Trigo.

extra grains Borlaug's genetically selected strains produced).

Edwin Wellhausen was CIMMYT's corn-breeding specialist. He had developed a high-lysine amino acid corn variety that would significantly raise protein levels in the tortillas that the Nuestros Pequeños Hermanos children ate at every meal. A tall, thin, bespectacled man in a straw sombrero, Wellhausen arrived with a trailer truck loaded with hundreds of white sacks. Some contained donated seed. Others were ammonium nitrate and urea: nitrogen fertilizers. The rest were pesticides and fungicides: Green Revolution laboratory-bred hybrids, forced quickly through generations to emphasize certain desired traits, lacked resistance to various bugs that grains like corn, a native to Mexico, had acquired over thousands of years of evolution.

By now, Father Wasson had a sizable staff, including many of his grown children who were helping to raise and teach the next generation of Little Brothers and Sisters. The appearance of all these chemicals, several of them poisonous, provoked a discussion about potential threats to the children and to the soils of their donated hacienda. Another concern was cost. This truckload was a gift, but after a quarter-century, the orphanage had learned that an act of charity rarely keeps giving forever.

It was a short discussion. They had too many mouths to feed. They would worry about it later.

———————

At one point during the twenty-five-mile drive from Mexico City to CIMMYT, the highway briefly passes through something startling: empty land. The bleak salt marsh is what remains of Lago Texcoco, the largest of five lakes that filled this high basin in central Mexico when Hernán Cortez's Spanish troops first saw it. The Aztec capital, called Tenochtitlán, was on an island, connected to the shore by causeways. After the conquest, the Spaniards drained the lakes; eventually, the basin refilled and overflowed—with people. Today, 24 million live in one of the Earth's greatest expanses of continuous concrete and asphalt, covering Mexico's Distrito Federal and parts of five surrounding states. The sheer weight of the city atop its overpumped aquifer has sunk it so low that sewage canals no longer flow outward. Especially when it rains, Mexico City is in danger of drowning in its own wastes, requiring construction of the world's longest sewer pipe: twenty-three feet across and thirty-seven miles long, tunneling nearly five hundred feet down to drain into a valley below.

Past the gray thorn scrub of the dry lake bed and some low hills composed entirely of automobile carcasses, urbanity resumes until the road reaches fields of wheat and maize surrounding the agricultural research center. A billboard near the entrance shows Norman Borlaug, who died in 2009 at ninety-five, in khaki shirt and pants, waist-high in dwarf wheat, notebook in hand. His many international awards are noted above the green and white CIM-MYT logo, including the 1970 Nobel Peace Prize. Only five years earlier, Borlaug and his team had put the hybrids they'd developed in Mexico to the test in India and Pakistan. Both were nearing famine, despite massive grain imports from the United States. By 1970, harvests in both countries doubled and imminent disaster was averted. Green Revolution crops and breeding techniques began to spread around the world. In 2007, the United States awarded Borlaug its Congressional Gold Medal for having saved more lives than anyone in history.

He was also widely credited for having scuttled the dour predictions of Thomas Robert Malthus, a British economist and Anglican vicar. Malthus's 1798 magnum opus, *An Essay on the Principle of Population*, warned that population growth would always outstrip food availability. This, Malthus concluded, doomed the masses to misery as their burgeoning numbers divided ever further what little pie was allotted to them. Many scientists, most notably Charles

Darwin, were directly influenced by his work. Most economists, however, bridled at the suggestion that growth—especially, in Malthus's time, growth of the labor force—was anything but wonderful. Malthus's pronouncements seemed so inherently dismal, so contrary to the natural impulse to add more life to the world, that his scholarly essay became universally notorious. More than two centuries later, both its unsettling power and notoriety continue, and his name has entered the language, usually as a pejorative: *Malthusian.*

In 1968, Malthus's ominous caveat was resurrected by a Stanford University ecologist, Paul Ehrlich, in a book titled *The Population Bomb.* By then, we had reached 3.5 billion—half of today's count. Ehrlich, an entomologist who studied population dynamics in butterflies, had begun to lecture and write about human population following a trip to India with his wife and collaborator, Anne. Their book[3] predicted widespread famines and accompanying disasters, beginning in the 1970s.

The year *The Population Bomb* appeared was also the same year that humans first got far enough away from Earth to turn around and take its picture. A

3. Anne Ehrlich was not credited as coauthor of *The Population Bomb,* due to a publisher's decision. Many subsequent books and articles have appeared under both Ehrlichs' names.

photograph by Apollo 8 astronaut Bill Anders of the Earth rising over the moon's horizon, so vividly alive compared to the surrounding black void, helped ignite a popular environmental movement that had been smoldering since *Silent Spring,* Rachel Carson's seminal book on pesticides sixteen years earlier. The following year, the United Nations declared the first Earth Day. By 1970, Earth Day was a worldwide movement.

With the Ehrlich book, population joined pesticides and pollution as a headliner on the environmental agenda. *The Population Bomb* sold millions of copies. In the United States, Paul Ehrlich became a celebrity, appearing on *The Tonight Show with Johnny Carson* more than twenty times. Like Malthus's name, his book's title entered and remains in the popular vernacular in many languages—even after its most urgent argument apparently proved wrong. The famines that it predicted would leave hundreds of millions Asians dead within a decade never happened. The Ehrlichs had not foreseen Norman Borlaug's astonishing Green Revolutionary boost to the world's food supply.

In the decades that followed, Ehrlich's and Borlaug's names became routinely linked, usually by the former's detractors. "Ehrlich was sure that 'the battle to feed humanity is over.' He insisted that India would be unable to provide sustenance for the two-hundred-million-person growth in its population by 1980," wrote Duke University engineering professor Daniel Vallero in a 2007 textbook titled *Biomedical Ethics for Engineers*. "He was wrong—thanks to biotechnologists like Norman Borlaug." This was a typical jeer: While the doomsayer Ehrlich prophesized starvation in India and Pakistan, Borlaug was bringing both countries to self-sufficiency in wheat production by the mid-1970s.

Through "technical optimism," Vallero added, "engineers 'mess up' the Malthusian curve by finding ways to accomplish this (e.g., Borlaug spoiling Ehrlich's predictions)." This was a typical conclusion: by enabling millions more to eat and live, Norman Borlaug had refuted Ehrlich and Malthus's panic-mongering about overpopulation.

That conclusion, however, was not shared by Borlaug himself. His Nobel Peace Prize acceptance speech ended not in triumph, but with a warning:

> ...we are dealing with two opposing forces, the scientific power of food production and the biologic power of human reproduction. Man has made amazing progress recently in his potential mastery of these two contending powers. Science, invention, and technology have

given him materials and methods for increasing his food supplies substantially and sometimes spectacularly.... Man also has acquired the means to reduce the rate of human reproduction effectively and humanely. He is using his powers for increasing the rate and amount of food production. But he is not yet using adequately his potential for decreasing the rate of human reproduction....

There can be no permanent progress in the battle against hunger until the agencies that fight for increased food production and those that fight for population control unite in a common effort.

The Green Revolution, Borlaug often said, essentially bought the world another generation or so to resolve the population problem. For the rest of his life, he served on the boards of population organizations, even as he continued crop research to feed the multiplying millions his work had added to the global census.

iv. Two Generations Later

At one end of Norman Borlaug's spacious former office in the two-story CIMMYT headquarters building,

Hans-Joachim Braun perches on the edge of a hardwood conference table, hunting for a PowerPoint slide on a Dell laptop. He sets it in front of Matthew Reynolds. "In the next fifty years," the screen reads, "we will need to produce as much food as has been consumed over our entire human history."

Reynolds nods. No argument.

Along with this office, Braun has inherited Borlaug's title, director of CIMMYT's Global Wheat Program. His CIMMYT colleague Reynolds heads an international consortium of geneticists, biochemists, crop breeders, and plant physiologists like himself, racing to improve wheat yields faster than expanding populations can eat them. Borlaug's semidwarf wheat was a jump of quantum proportions, increasing harvests up to sixfold. Since then, however, gains have slowed dramatically, below 1 percent annually. Meanwhile, world population is still growing faster than that, and not peaking anytime soon: In seven of the new century's first ten years, more wheat was consumed than produced. To keep up, they figure that somehow they must increase yields 1.6 percent annually by 2020.

How can they possibly do that? Clearing more forests isn't an option, if only because when trees go, so does water. Braun is still fuming over a recent meeting at the United Nations. "We talk about global warming, we talk about all the problems, but the underlying, biggest problem—*population growth*—wasn't mentioned once." With his gray-bearded chin, he gestures at the laptop.

Not that the problems are unrelated. Like most crops, wheat is temperature-sensitive. For every degree Celsius that temperature rises, agricultural scientists calculate, wheat yields drop 10 percent in the Earth's hotter midriff. Many agronomists (and economists) had speculated hopefully that global warming might actually help yields in cooler regions, but during recent European and Russian heat waves, losses spiked beyond 30 percent. The only thing that indisputably grew with added heat was the population of crop-devouring insects.

Temperature is rising, Braun and Reynolds agree, because more people are burning fuel and eating food made from it. The number of people is rising because there's more food available. The Green Revolution's two biggest success stories are in danger of choking on their good fortune: Before 2025, India will surpass China as the world's most populous nation. Pakistan is now one the fastest-growing countries on Earth, its numbers tripling since 1970, to 187 million. Unable to generate jobs to keep up, especially for millions of frustrated young men, it's also among the world's most unstable places—and happens to be a nuclear power.

But not just more people: paradoxically, enhanced food production has resulted in a planet with more hungry people than ever before—around a billion. Thanks to agro-technology, the percentage of malnourished humans has dropped, but in creepy echoes of Malthus, the sheer number that survives to reproduce stays ahead of the pace that food reaches their tables.

"Though I have no doubt yields will keep going up, whether they can go up enough to feed the population monster is another matter," Norman Borlaug said in 1997. "Unless progress with agricultural yields remains very strong, the next century will experience sheer human misery that, on a numerical scale, will exceed the worst of everything that has come before."

Unless his successors can do something, fast, both the numbers and the percentage of the world's hungry will rise, along with their tempers. But there aren't many tricks left to try. "Reaching the moon was an engineering problem," says Braun. "To produce the food we need in the next forty years is much more complicated. It will require more investments to solve than what was invested in the Apollo program. And we don't see enough of them."

Especially, they worry, there's not enough research funding for wheat, which, they argue, with more protein than rice or maize, is the most important food crop. The reason is that, unlike corn, wheat is self-pollinating, so farmers can use their own grain to replant. "There's five times as much invested in maize," Reynolds says, "because farmers have to buy maize seed every year. Wheat, they keep the same seed. So it's not related to food security; it's related to making money." His fist hits the table. "If we were taking food security seriously, those numbers would come closer together, wouldn't they?"

It exasperates him to think of agriculture's driving incentive being not to feed, but to profit. Reynolds rises and stalks to the window. Both these men have made their careers here, working alongside Dr. Borlaug, authoring papers with him. A Nobel Peace laureate, and yet money to continue his work on the veritable staff of life that launched human civilization, and on which it still depends, is so damned scarce. Gazing out at the brown December fields, Reynolds pulls his fleece vest tighter. Beyond the test rows of hybrid corn, each with a sign explaining its complex crossbred lineage, a dozen Mexican graduate students in blue CIMMYT caps are assessing a conservation agriculture experiment to produce more food with the least damage.

What's being conserved is fertility, and possibly the atmosphere: this is CIMMYT's version of the recent trend in no-till farming. Usually, farmers burn organic detritus after harvest or feed it to their animals, then plow and harrow to eliminate weeds, mix in fertilizer, and loosen the soil for seeding. Whether by hoe, draft animal, or tractor, this takes time — often, a week or more — and energy. It also destroys soil structure created by worms, insects, and bacteria.

Not plowing, however, keeps the soil and its biological activity intact; by leaving crop residues in place, they become a nutrient sponge that holds water. Theoretically, no-till farming also keeps carbon dioxide bound in the earth.

In thirty-two CIMMYT no-till test plots, the students measure moisture, crop growth, weeds, earthworms, added benefits of rotation with legumes, and greenhouse gas emissions. Disappointingly, carbon retention isn't proving significant, although there's clearly a savings on tractor fuel. Weed control is another problem; without tillage, they're needing more herbicide. But as in nature, the system is extremely productive: wheat rows sowed with tools they've developed to punch seeds through the previous harvest's litter are twice as lush as the clean, conventionally plowed control rows. It's not organic cultivation, however; the tools — some hand-operated, some mechanized — also inject nitrogen fertilizer into the soil. No-till helps, but not enough, by their reckoning: With so many people to feed, and with half the world's calories coming from grains, CIMMYT can't see how to avoid global chaos without continuing to force-feed crops with chemicals.

The one bit of magic that might make a difference, the one for which Matthew Reynolds's worldwide consortium needs money, would be to supercharge the way plants turn air and sunlight into biomass in the first place: photosynthesis. Some increases may simply emerge from imaginative physics: Reynolds has a Chinese mathematician studying how light bounces around in a wheat field. "In a forest canopy," he explains, "light reaching leaves at the bottom is completely different from what a leaf in full sunlight receives. They also get different amounts of nitrogen. A field is a microcosm of that canopy—if we understand it better, we can improve the efficiency of photosynthesis just through better light and nitrogen distribution."

But there's only so far that can go. Borlaug's improved wheat already captures 90 percent of the solar energy it receives. The only thing left is to tinker with RuBisCO—the enzyme that actually turns atmospheric carbon dioxide into cellulose, lignin, and sugars. RuBisCO,[4] in essence, is the basis of all plant and animal life. To ratchet up its carbon-fixing capacity would require genetic modification.

----

4. An abbreviation for Ribulose-1,5-bisphosphate carboxylase/oxygenase.

In the mechanics of photosynthesis, wheat and rice are known as C3 plants — which means that the initial building-block hydrocarbon molecules they make from the CO_2 they inhale have three carbon atoms. Corn and sorghum, which evolved later, are C4 plants. At a CIMMYT sister institution, the International Rice Research Institute (IRRI) in the Philippines, plant geneticists are trying to rearrange the cell structure in rice leaves to kick it up from C3 to C4, which could raise its photosynthetic efficiency by up to 50 percent. If they're successful, CIMMYT hopes that the same ploy will work with wheat. But IRRI scientists expect it will take at least twenty years to produce commercially viable C4 rice. They also have another goal: as well as increase yields, they want to hot-rod rice with enough energy to fix its own airborne nitrogen, to lower or eliminate its dependency on synthetic fertilizer's costly fossil-fuel feedstock. Adapting any technology IRRI produces to wheat could take even longer, which doesn't help the immediate problem of feeding more Pakistanis before food wars erupt.

A British researcher Reynolds knows recently increased biomass growth by 40 percent in a tobacco plant by manipulating a single bacterial enzyme. Learning whether this might work for wheat will also require precious time and funding. Everything does:

even introducing a new variety just by crossbreeding plants takes ten to twelve years. To successfully insert genes into wheat would take twice as long and cost between \$25 to \$100 million—all before facing a gauntlet of international regulation and consumer fears of genetically modified plants.

The floor-to-ceiling white metal shelves of the Wellhausen-Anderson Genetic Resources Center, CIMMYT's gene bank of wheat and corn germplasm, contain the largest collection of maize landraces in the world: about twenty-eight thousand, mostly from Latin America, where corn originated. Landraces are varieties that farmers themselves have bred and selected over thousands of years. All trace back to a grassy weed called teosinte, corn's wild Mexican progenitor, which is also here. The yellow, white, blue, and red maize varieties are stored in plastic jugs. The wheat collection, about a hundred forty thousand modern cultivars and ancient landraces from all over the world, is hermetically sealed in aluminum pouches packed inside long cardboard boxes. Everything is bar-coded and kept at 0°C, and duplicated in a long-term collection a floor below at −18°C.

An identical set is housed at the National Center for Genetic Resources Preservation at Fort Collins,

Colorado, and yet another goes to the Svalbard Global Seed Vault in a cavern deep in the Norwegian permafrost: the so-called doomsday repository for the Earth's botanical diversity, should seed banks elsewhere be lost to disaster or war, or their source varieties succumb to climate change. The purpose of this gene bank is to dole out genetic material, five grams at a time, to breeders developing new strains. But it is also a hedge against emergencies, such as when stem rust, a dreaded wheat fungus, broke out in Uganda in 1999, and CIMMYT air-freighted hundreds of kilos of resistant seed to East Africa.

Over the coming years, CIMMYT intends to genetically classify its entire germplasm collection. Along with historic strains, it holds seeds that Norman Borlaug archived during all the steps that led to his Green Revolution varieties, believing that eventually biotechnology would allow them to see exactly what they did to improve wheat over the last few decades. They'll begin with several thousand lines whose useful traits—high yield; resistance to disease or drought—have already been identified. Taking seeds from each, they'll grow at least one plant apiece in a greenhouse, then send fresh leaves to a genotyping service, to extract DNA and produce genetic sequences for every line.

Their hope is that decoding this vast genetic heritage will reveal how, whether through transgenics or more ingenious hybrids, to keep increasing global yields without putting any more of the planet's land under cultivation. That is a widely shared ecological urgency, but at CIMMYT it's also a point of pride. The oft-repeated rejoinder here to environmental outrage over the Green Revolution's fossil fuel gluttony, its river-fouling fertilizers, its drug dependence on poisons, and its monocultural menace to biodiversity is that without improved crop varieties, billions more acres of the world's forests and grasslands would . have been plowed to keep everybody fed.

It's a claim that recognizes that a world losing its trees and other native flora is a world on the brink, yet one that neglects CIMMYT's own responsibility for the surfeit of hungry humans whose existence threatens them. Saving more lives than anyone in history also means there are more lives, period— which then beget even more. CIMMYT's dilemma is a microcosm of the world's: how to keep growing even more, in a space that does not grow.

Each new success only squeezes things tighter, and heightens the demand for still more. Even the elegant mathematics of genetic sequencing can't square a vicious circle.

More than thirty years have passed since Nuestros Pequeños Hermanos turned their donated hacienda in the Mexican state of Morelos into a home and a Green Revolution farm to feed orphan children. Father William Wasson has passed on as well, in 2006, at age eighty-two—but not before founding more branches of their family in Honduras, Haiti, the Dominican Republic, Guatemala, El Salvador, Nicaragua, Bolivia, and Peru. Many of the fifteen thousand children he raised now help run these new homes.

The original home in Mexico is still the biggest, but its population has dropped from a high of twelve hundred to around eight hundred. This change reflects Mexico's own demographic shift, from a country doubling every twenty years when Wasson took in his first homeless boy in 1954, to its current annual growth of less than 1 percent. If that pace continues, Mexico will double again in seventy-one years, but the rate of increase, now barely above replacement, is still falling. As *planificación familiar* became established in Mexico, women chose to have fewer babies, and their daughters have had fewer still. Most Mexicans now live in cities, where they don't need extra hands to tend flocks or fetch firewood. Most Mexican women want or need to work, and can't be tied down to eight kids at home.

Even though they mostly stop at two, their grandmothers didn't, and the rural villages surrounding the orphanage's hacienda are now overlapping towns. The hacienda's former sugarcane cribs are now dormitories, and a primary and secondary school have been added. Across the lawn from where children play volleyball is a life-sized bronze of three figures by sculptor Carlos Ayala, who grew up here: a seated Father Bill, talking with a boy and girl.

Behind the dormitories are the fields. Next to a galvanized steel silo, five girls shuck ears atop a mound of white corn. In the silo are a few bags of nitrogen fertilizer, the gift of a German donor. Sheep graze around fish ponds and a tilapia hatchery. There are pig pens and a chicken house. In a newly donated greenhouse, a dozen children are sowing two varieties of winter tomatoes. A drip-irrigated vegetable patch produces beets, watermelon, cabbage, lettuce, chili peppers, cauliflower, and carrots; a different child is in charge of planting and weeding each furrow.

Luis Moreno, the veterinarian in charge of the farm, inspects an ear of corn. He's grateful that the yield this year from the eight hectares they still have planted of the original forty was decent. Still, the twelve-ton harvest will provide for just one hundred days of tortillas. It's a good thing that the population is dropping, because when he arrived three years earlier, he was shocked at the condition of the soil. Decades of intensive chemicals had left fields "looking like they'd been napalmed." In some places, not even weeds grew. It reminded him of reading about the Oklahoma dust bowl in the 1930s. He could barely believe the neighbors and older children who told him how much corn used to grow here.

He's switched to no-till cultivation, and smaller plots. The owner of a nearby fertilizer plant, who underwent a sort of agro-religious conversion, now sells them organic nutrients titrated with beneficial bacteria and fungi, which Luis is applying in a fifty-fifty mix with synthetic nitrogen. In the greenhouse and truck garden, they're trying to go all organic.

"Someday I hope we're completely natural. Manure is slower, but it's long-term. Chemical fertilizer is gone in twenty days, and leaves everything saline." Slowly, by spreading animal and corn wastes, they're letting the rest of the land recover. Birds and earthworms are returning.

He looks at the girls, filling plastic pails with white corn kernels. "We don't want more dust bowl children."

CHAPTER 4

Carrying Capacity and the Cradle

i. God, Country, and Mrs. Sanger

In 1948, José Figueres Ferrer executed what may be the most original coup d'état in world history. In the aftermath of a stolen presidential election, Figueres, a coffee grower who stood all of five foot three, cobbled together an army of seven hundred irregulars that overthrew Costa Rica's government. Then, as the leader of the new ruling junta, his first act as commander in chief of the military was to abolish it.

Figueres reasoned that it was easier—and cheaper—to keep the citizenry pacified with schools, health care, and social security than with a standing army ready to suppress internal unrest. On his coffee finca in southern Costa Rica, he'd learned that paying laborers fairly, and providing them medical care and free milk for their children from his dairy, assured him of a loyal workforce. Within a year of his coup he had converted former army barracks to schools, held elections, and stepped down from the interim presidency. A few years later, he was elected democratically, and reelected twice thereafter.

The success of his revolution involved some lucky timing. With a Cold War between world capitalism and world communism incubating, the United States was too preoccupied with a sinking situation in Korea to worry about a Central American backwater. Had Costa Rica happened five years later, post–Korean War, Figueres's fate might have been that of Guatemalan president Jacobo Árbenz Guzmán, whom the CIA removed in 1954 before his land reforms could expropriate United Fruit Company banana plantations — or that of Iranian prime minister Mohammad Mosaddegh, ousted in 1953, also by the CIA, for nationalizing Iran's oil industry.

By then, Figueres had long since nationalized Costa Rican banks, enfranchised women and black voters, extended health services, and guaranteed higher education throughout the country. The resulting stability was so applauded by labor and business alike that the United States overlooked his suspect populism, especially after Fidel Castro's 1959 Cuban revolution. With Soviet money propping up Cuba like a billboard for communism in Latin America, the United States needed one for capitalism, and the most dependable democracy in the region was the obvious choice. In 1961, President Kennedy created the United States Agency for International Development, to lavish generosity on countries friendly to U.S. interests. USAID's mission in Costa Rica was one of its biggest, bestowing eight times more foreign aid per capita than anywhere else in Latin America.

It was also among the first places where the United States sent contraceptives. At the time, Costa Rica had one of the world's fastest-growing populations, with families averaging between seven and eight children. Thanks to the improved public health care Figueres instituted, most were now tending to survive—a blessing that resulted in an unexpected explosion of numbers. America's foray into family planning abroad, like its policy of buying foreign friendship, was not without controversy. The pills that USAID began distributing in Costa Rica in 1966 were the result of drug trials conducted on a Caribbean island that, to this day, still besmirch the cause of reproductive health.

In 1934, the United States began its first governmental birth control program—in Puerto Rico, which

Theodore Roosevelt had persuaded his government to keep as spoils of the 1898 Spanish-American War. Roosevelt's plan for Puerto Rico was a U.S. naval base and coaling station for ships using the canal he dreamed of digging through the Central American isthmus. Eventually, it all came to pass: The Panama Canal made the United States a world economic center, and the biggest American naval base, on Puerto Rico's eastern shore, helped make it a world military power.

Unlike the transcontinental country to which it now belonged, Puerto Rico was an island only a hundred miles long and thirty-five miles wide, without much room for its population to expand. Yet it was doing so anyway. Beginning the nineteenth century with a hundred fifty thousand people, Puerto Rico ended it with a million. The acquisition of a small, crowded isle of brown-skinned people who didn't speak English alarmed more than a few Americans. Although Puerto Ricans would be granted citizenship in 1917—in part to blunt accusations that the United States, born of a revolt against colonialism, was now a colonial power itself—even today they are denied voting in Congress or in national elections.

But Puerto Ricans could be useful. Since World War I, they have been drafted, with many dying in U.S. foreign wars. During World War II, Puerto Rican soldiers were experimentally sprayed with mustard gas to see if they were more resistant than Caucasians. And in the 1950s, Puerto Rican women became human lab mice for testing birth control pills that later were sent to Costa Rica—although by then, with only one-third of the estrogen and one-hundredth of the progesterone of those used in the Puerto Rican trials.

Scores of Puerto Rican women taking the original high-dosage pills experienced nausea, dizziness, headaches, blurred vision, bloating, or vomiting. Some suffered blood clots and strokes. The ones who died were never autopsied. None, it has been widely reported, had been informed that, except for a short trial in Boston, the new medication from G. D. Searle and Company wasn't field-tested—nor that *they* were the test. They were simply told that the tablets prevented pregnancy.

When the truth emerged, no one was particularly surprised. Puerto Rican women had already been subjected to what, until Zyklon B started hissing out of Nazi showerheads, was the most sweeping policy ever based on eugenics, a pseudoscientific distortion of Charles Darwin's theory of natural selection. During the first three decades of the twentieth century, eugenics was taught in hundreds of European and American universities, including Harvard and Yale.

Among its advocates were Theodore Roosevelt, Winston Churchill, Alexander Graham Bell, breakfast cereal magnate J. H. Kellogg, several Scandinavian governments, and Margaret Sanger, the founder of Planned Parenthood. Although Darwin himself was not a proponent, his son Leonard presided over the First International Congress of Eugenics, held in London.

The term *eugenics* is attributed to Darwin's cousin, Sir Francis Galton, a scientist who claimed a biological rationale for Britain's ruling classes: namely, superior genes. This assertion soon broadened into a theory of social and economic survival of the fittest called *Social Darwinism*. Its purported scientific logic reassured elites that some races, especially their darker-skinned colonial subjects, were inferior to others. In America, eugenics became the pretext for legitimized prejudice, including anti-miscegenation laws in several states. It spawned organizations such as Kellogg's Race Betterment Foundation, which promoted the improvement of humanity by careful breeding through racial segregation, lest the gene pool be tainted.

Margaret Sanger's embrace of eugenics involved not so much qualities to be nurtured as those to be eliminated. Her belief that the "mentally unfit" should be sterilized, conflated with her work to bring contraception to minority groups, made Planned Parenthood suspect of racism and even of plotting genocide against minorities. These charges still surface, even though luminaries like Martin Luther King Jr. were among Sanger's supporters. Although she had helped secure funding that led to development of the pill and its Puerto Rican field trials, the genocide claim concerned something with which she had little direct involvement: a mass sterilization program in Puerto Rico that began during the 1930s, and which never really ended.

Its messy context was the inept relationship of the anticolonial United States to its colonial possession. Until the late 1940s, every governor of Puerto Rico was an appointed male Caucasian mainlander, who could veto anything passed by its legislature. English was mandatory in federal courts on the island (it still is) and in schools, resulting in Spanish-speaking teachers being required to teach Spanish-speaking students in a language neither understood very well.

The prevailing acceptance of eugenics contributed to the widespread prejudicial notion on the mainland that Puerto Ricans were somehow inferior. Not until Hitler, eugenics' most ardent devotee, would the criteria of scientists who propounded it be questioned. For years, Harvard genetics students were taught that alcoholism, criminal behavior, and "feeble-mindedness"—a term Margaret Sanger also used—were inherited traits to be rooted out through breeding. According to Harvard science historian Everett Mendelsohn, their textbook stated that "the biologically poorest elements" reproduced faster than "the intellectual and cultural elements."

Against this stacked deck was the fact that Puerto Rico was becoming seriously overcrowded. By the 1930s, nearly another million had been added. (Like the planet, Puerto Rico's numbers would quadruple in the twentieth century; its current population, 4 million, doesn't include 4 million more *puertorriqueños* living in the mainland United States—to which, as U.S. citizens, they can emigrate freely.) In 1934, with unemployment rising as fast as the population, sixty-seven federally funded birth control clinics were opened on the island through a special Puerto Rican Emergency Relief Fund. With the situation classified as an emergency, doctors were literally encouraged to cut with surgical swiftness.

Back then, there weren't many options for reliable contraception. Margaret Sanger herself imported the first diaphragms and French pessaries—cervical caps—into the United States, in open defiance of the 1873 Comstock Act that outlawed sending "obscene, lewd, and/or lascivious" materials through the mail. Even condoms were illegal until Sanger finally won court judgments acknowledging their role in preventing disease (sadly, too late to benefit U.S. World War I servicemen, who had the highest gonorrhea and syphilis rates among Allied forces). Sanger, an Irish-American Catholic whose mother died at forty after eleven children and multiple miscarriages, was a nurse and reformer for women's rights. Each time she went to jail, Sanger amassed more support for her contraceptive cause—but those supporters also included eugenicists, appalled at how "the unfit" were multiplying.

In several U.S. states, tubal ligation—severing or blocking a woman's Fallopian tubes—was allowed for enforced sterilization on alleged mental defectives, criminals, and others deemed genetically unsuitable, including people born with physical impairments. In Puerto Rico, sterilization was considered simpler and more reliable than the prophylactic or barrier devices Sanger eventually got legalized. It was usually performed postpartum, to insure that a woman's latest pregnancy would be her last. Routinely, however, she wasn't told that it was permanent. (According to women's groups against imposed sterilization, the euphemism *getting your tubes tied* implied that the procedure was reversible.) Even after the shock of Hitler cur-

tailed the American eugenics movement,[1] the program in Puerto Rico grew. By the mid-1960s,
according to numerous studies, more than one-third
of Puerto Rican women of child-bearing age had been
sterilized—ten times the mainland rate. To put that
in perspective: In 1977, when a coercive mass sterilization program in India tumbled the government of
Prime Minister Indira Gandhi, the figure was 5
percent.

Today in Puerto Rico, the phrase *la operación*
remains synonymous with sterilization. However, even
as feminists and Puerto Rican *independentistas* alike
cite it as proof of the colonial power's racism and sex-
ism, the reaction of most Puerto Rican women has
been simply to shrug. For decades now, they mostly
live in cities, want jobs, and want to stop having children after two—or even fewer: Puerto Rico's fertility rate has now dropped to 1.62 children per woman.
A tubal ligation is easier than getting men to wear
condoms, or keeping track of—or having to buy—
birth control pills. Despite abuse investigations that
eventually led to sterilization guidelines on both the
island and the mainland, by the 1980s the percentage of *puertorriqueñas* who had *la operación* climbed

---

1. With notable exceptions: California, which led the United States in
forced sterilizations, continued them into the 1960s. North Carolina's
Eugenics Board remained active until 1977.

past 45 percent, the highest in the world. Among Puerto Rican women wherever they live, says anthropologist Iris Lopez, "It is now a tradition."

As Ronald Reagan would note with wonder when he first visited Latin America as president, "They're all different countries down there." Latin American tastes toward family planning vary by locale, and Costa Rica, unlike Puerto Rico, wasn't the USA's colony, but its billboard. A bludgeon approach to population control by foisting tubal ligations on independent Costa Rica would have been no way to treat a poster country.

"In fact," says Hilda Picado, tapping her desk with brown-rimmed rectangular glasses, "sterilization was a titanic struggle here. A doctor had to agree the need was urgent. The husband's permission was required. And it was only allowed if a woman already had three children." A 1998 law finally gave Costa Rican women the right to choose it for any reason. But in a country where Catholicism is still the official state religion, reproductive rights were won in slow increments.

Hilda Picado is director general of the national Asociación Demográfica Costarricense. Her office is in a pastel condominium in La Uruca, a former coffee finca in Costa Rica's central highlands northeast of the capital, San José. Two generations ago, San

José was small enough that the aroma from mounds of coffee beans in the central market pervaded much of the city. Then, the children of Costa Rican women, who had been reproducing faster than almost anyone else on Earth, reached adulthood and spawned their own families. San José soon engulfed ten surrounding villages, including La Uruca, and now smells mainly of diesel and damp concrete.

Hilda Picado's father was one of twelve. Two of her uncles also had twelve. "Twelve wasn't that many. I knew families with sixteen, eighteen, twenty." Picado, born in 1960, was one of six. Her mother would have had more, but toward the end of the 1960s, two things happened.

The first, in 1966, was USAID's infusion of birth control pills into the clinics that President Figueres built, along with money to develop the organization Hilda now directs.

It was no coincidence that this occurred shortly after the Second Vatican Council ended. Convened by Pope John XXIII early in his five-year papacy, Vatican II was intended to modernize Catholic Church practices. It permitted vernacular language in the previously all-Latin Mass, embraced ecumenism, unveiled women, and was widely welcomed as refreshing spiritual renewal. Many Catholic intellectuals, theologians, and even clergy believed that, especially with the recent appearance of birth control pills, a major shift of church doctrine regarding contraception was now inevitable. The Pope even appointed a commission to study the matter. Although John XXIII died of stomach cancer before the study was completed, momentum for change seemed great; even his more conservative successor, Pope Paul VI, continued Vatican II and expanded the contraception study, and it was widely assumed that the Church's proscription on birth control would be overturned.

That was especially true in Latin America, where the divergent spirits of Vatican II and the Cuban revolution intersected in a movement called Liberation Theology. Throughout the region, nuns doffed their habits and dressed like the people they served, and priests preached against social and economic injustice. Liberation Theology's defense of the oppressed especially embraced women. Amid this exhilaration, the introduction of oral contraceptives into Costa Rica and its Latin American neighbors met only token opposition from Catholic clergy.

In 1966, by a 69–10 majority, clerical and lay members of the Papal Commission on Population and Birth Control voted to annul the church's prohibition. Five minority members submitted a dissenting opinion, based largely on the writings of a Polish archbishop, Karol Wojtyła, who would later become pope himself. To reverse the proscription on birth control, the dissenters held, would undermine papal infallibility. After both opinions were leaked to the press before any papal action had been taken, an angry Pope Paul VI responded with an encyclical, *Humanae Vitae,* that sided with the minority.

Humanae Vitae was a shock, but it came too late. By 1968, pills were everywhere. In officially Catholic Costa Rica, even the Ministry of Health distributed them, through its new Office of Population. The popularity of its family-planning program was aided by the second thing that dissuaded Hilda Picado's mother from having more children: a message coming over the radio into the Picados' kitchen, never heard before on Costa Rican airwaves.

"Let's not be embarrassed to discuss what God wasn't embarrassed to create," it said.

It was church-sanctioned sex education programming, including information about how to acquire and use birth control. But the clergy behind the broadcasts weren't Catholic: after *Humanae Vitae,* priests or nuns who counseled their flocks to use contraception did so at peril of excommunication.

"It was *los evangélicos!*" recalls Hilda Picado, beaming. They were Pentecostals, Baptists, Wesleyans, Methodists, Moravians, Mennonites, Presbyterians, and others that had banded together to form the

Evangelical Costa Rican Alliance, after José Figueres's peaceful coup. With this united front against anti-Protestant pressure from the official Catholic Church, their hope was to gain space for alternatives in the new Costa Rica. Even before the pill, they had spotted and begun to exploit their adversary's weakness.

By the early 1960s, evangelical "Good Will Caravans" roamed the country, spreading contraceptive advice and even offering vasectomies along with the Gospel. When birth control pills became available, they included that information with the other good news on their radio programs and helped the government distribute them. God, they assured listeners, loved them for wanting to have the number of children they could comfortably support. No one was going to hell, nor even had to ask forgiveness for something so reasonable. Having fewer children, they said, meant a better chance to escape poverty. By stressing that preventing pregnancy in the first place was the best way to avoid having an abortion, they beat the Catholics at their own game.

"The Bible gives you the freedom to decide what to do with your own life," says Hilda Picado, a Jehovah's Witness. To explain in part Costa Rica's incredible reversal in fertility rates — from 7.3 children per family in 1960 to 3.7 by 1975, to 1.93 by 2011 —

and the reason why nearly all of Latin America is approaching replacement rate, she points to the simultaneous defection rate of Catholics who have joined evangelical sects in the last fifty years: By some estimates, Latin America will have a Protestant majority before the end of this century.

Picado is currently battling conservative Catholic groups like Opus Dei to legalize the morning-after pill. "You need a backup if whatever you're using fails. Condoms break, or sperm spills over. Women forget to take a pill. Most important, women who get raped need it."

Without it, she reminds opponents, the only other backup is abortion, which is illegal in Costa Rica, and which neither Picado nor her organization supports, even though they're part of the International Planned Parenthood Federation. She cites a 2007 study that estimates twenty-seven thousand annual illegal abortions in Costa Rica. As everywhere, they account for more emergency hospitalizations than nearly anything except traffic accidents.

"The more family planning, the less abortion. That truth is as simple as the existence of water." She's proud that her country was the first in Latin America after Cuba to reach replacement rate. She's proud that her church supports her work. Some Jehovah's Witnesses, she says, aren't having children at all, taking environmental destruction and rising world tensions as signs of the End Times. Contraceptives make it easy to wait to have their families after the eternal resurrection on Earth commences.

"It's a religion that makes sense, not one that emotionally jerks you around."

ii. The Rivet Poppers

Five hours south of San José, Gretchen Daily stands in a coffee field just above the Panamanian border, afraid to move, because the pregnant fruit bat hanging from her forefinger has clearly fallen asleep, and Gretchen doesn't want to wake her. "Hey, guys, how long am I supposed to stand here?" she asks her two Stanford graduate students seated at a nearby white plastic field table.

Chase Mendenhall and Danny Karp, headlamps trained over the specimens they're measuring with calipers, grin at each other and don't answer.

It's an hour after dusk. Costa Rican researchers and more Stanford biology students are bringing in the catch from twenty mist nets they set out twice a day: at 4:30 a.m. to trap birds, and at dusk for bats. The gossamer nets, twelve meters long, woven of black polyester thread the thickness of a human hair, are invisible before sunrise and after sunset. The students string them like phantom volleyball nets from bamboo poles between the rows of coffee plants, across flyways that connect silhouetted patches of forest that edge the plantation.

This is a pretty good haul, Gretchen sees, as she waits for her bat to awaken. Because it seemed stressed by its entanglement with the mist net, after banding, Chase laid it in the "bat ICU"—a cardboard box containing a hot-water bottle—until it calmed. He then hung it on Gretchen's finger, but rather than flying off, it swung serenely and dozed off. Meanwhile, from soft cotton bags, the students are handing Chase tent-making bats, broad-nosed bats, orange nectar bats, a pale spear-nosed bat, a Sowell's short-tailed bat, a tiny insectivorous hairy-legged myotis, and a chestnut short-tailed bat. Once again, no Spix's disk-winged bat—a beautiful, long-eared, reddish-brown and cream-colored creature that clings to the insides of curled-up heliconia leaves—but they know they're around: they've recorded their calls. There are sixty-one native bat species here—nectar feeders, seed eaters, insectivores, and fruit eaters—but except for isolated ribbons, their forest has been turned to coffee plantations.

This is Coto Brus, a 360-square-mile canton in southern Costa Rica's Pacific watershed. Until the early 1950s, its jungles were barely touched by humans, other than indigenous Guaymí hunters. Then, several Italian families who'd lost their farms in World War II were offered homestead grants to settle this ostensibly empty land in exchange for declaring loyalty to Costa Rica, which needed settlers to discourage Panama's expansion interests.

Within a decade, exploding population was also pushing native Costa Ricans to this remote outpost. Clearing land was the way to stake a claim, and they used the fastest way possible. The dollar and ecological value of precious hardwoods that vanished in smoke during what is remembered as *el fosforazo*—"the torching"—is incalculable. By the late 1970s, three-fourths of the rainforest was gone. What remained was mostly on slopes too steep to cultivate.

The Stanford researchers are trying to determine how much biodiversity this fragmented countryside still sustains, and whether that biodiversity somehow contributes to the success of the agriculture. If coffee plants closest to the forest turn out to be the healthiest—meaning free of pests such as *la broca,* a tiny black African coffee-bean borer that recently turned up in Costa Rica—that would suggest that something from the forest is eating them. In Africa, where coffee originates, *la broca*'s natural predators are tiny wasps; Brazil tried importing them as a natural pest control, but they didn't thrive there. The fact that Costa Rican coffee has been spared until recently, Gretchen Daily's team surmises, may be due to any of several small insectivorous birds — rufous-capped warblers, slaty- and pale-breasted spinetails, or tropical gnat-catchers — that reside in thin bands of remaining forest in the most rugged parts of this green landscape. Or it may be these bats: in the coming weeks, Danny Karp will spend most of his waking hours collecting and preserving bat and bird guano from plastic sheets laid below the mist nets, carefully noting which species hanging in the mesh corresponds to which pile of poop, which he and laboratory techs back at Stanford will then analyze for *la broca* DNA.

This is a lot of work. Chase has a study under way to quantify the benefits from single trees still standing in farmers' fields. By her own description, Gretchen nearly went blind one year here at a microscope, trying to distinguish some six hundred species of local native bees by minute differences in how hairs grow on their heads. Since no one here can keep European honeybees anymore since they turned lethal after crossing with African killer bees, she was searching for possible native pollinators.

Eventually she found twenty bee species with coffee blossom pollen on their bodies. All live in the forest and don't like to fly very far from it. When she and her team explained in agricultural extension offices that they were testing whether Costa Rica's most important commercial crop, coffee, depended on the number of bees available to transfer pollen, they were told that of course it didn't: modern cultivars are self-pollinating, and don't need help from insects. Daily, whose thick blond hair and jogger's frame belie the fact that she's in her late forties, took this assertion that pollination is irrelevant as the latest government malarkey she's heard throughout her career in various countries, including her own. Recent research she'd seen suggested that coffee yields were lowest in tropical countries with the least amount of rainforest left. Since wherever coffee grows in the Americas was previously rainforest, she had a hunch that the difference might be due to missing pollinators.

So they've counted the beans harvested from dozens of individual coffee bushes at varying distances from the forest patches. "We've found that yields from bushes adjacent to rainforest were 20 percent higher than plants a kilometer away," she says, as the fruit bat dangling from her index finger finally stirs and flaps back into the night. "For one farm, the difference the rainforest made added up to $60,000 per year."

Next came seeing whether birds as well as bees

also help agriculture, and now they've added bats. Besides continual netting and banding, the bird research has included years of pinpointing the range of local species by using false eyelash glue to attach radio transponders the size of an M&M onto 250 of them—including tiny ones like white-ruffed and blue-crowned manakins, which weigh around a third of an ounce.

The reason for taking all these pains is that Gretchen Daily and her colleagues at Stanford's Center for Conservation Biology believe that the future of biodiversity will be determined by what happens in agricultural countrysides across the Earth's tropics. In a world where 40 percent of the nonfrozen landmass is either cultivated or grazed, there is logic in this idea. However, to many conservationists, suggesting that human-altered ecosystems can support biodiversity is sacrilege.

"Whenever we publish a paper," says Daily, "some reviewer calls it dangerous, or 'highly emotional.' We're told that as conservationists, we're supposed to be concentrating on saving the rarest of the rare."

She has no objection to anyone's efforts to do that. Unfortunately, however, "rarest of the rare" often means functionally extinct—species such as California condors, with so few individuals left they no longer play a role in the ecosystem. In the meantime, every species that still does play a role is clinging ever more precariously to the planet where they make their living. Ensuring that they still can has her attention now, especially since one of those species is her—our—own.

Besides, she is used to controversy. She springs from a veritable royal academic lineage of it.

Gretchen Daily came to her life's work through a case of mistaken identity. In the mid-1980s, she was a junior at Stanford, still sampling majors and needing a job to make tuition. A posting caught her eye; a professor named Paul Ehrlich was hiring people to check data entries for his research. Gretchen recognized the name—or so she thought. The daughter of a U.S. army doctor, she had grown up partly in Germany, where the federal agency that regulates vaccines and medicines is the Paul-Ehrlich-Institut. She wasn't aware that its namesake founder, who won a Nobel Prize for developing chemotherapy, had been dead since 1915.

She took the job, and found that it was a different Paul Ehrlich. This one was a lanky, joking biologist who handed her thousands of records dating back to 1959 of checkerspot butterfly catches he'd made in Colorado, which she was to verify for accuracy. It turned out to be easy work, as Professor Ehrlich had entered everything correctly. But she was intrigued by his meticulous investigation, how data accumulating over time revealed fascinating detail about these beautiful insects and the mountains they inhabited.

She switched her major to biology and gradually became acquainted with her boss. She soon learned that while butterfly populations were his passion, he was better known — notorious, by some accounts — for his forays into the ecology of human population. After reading *Extinction,* the latest book he'd written with his wife, Anne, that connection made perfect sense to Gretchen. Its preface, written as a parable, had become as famous within ecology circles as *The Population Bomb* was to the outside world.

It imagined a passenger who notices a mechanic popping rivets from the wing of the airplane he's boarding. The mechanic explains that the airline gets a great price for them. But it's no problem, he assures the aghast passenger: with thousands of rivets, the plane surely won't miss a few. In fact, he's been doing this for a while, and the wing hasn't fallen off yet.

The point is that there's no way to know how many missing rivets is one too many. To the passenger, it's insane to remove even one. Yet, the Ehrlichs noted, on the spaceship called Earth, humans were popping them with increasing frequency. "An ecologist can no more predict the consequences of the extinction of a given species than an airline passenger can assess the loss of a single rivet."

As Gretchen Daily came to understand, one reason why Paul Ehrlich was obsessed with butterflies was that, like birds, they were valuable environmental indicators, because they're easy to identify and sensitive to changes—especially changes caused by humans. Sooner or later, the changes affecting butterflies would be affecting the humans as well.

Ehrlich invited her to the Rocky Mountain Biological Lab field station near Crested Butte, Colorado, where he and Anne went every summer. They lived in cabins in a 9,500-foot alpine valley flanked by ridges only briefly free of snow, and rose at dawn to track birds and checkerspots flitting among groves of spruce and quaking aspen, and in meadows filled with sunflowers, bluebonnets, yellow glacier lilies, and purple larkspur. In the evening, Gretchen joined them and Paul's best friend, a bearded UC-Berkeley engineer and physicist named John Holdren, who was writing a book on energy, and his biologist wife, Cheri, over dinners of trout that Holdren and Anne Ehrlich caught while Paul and Cheri were catching butterflies.

Gretchen, dazzled by the minds discoursing across the table, contributed pies she made with local apples and cherries and her rapt, shy attention. She was disarmed by these gifted people: Paul, tall and black-haired, so solicitous and adoring of the wife he towered over; John Holdren with his intelligent gaze; Anne and Cheri's glowing skin that to Gretchen reflected inner brilliance. Cheri was writing a book on environmental toxins; Anne, who never finished her degree when the birth of their daughter intervened, had published so many papers and books that she'd earned two honorary doctorates. They were all so healthy, fun, relaxed, and made so much imaginative sense that Gretchen wanted to become like them.

In 1969, a year after *The Population Bomb* appeared, Paul Ehrlich and John Holdren had responded in the journal *BioScience* to a frequent objection to the book: that modern technology would surely solve the shortages of food, water, energy, and sea harvests that Paul and Anne Ehrlich had predicted if population kept growing.

Holdren contributed math projecting an alarming tonnage of synthetic fertilizer that would be needed indefinitely to feed ever-expanding human civilization, and its inevitable chemical consequences. He calculated that nuclear plants, then touted as the answer to the future, would run out of uranium long before the world could be powered by atomic energy.

He also mentioned a fact largely unnoticed in the

1960s: atmospheric CO_2 had risen 10 percent since the beginning of the century. Factoring that news with soaring energy demand and waste heat that power plants generate, including the ones in vehicles, he and Ehrlich calculated that in less than a century, the Earth would be looking at drastic, if not catastrophic, climatological changes.

Over the next two years, Ehrlich and Holdren wrote eighteen articles for the national magazine *Saturday Review,* discussing the fallout of overpopulation in lay language. They boiled human impact on the environment down to a single expression, multiplying the number of people by their consumption level and by the technology needed to produce whatever they were consuming. The resulting equation, simple enough for anyone to understand, is now a standard in ecology:

$$I = PAT$$
(impact = population X affluence
X technology)

In 1977, with Anne Ehrlich they published a textbook called *Ecoscience.* At 1,051 pages, it was a compendium of how the planet's land, sea, and atmosphere interact. To the Ehrlichs' biological research, John Holdren added hard numbers and expertise in energy to estimate what it might take for humanity to forge a sustainable relationship with the rest of nature. *Ecoscience* showed how quickly resource levels were changing, and projected how long it might take civilization to change course. It speculated how fast technology needed to evolve to maintain a decent standard of living if human numbers kept surging.

It was a hugely comprehensive, successful textbook, but it also became known beyond academia because of its analysis of how runaway population growth might be slowed. As scientists, the authors had researched every theoretical possibility ever broached. Three decades later, some of them would be selectively resurrected when President Barack Obama appointed Holdren as his science advisor.

Holdren's attackers disregarded the fact that in the same sentence that discussed adding a human sterilant to drinking water supplies or staple foods, he and the Ehrlichs rejected it as horrifying to the public and to themselves. Another option envisioned 30-year contraceptive capsules to be inserted in women at puberty, removable "with official permission, for a limited number of births." Acknowledging how chilling this was, the authors reiterated why they were raising such repellent conjectures: Unless current trends in birth rates were reversed, some countries might soon resort to compulsory birth control.

A year after *Ecoscience's* publication, China announced its one-child policy.

An inserted contraceptive capsule, the Ehrlichs and Holdren allowed, might be acceptable if it could be removed whenever a woman chose, then replaced after childbirth. This would solve what many family planners call the biggest problem of all: the fact, as studies even today show, that around half of all pregnancies are unintended.

"Unwanted births and the problem of abortion would both be entirely avoided," they wrote. But, they added, the logistics of keeping the entire female population on a continual steroid dosage rendered this contraceptive prospect prohibitive as well. Nevertheless, in 1983, Norplant, a hormonal-releasing capsule worn up to five years beneath the skin of the upper arm, would appear. Along with several others, it is still used widely.

Holdren and the Ehrlichs considered legal bases for population laws. As the U.S. Constitution balances individual rights with a society's compelling interests, they noted, a mandated limitation on family size might be no more unreasonable than requiring men to serve in the military. But, they correctly guessed, the reaction to this opinion among conservatives who advocate both minimal government intervention in people's lives and robust national defense would be outrage.

"Compulsory control of family size," they concluded, anticipating the outcry, "is an unpalatable idea, but the alternatives may be much more horrifying."

So much so, they warned, that conceivably someday people might actually demand such control. Before scarcity and civil order devolved into food riots and water wars, "A far better choice, in our view, is to expand the milder methods of influencing family size preference, while redoubling efforts to ensure that the means of birth control are accessible to every human on Earth within the shortest time possible."

John Holdren went on to a chair at Harvard's Kennedy School of Government and to become president of the American Association for the Advancement of Science. He was elected to the National Academy of Sciences, the National Academy of Engineering, and the American Academy of Arts and Science. He shared in the 1995 Nobel Peace Prize, for which he gave the acceptance lecture. His appointment as Obama's science advisor occurred early enough, when Obama enjoyed a Senate majority and the opposition had yet to shape its paralyzing strategy, to assure confirmation. During his hearing, in reply to a Republican senator, he stated that he did not believe in forced sterilization or any coercive form of population control.

He also responded to an issue raised at the end of *Ecoscience*. He and his coauthors had imagined a superagency they dubbed a "Planetary Regime," which might one day combine the UN's environmental and population programs and expand the UN treaty called the Law of the Sea to manage all natural resources. It would be a steward of the global commons, empowered to control pollution of the atmosphere, oceans, and transboundary waters. Such an agency, they added, also "might be given responsibility for determining the optimum population for the world."

In his confirmation, Holdren testified that he did not believe that determining optimal population is a proper role of government.

The title they gave the superagency became fodder for Obama foes seeking proof that his administration belonged to a world socialist conspiracy. After someone broadcast quotes from *Ecoscience* on the Internet, Paul and Anne Ehrlich responded to the out-of-context selections of their views and those of their former colleague:

"We were not then, never have been, and are not now 'advocates' of the Draconian measures for population limitation described—but not recommended—in the book's 60-plus small-type pages cataloging the full spectrum of population policies that, at the time, had either been tried in some country or analyzed by some commentator."

During Gretchen Daily's second summer at the Rocky Mountain Biological Lab, while she and Paul Ehrlich hiked back one afternoon after a day of tallying mating butterflies, they spotted a male red-naped sapsucker, a small western North American woodpecker, chiseling a rectangular patch of bark from a willow, then drinking the sugary sap that flowed down the exposed bare surface. Surrounding branches were pocked with other sap wells, indicating that sapsuckers regularly feasted there.

The next time Gretchen returned, she found an orange-crowned warbler and two kinds of hummingbirds imbibing at the sap well. Further observation—more than fifty hours' worth, at her mentor's encouragement—revealed forty species of birds, insects, squirrels, and chipmunks feeding off the sapsuckers' labor.

Over the summer, intricate dynamics of alpine ecology revealed themselves to her. Sapsuckers needed willows to nourish themselves and their young, and a surrounding aspen grove for shelter. They also depended on a heartwood fungus that rots aspen trunks, enabling them to peck nesting cavities. Willow, aspen, and fungus had to occur together for sapsuckers to be there. To confirm, Daily and Ehrlich surveyed thirteen thousand quaking aspens at varying distances from willows: those that bore telltale sapsucker holes were the closest ones. They also examined all the willows: those far from aspens were unscathed by sapsuckers.

The sapsuckers, in turn, provided a significant source of food to a host of other animals. Since they drilled a new nest hole each year, their former homes were used by seven other bird species that couldn't dig their own, including two kinds of swallows that appeared only where sapsuckers were present. An entire community of plants and animals all depended on a complex of keystone species: sapsucker, aspen, willow, and fungus. Take away any, and the others would decline or disappear.

This interdependence among plants, birds, insects, and mammals resulted in Daily's first professional publication, coauthored with Ehrlich, just as she was starting her master's degree. It was the beginning of her understanding of how losing a single species could touch off a cascade. After a year back in Germany to look at acid rain's effect on Bavarian forests, she returned to Stanford to begin a doctorate, joining the Ehrlichs at their other perennial research site, the Las Cruces Biological Station in Coto Brus, Costa Rica.

It was the perfect place, Paul told her, for documenting what happens to wildlife when forests go. The massive bee study that kept Gretchen chained to a microscope for many months was led by Ehrlich and his own mentor, Charles D. Michener of the University of Kansas, the world's greatest living bee authority.[2] Besides confirming that forest bees pollinated farmers' crops, something else surprising had turned up: Bee populations were actually thriving in the cleared spaces. So, Ehrlich had discovered, were butterflies and moths.

Possibly, they reasoned, this was because flying insects easily move between altered landscapes and where they actually live. Over the following years, they looked at less-mobile reptiles, amphibians, and nonflying mammals. They tracked and trapped frogs, toads, snakes, lizards, anteaters, pygmy squirrels, opossums, sloths, pacas, long-tailed weasels, puma, ocelots, river otters, and two species of monkeys. With all these, too, they found a higher capacity than expected of farmed countryside to sustain even threatened and endangered species.

---

2. Michener, author of the magnum opus *The Bees of the World*, was still at work in 2013 at age ninety-four.

The key in every case, they finally realized, was linked to trees. Wherever farmers left some standing, biodiversity hung on.

Not that a human-worked landscape was any substitute for native forest: Seven species—jaguar, tapir, white-lipped peccaries, howler and spider monkeys, giant anteaters, and an aquatic opossum—had disappeared. But a huge portion of the world's land was now being used by people, and they were seeing that countryside that still contained some native vegetation cover could support a surprising percentage of native fauna. Such land could still provide services that humans needed: it could hold and filter water, replenish soil, and harbor creatures that pollinate crops and control pests.

Many scientists, they knew, would protest, contending that this conclusion could harm the worldwide conservation movement's efforts to preserve remaining wilderness habitat for precious species. But the tiny percentage of the planet in nature reserves alone could only save a fraction of the world's biodiversity. The concept of conservation had to be enlarged to include nonreserve lands as well. The challenge was convincing people who lived there that it was in their interest to coexist with whatever else still did, too.

*   *   *

In 1992, Gretchen Daily took a postdoctoral fellowship at Berkeley's Energy and Resources Group with John Holdren. She needed to learn about energy: The modern agriculture that was transfiguring the land ran on the same fuels that stoked the planet's engines of urbanity. The vast fertilized monocultures of the Green Revolution, where no trees were left standing — no anything but the cash crop — turned oil into food but failed to compost the carbon released in that chemical exchange.

At Berkeley, Holdren had her look at the converse: could agriculture grow fuel? Under the decade's new watchword, *sustainability,* if living plants rather than their fossilized ancestors were the feedstock for the hydrocarbons that civilization now depended on, each new plant generation would inhale the CO_2 released by the last one when burned. Theoretically, their carbon contributions to the atmosphere would zero out. But would they really? How much energy was needed to harvest and refine vegetation into biological fuel? How much would it compete with food production? Did it make sense to raise fuel crops on the same land as food crops? Or if biofuels were restricted to degraded lands, could anything grow there that would produce enough energy to make it worthwhile?

That same year, more than a hundred heads of state and thousands of scientists, activists, journalists, politicians, and emissaries of industry gathered in Rio de Janeiro for UNCED, the 1992 United Nations Conference on Environment and Development. The Earth Summit, as it became known, was portrayed as the watershed moment that might determine both the fate of the global ecosystem and the survival of the human race.

For two years before the meeting, ferocious parlaying ricocheted among member nations and thousands of entities whose interests were vested in the Earth Summit's outcome. Besides environmental groups, these included women's networks, human rights defenders, and religious leaders, from shamans to Vatican curia officials. Fifty of the biggest transnational companies pooled their clout to form the Business Council for Sustainable Development, predicated on hopes that economic growth could proceed unabated if ecological impact declined.

Everything on Earth was on the table—except for one. Despite a declaration by Earth Summit secretary-general Maurice Strong that "either we reduce the world's population voluntarily, or nature will do this for us, but brutally," by the time UNCED began, the topic was effectively taboo. Although groups named Population Action International, the

Population Institute, and one Paul Ehrlich founded, Zero Population Growth, were among the multitudes in Rio, they were, fittingly, outnumbered.

Detractors, who called them "population controllers," included developing countries that protested being blamed for the world's environmental woes, when the real culprit, they insisted, was clearly the runaway consumption of rich nations. They rejected as racist neocolonialism the idea that limiting a poor country's greatest strength—numbers—could be touted as some sort of solution. Feminists added that women in poor countries were doubly abused: traditionally exploited, then forced to submit to involuntary sterilization or Norplant insertions they couldn't remove by themselves.

The dilemma for population advocates was that they substantially agreed with the grievances of their accusers, and with their goals. Eliminating poverty, guaranteeing women's reproductive rights, educating everyone, and social justice for all were aims they saw as crucial to achieving their own. The difference lay in strategy. While population groups believed that letting women control the number of children they bore was the swiftest way to reversing their plight, feminists had run out of patience with waiting for something else, such as wide implementation of family-planning programs, to happen before women had equal rights and opportunities. Anticonsumption groups insisted that the first order of business was to eliminate greed, not more greedy people. Arguments that the path to the success of any of these was to pursue them all simultaneously were lost amid the squabbling.

Their divisions proved useful to the Vatican. Invoking the sanctity of human life, it defended the contention that the world's poor were victims, not the cause, of ecological degradation. As the Summit's setting, Brazil, had the largest Catholic population in the world, the Church had considerable leverage in pre-session negotiations, and succeeded in deleting the terms *family planning* and *contraception* from UNCED draft agreements.

By the final version, the sole remaining reference to population was a single phrase, calling for "responsible planning of family size, in a spirit of liberty and dignity and in accordance with personal values, taking into account moral and cultural considerations."

"The Holy See has not attempted to eliminate any wording relating to population, but only to improve it," the Vatican announced when satisfied.

For the transnational companies that were major funders of the conference, more people meant both cheaper labor and expanding market bases, a point articulated eight years earlier at the 1984 World Population Conference in Mexico City. To the shock of the host country, Mexico, diligently trying to no longer be the world's fastest-growing nation, the United States announced it would no longer support UN family-planning programs. Not only did they abet abortion, of which President Reagan's administration did not approve, the U.S. representative explained, but the more people on the planet, the more consumers for the products of capitalism.

Since the United States was the UN's biggest funder, and among the original patrons of its contraception programs, it was a policy flip that shook international family planning for years to come. Now, at the Rio Earth Summit, another unexpected reversal was occurring, as the United States stunned everyone by rejecting UNCED's Convention on Biodiversity, under which every other nation agreed to identify and set aside reserves to protect genetic resources. This time, the U.S. complaint was that a provision for "fair and equitable sharing of benefits" from developing those resources constrained the intellectual property rights of biotechnology firms and pharmaceutical companies to products they might derive from tropical plants.

To American ecologists like Paul Ehrlich, such defiance could not be more perverse. For energy experts like John Holdren, things became even worse. As the eleven-day Earth Summit continued, U.S. president George H. W. Bush stayed in Washington, refusing to participate if another principal UNCED document, the Convention on Climate Change, established specific targets for emission reduction. Once again, every other signatory had agreed to limit CO_2 emissions to 1990 levels by the year 2000. A prolonged, rabid debate ensued, led by countries that argued for a valid convention, even if it left the United States in glaring isolation. Ultimately, the rationale prevailed that any accord was meaningless without the world's most powerful country and biggest polluter. The pact was diluted to meet U.S. demands, and the day before the conference ended, Bush arrived in Rio.

"The American way of life is not negotiable," he said when he addressed the gathering.

———

The 1992 Earth Summit confirmed that only one species, *H. sapiens,* had a vote in deciding the fate of the Earth, as it was the only species at the table. In the long run, that vote will be meaningless: insects and microbes will likely have the last laugh, if they laugh at all.

The question, however, is when, exactly, is the long run? No one who has tried to predict that with any precision has been right thus far. Nevertheless, the failure of seers, or of skewed interpretations of Nostradamus or of Mayan calendars, should not lull anyone into complacency. Although outmuscled by politicians and lobbyists, scientists at the Earth Summit had plenty of reason to be concerned about our trajectory if things proceeded as usual.

A year later in Cambridge, England, at the First World Optimum Population Conference, Gretchen Daily and the Ehrlichs offered what they called a tentative, back-of-the-envelope calculation. They were not trying to pinpoint the end of human civilization, but rather to determine the opposite: how many humans could safely fit on the Earth without capsizing it?

Their presentation, twenty-five years after *The Population Bomb* was published, drew from a discussion of carrying capacity in Gretchen's doctoral dissertation. Optimum population, they stated, did not mean the maximum number that could be crammed onto the planet like industrial chickens, but how many could live well without compromising the chance for future generations to do the same. At minimum, everyone should be guaranteed sustenance, shelter, education, health care, freedom from prejudice, and opportunities to earn a living.

That didn't mean ending inequality. "While it is

in nearly everyone's selfish best interest to narrow the rich-poor gap, we are skeptical that the incentives driving social and economic inequalities can ever be fully overcome. We therefore think a global optimum should be determined with humanity's characteristic selfishness and myopia in mind."

Nor did they mean a pastoral, preindustrial existence. "[Optimum population] should be big enough to maintain human cultural diversity," and in places dense enough to allow "a critical mass of intellectual, artistic, and technological creativity"—enough people to have "large, exciting cities and still maintain substantial tracts of wilderness."

Yet it must be small enough to ensure that biodiversity is preserved. Their reasons were both practical— humans can't live without the nourishment, air, materials, and water that nature provides—and moral:

"As the dominant species on the planet, we feel *Homo sapiens* should foster the continued existence of its only known living companions in the universe."

To estimate optimum world population, they used a scenario developed by John Holdren. In that year, 1993, the planet's 5½ billion people were consuming 13 terawatts—13 trillion watts—of human-generated energy. Nearly three-quarters of that were used by 1½ billion in industrialized countries, averaging 7½

kilowatts per person. If everyone used that much—
in the developing world, the average was 1 kilowatt
per person—and the world kept growing at the current pace, sometime in the twenty-first century there
would be 14 billion humans and energy demand
would be eight times higher.

Well before then, they feared, either oil or the ecosystem would collapse, or both. So Holdren had
looked at what might be practical if everyone had
equal access to energy. If demand averaged 3 kilowatts per capita (triple a poor person's allotment; one-
fourth what a typical American used, possibly
achievable if energy efficiency were maximized), and
if population growth rates eased enough to increase
only to 10 billion,[3] the total needed would still be
30 terawatts.[4]

Taking those figures, Daily and the Ehrlichs calculated backward. Since the 13 terawatts used in
1993 were already stripping the planet and scram-
bling atmospheric chemistry, they knew their total
had to be lower. Assuming widespread adoption of
clean technologies—some known, some yet to be
developed—on the back of their envelope they haz-
arded a wild, wishful guess that it might be possible

---

3. Currently, the UN projection for around the year 2082.

4. Almost double that of 2012.

for the human race to use 9 terawatts every year without trashing the environment.

To allow for unforeseen consequences, which invariably accompany technologies, they proposed a 50 percent margin of error. That left 6 terawatts. From there, it was just a matter of long division.

The total number of people, each using 3 kilowatts of energy apiece, that could live in a world using no more than 6 terawatts was 2 billion.

Two billion was the population of the Earth in 1930, when the Haber-Bosch process had just become commercially available worldwide. Nearly everyone on Earth was still living off plants growing on sunlight, not fossil fuel. At 2 billion, the world's population could be fed with little or no artificial fertilizer, relieving pressures on the soil, on downstream waters, and on the atmosphere: agricultural nitrogen is a major source of nitrous oxide, both a pollutant and the most potent greenhouse gas after CO_2 and methane.

In 1930, the world's 2 billion used just over 2 terawatts of energy annually: slightly more than 1 kilowatt per person. It was a world without television, computers, fewer automobiles per family, minimal appliances, and no jet air travel. By today's living standards, an allotment of 1 kilowatt per person per year would mean we'd all be considered underdeveloped, an option desired by few beyond survivalists and some remaining hunter-gatherers.

The Ehrlichs and Daily acknowledged that it was unlikely that even their calculation, which would give each of us triple that amount, would be very appealing. So they offered another alternative: in a world of 1½ billion people, everyone could have 4¾ kilowatts. That figure, nearly two-thirds the per capita energy usage of rich countries, was feasible without any major technological breakthroughs, simply through better insulation, better gas mileage, and increased use of inexpensive solar water heaters.

They did not discuss how to bring the population back down to 1½ billion people—approximately the global population at the beginning of the twentieth century. However, one country had already embarked on a plan that, were the whole world to adopt it, within a century would bring the numbers back exactly to those of 1900. That was China, whose one-child policy was considered unacceptably brutal.

Neither the Ehrlichs, Gretchen Daily, nor nearly anyone else knew in 1993 that in an equally inscrutable, large country in another part of the world—a Muslim country—an alternative to China's coercion was under way in which citizens would voluntarily reduce their high birth rate even faster than China, though years would have to pass before its extraordinary success would become apparent.

Two decades later, at eighty, Paul Ehrlich would still be presiding over Stanford's Center for Conservation Biology. When asked why, he would reply, "To free up Gretchen Daily." She was now the Center's nominal director, winner of several of the world's highest honors in science for her efforts to find a workable balance between people and nature.

To do that requires research into what species and ecosystems would continue to exist in the future. That raises a corollary, excruciating question, one that most scientists are loath to touch: Which species, from the perspectives of both science and human society, are so important that they and their habitats most merit protection?

To judge that a charismatic polar bear or cuddly panda is more significant than some inconspicuous brown bird hopping unnoticed on a forest floor, and therefore more crucial to save, is the ecological equivalent of Sophie's Choice. No one, least of all Gretchen Daily, wants to make such a decision. Yet this is a world where many people are skeptical that species other than edible domestic animals are particularly important at all. Europeans, after all, are among the healthiest humans on Earth, despite having purged their continent of much if not most of its biodiversity. What is the justification for keeping every variety of flora, fauna, and mushroom intact—or what is the danger if we don't?

This, Gretchen knew, was the tyranny of the Netherlands Fallacy: all Europeans were as dependent on a robust planet as any fisherman in the Philippines or hunter-gatherer in the Amazon. The resources that afforded Europe's exalted standard of living came from farther away than Europeans could see, courtesy of all the imports their euros could buy. Rich countries fly high on the wings of distant lands that still have enough rivets in place.

Now, however, they were popping fast. Every decision of which rivet was more important than another was playing Russian roulette with the global biosphere. The truth that Gretchen Daily lived with was knowing that there will inevitably be a certain amount of Sophie's Choice. "We can still bring a lot of life along with us," she told her students. "But we can't bring everything."

No one knows which, or how many, are the essential minimum. Nevertheless, the ecologists' job was to show that there are definitely some we can't live without, such as pollinators and water conservers, and to help us realize that those species, in turn, can't live without a habitat to sustain them.

As the years went by and the century turned, the estimate that Daily and the Ehrlichs had conjured from John Holdren's energy arithmetic of how many humans the global habitat could safely sustain remained unchanged. No new technological miracle had stretched the planetary playing field.

All that did change was the number of players. There were 1½ billion more of us, all competing for space and sustenance with every other living thing.

PART TWO

CHAPTER 5

Island World

i. The Xenophobe

The River Severn is Britain's longest, rising in a Welsh peat bog and arcing east through the Midlands until it turns south, swelling into Bristol Channel and the Atlantic. Much of its course lies in Shropshire, where, about a third of the way, it loops through Shrewsbury, a market town since medieval times.

As a boy, Charles Darwin learned as much along the banks of the Severn as he did at Shrewsbury School. His family's garden path led down to the river, where he walked before breakfast, returning with beetles he'd collect. He encountered birds no longer seen here, such as corncrakes and nightingales, and others that still are, such as Britain's three species of swan: mute, Bewick's, and whooper.

Nearly every geologic period in Earthly history appears in outcroppings along the Severn's Shropshire drainage; some of the remnant corals, limestone, marine fossils, and quartzite date to half a billion years ago, when the Midlands were on the opposite side of today's equator—apt inspiration for young Darwin, who, at age twenty-two, was headed there himself. Upon his return in 1836 from the epic five-year voyage on H.M.S. *Beagle,* his first night was spent back in Shrewsbury, where he dined at the Lion, a sixteenth-century inn.

One hundred and seventy-five years later, Simon Darby sits in the Lion, frowning over his shepherd's pie. In his mid-forties, he has pale blue eyes and thick flat eyebrows, with tightly cropped black hair that feathers into a thinning widow's peak. Darby was also raised in the Midlands, just outside industrial Birmingham. In 1709, his ancestor Abraham Darby invented the coke-fueled blast furnace that made the Industrial Revolution possible. Darby cast-iron foundries changed the future of England, and of the planet. The world's first iron bridge still spans the Severn. The first iron-framed building, a flax mill on Shrewsbury's outskirts, is the ancestor of today's skyscrapers. The Darby company also built the world's first steam locomotive.

Both the Industrial Revolution and the family fortune had vanished into history by the time Simon Darby was born. Like Darwin, he studied biology and chemistry, but he never used his degree. He got into computers, and then into postindustrial Midlands politics, ending up as deputy chairman of the far-right British National Party. He often stands in for the BNP chairman, Cambridge-educated Nick Griffin, who has been charged more than once for inciting hatred toward Jews and Muslims. In 1998, Griffin was convicted for a series of articles that mocked the Holocaust. Yet by 2009, he and Darby had recast their fringe party's former skinhead-and-leather image with neat haircuts and neckties, and Griffin was elected to the European Parliament, representing North West England. The British National Party polled nearly a million votes nationwide.

As party spokesman, Darby has earned his own notoriety, most famously for a reply to the Archbishop of York, a Ugandan native, who'd criticized a BNP demand that black and Asian Britons be described as "racial foreigners."

"He said everyone who wanted to be English could be English," Darby explains in the Lion's restaurant. "But what about the real and proper English? That's *my* heritage. It cheapens my own identity, you see." Even as his color rises, his voice remains a soft tenor. "So I said that if I went to a Uganda village and told them that they were all genetic mongrels and that anyone could be Ugandan, I'd still be picking spears out of myself."

He shrugs. "It was a perfectly rational thing to say about a nation whose coat of arms has spears on it." He sets his fork down. "Look: We've got an increasing generation of people who don't really belong to the island. They don't have a common history here. They don't feel that it's their heritage, and they don't look after it. I mean, why would they?

"There's an Oxford demographer," he continues, "who is debunking this mongrel Briton kind of assumption. He says that 90-odd percent of everyone with a maternal grandparent born in this country can trace their ancestry back ten thousand years. Right to the Ice Age. I put it to the test: I used genetic mapping on both my maternal and paternal DNA. And sure enough, I'm what was referred to in the database as a native son of Europe. Which is good enough for me."

A waitress appears, wide-cheeked, with blond hair pulled behind her ears. "Excuse me," she says. "Are you finished?"

Darby stabs a final bit of shepherd's pie. "Yeah." He stares at her as he chews, until their blue eyes lock. Her prim smile turns puzzled.

"Everything was...fine?" she asks.

"Yeah." He leans forward and squints. "Are you from Poland, actually?"

"Yes. Why?"

"I just noticed the accent."

"My accent. Yes."

"There's a program on the BBC called *Lead Balloon*. Have you heard of it? A girl on there called Magda who plays a Polish girl."

On the program, the character Magda, an eastern European housekeeper, is regularly perplexed by the ways of the British. "She has the exact same accent as you."

"Exactly the same?"

"Exactly."

"What's the program of this? *Red Balloon*?" she asks, gathering plates.

"*Lead* Balloon. L-e-a-d."

"Okay. Thank you." She retreats.

He leans back. "Nice lady. Does her job. But how do our people feel when they need a job and she'll work for a lot less than they do? I quite like Polish people. But I've asked them, how would you feel if the Polish government told you, 'We're going to import millions of Vietnamese, who will undercut your wages and work for next to nothing'?"

He swirls his empty glass, clinking the ice cubes.

"They wouldn't put up with it, would they? There would be riots in Poland."

But the European Union–sanctioned labor mobility that allows thousands of hardworking Poles to seek employment in the UK is merely an irritant to Simon Darby's British National Party, compared to what they and their counterparts in other western European nations see as a far deeper threat.

"There is now a war on Western civilization—a cultural war on white society. Muslims in this country have six children as an average, whereas we don't even maintain our own population. Muslims believe that the more kids they have, the more power they'll have. This country's population is headed to 70 million. That is simply not sustainable."

Currently, there are nearly 63 million Britons. "Right," he says, standing. "And we've got all the overpopulation problems: transport, stress levels, the violence when people live on top of one another. It's bad enough in a monocultural society. In a multicultural society, it's destabilizing."

Outside the Lion Hotel, Shrewsbury seems a postcard of stability. Some cobbled streets have given way to asphalt, but their configuration hasn't changed since medieval English was spoken here. The palette of the pedestrians is richer than in Darwin's monochromatic era, but there is no overwhelming Muslim presence—although the next parish to the east, Telford, near the famous Iron Bridge, has thirteen mosques and is one of the UK's fastest-growing towns.

"And Bradford in Yorkshire is an Islamic town now. They run it. In much of Birmingham, we people don't show up anymore. In London now, only 17 percent of the kids are like me."

It is June; the sun has pushed morning's clouds to the green horizon. In shirtsleeves, Simon Darby heads toward the English Bridge, where steps lead down to the river. Two girls in hijabs and blue jeans exit an herbal shop and pass without a glance, intent on their mobile phones.

Darby shakes his head. "They'll push us out."

It's a fear that oozes through much of western Europe, giving rise to quasi-fascist political movements in previously welcoming, liberal places like Denmark and the Netherlands. This fear is often summed up with a vivid neologism: *Eurabia*. A virtual epidemiology of lurid Internet videos mutate around a theme of Europe becoming a vast Islamic nation by mid-century. Among their claims:

- French Muslims average 8.1 children per family. Southern France already has more mosques than churches. Thirty percent of French children are Muslim. In Paris, 45 percent. By 2027, one in five Frenchmen will bow to Mecca five times daily.

- Fifty percent of Dutch newborns are Muslims, as will be half the Netherlands by 2023.
- A quarter of Belgians and 50 percent of newborns are Muslims. In Brussels, the EU says that one-third of European children will be Islamic by 2025.
- With just 1.3 children per woman of childbearing age, the collapse of the German population is irreversible, and by 2050, Germany will be a Muslim state.
- Forty percent of the Russian army will be soon be Islamic.

None is remotely true. The high range of projections suggests that Europe's 20 million Muslims—about 5 percent of the population in 2011—will increase to 8 percent by 2025. What is real, however, is Islamophobia. At the English Bridge's stone arch, Simon Darby gestures at riverbank strollers and anglers casting for pike below, all who appear to be Caucasian.

"Those people have mortgages. They've got kids and pets and pay council taxes. But a third-world immigrant can live in a flat for twenty-five pounds a week. He's got no overhead, so he can afford lower wages. So our guy loses his house. My people have rights, too. Japanese do what they want in their own country. We feel we should remain dominant in this country. Because it's ours."

He pauses on the steps. "If I went to Iran, I wouldn't expect churches. But if I do the same in this country, then I'm a racist villain."

But below, where huge old riverbank willows droop over the water, Simon Darby is not a villain, but a boy again. The petulant ultranationalist fades, and the naturalist reemerges. He delights in swallows and martins dipping above the river's surface. "And those swifts—beautiful little birds. All the way from Africa!" He spies a brood of cygnets following a mute swan hen. "This is our biggest British bird. We have three swans in Britain: these resident mutes, and the wintering whooper and Bewick's swans, which come from Russia and that area. Some like it so much they've settled here," he says proudly.

"But it's not the same. People trap and eat them now. Eastern Europeans. Very unfortunate." He points at a big mute swan probing the bank with its yellow bill. "They see something like that as a free lunch. They aren't rooted in the ecology, the nature of this island."

Darby's party frequently plays the environmental card, calling for halts to fracking and bans on shale gas exploration, claiming agreement with its political opposite, the Green Party. They embrace the tenets of an organization of distinguished British doctors, activists, and scientists, the Optimum Population Trust.[1] Although the embrace is not returned, some of their concerns do coincide: This is an island ecosystem, its limits starkly delineated by its shores. The 70 million that Darby cites are expected by 2030. That will be the equivalent of adding another London, the biggest city in Europe, to this increasingly crowded British isle.

More than two-thirds of that increase will come from foreign immigrants and their offspring. As an EU member, Britain must welcome job seekers from any other EU country, on top of its custom of accepting subjects from its former empire (via a system that has segued over the years from unlimited entry to work permits, then to selective, points-based immigration). Back when that mainly meant Canadians, Australians, and New Zealanders, nobody much noticed. Later, the unexpected arrivals of citizens from so-called "New Commonwealth" countries—the Nigerias, Pakistans, Jamaicas, and Bangladeshes—gave rise to nationalists like Simon Darby.

There is environmental justification, he says, for

---

1. In 2011, to avoid the controversy of suggesting an optimum figure, Optimum Population Trust changed its working name to "Population Matters."

his party's goal of stopping immigration and "deporting all the illegal immigrants." As this presumably would take time, the BNP also advocates financial penalties for "communities that continue to have excessively large families."

The ideal number of United Kingdom citizens they propose is 40 million. Leaving aside the environmental and economic implications of such an implosion, census figures show that more than 50 million Britons are white. Evicting every person of color from Great Britain would still leave more than 10 million extra Caucasians.

Of UK nonwhites, just 2.7 million are estimated to be Muslim. Yet what Simon Darby sees is the Britain he thought he inherited disappearing under an unfamiliar sea of sepia, where one of six Britons no longer looks like his image of the English, Welsh, or Scottish.

"It's sad. The idea that we're now a rich rainbow of cultures is nonsense. Go to Birmingham, where I was born. See the Islamo-Marxist liberals who hide their own inadequacies by destroying the very system that makes them inadequate. They drag it all down."

He walks back into the old streets of Shrewsbury. "This city produced Charles Darwin. My ancestors invented industry. We Brits were clever and strong.

We were wealthy. We had pride. We used to build the Concorde. Now our aircraft industry can't make anything but the wings for the Airbus. Jaguar is owned by an Indian company. British Land Rover is gone, MG is gone. No steel industry, no coal, no shipping, our fishing industry barely clinging."

He turns his palms up helplessly. "All that, in my lifetime."

ii. The Rainbow

Birmingham, England's second largest city, is where Simon Darby's forebears cast iron, forged steel, and mounted their great Industrial Revolution. The original Anglo-Saxon hamlet here was just south of today's city center, in an area now called Highgate. It is characterized mainly by its lack of character: a succession of blank high- and low-rises, built atop World War II Birmingham Blitz rubble. The striking architectural exception in Highgate is the Birmingham Central Mosque, one of the largest in western Europe.

The rectilinear red masonry exterior of its first two stories recalls the factories of Birmingham's past. It then rises into the postindustrial, multicultural present with a dramatic white dome—and twice the height of that, a single minaret topped by a crescent, its points heavenward.

Three to four thousand fill its green-carpeted prayer hall and women's galleries every Friday. On festival days, twenty thousand may appear. Birmingham also has 290 smaller mosques, serving a Muslim population of about two hundred fifty thousand, around one-fourth of the city's total. The assorted mosques reflect an immigrant tendency to congregate with fellow nationals: Bangladeshi, Pakistani, Indian. Although most are Sunnis—as were the Islamic lands once ruled by the British Empire—the Central Mosque is nondenominational—"to promote thinking, not religious laws," says its Indian-born founder, Dr. Mohammad Naseem.

A slight man in his eighties in a high-button black pin-striped suit, Naseem has seen the number of Muslims here quadruple, a growth now slowing as immigration tightens. Also, he notes, as succeeding Muslim generations whose language is English spread beyond the nationality enclaves of their parents, they don't have eight children like their Bangladeshi or Pakistani mothers. There is no injunction in the Qur'an against contraception—there is even discussion of the seventh-century version, coitus interruptus, in the Hadith commentaries. It's common today to see women in headscarves in the waiting rooms of local family-planning clinics.

"But the damage was already done," says Naseem, a medical doctor. "Their parents arrived with a history of centuries of children dying, of always needing more hands to do the work. A new passport doesn't instantly change that."

Only time does, he says. The present generation might have far fewer children, and Muslim girls might now prepare at Oxford and Cambridge for careers, but it is a much larger generation, so for a while their swathe in the tapestry of British society will continue to widen. In the meantime, a new growth spurt in the Muslim community is due neither to procreation nor immigration.

"Converts are increasing. West Indians, even indigenous white Britons," he says, as a white-robed, bearded Caucasian British acolyte appears with a tray of tea.

"The majority," interjects the acolyte, "are women."

Why are Englishwomen converting to Islam?

"Because of the protection that Islam offers them. They say they feel more secure covered by a hijab or wrapped in a chador. Safer."

———

"Fifty countries, and one-fifth of the planet's people are Muslim," says Haji Fazlun Khalid. "Some fear that. I see it as an opportunity. The Qu'ran tells us to remember Allah's blessings and to not defile the Earth. If Muslims heed that, we can make a big difference."

Khalid, founder of the Birmingham-based Islamic Foundation for Ecology and Environmental Science, sits on the café terrace of the public library in Burton-Upon-Trent a half-hour north, drinking lemonade. The view overlooks the Trent Washlands, a chain of river meadows dotted with old pollarded willows and marsh marigolds. Khalid, a tall, bald man in wire-rimmed glasses with a trim beard, often comes here to think.

An immigrant from Ceylon (today Sri Lanka), after serving in the Royal Air Force and then for years as Midlands director of Britain's Commission for Racial Equality, he resigned the civil service to take a graduate degree in Islamic theology. Having watched the jungles of his boyhood razed for tea plantations and then seen the Midlands countryside where he hiked fill with houses, he was curious to know if Islam offered guidance about the besieged environment.

Early in the Qur'an, in a surah that describes how Ibrahim embraces monotheism, he found that the Prophet Muhammad appointed Muslims as *khalifas*, guardians of the Earth, and warned against excessive exploitation. In the *Sunnah*—collected sayings and acts of the Prophet that, with the Qur'an, form the basis of shariah law—Khalid read that Allah is the sole owner of the Earth and everything in it. He loans the world to humans to use, but not to abuse.

His nonprofit group has published Green Guides for Muslim households and mobilized urban Muslims into "Clean Medina" campaigns. They've held conferences on whether genetically modified food is permissible halal and on the Qur'anic grounds for recycling. They've helped establish a shariah-based conservation zone in the Zanzibar archipelago to save Indian Ocean coral reefs, and given workshops there to dissuade fishing with dynamite. In Indonesia, home to the world's largest Muslim population and one of its richest ecosystems, they convinced Sumatran religious scholars to issue the world's first environmental fatwas, warning that illegal logging, mining, and burning forests are *haram:* forbidden under divine law.

The 2007 Live Earth Initiative named Fazlun Khalid one of the world's fifteen green religious leaders, along with the Dalai Lama, the Archbishop of Canterbury, and the Pope. "Many of the world's nearly 1.5 billion Muslims are from poor countries that use far less fossil fuel than the rich," he says. "But many also live in fabulously wealthy nations that produce oil. We are equally culpable. Rich petroleum states by their sheer wealth, and the rest of Muslims by our sheer numbers."

In the Qur'an, Khalid says, the Prophet counsels people to have no more children than they can provide for. Countries awash in oil, he adds, also have a sacred responsibility for the consequences of their industry. "The Maldives are now destined to vanish under the sea. That means the first country to disappear from the face of the Earth due to climate change will be a Muslim nation."

He has advised the Secretary General of the United Nations, and consults to Prince Charles. But he's not sure how well they've listened.

"At the root of the environmental crisis is our financial system. Banks charge interest, and create money out of nothing." In four different surahs, the Qur'an prohibits *riba,* or usury, as one of Islam's most heinous sins. But he considers Islamic banking, which avoids charging interest through machinations that still earn banks profits from borrowers, to be an oxymoron.

"If we continue to create money infinitely and then apply it to resources Allah created as finite, the only long-term scenario is environmental destruction. Money is a virus. If we cure it, we will heal our environment. Population and consumerism will take care of themselves."

But the global financial system is now as intrinsic to civilization as the atmosphere. Can it be changed? Gazing at the River Trent, golden in the afternoon sun, Khalid quotes from the Qur'an, Surah 30:41: " 'Corruption has spread far and wide over the land and sea, due to the actions of humankind. Allah will make them taste of their own actions as a means to find a way back to Him.' It means that God will make us feel the error of our ways, then give us a second chance. We must seize the chance God gives us," he says. "In our race to grow to infinity, we put too much pressure on this Earthly space. If pressure is instead placed on our population, universally and fairly, that may be a good step."

iii. The Optimum

The 1993 World Optimum Population Conference in Cambridge, where the Ehrlichs and Gretchen Daily presented their calculation that the Earth could safely handle a population of 2 billion humans, was organized by the Optimum Population Trust. An environmental think tank, OPT had been founded a year earlier by David Willey, an Oxford classics scholar who started language schools throughout Europe. A world traveler, he'd lately noticed how crowded the planet had grown, and wondered what might be done.

OPT's mission was to promote research that might determine the optimum, sustainable human population for given regions, as well as for the entire world. Although its goals were grand and it attracted illustrious patrons — esteemed naturalist and BBC broadcaster Sir David Attenborough; primate biologist Dame Jane Goodall; and former UK representative to the UN Security Council Sir Crispin Tickell — its research resources were limited. Its chief focus became its campaign to lower the population of the United Kingdom.

It was a campaign that inevitably risked accusation of encouraging racial politics that spawn the likes of the British National Party. OPT's members and patrons would respond that in 1973, long before Europe's current wave of xenophobia, a UK government population panel had concluded that the Britain must accept that its "population cannot go on increasing indefinitely." As nothing had been done since to enact the panel's recommendations, the Optimum Population Trust formed to urge government to integrate population policy into its decision making.

Nevertheless, being called bedfellows to racists hearkens uneasily to old associations of birth control with eugenics. Their reason for seeking to determine the optimum population for their island nation was based on environmental carrying capacity, not hatred or exclusionary politics, yet with two-thirds of Britain's population increase due to immigration, it was a delicate job to convince others that to oppose more immigration didn't mean opposing immigrants themselves.[2]

OPT had two further goals, neither apt to make it more popular. One was to "oppose the view held by many politicians and economists and those in the commercial world, that a perpetually expanding economy, alongside perpetual population growth, is desirable and possible."

The other, ominously: "To make it widely understood that failure to reduce population is likely to lead to a population crash when fossil fuels, fresh water and other resources become scarce."

June 2010: Roger Martin, chairman of the Optimum Population Trust, finishes his afternoon tea in the bar of the Hotel Russell in Bloomsbury, central Lon-

---

2. In the United States, both the Sierra Club and Zero Population Growth (today, Population Connection) endured wrenching battles over whether to oppose immigration. The Ehrlichs and Gretchen Daily have debated immigration in the scientific literature with physicist Albert Bartlett, who has called for halting it.

don, and heads up the street to the St. Pancras Church, where the debate will take place. A tall, thin, graying man, he wears a dark red tie and lightweight suit with a white pinstripe. His leather briefcase looks as though he's carried it for years. He is a retired foreign officer who returned after years in Africa with an idea of what was going very wrong in the world, and he looks weary from knowing.

The debate is in conjunction with an art installation about overpopulation in the Crypt Gallery, a converted catacomb beneath the church. Like many such crypts in London, this one was dug in the early nineteenth century to answer a need for more burial space, as rising Industrial Revolution populations filled village graveyards to overflowing. After a few decades, church crypts were closed to further interments for health concerns, presumably because smallpox could linger in long-dead corpses, but the brick-lined tunnels here still hold the remains of 557 people.

The exhibit features fifty canvases by British painter and environmental architect Gregor Harvie. Each has a distinct palette, but all resemble swarms of proliferating cells as viewed under a microscope. Tightly hung under the cramped ceiling, the effect is of the swarms mutating from canvas to canvas, out of control. They are accompanied by fifty "elegies" on wall-mounted placards, by the painter's wife, writer Alex

Harvie. Each memorializes a past society in which rapid growth was followed by collapse. They start in the Pleistocene, when the first Australians and North Americans expunged the resident megafauna from their new homes. They range through the tragedy of Sumerians who turned Garden of Eden soils between the Tigris and Euphrates into sterile salt flats; the stripped, treeless hills that were the undoing of classical Greece; Peru's vanished Nasca people and Mexico's Olmec; the acidification of once-lush British moors by Bronze Age tin smelters; the hapless Viking farmers who perished in Greenland when the climate shifted.

They conclude in recent memory: China's Great Leap Forward, which overshot its capacity to produce food, starving 40 million; the massacre of Tutsis by Hutus in bursting Rwanda; the calamitous shriveling of the Sahel; the horror of Haiti; Madagascar's red soil bleeding away to sea. It is unsettling to read them in a crypt, alongside plaques commemorating those interred here.

The debate takes place aboveground, in the church's main sanctuary. Yet again, the topic is what to do about rising population. Six people are on the panel, three associated with OPT, including Roger Martin. The others include a woman who heads a relief agency for urban African street children, a Cambridge University minister, and an environmental writer for *New Scientist* magazine. The host of a BBC Radio 4 science program is the moderator. The panelists sit at a long table in front of six marble-painted pillars in the church's colonnaded, semicircular apse, facing an audience of about a hundred fifty in dark oak pews.

The first to speak, Dr. John Guillebaud, is professor emeritus of family planning and reproductive health at University College, London. Guillebaud, his dark suit punctuated by an orange daisy in his lapel, notes that every year the world adds the equivalent of another Germany or Egypt. He invites people to try to imagine where to fit another of either on the planet. He talks about the human gluttony behind the recent BP—née British Petroleum—outrage in the Gulf of Mexico in pursuit a bit more of the world's remaining known oil.

"Resource shortages are mainly caused by 'longages' of people," he says. "If the world were run by biologists and not economists, everyone would know that no species can go around multiplying indefinitely, humankind included, without eventually running out of vital resources like food, and ultimately ending with the collapse of numbers through deaths. Unremitting growth, folks, is the doctrine of the cancer cell."

He speculates as to why something so logical has

become such a taboo, concluding that it's become inextricably tangled with our fear of being coerced. The phrase *population control,* he says, has become repellant.

"It suggests China; control by Big Brother. Please don't say *population control.* It does damage." He ends by explaining that even though worldwide birthrates are going down, "Due to a bulge of births from previous high birth rates, we are still in trouble. It's called population momentum, and it's the reason why we're absolutely certain to get at least another two billion more people, because all of tomorrow's parents are alive today."

Next is the one whose presence qualifies this event as a debate, because he's the only person on the panel expected to take a contrarian view. Fred Pearce, writer for *New Scientist,* recently published a book whose title in the UK, *Peoplequake,* is less to the point than its American title: *The Coming Population Crash.* "The truth," he says, reiterating the book's premise, "is that the world is now defusing population bombs."

The world's total fertility rate is down to 2.6 children per woman, he explains, when little more than a generation earlier it was at 5. Not just in wealthy countries, where career women don't want to be tied to the house by too many children. "It's being done by the world's poorest and least educated women, who other people often see as villains in the population story."

Even in Bangladesh, where women marry in their teens, the average is down to 3, he says. In the world's biggest Catholic country, Brazil, "Most women have two children now. Nothing the priests say can stop millions of them from getting sterilized. What's going on? Something very simple: Women are finally choosing to have smaller families, because for the first time, they can."

Pearce, with sandy gray hair parted in the middle and a scruffy gray beard, says he wants to focus on the good news that the world is winning the population battle. By the stony silence, it's not clear that this audience is convinced, let alone the other panelists. He explains that with modern medical advances, mothers no longer need six children so that enough survive to ensure a next generation.

"It took a while to realize that. While people were still having five or six and most reached adulthood, that's when the population bomb happened. That's why world population quadrupled in the twentieth century. But we're reaching the end of that phase. Two or three is enough, we now realize. Rich or poor, socialist or capitalist, Muslims or Catholics, secular or devout, tough government controls or not, small families are the new norm in most of the world."

The trouble, he acknowledges, is that even at this new, decreased fertility rate, the world is likely to add another 2 billion people by mid-century before numbers begin to decline because of the population momentum that John Guillebaud described.

"But rising consumption today, in my view, is a far greater threat to the planet than a rising head-count. The richest 7 percent are responsible for 50 percent of carbon dioxide emissions. The poorest 50 percent are responsible for 7 percent of the emissions. There's no way that halting population growth will do something about climate change. The population bomb is being defused. We haven't begun to defuse the consumption problem."

His book made the same points: population is already coming under control nicely, and to worry about it distracts from the real menace, consumption. It went further, saying that thanks to the Green Revolution "with one bound, the world was free of its Malthusian [and] Ehrlichian bonds." And in a chapter titled "Winter in Europe," he warned that "a birth dearth is about to plunge the continent into a tailspin of ever-declining numbers. . . . Demographically, Europe is living on borrowed time."

It is his images of empty Sardinian villages and former East German towns now overrun by wolves that OPT chairman Roger Martin has in his mind as his turn arrives. His voice is calm, but color singes his pale cheeks. "It's not either-or, either consumption or numbers. It's obviously both. The total impact is one multiplied by the other."

He quotes OPT patron Sir David Attenborough: " 'I've never seen a problem that wouldn't be easier to solve with fewer people, and utterly impossible if there were more.'

"We all agree that the solution is to empower women to control their own fertility. It doesn't help, frankly, for people to say, 'That's happening anyway, don't worry.' This is not an automatic process that will happen if no one tries to make it happen. It needs priority in budgets to fund programs to make it happen."

Martin turns to face Pearce. "This is *not*, Fred, us blaming the poor" — adding, as he turns back to the audience, "a phrase he likes to use about us. It is helping the poor to achieve what they want to get, which is stable populations."

He acknowledges that the rich must emit vastly less carbon. But he also points out that to achieve some semblance of equity, the poor will have to emit *more* carbon. "And that figure will be much higher, the more we are. The sooner we cut our numbers, the more carbon we can emit and the better quality of life we can support."

His candor causes a stir in the audience. Discussions of carbon emissions usually lead to calls for clean renewables to replace dirty fossil fuels immediately. Martin, however, has alluded to the growing understanding that this can't happen anytime soon, if ever: renewable technologies potent enough to run all the world's factories, vehicles, heating, and cooling simply don't exist yet, even if the political will to switch tomorrow existed. And the amount of fossil fuel required to mine component metals and to build solar and wind power installations incurs an emissions debt that takes decades to environmentally amortize before their output can be considered truly carbon-free. In the meantime, he argues, the best hope to keep the planet livable is to reduce the number of us making all the demands.

"Otherwise," Martin concludes, "every additional person simply ratchets down everyone else's carbon ration."

And with that, the fireworks are mostly over. The Street Children Africa director, a British-educated Belgian named Savina Geerinck, poses the pertinent question *Are street children the visible manifestation of overpopulation?* and responds by noting the obvious: Most would not be on the streets if their parents had had access to family planning.

"If young people are targeted for sex education,"

she warns, "street children should be a top priority. Sixty-three percent have a sexual encounter within their first week on the streets. And 90 percent of it will be unprotected." Her organization, she adds, is now dealing with third-generation street babies.

Zoologist Aubrey Manning, OBE, the august, eighty-year-old presence on her left, swiftly summarizes the biology pertinent to the population matter: "Human beings are rapidly becoming a monoculture—a voracious monoculture. We suck resources in at the cost of the rest of life on the planet." Every plan for the future, he says, "is totally anthropocentric: What can we do to make *us* better? Let us also recognize that by diminishing the planet's resources, we are threatening our own existence. Because, like all other plant and animal species, we rely on a planet being able to renew clean air, clean water, and fertile soils to keep us alive."

Like other biologists of his generation, he is confounded that his own kind is perpetrating an extinction the likes of which the planet has seen only five times previously over the past 4 billion years—and previously, always due to some monumental upheaval of geology, or a disaster of cosmology when an errant bit of creation collides with our own. "I am sickened by the destruction of so many of our fellow creatures. Our descendants will be diminished as human beings if they can't share the planet with a rich biodiversity. We will have to reduce the strain on the Earth, reduce our carbon footprint, and stop having third children. Numbers count."

There is an easy way to evaluate the population debate on moral grounds, suggests the Reverend Jeremy Caddick, whose Cambridge chapel was the first in Britain's Anglican church to bless gay unions.

"In a traditional moral debate about say, abortion rights, usually somebody says, 'Well, that's your opinion. I think differently.' But if you say, 'Adolf Hitler believed that exterminating whole races of people was acceptable; that's just his opinion,' that's less credible. If the issues in the population debate are connected to the very survival of our species and culture, then the notion that different views are just people's opinion is frankly ridiculous."

If the future of the human race indeed depends on tackling population increase head-on, it must be asked if it's feasible—and if so, how quickly can or must it happen.

"It probably will take care of itself, mostly," offers Fred Pearce in the discussion afterward, but tonight he's alone in that opinion. This is London, which has added more than five hundred thousand people since the millennium turned, and a million more are expected by 2020. Boroughs are warring over how many housing units developers can build, and how many the city can sustainably tolerate. With England feeling more mashed each year, its reservoirs strained, and 15 million more people projected by mid-century, it doesn't feel like the problem is taking care of itself. The Office of National Statistics projects that thanks to health care, a third of UK babies will celebrate their hundredth birthday, and that by 2035 the number of centenarians will increase eightfold. By 2050, the United Kingdom will be the biggest country in western Europe.

"I think we pussyfoot around this word *coercion*," says Aubrey Manning. "Let's remember that for centuries, governments and churches have been coercing people into having *more* children. We have to give governments the courage to recognize that we're overpopulated and the best thing that could possibly happen is population decline." He's applauded.

Even at today's slowing growth rate, world population still will hit at least 10.9 billion by 2100, a figure that terrifies ecologists, who warn that the 7 billion we're already at is stretching the world beyond its breaking point—and that 10.9 billion people likely will never happen, because 7 billion of us are already turning the atmosphere into something unlivable. The UK, however, is actually growing faster than at any time in the last two hundred years. By 2033, it is projected to reach 72 million (and the United States, the other developed nation that is still growing, will approach 400 million). With the UK adding the equivalent of ten more Birminghams by 2033, Optimum Population Trust's own goal for a sustainable Britain is even more radical than the British National Party's 30 million. Despite recently dropping the phrase *optimum population* for its new working name, Population Matters, publications on its website still advocate one for the UK: between 17 and 27 million.

The BBC moderator is upset that Manning invoked the c-word. "At what point does any kind of policy merit the term *coercive?*" he wants to know.

At no point, apparently. Their applause notwithstanding, everyone here abhors China's one-child policy and the enforced sterilizations of India Prime Minister Indira Gandhi's regime. But since it's unclear how to speed toward their goal otherwise, this question raises the objection that it should be a woman's right, not a government's, to decide for herself how many children she wants. Suddenly, the apparently united crowd divides over whether women will be victims or beneficiaries of hard decisions that protect nature from being crushed by human excess.

A male in the audience stands up. "When you promote family planning on the basis that too many children will doom the environment, you're using the politics of fear and moral blackmail. You're not giving people a choice; you're giving them an ultimatum. This is naked moral coercion of women to make the right choices as defined by you, or they will single-handedly destroy the planet by daring to have too many children. I challenge the idea that family planning in the Third World is about female empowerment. Every Malthusian in history has been wrong. So has Paul Ehrlich."

He gets applauded, too, demonstrating how truly emotionally confusing the thought of restraining our natural urge to procreate is.

"That's the popular position of rich people in the world," retorts Aubrey Manning. "The Earth is limitless. You just fiddle with technology, and increase food supplies. But we are now climbing a down escalator. It's unimaginable how anybody can suppose that population growth could go on indefinitely. It's the idea that we have some kind of right to go on the way we're going. We are living in cloud-cuckoo-land if we believe that the Earth will go on providing. As for decisions, who's going to speak for orangutans?"

Another ovation.

Strangely, two things go unmentioned. One is Europe's aging demographics. A book currently selling in England, propounding the same crashing-population theme as Fred Pearce's, is *The Empty Cradle: How Falling Birthrates Threaten World Prosperity and What to Do About It*, by an American, Phillip Longman. It urges western Europeans to have more babies, lest their pensions and their economy collapse.

The other omission is apparent from the complexions of the evening's attendees: Everyone present is white. A two-hour discussion on overpopulation has taken place in London without any reference to the politically touchy fact that the United Kingdom's growth is mainly due to immigration. The missing elephant in the room is anyone resembling an immigrant.

This odd fact recalls a comment earlier in the evening by Fred Pearce that evoked no response: a large Muslim country, he said, with no coercion à la Mao Zedong or Indira Gandhi's zealot son Sanjay, has managed to bring their once-high birth rate below replacement level.

"In the past twenty-five years, behind the veil," Pearce said, "the number of children Iranian women are having has crashed, from eight to less than two — 1.7, on average. Women in Tehran today have fewer children than their sisters in New York, believe it or not."

Nobody seemed to have heard.

CHAPTER 6

Holy See

i. Sancta Scientia

Behind St. Peter's Basilica is a narrow road leading north past a gauntlet of gendarmerie and up a gentle slope. Where it crests, the pines and cedars of Lebanon that shade the Vatican Gardens' lawns give way below to an illusion of climate shift, in the form of a stand of date palms from the Canary Islands.

The palms flank an oval marble courtyard and a sumptuous villa encrusted with ornate stucco reliefs, a building begun in 1558 as a summer home for Pope Paul IV, who died before he ever slept there. Three years later, it was completed by his successor, Pope Pius IV, who directed its architect to sculpt an extravagant exterior montage of what at first seems to have little to do with Christianity. Instead, the imagery hearkens to mythology: Apollo, the Muses, Pan, Medusa, and even Bacchus, with the heavens represented by the zodiac. But to the erudite Renaissance mind, Casina Pio IV's façade symbolized the Church's triumph over pagan beliefs that preceded it, which reduced icons of Greece's classical pantheon to allegories of the victorious Christian world. On the gleaming white walls, Hercules and Cybele evoked Christ and the Virgin—as did, on the casina's fountain loggia, Adonis and Venus, and Jupiter and Amalthea.

Above the tabernacle facing the courtyard was Pius IV's coat of arms followed by the words *Pontifex Optimus Maximus:* pontiff supreme. The casina's interior featured the prevailing canon, its vaulted ceilings lavishly frescoed with scenes from Genesis and Exodus to the life and agony of Christ and his encounters with various saints.

Since 1936, Casina Pio IV has housed the Pontifical Academy of Sciences. Intended to demonstrate that faith and science are compatible, it dates to 1847, when shortly after his election, Pope Pius IX resurrected a former Roman scientific academy once led by Galileo. Today, about eighty scientists from around the world are members, a quarter of them Nobel laureates. Its roster includes non-Catholics, and even suspected atheists such as physicist Stephen Hawking. Several times a year, its scientists meet to

Casina Pio 4, Vatican
PHOTOGRAPH BY CATARINA BELOVA/SHUTTERSTOCK.COM

discuss relevant contemporary issues and publish the proceedings.

In the early years of his nearly thirty-two-year reign, the Academy's founder, Pius IX, was a popular liberal reformer. He was also the last head of the Papal States—land that encompassed much of today's central Italy, which the Church had acquired from wealthy adherents, including emperors Constantine and Charlemagne. Italian nationalists, however, eventually stripped the church-state of all its territory save 110 acres that comprise today's Vatican City—and turned the populist pope into a reactionary. Pius IX is best recalled not for his enlightened incorporation of a scientific body within the Church, but for convoking the First Vatican Council in 1868 to bolster Catholicism against rising secular tides.

The most memorable achievement of Vatican I was the declaration of the dogma of papal infallibility. Unprecedented in Church history, it stated unequivocally that on matters of morals and faith, the Pope's teachings are divinely inspired by the Holy Spirit, and thus irreversible. That declaration would later bring the Church and Pius IX's Pontifical Academy of Sciences to an embarrassing impasse.

Monsignor Marcelo Sánchez Sorondo, chancellor of the Pontifical Academy of Sciences, sits at a long, polished hardwood table in Casina Pio IV beneath a Zuccari fresco of the Mystic Marriage of St. Catherine. He is Argentine, in his early seventies, tall with a straight nose, thick eyebrows, and a receding gray hairline that has reached the top of his head. A gold cross on a chain and rimless reading glasses hang over his black jacket and black clerical shirt. A professor of philosophy, Msgr. Sánchez Sorondo assumed his position here five years after the events of 1994 that caused that impasse and enraged Pope John Paul II, who appointed him.

In September 1994, the third decennial United Nations Conference on Population and Development was scheduled to meet in Cairo. Two years earlier, the Vatican had scuttled efforts by ecologists to address the matter of population at the Earth Summit in Rio de Janeiro. Now, it again had to ensure that, as the Pontifical Council for the Family described it that spring in a treatise titled *Ethical and Pastoral Dimensions of Population Trends,* "alarmist views concerning world population" would not prevail among attending nations.

Strategizing to thwart family-planning programs was nothing new here. For decades, the Holy See had infiltrated groups such as Planned Parenthood with moles. After years of pressure, Catholic U.S. congressmen, backed by the U.S. National Conference of Catholic Bishops, had forced out the director of USAID's Office of Population, Dr. Reimert Ravenholt, author of the agency's international family-planning programs since its inception. For the coming UN population conference, John Paul II directed the Pontifical Academy of Sciences to prepare a white paper on the state of population on the planet. He had reason to feel confident: The Pontifical Council for the Family, which he created in 1981, was reporting that world population growth rates had peaked between 1965 and 1970 and were now naturally declining. In the coming century, they predicted, there would be no more quadrupling; growth rates might be only one-third of the former exponential frenzy.

The Pontifical Council for the Family was comprised of cardinals, bishops, and married couples, but no scientists. Now, three members of the Pontifical Academy of Sciences, along with demographers and an economist, were chosen to produce a report that ostensibly would concur with the Council, and validate the Vatican's position at the Cairo population conference.

In June 1994 they released their report. Over seventy-seven pages, *Popolazione e Risorse* (*Population and Resources*) tracked global and regional demographic and economic trends. It examined natural resources, technological development, water, and food production, including the Green Revolution. It considered education, family issues, women's issues, labor, culture, religion, morals, and ethics. Taking into account the time frame in which all these variables interacted, it concluded:

It does not seem possible that population can grow indefinitely in the long term. With the capacity humans have acquired to control sickness and death, which will plausibly increase, it is now consequently unthinkable to sustain *indefinitely* a birthrate beyond 2.3 children per couple to guarantee replacement. The contrary demographic consequences would be unsustainable to the point of absurdity.... [Given] the long-term consequences created by the decline of mortality, there is an inescapable need for a global *containment of births,* which must be met with scientific and economic progress and all the intellectual and moral energies of mankind to assure respect, equity, and social justice among all parts of the planet, and between present and future generations.

"That," snaps Msgr. Sánchez Sorondo, "was the committee's opinion. Not the Academy's."

In the days that followed the report's release by the Italian bishops' conference, Vatican spokesmen attempted to parse the Vatican's policy from the recommendation of its own august scientific body.

"It was not," declared the secretary of the Pontifical Council for the Family, "a synthesis of the work done, but merely an illustration of the data and of the problems which emerged, accompanied by some editorial considerations."

"The Academy's task," said Vatican Radio, "is to contribute to scientific progress, [not to be] an expression of Church teachings or of the Holy See's pastoral strategies."

The Pope, reportedly livid, may have wondered why he hadn't assigned the task to a new advisory team of scientists he had recently founded, the Pontifical Academy for Life, to support the Vatican's anti-abortion and anticontraception campaigns. But with its Nobel laureates and international credibility, he did not have the option of disbanding the esteemed Pontifical Academy of Sciences.

Five years later, when Msgr. Sánchez Sorondo became the Academy's chancellor, following a study week titled Science for Survival and Sustainable Development, Academy members issued another provocative statement:

> Our planet is threatened by a multitude of interactive processes—the depletion of natural resources; climatic changes; population growth (from 2.5 billion to over 6 billion people in just 50 years); a rapidly growing disparity in the quality of life; the destabilization of the ecological economy; and the disruption of social order.

Like the warnings of Greek choruses depicted on Casina Pio IV's façade, voices of Academy scientists rise to counsel cardinals and Popes about extraordinary developments at an extraordinary point in God's creation, warranting extraordinary measures. Today, with population at 7 billion and racing beyond 10, what is the Church's response?

"When I was in the seminary," says Msgr. Sán-chez Sorondo, "people said a time was coming when we wouldn't be able to eat because of population growth. It never happened. When sociologists of my generation recommended birth control, the Pope opposed it. Now, it turns out, the Pope was right. You don't hear of overpopulation anymore. Today's sociologists are worried about population decline. Europe's population is diminishing."

Not exactly yet, although population growth on the European continent has, in fact, slowed to the point that decline could one day set in. In few places is that truer than Catholic Italy, where the birth rate is below 1.4 children per fertile woman.

"This a big concern," says Sánchez Sorondo, rocking in his leather chair. "It's more than just being a Catholic country: Italy's tradition *was* the family." He touches his fingertips together. "We bishops are very alarmed."

Yet Italian public schools aren't full of empty seats and desks, because immigrant children from over-flowing Africa and Asia, as well as eastern Europe, are filling the breach. Italy has its own counterpart to the British National Party, the anti-immigrant—and especially anti-Muslim—Lega Nord. Unlike the fringe BNP, Lega Nord is among the most powerful parties in northern Italy, for which it has advocated autonomy—and at times outright secession—from the rest of the country.

Anti-immigration politics is problematic for the Church, which ministers to refugees in Italy. The refugees' very existence, however, underscores an uncomfortable reality: Other continents have more people than can be fed. Such hungry hordes produce many more children than Europeans, whose infant mortality rates are nearly zero, whose family livelihoods don't depend on child labor, and who have ready access to contraceptives, even in the long shadow of St. Peter's.

In 2009, Pope Benedict XVI addressed this convergence of poverty and population in his encyclical *Caritas in Veritate (Charity in Truth)*. In it he denounced the global market economy for squeezing salaries, social security, and workers' rights to maximize profits, locking poor countries into competing in a race to the bottom of wages and benefits for factory jobs that bring more misery than actual development. He condemned consumer temptations that undermine people's values and their planet.

During his papacy, the first of the new millennium, Benedict XVI became known as the "green Pope" for installing thousands of photovoltaic cells atop the Vatican auditorium, and for his open disgust at the failure of the 2009 climate talks in Copenhagen. In *Caritas in Veritate,* he declared: "The

Church has a responsibility towards creation and she must assert this responsibility in the public sphere. In so doing, she must defend earth, water and air as gifts of creation that belong to everyone."

But he rejected any conflict between that moral environmental imperative and maintaining a growing population:

> Human beings legitimately exercise *a responsible stewardship over nature,* to protect it, to enjoy its fruits and to cultivate it in new ways with advanced technologies, so that it can accommodate and feed the world's population. On this earth there is room for everyone: here the entire human family must find the resources to live with dignity, through the help of nature itself—God's gift to his children—and through hard work and creativity. At the same time we must recognize our grave duty to hand the earth on to future generations in such a condition that they too can worthily inhabit it and continue to cultivate it.

Nature will help humans if humans help nature: It sounds simple, except the number of humans keeps increasing, even as nature's bounty does the opposite. How to feed "everyone" without sacrificing our remaining carbon-absorbing forests, says Msgr. Sánchez Sorondo, is what the Pontifical Academy of Sciences has been charged to solve. And he believes they have.

He turns to the shelves behind him, lined with leather-bound volumes. Their gold-embossed titles glint beneath crystal wall sconces retrofitted with multiple compact fluorescent bulbs. Not finding what he wants, he calls toward the doorway in a sonorous baritone amplified by the vaulted ceiling. A priest appears with the proceedings from a recent Academy study week, titled Transgenic Plants for Food Security.

"Food isn't running out," he says, opening to the report's table of contents. "New crop species are coming in. Developing countries are living off them — Mexico, Brazil, Argentina, most of all. They're producing nothing else, and selling them in Asia. People who were poor are getting rich — they're making more by growing transgenic soy than by raising cattle."

Some articles in the proceedings describe the case of golden rice, a genetic modification that inserts genes from daffodils, corn, and soil bacteria into rice to make it produce beta-carotene, which in turn produces vitamin A. The idea was to combat the world's millions of cases of blindness and death from vitamin A deficiency. Golden rice was first developed in Switzerland, with subsequent improvements by affiliates of IRRI, the International Rice Research Institute, in the Philippines, the tropical counterpart to CIMMYT, Mexico's wheat and maize center. Its grains are golden-orange like a sweet potato, for the same reason: beta-carotene.

Although its flavor is indistinguishable from white rice, and it was developed more than a decade ago, golden rice has yet to become available due to wide opposition to genetically modified crops. One fear is that transgenic plants might crossbreed and permanently alter strains in nature, meaning a loss of crop biodiversity.[1] The Vatican study was devoted to disabusing that notion, on the grounds that today's crops have been selected by humans over millennia to improve them, so none remotely resembles its ancestors.

Msgr. Sánchez Sorondo turns to an entry by renowned ecologist and Academy member Peter Raven, longtime director of the Missouri Botanical Garden.

"Dr. Raven says transgenics actually help conserve biodiversity." During the study, Raven presented a paper stating that at the rate species are being killed

---

1. Some critics also contend that modified golden rice delivers far less vitamin A than naturally vitamin-rich leaves, vegetables, milk, and eggs.

off worldwide, by 2100 two-thirds may be gone: an extinction equivalent to the event that obliterated the same proportion of the world's life-forms 65 million years ago, including the dinosaurs. In that case, an asteroid the size of a small town smashed into the Yucatán Peninsula; in this case, the asteroid is the human race. One thing that might help, Raven proposed, is planting transgenic crops, which can be grown intensively and therefore take less land away from other plant species than conventional agriculture. He dismissed as a myth the concern that these genetically altered strains might hybridize so readily with their wild relatives that the latter would vanish.

If Sánchez Sorondo is aware that Peter Raven's scientific prestige dates to a classic 1964 paper on the coevolution of butterflies and plants he coauthored with an entomologist named Paul Ehrlich, it is a detail he ignores.

"If transgenic food wasn't healthy," he says, "nature would rebel against it. Like when you feed meat to a cow, you get mad cow disease. The Church believes that if things were only better regulated economically, there would be plenty of food for everybody."

In part, this argument refers to Pope Benedict XVI's invectives against food becoming less human sustenance than marketable commodity. But it may also respond to American diplomatic persuasion. Having ingratiated itself in Rome by defunding foreign aid for any family-planning program that mentioned abortion, the George W. Bush administration lobbied the Vatican on behalf of biotech agro-industries, asserting that the way to feed the world's hungry is with GM crops. This lobbying effort was intended to counter Catholic clergy in poor countries who oppose genetically altered grains. Because new genetic strains are hybrids that often can't reproduce or lose their vigor if they do, farmers must buy new seed every year, as well as the fertilizers and chemical protection needed to cultivate them. Even the conservative African Synod of Catholic Bishops has accused agro-technology of "risking the ruin of small landowners by abolishing traditional methods of seeding, and making farmers dependent on companies" that produce GMOs.

Apparently, they have been overruled. "As the Holy Father said, there will be enough food in the future for all," repeats Sánchez Sorondo. "The Church is showing that the new transgenic methods can help bring this about."

Yet scientists at both IRRI and CIMMYT warn that transgenic leaps to feed the world are decades away from being viable—let alone discovered. And Green Revolution founder Norman Borlaug insisted that it will be impossible to keep feeding the whole world unless population growth is also checked.

"That's not what the Church believes. The Church believes in Providence. That fellow apparently didn't."

But how far does Providence extend? When Pope Benedict XVI wrote of enough room and resources for everybody, did he mean every living species, not just human beings?

"Both humans and animals are subject to natural laws that have taken scientists time to decipher and understand," Sánchez Sorondo replies after a pause. "We have to respect the natural laws."

Another pause. The Academy, he admits, has never actually studied how human population growth might trespass on biodiversity. "But to respect nature doesn't mean that you just stand there admiring it. Pope Paul VI once said that the goal of a scientist should be to develop the potential of nature for the benefit of man and of nature itself. We must understand how nature functions, what its laws are. And then, perfect it."

ii. Heaven and Earth

Is natural law immutable? Or is it law that changes with time, circumstance, or interpretation? It might be said that biological laws evolve, but the laws of physics don't: a chance mutation might skew a living lineage off on some wild new angle, while the law of gravity seems unlikely ever to be repealed. But in the Catholic Church, law became immutable from the moment in 1870 when Pope Pius IX and his advisors realized that, bereft of their Papal States, their territory reduced to less than half a square mile, with only a thousand or so citizens (nearly all male, as today) their power was essentially gone. Unless...

Thus Vatican I, which sealed the notion of papal infallibility. It was an idea that had been broached over centuries, with arguments pro and con even among Popes. It was also suspected of being a Protestant rumor meant to vilify the Catholic Pope for such a presumptuous claim. But now, for the first time since biblical prophets and apostles, the word spoken by a man — the Bishop of Rome — on matters of faith and dogma would be not mere opinion or command, but divine revelation. The authority of God Himself was infused in the Pope.

Power restored. But papal infallibility was a sword that cut two ways. As the late Vatican historian Father August Bernhard Hasler noted, if the Pope's teachings were infallible by virtue of being Pope, then the teachings of all Popes were infallible. A new Pope was locked into—and limited by—what was now the inviolable word of his predecessors. Overturning precedent was not an option.

Therefore, on controversial positions that perplex modern progressive Catholics over their Church's seemingly ossified stance against contraception, ordination of women or married men, or acceptance of homosexuals, the reality is that the Church has little choice, because it has painted itself into an ever tighter corner. As Karol Wojtyła, the future Pope John Paul II, would write for the dissenting opinion to the overwhelming (69–10) majority of the Papal Commission on Population and Birth Control that advised Paul XI to relax the sanction against artificial birth control:

> If it should be declared that contraception is not evil in itself, then we should have to concede frankly that the Holy Spirit had been on the side of the Protestant churches. . . . It should likewise have to be admitted that for a half century the Holy Spirit failed to protect Pius XI, Pius XII, and a large part of the Catholic hierarchy from a very serious error. This would mean that the leaders of the Church, acting with extreme imprudence, had condemned

thousands of innocent human acts, forbidding, under pain of eternal damnation, a practice which would now be sanctioned.

Those words provided a key passage in the minority opinion that persuaded the Pope to write *Humanae Vitae*, rejecting the majority that favored contraception. To do otherwise would have undercut the stoutest remaining pillar of the Church's foundation: the absolute authority of the Pope.

"The Church has never been against birth control," says Cardinal Peter Kodwo Appiah Turkson. "It's just a problem of method."

Cardinal Turkson heads the Pontifical Council for Justice and Peace. Although its official mandate mentions neither nature nor ecology, in one of the mysteries of the Roman Catholic curia, it is the branch of the Vatican's bureaucracy that takes the lead on environmental issues. Before becoming its president in 2009, Turkson was archbishop of the ecclesiastical province of Cape Coast in his native Ghana. With the world's highest birth rates, Africa also is where Catholicism enjoys its fastest growth; Turkson's former archdiocese is famous for training and exporting priests to other countries where Catholic clergy have become an endangered breed, such as the United States.[2]

The Pontifical Council for Justice and Peace is housed in Rome's seventeenth-century Palazzo San Callisto, a four-story complex three miles from the Vatican, owned by the Holy See as an extraterritorial property under treaty with Italy. Its office is spare, with pale walls and plain, dark wood-trimmed doorways and windows. Portraits of popes past and current hang above cases of multilingual pamphlets and books published by the Council on topics such as ethical development, disarmament, and fairness in global financing. Compared to the opulent Pontifical Academy of Sciences, its modest countenance resembles that of a human rights NGO.

Cardinal Turkson has a broad, gently smiling face, with a cloud of gray frizz above a high, prominent brow. He explains that the Church, in fact, supports several kinds of contraception—each based, he says, on the fact that "a woman can always tell if she's ovulating."

He actually took a class in Australia, he adds, in a

---

2. Since *Humanae Vitae,* the number of U.S. Catholic seminarians studying for the priesthood has dropped by more than half. Only 1 percent of nuns today in the United States are under forty. (Source: Center for Applied Statistics for the Apostolate, Georgetown University.)

technique known as the Billings ovulation method. "They called me their first bishop student." The Billings method teaches a woman how to recognize the fertile stage of her menstrual cycle. "Without even inserting any finger into anything—just by, you know, touching—she can feel the mucus that begins to appear and notify the husband. Something like that, we encourage."

There are several ways, he says, for women to alert their spouses. "Some put a green leaf on the bed. That indicates to your husband that you're ovulating. When you see it's over, you put a red leaf."

It is disconcerting, if not surreal, to hear a Catholic cardinal—and one frequently mentioned as a prospect for the papacy—discuss vaginal mucus, especially when the topic was supposed to be the environment. But all environmental issues quickly lead to the fact that there are more humans than the system can comfortably hold, including the issues Cardinal Turkson himself lists: the need to clean the air, cut CO_2, and slash Rome's satanic traffic. Lamenting the hours that Italians lose hunting for a parking place, he calls for more mass transit, and bicycles to save fuel. He considers it a crime that a crucial measure of economic success in Europe is how many cars people can be convinced to buy.

"When the Volkswagen was invented, their slogan

was *ein Auto für jedermann:* 'a car for everybody.' Then when everybody has one, there's hardly any space to park, so cars get smaller and smaller. Then, you know what happens next: Families want two cars, and you double the problem."

Overconsumption is unquestionably deplorable, but taken alone, it also deflects from the obvious: that too many cars result from too many people. That, in turn, results in the awkward spectacle of a kindly, intelligent man who someday might be leader of the world's Christians—at least according to the Roman Catholic Church—pretending he doesn't know that sperm can live inside a woman for up to six days preceding ovulation, regularly foiling contraceptive methods based on mucus, temperature, or calendars.

Lurking behind such contortions of learned men who are genuinely worried about melting poles and deepening droughts, yet who still insist that a million more of us every four days or so is a blessing, is a simple accounting cipher. Even an infallible pope has little power if his flock shrinks too far. Like Yasser Arafat's womb-weapon and the overbreeding of Israel's *haredim,* the Church has a fundamental, vested interest in bodies. The more Catholics there are in the world, the more the judgment of the 1,000 male citizens of Vatican City matters.

Cardinal Turkson has seen enough African suffering and starvation in a world with 7 billion to know what it will be like with 10 billion. Moreover, he heads a Vatican council charged with moral guidance regarding questions now shaking seven continents and roiling the seas: questions such as ethical dilemmas over which species to save and which get sacrificed, dilemmas that might never arise with fewer people cornering all the room and resources. Yet his Church insists there's room for everyone, and that it's a punishable sin to use effective means to prevent adding more.

Cardinal Turkson knows, yet he can't disobey dogma. He cites Pope Benedict's 2009 annual World Day of Peace message, when the pontiff said that we need to live in solidarity with the future and with other dependents on the Earth. "You know. Like animals."

Yet ecologists contend that this not just about expressing solidarity, but about mutual survival. Can there be a home for humans here without a supporting cast of characters, whose numbers perhaps only God can know?

In his plain wooden chair, he sinks into contemplation of this question. "When God began to create the world," he finally says, "it was chaos. Then God said *let there be this* and *let there be that*. The chaos transformed into a cosmos, into a beautiful, orderly system. That transformation was through the Word of God. For me as a Christian, that means that without the Word of God, we're likely to go back to chaos again. I would be worried if I was not a man of faith. I would be worried if I didn't believe in a God who our Scripture says has not created this world to be in chaos."

But if we have entered a time where our planet seems to be bursting its seams and popping its rivets, might there be Scriptural justification for thinking about restraint?

The cardinal takes a deep, thoughtful breath.

"It makes a lot of sense to practice restraint. There are biblical instances of a time to do this, and a time not to do that. Unfortunately, our culture has gone through an evolution that makes it difficult to hear Ecclesiastes saying that there is a time to embrace and a time to refrain. Now, there's always time to do, and never a time to refrain from anything. Everybody knows how to celebrate Mardi Gras, Fat Tuesday, but nobody thinks about the abstinence that Ash Wednesday calls for. Does Mardi Gras make sense if it's just Mardi Gras?

"As for restraining from sex: in the animal world, a dog or a cat will not accept a mate unless it's in heat. It's only human beings who make love both in and out of season. But there is a viable alternative to which we could invite people..."

He stops and looks at the floor. Then he raises his eyes.

"I was going to say that if we lived our celibacy faithfully, we could offer it as an eloquent message to the world that such action is possible," he says softly. "But the eloquence of this message has been badly compromised."

iii. *Belle donne e bambini*

It would seem that the spectacle of a Church exposed for abetting widespread serial child rape might finally mute its dicta that sex is only for "responsible procreation," not pleasure or entertainment. But the Vatican is the oldest of political echo chambers, St. Peter's resonant dome enlarging its proclamations in the ears of the proclaimers—even as right outside Vatican walls, few hear or care. Studies show that 98 percent of the Catholic women in the United States have used contraception; in Catholic Italy, the figure may be lower—but only due to a lingering cultural preference, particularly in conservative northern Italy, for coitus interruptus, also a forbidden sin to the Vatican. The fact that Italy nevertheless has one of the lowest fertility rates anywhere is partly explained by the success of parliamentarian Emma Bonino to legalize abortion in 1978, a campaign instigated after her own clandestine abortion. Church attempts to muzzle her were ignored; her long government career includes serving as vice president of the Italian Senate and as foreign minister.

In the 1990s, Italian women had the world's lowest birthrate, 1.12 children apiece, only to be passed in 2001 by Catholic Spain. With one of the world's highest percentages of women with doctorates—more Italian women have PhDs than men—Italy is posterworthy proof that education lowers birthrates. Yet the details are complicated.

Sabrina Provenzani sits on the floor with her old college friend, Licia Capparella, whose three-year-old twins, Michelangelo and Adrian, are investigating her luxurious thick hair, comparing it to their mother's long brown curls. It is January 2011; Sabrina, a producer for the public broadcasting network Radio Televisione Italiana, has the day off because the CEO has once more suspended her program under pressure from Prime Minister Silvio Berlusconi. The prime minister—whose days finally seem numbered—is lately mired in one of his more lurid scandals, involving a seventeen-year-old Moroccan immigrant dancer.

Because Sabrina's program covered the affair, Berlusconi is again threatening them.

What infuriated Sabrina most were the wiretaps that surfaced: hearing parents and siblings of several girls saying yes, go with him, he's a generous man, it will set our future. These days in Italy, it's easy to find girls who'll leap to earn €7,000 in one night, rather than €700[3] a month. Women may be Italy's most educated sector, but they're also the worst compensated. For more years than she cares to remember, Sabrina has been working twelve hours a day producing a TV show with 1.6 million viewers, but getting paid the same as a Fiat factory worker. The network deftly sidesteps a law prohibiting too many consecutive monthly contracts by paying her *weekly* as a consultant, not as a staffer eligible for benefits.

She and her husband, Emilio, a software designer, have now reached their late thirties, a time they'd always hoped to have enough economic stability to start a family. But as Licia is reminding her, working women who dare to have children risk everything.

For years, Licia worked for one of Italy's oldest nature NGOs. She wrote about animals, ran their website, and loved her job. She worked from 9:00 a.m. to 7:00 p.m., often came in on weekends, and

---

3. About US$934.

was loved in return by her superiors—until she got pregnant.

"Silly me. I came running into work, all excited to tell my boss."

Despite the frigid reception, she kept working. Even when she'd faint in the subway, she kept going to the office, working through the summer when nobody else wanted to. "After six months, when I got too fat with the twins and took maternity leave, I kept calling in to see if I could help by working from bed, even though that's illegal. That's when they told me they weren't renewing my contract."

Actually, they'd never given her a legal contract. For three years she'd had a string of temporary six-month contracts, even though the law required full contractual health benefits and five months' maternity leave following the second renewal.

"Yeah, right," says Sabrina.

Licia nods. At the NGO, they gave her a choice. After she had her babies, she could return, but she would lose her seniority and have to start all over. She is now working as a park guide two days a week, without a contract. "Nobody checks, and I need the work so badly, I accept it."

What she didn't accept was her treatment by the environmental nonprofit. She sued for €65,000, the additional amount she would have made if she'd had the correct contract in the first place. Wonder of wonders, they offered to settle for €35,000. The judge, a woman, commented tartly that if they were willing to pay that much, they were in effect admitting their guilt and by rights should pay the full sum. But in the end, to avoid further battle, Licia agreed to that amount plus her legal costs.

With two babies, the money was a godsend, but reinstatement in her former position was now out of the question.

"Still, we're lucky. We have two bedrooms. We know people with children sleeping on the sofa. Or they've stopped eating meat. All these qualified people, barely making it to the end of the month. One of my friends has a doctorate in biology, but all she can find is work in a call center, for €1,000 a month. We're like medieval serfs. We're Italy's new poor."

In France, she says, they make it easier for parents, with state funding for day care and kindergarten. "In all of Rome, there are maybe three or four day-care centers. You're really thinking of having kids?" she asks Sabrina.

"We're talking about it."

"Good luck. No one helps." There is the "Berlusconi bonus"—a €1,000-per-baby government incentive to raise the birth rate. "It won't even buy diapers. And now they're cutting kindergarten to half-days, because the government needs to cut the education budget. Meanwhile, government funding gets siphoned to private Catholic schools so Berlusconi can get support from the Church."

Licia's father was one of fourteen children. She is one of four. Had she not been blessed with these adorable twins, her child would have been one of one. "I'm happy that we have these two. But it's twice as hard for us."

A generation ago, men and women married in their twenties. Women had babies earlier, and had more of them. Even so, family size had been dropping ever since the Industrial Revolution turned farming villages into manufacturing towns and women became part of the labor force. Today, being so well educated, they're still hired as long as they're single and childless, even as Italian men now live with their parents into their thirties, trying to save enough to get married. By the time they and their underpaid working girlfriends do so, there's usually only time and money enough for one.

"Today," says Licia, "a thirty-year-old is still a girl. I'm forty, and I'm just settling in to being a mother."

Her friends are all leaving — for Germany, Australia, even Spain. There aren't jobs there, either, but supposedly they do more to help women. Sabrina and Emilio have toyed with going somewhere, too.

What a century: Italians aren't having babies because it's too expensive, or they flee Italy to have them somewhere else. Meanwhile, Italian schools are overfull, because immigrant children are taking the place of missing natives.

"If we have kids, what future will there be for them?" Sabrina asks. She and Emilio are having dinner in the home of their friends Claudia Giafaglione and Vincenzo Pipitone.

Claudia, who's Sicilian, is serving grouper with couscous and a salted brioche stuffed with smoked salmon, ricotta, and chives. She has dark hair, round dark eyes, and a heart-shaped face, reminding Sabrina of a beautiful pet cat. She also has a degree in pharmacology and biology, and another in nutrition. Vincenzo, her tall, slim, handsome husband, is an army surgeon. They are more secure financially than most Italians their age—Claudia has just turned thirty-five—yet like Sabrina and Emilio, they are terrified by the idea of having children.

Emilio, whose latest app design is a guide to olive oil, translates his own fears into hard cash: "I earn about three thousand euros[4] a month. We use contraception because we're afraid we can't afford kids.

---

4. Approximately US$4,200.

Yet suppose in ten years we have a bigger house, and can afford a better school. Ten years later, my pension will be about five hundred euros. So in twenty years I'll be poor. If we wait ten years to have a baby, how will we afford to raise it?"

"I agree with Emilio," Claudia says.

"This is stupid," says Vincenzo. "When I go on military mission to Afghanistan, I see people as poor as animals. No electricity, no security. Yet they have families. Italy may be crazy, but at least we have peace here. We must be happier than they are. Yet we think so much about what we don't have. The national sport in Italy is complaining."

For a few minutes, they take turns at that sport, excoriating their beautiful, frustrating country that has so many ancient wonders — and ancient infrastructure to match. When Vincenzo was a medical student, he was assigned to a hospital forty-five kilometers from where he lived: without public transport, his commute was three hours.

"My brother never sees his daughters," says Emilio. "They're asleep when he leaves for work and asleep when he returns. He's working so hard to send them out of Italy to study, meaning he'll see them even less. But it's the only way they can escape this economy that he's sure won't ever offer them decent jobs."

"That's so paranoid!" moans Sabrina. But it's

exactly what they fear for themselves, if they ever have the child they're still too scared to have.

"We figure that by the time the kid is fourteen, he'll already be out of the house, in England or China. Or India," says Emilio glumly.

"It would be a strain for her to live here," says Sabrina. "Nothing moves. We're stuck in a past that we didn't build. I just watched an edition of my show from ten years ago. We had the same guests on, talking about the same problems."

But Claudia isn't even thinking about Italy. She has far bigger worries.

"How can we even think of bringing children into this world anyway?" she asks.

Two days earlier, she went to the annual Rome Science Festival. This year's theme was "The End of the World: A User's Guide." The opening session was a National Geographic Channel film titled *Sovrappopolamento*—"Overpopulation." Its premise imagined 14 billion people—the United Nation's high projection for 2084, should family-planning programs founder—trying to fit on the Earth. It showed Mexico City literally crumbling under its own weight, then pulled back to describe a planet that in 1930 had a comfortable population of 2 billion. Ever since, it's been adding the equivalent of ten more New York Cities annually. The film then showed Asia rapidly doubling, interspersed with animations of entire cities suddenly collapsing. Apartment buildings two hundred stories tall went up, then came down—as did forests, flattened for more farmland. Bridges fell under the relentless tonnage of trucks hauling food. Grimy clouds from four new Chinese coal-fired plants each week fouled the air from London to Los Angeles. Shit gushed from overflowing Manhattan sewers, followed by rats bearing meningitis. Countries desperate to feed people slathered the land with chemicals.

Finally, after thirty-five years of bending under the burden of 14 billion-plus, famine wiped out 80 percent of humanity. Population stabilized at 4 billion. At the film's end, ecosystems began to revive. Fish refilled the oceans. Greenery burst forth. People grew enough food, and birds sang anew.

When the lights came on, Claudia saw that several middle schools had brought classes to the science festival. She shuddered to imagine what these fourteen-year-old schoolkids would be thinking to see in an alleged documentary the world where they'd barely begun to live hell-bent for cataclysm within their own lifetimes.

"I'll bet they find a solution before it gets that bad," said a girl in a navy blue sweater and jeans as her class filed out. "Someone will invent something."

"They'd alert us before something like that happens," said the girl behind her, dressed identically except for her knee-high suede boots.

"I'm not having any kids," said another in a purple scarf.

"If we all have to farm, you'll need them," a boy in a blue stocking cap interjected.

The girls exchanged alarmed glances at the prospect of having to farm.

"We are just too many!" says Claudia as she serves warm chocolate cake with a molten center. "We will be like a bacteria colony, living off our own wastes! How do we bring a child into this world of trouble, when we are destined to die?"

Vincenzo reaches for the wine, changes his mind, and produces a bottle of grappa from a cupboard.

It emerges that Claudia, appalled at Earth's deteriorating ecosystem, is writing a spy romance set in the most polluted place in the world. She went to the science festival for ideas about settings: she's considering the saline wasteland left by the now-vanished Aral Sea, the island of floating plastic spreading over the Pacific, or methane geysers in the melting Arctic.

"Maybe when you're done writing about something so dark, you'll be willing to think about a baby—" Vincenzo says, but stops when he sees her stricken look.

He lifts his glass of grappa. "Our future children," he says, "who could live to see the end of the world." He shakes his head, then downs it. Sabrina and Emilio stare at each other across the table.

For a long moment, all is silent. "Coffee?" Claudia finally says. Relieved, everyone laughs.

"I think Claudia and I are thinking too much," says Vincenzo, standing behind her with his arms around her waist as their guests leave. She looks up at him with her round cat's eyes.

Under the yellow streetlamps of the Lungotevere della Vittoria alongside the Tiber, Emilio and Sabrina walk to their car, holding hands. Later that year, the answer to whether or not to bring a child into a frightening century will be instantly clear to them, upon learning that Sabrina is pregnant—the answer being, *Of course you do.* A child is not just a child, but the future incarnate. Despair vanishes when there is truly something to hope for: a world for your child. You'll do anything to assure there'll be one. It may have colossal problems, but your baby is part of the solution, as will you be: there's no more compelling reason to save the Earth than parents wanting to protect their offspring, one of whom may invent the miracle that changes all the odds.

Two months before she is to give birth, Sabrina leaves her job, packs up their apartment, and boards a British Airlines flight to London. Emilio has been there for nearly a year; she conceived when he came to see her on holiday. He is designing mobile apps for a thriving clothing company, and has already been promoted.

Sabrina is the newest immigrant to the UK. When their daughter, Anita, is born, should they remain four more years, she will be a British subject.

CHAPTER 7

Gorillas in Our Midst

i. The DNA

Dr. Gladys Kalema, barely out of veterinary school, looked at the tranquilizer dart she'd just filled with anesthetic, then looked again at the mountain gorillas. She counted three females, two juveniles, three infants, two black-backed adult males, and naturally, a silverback—the patriarch. This one, Gladys saw, approached five hundred pounds, about as big as they come. He had a conical forehead head atop a pumpkin-sized jaw, arms that bent entire treetops toward a wide mouth flashing with oversized canines, and long, thick black body hair, except for the saddle-shaped, silver-gray patch on his well-muscled back. His close-set, round black eyes ignored the nervous park rangers and fixed on Gladys, as if he knew what she was planning.

Two hours earlier, Gladys, the rangers, and a visiting Kenyan vet had hacked their way into southwest Uganda's Bwindi Impenetrable Forest, following three trackers who'd been there since dawn. After lurching uphill, they'd finally found this band in a stand of corkwoods, the juveniles in the trees, swinging among the newest leaves, the adults lolling on the ground, pulling branches toward their mouths and within reach of the babies.

Less than half the size of Chicago, the Bwindi forest crowns a biologically fabulous escarpment containing more endemic species than anywhere else in Africa. The estimated four hundred Bwindi mountain gorillas account for nearly half those remaining in the world — the rest are scattered through Rwanda and the Democratic Republic of the Congo, mostly in the Virunga volcanoes thirty miles south, where those countries and Uganda meet.

Sometimes called the Switzerland of Africa for its 8,500-foot inclines, Bwindi owes its great biodiversity both to elevation changes and to being one of the oldest forests on Earth, dating back at least twenty-five thousand years, before the last Ice Age. It wasn't until the latter part of the twentieth century that biologists knew that the apes raiding surrounding settlers' fields were, in fact, rare mountain gorillas.

The gorillas might have claimed the opposite: they were the ones who'd been raided. Once, this cool forest and the Virungas' skirts formed an unbroken rainforest canopy along the Albertine Rift, a western branch of Africa's Rift Valley that forms the Uganda-Rwanda-Congo border. The sole human presence was forest-dwelling Batwa pygmies, who hunted bush pigs and duiker and gathered wild honey, coexisting peacefully with their primate cousins.

But over the past few centuries, Bantu farmers, who cut and burned forests for fields, kept coming. The jungle that filled the Rift was chopped into three discrete fragments, their gorilla populations isolated from each other. Later, when British colonials introduced tea as a cash crop, the fragments kept shrinking as dark green tea rows advanced. Gladys Kalema first saw Bwindi Impenetrable Forest in the early 1990s, when confirmation of mountain gorilla presence led Uganda's government to elevate it to national park status. By then, Bwindi resembled a shaggy green toupee plopped atop fields of tea, cassava, banana, millet, maize, sorghum, and pink potato flowers that smacked hard against the forest's edge.

And that, Gladys had guessed, was the source of the trouble that had pulled her across the country from Uganda Wildlife Authority headquarters in Kampala, the capital, where she'd just begun as the UWA's first full-time veterinarian. A distress call had come from the Bwindi park rangers: gorillas were losing their hair, leaving patches of scaly white bare skin, big enough to be noticed by tourists. The whole reason for the national park was that Europeans and Americans would pay $500 apiece for a chance to glimpse these creatures. The park's boundaries had been gazetted, Batwa pygmies had been expelled, and teams of biologists had trudged through Bwindi's dense lianas and hardwoods, counting gorillas by measuring the different sizes of dung left in their night nests. Then they'd focused on acclimating two of the thirty-eight separate gorilla bands to human presence, creeping a few meters nearer each visit, not retreating when the silverback charged, hoping he remembered that he was a vegetarian.

After two years, they could get within seven meters without the silverback threatening or the other gorillas fleeing, and they began to bring in tourists. As gorillas and humans share about 98 percent of their DNA, they kept people and these lucrative primates a full seven meters apart: a bad measles outbreak among mountain gorillas in Rwanda a few years before had probably come from humans. It had taken more than ten years after the ouster of macabre dictator

Idi Amin, who exterminated hundreds of thousands of his citizens during the 1970s, to finally convince tourists to return to Uganda, and they couldn't risk something else going amiss.

Before the ten-hour trip over unpaved roads to Bwindi, Gladys called a doctor in Kampala. "What's the most common skin disease in people?"

"Scabies."

Gladys had done her veterinary studies in London; her mother was a Uganda parliamentarian who entered politics after Gladys's father, a government minister, was among the first that Idi Amin killed after his 1971 coup. In England, people hardly ever got scabies. But hygiene was wretched in rural Uganda, and from what the rangers described, the gorillas might well have human scabies.

Now she would see. The rangers were used to viewing gorillas, but not to taking skin scrapings and blood samples from them. A six-year-old with a half-bald back was in the worst shape, but if Gladys approached him, the silverback was sure to charge. The rangers would be no help, she saw, and the Kenyan vet looked terrified: Kenya might have lions, but not 500-pound gorillas. Sighing, Gladys stood, all of five foot four, faced the silverback, and started clapping and shouting. During Rwanda's measles outbreak, she had seen vets do this with gorillas habituated to humans a lot longer than these. She hoped it would work. The massive creature moved a few meters away, clearly upset, but kept his distance as she advanced and fired her air gun into the juvenile's thigh.

Ten minutes later, she had taken samples from the sorry creature, so afflicted that he kept scratching under anesthesia. As he began to stir, to the rangers' amazement the young veterinarian lifted the fifty-pound youngster in her arms and carried him back to the silverback. A few days later, the scabies diagnosis was confirmed—a relief, because ringworm would have been much harder to treat. The following morning, Gladys returned to the forest with enough darts and ivermectin to cure the entire gorilla band with a single dose.

She had a hunch how they'd been infected. Once, the fields and land beneath local wattle-and-daub huts and tourist lodges were part of their range. Habituated gorillas, having lost their fear of humans, ignored park boundaries more than ever, especially since farmers were growing bananas, whose succulent stems and leaves they savored. One reason people here had big families, Gladys learned, was because they needed kids to shoo gorillas from their crops.

But children couldn't throw rocks and bang on pots day and night, so they'd make scarecrows, dressed in discarded clothing. Every one Gladys tested was crawling with the same scabies species. More curious than frightened, apes were examining the clothes and picking up mites.

In her report, Gladys wrote that people needed to learn basic hygiene for their own good and for the sake of wildlife that brought income to their communities. That wouldn't be easy: nobody had toilets or piped water, and most couldn't afford soap. The Uganda Wildlife Authority and the International Gorilla Conservation Programme asked her to design an education program for the Bwindi region. With a conservation ranger, she arranged workshops in eight villages for more than a thousand people. She came armed with flip charts. "Gorillas can get our parasites, our measles, dysentery, pneumonia, and tuberculosis," she explained. Uganda had one of the world's highest rates of TB. A quarter of the chronic coughers in communities surrounding the park tested positive, as did 5 percent of Bwindi's park staff.

She was about to flip to a list of solutions, such as using charcoal to wash when there was no soap, when the ranger touched her arm. "Let them suggest solutions," he said.

A city girl who'd studied abroad, she'd assumed that uneducated people were ignorant. They actually knew their own situation best, once they understood the problem. Gladys listened. They wanted closer health services. They wanted safe water. They needed more and better pit latrines, and covered trash heaps.

They discussed what they could do themselves and what required government assistance. They needed help scaring the gorillas from their fields, so that they weren't putting their children at risk. That eventually resulted in "HUGOs" — human-gorilla conflict resolution patrol teams, paid with gum boots and rain slickers from a gorilla conservation NGO, cornmeal rations from park headquarters, and the respect of the community: a commodity that Gladys learned was especially prized.

After two years as veterinarian to the Uganda Wildlife Service and two more getting a master's in public health in the United States and marrying a Ugandan telecommunications specialist, Gladys made a decision. To really safeguard mountain gorillas, she needed her own NGO: There was another human health issue to confront for wildlife conservation to stand a chance, and no one in Uganda's government was doing it.

ii. Alphabet Soup

July 2010: Dr. Amy Voedisch puts down her ring forceps and speculum, removes her exam gloves, thanks the nurses for a good day's work, and walks out of the Bwindi Community Hospital's maternity ward into afternoon sunlight. In the courtyard, women in flowered cottons sit in the shade of the plastered walls. Most walked for hours to stay at the hospital's hostel for mothers waiting to give birth. Amy saw four of them today. For the Uganda shilling equivalent of US$1.50, a woman can buy a voucher to cover prenatal care, her stay in the hostel, delivery, and postnatal care. The vouchers are subsidized by Marie Stopes International, Britain's analog of America's International Planned Parenthood Federation,[1] although the program is running out, and they have yet to find a new sponsor.

The Bwindi hospital literally began under a tree. When the park was founded, about a hundred Batwa pygmy families had been evicted and left to fend for themselves on the bare margins of an already marginal setting. Landless, considered subhuman by the Bantu, their hunting skills and their uncanny ability to smell honey now useless because they couldn't forage in their former forest home, they were among the poorest of Africa's poor. Most Batwa children died, and life expectancy was twenty-eight years. In

---

1. Marie Stopes was mentored by Margaret Sanger when the latter fled to England in 1916 to avoid arrest on obscenity charges. In succeeding decades, however, the two warriors for women's reproductive rights came to despise each other, and competed.

2003, an American missionary doctor named Scott Kellermann held an impromptu outdoor clinic for the Batwa. But as he learned, beyond some drugstores, the hundred thousand Bantu in villages ringing the national park had no more medical care than the dispossessed pygmies. He ended up starting a foundation to raise money for a hospital.

By the time Amy, an OB-GYN from California in her early thirties, arrived, Bwindi Community Hospital comprised four reinforced concrete buildings. They included a maternity ward recently expanded to forty beds through a Japanese Embassy donation. Even as it was inaugurated, however, the Kellermann Foundation was already seeking bunk beds to double those numbers. In a country with one of the world's highest fertility rates, where many men have multiple wives—the 33 million Ugandans will more than triple by 2050—Bwindi is on the high side of the national median, with families of eight children or more common.

A breeze rustles the flame trees as Amy follows a footpath from the hospital, past a billboard proclaiming that "Smaller Families Are Richer Families" and through a thicket where sunbirds dart at peach-colored hibiscus blossoms. It leads to a road filled with barefoot women clutching plastic jerry cans of water and balancing baskets of fruit on their heads. They are headed home from the dusty market at the center of Buhoma, the village at the entrance to Bwindi Impenetrable National Park, two kilometers from the Congo border. Amy's destination, just across the road, is marked by a small white wooden sign protruding from the foliage. It reads, "CTPH — Conservation Through Public Health: Field Clinic for Mountain Gorillas and Other Species," the NGO that Dr. Gladys Kalema-Zikusoka and her husband, Lawrence, founded.

A voice calls out. Amy doesn't speak Rukiga, the local Bantu dialect, but she turns. A skinny woman who looks around sixty, walking with a stick between two banana-laden companions, is hobbling toward her, smiling toothlessly, arms widespread to embrace her. The day before, Amy delivered this woman's tenth child, a daughter. Afterward, through a nurse-interpreter, Amy asked if she wanted any more.

The woman, who is actually thirty, had burst into tears. "Lord, no!" she whispered. She was HIV-positive, and already had suffered one stroke. "I'm too weak to go through this again." Her husband, however, had other ideas. So Amy had explained that she could put something in her uterus that would keep her from conceiving for the next twelve years. "Right now, if you want."

She wanted.

*   *   *

Her dark blond hair tied back in a ponytail, Amy stands before fourteen women and twelve men seated in wicker chairs under a thatched roof on CTPH's patio. These are family-planning peer counselors recruited in surrounding villages, who are paid with soap and goats. Their job is to educate their neighbors about the availability and comparative advantages of condoms, daily birth control pills, Depo-Provera injections that last three months, and hormonal upper arm implants that last five years.

Gladys Kalema-Zikusoka and five of her staff are also present. There was no way, Gladys had concluded while getting her master's, that she was going to save any gorillas if she didn't deal with western Uganda's double bind. Like so many of the world's biological hot spots, for the same fertile reason that animals abound here, so do humans. Even with no city for hundreds of miles, nearly a third of Ugandans live in their country's southwest quadrant around Bwindi, one of Africa's most densely populated rural regions. More than half were under fifteen years old, and farms already had been subdivided so many times that most were now under a hectare.[2] Eventually, Gladys knew, hungry people would

---

2. 2.47 acres.

convince park officials by bribes or threats to let them keep chipping at the boundaries.

To keep animals healthy, she had to keep people healthy. But the healthier people were, the more they survived, and the longer they lived. So many were already pressing up against the Bwindi forest that its gorilla habitat was imperiled, and with better health care, there would be even more. The logical thing was to limit the amount of healthy people, by providing them incentives, and the means, to limit themselves. Having earned the public's trust in campaigns against scabies and tuberculosis, CTPH now added family planning. Managing the number of humans was the gorillas' only chance.

A factor in Gladys's favor was the importance of gorilla tourism to the area: 20 percent of park fees were shared with surrounding communities. Nobody wanted to jeopardize that. Everyone remembered the day in 1999 when a Hutu death squad that had fled into the Congo jungle after the Tutsis won in Rwanda crossed into Uganda, entered Bwindi Impenetrable National Park, and captured fourteen tourists and a park warden. Their targets were British and Americans, whose governments had supported their overthrow. The Hutus let German and French tourists go free, including a deputy French ambassador. The two Americans, four British, and two New

Zealanders who got lumped in with the other English speakers they hacked to death with machetes. A warden who tried to stop them was bound and burned alive. It took three years for tourism to recover, while the entire region reeled.

"If we have too many babies and keep growing bigger," Gladys explained, "people will cut more forest to grow more crops, we'll lose the gorillas, and tourists will never come back." Women needed little convincing. The local tradition of respect accruing from having many offspring was rooted only in men. Women simply accrued each other's commiseration as their broods grew.

The concept of family planning doesn't exist in Rukiga, so women soon learned to say it in English. But willingness to have fewer was useless without access to the means. One obstacle was Uganda's president, Yoweri Museveni, a popular leader who had restored calm after years of bloody chaos under Idi Amin. Now in his second quarter-century in office, President Museveni believed that the surging economies of China and India were due in direct proportion to their vast populations—so the more Ugandans, he reasoned, the better off Uganda would be.

He saw the fact that the country's population had doubled in just seventeen years as a window of opportunity to leap through: Population growth meant more people earning more money to buy more domestic goods, and paying more taxes to fund more education to teach even more people, and so forth. His government didn't prohibit contraception: the health ministry even offered it. But its meager budget depended on foreign donations, and didn't reach half the country's fertile women. In 2008, only 6.4 percent of it was actually spent, much of it on hand-held abacuses that the president's wife advocated for calculating ovulation days. Known as Moon Beads, this variation on the rhythm method resembled prayer beads, and was about as effective in averting pregnancy.

"Yebare munonga," says Amy, exhausting most of her Rukiga vocabulary as she thanks her audience of community-conservation health workers, as they call themselves. In English, she explains that she is a women's doctor who came to share an important family-planning tool, one that lasts much longer than ones they already have. She pauses as one of Gladys's colleagues translates. Like Amy, he wears a gray T-shirt with the CTPH logo: a mama and baby gorilla with a human couple.

Amy holds up a ParaGard T-380A, the American-made intrauterine device she has been inserting since her arrival earlier in the week. She passes the T-shaped IUD around. It is an inch long, made of milky polyethylene, with two nylon monofilaments dangling from the end. Fine copper coils circle the stem and the arms of the T, which are about 1/32 inch in breadth. Its cost here, courtesy of Population Services International, a U.S. NGO, is under a dollar.

The women heft it: it is practically weightless.

"How does it work?" one asks.

"The copper," Amy explains, "releases ions that block sperm from reaching the egg." A lengthy translation ensues.

"How long does it keep working?"

"Twelve years. You can put a new one in when the old one is removed."

"What about side effects?" This was always the biggest concern. Many birth control myths, often traceable to men, circulated in Uganda, such as women on Depo-Provera retaining so much menstrual blood that their uteruses rot.

"An IUD has none of the side effects of hormonal methods, like headaches or weight gain or mood changes," Amy replies. "In some women it does make menstruation heavier."

Groans follow the translation. "But that usually normalizes after a few months. In my experience, very few women are unhappy with it. If heavy bleeding persists, it's easily removed by these cords that hang into the vagina."

"Can the man feel them?"

"The strings are clipped, and they curl up where he can't reach them. They're invisible."

From a bag she produces an oversized leather model of a uterus, Caucasian-flesh pink. Everyone titters. Using an instrument resembling a small forceps with a loop at one end, Amy demonstrates how easily the IUD is inserted and removed.

"It doesn't move around inside you?"

Amy shakes her head. The advantage, she explains, is that this is a long-term method that's completely reversible. No need for another Depo shot every three months, no trek to the clinic for a new implant. A young woman might insert one until she's ready to have a baby. After giving birth, she can replace it, then remove it when she wants to have another. An older woman with enough children could put one in and leave it for the next dozen years, at which point she wouldn't need contraception anymore.

"And," Amy adds, "one of the easiest times to insert an IUD is in the forty-eight hours after giving birth, when you're already in the hospital anyway."

She pauses to let this sink in. "And the husband wouldn't have to know?" asks a woman swaddled in orange.

"Not," Amy replies, "unless his wife tells him."
Everybody grins.

Several peer counselors here have been trained to give Depo injections in their villages. None is qualified to insert an intrauterine device, but they can refer women to the hospital, which will offer postpartum IUDs for free. They scoot their chairs into groups of three to role-play referrals. Amy gives each a scenario. In one, a twenty-seven-year-old woman with tuberculosis wants long-term birth control. The proper response is to counsel her to get an IUD, because there are no hormonal side effects to complicate her illness or conflict with other medications. A twenty-year-old woman, eight months pregnant, wants space between her first child and subsequent births—what kind of family planning should she use? In this case, all methods from condoms to chemicals to intrauterine devices should be explained, so she can decide which fits her circumstances best. But it's a good idea to mention that, other than requiring a hospital visit to remove it, a postpartum IUD is the least worrisome. Once out, she can get pregnant the next time she ovulates.

They go through other situations: a thirty-two-year-old tired of injections every three months; a wary twenty-year-old who would like the ease of an IUD but has heard that they can migrate in a woman's body all the way to her heart—or that it can fail and wind up inside a baby's head. Everyone takes turns playing client and counselor; afterward they critique each other. Did they remember to say that an IUD is reversible? Did they tactfully ask a mother of eight if each new child brought more happiness or more problems? Did they mention that besides being an effective, nonchemical form of contraception that can't be detected by a libidinous husband, the option of receiving a postpartum IUD is another good reason for having a hospital birth?

That's important, they're reminded by a nurse who's worked with Amy all week, because mortality of women having babies in hospitals is 80 percent below the national average. "It's the same for infant mortality," she adds. "If you die in childbirth, the chances of your baby surviving without you aren't good."

An arm around each of her two toddler sons, Gladys watches from the back, her long curls framing her wide smile. Four years have passed since CTPH added family planning to its mission, after building trust by raising awareness about parasites and disasters like TB, Ebola, or polio that could leap between humans and their hairy relatives. Until now, family-planning programs had rarely reached western Uganda. Now they had teams of field counselors, and a hospital embracing the program.

This has taken much work, much of it involving neither women nor gorillas. Like every charity, she must constantly find new funding as old sources become exhausted. During her master's at North Carolina State, Gladys learned to write grants, and to register CTPH as a nonprofit organization in the United States. Her first funder was the Washington-based African Wildlife Foundation. From there, she tapped the John D. and Catherine T. MacArthur Foundation, the Irish government, the U.S. Fish and Wildlife Service, and Bayer, the aspirin maker. Her expansion into reproductive health was abetted by a fortuitous meeting with an exuberant, copper-haired American who now sits to her left, jotting notes and nodding as Amy's workshop proceeds. She is Dr. Lynne Gaffikin, a public health epidemiologist who brought Amy Voedisch to Buhoma, and who connected Gladys to the funder of so many of the world's struggling family-planning efforts: USAID.

Lynne Gaffikin had spent her junior year of college abroad, sorting fossils for paleoanthropologist Richard Leakey at the University of Nairobi. With two fellow exchange students, she hitchhiked across Kenya and Idi Amin–controlled Uganda to see chimpanzees and mountain gorillas in the wild. Four years later, in 1978, she returned with a Fulbright to study

African culture. Her anthropology career, however, derailed in Kenyan villages she'd visited years earlier, now engulfed by children with flies in their eyes. Back in high school, she had read *The Population Bomb* and even belonged to a Zero Population Growth chapter. Now she saw what Ehrlich meant. The following year she returned to UCLA, to begin a master's in public health.

There she met Dr. Paul Blumenthal, an OB-GYN from Chicago on leave from Michael Reese Hospital and Planned Parenthood. Lynne told him about Africa, about seeing mountain gorillas peaceful as Buddhist monks, and how tourists turned silent and reverent in their gentle presence. There were so few left, and the land supporting them was being overrun by their human primate relatives. Unless something changed, both people and gorillas were going to lose.

After they married, Lynne Gaffikin earned a doctorate in community health and epidemiology, and Paul Blumenthal eventually became director of reproductive health at Johns Hopkins. Through the 1980s and 1990s, both were frequently in Africa and beyond. Lynne became an advisor to Kenya's Ministry of Health and to the Mountain Gorilla Veterinary Project, a legacy of Dian Fossey (another Leakey protégée—in this case, Richard's archeologist father, Louis, who also sent Jane Goodall to study chimpanzees).

They spent two years in Madagascar, a global biodiversity hot spot where a traditional wedding blessing, "May you have seven sons and seven daughters," reflected a population doubling every two decades. However, a new president, declaring that the health of the economy and the island itself depended on sustainable human numbers, renamed Madagascar's health ministry the Ministry of Health and Family Planning. Paul was an advisor there while Lynne, a fellow of a new USAID program titled Population, Health, and Environment—PHE—coordinated African sustainability initiatives.

In 2007, Paul was invited to direct family planning at Stanford, where he started a program that in its first year saw two hundred eighty thousand women in fourteen countries receive IUDs. In California, Lynne reunited with her old hitchhiking companions from Nairobi, now married to each other. The wife, children's book author Pamela Turner, returned to Africa with Lynne to write one about mountain gorilla veterinarians. There they heard about a young woman vet who had stopped a gorilla scabies epidemic in the Bwindi Impenetrable Forest.

A few years later, Dr. Amy Voedisch, who had spent her honeymoon in Rwanda watching mountain gorillas, saw a copy of Turner's *Gorilla Doctors*. Not long thereafter, she was off with the epidemiologist in the book to teach about postpartum IUDs at Gladys Kalema-Zikusoka's veterinary-cum-maternity NGO.

After the workshop, the community-conservation health workers pose with Amy for a group portrait. The USAID grant that Lynne Gaffikin midwifed to enable CTPH's family-planning program has now run out, although a bit more sluices through a program run by the Bronx Zoo–based Wildlife Conservation Society, which has an office in Uganda. By piggybacking environment, public health, and family planning, Gladys can troll for donations in all three arenas. Still, each year is a survival trek through the impenetrable jungles of philanthropy. Every NGO in every developing country competes for the same pool of charity—which, as economies contract and populations grow, is shrinking like Arctic ice.

All week, Gladys and Lynne have worked on a CTPH evaluation to present to funding agencies, Lynne translating it into the acronym-studded bureaucratese she's mastered to keep family-planning funds flowing. A grateful Gladys feels like she's swimming in alphabet soup when Lynne effortlessly produces donor-dazzling sentences such as: "USAID early recognized the lack of access to RH/FP services in the BMCA, and for close to a decade it funded CARE to implement CREHP in the area."

They each hug Amy good-bye. Lynne is headed to Kampala, the capital, to consult to urban NGOs battling with fragile supply lines: from fickle funders to corrupt bureaucrats to inept warehouse managers who let medical supplies overheat; from shady middlemen and lazy drivers to aging delivery trucks, impassable roads, mislabeled shipments, overwhelmed clinics, and overworked nurses, the chain can break anywhere and frequently does. Not long ago, the entire country ran out of condoms. After all the effort to raise awareness and educate women about their options, a week's delay in restocking birth control pills or injectables can mean hundreds of unintended pregnancies.

Gladys is off to an emergency at Queen Elizabeth National Park fifty kilometers to the north. An open savannah with two lakes connected by a natural channel, it is where thousands of fishing families, goats, cattle, elephants, cape buffalo, waterbuck, crocodiles, leopards, and hippopotami converge. Now an outbreak of anthrax has claimed sixty-seven hippopotami. Amid growing scarcity and growing numbers, people have been increasingly poaching hippo meat, and Gladys is praying that no one's infected. Somehow, she needs to burn or bury a lot of three-ton hippo carcasses before hyenas and vultures start spreading anthrax spores all over the Rift.

At the word *anthrax,* Amy shudders: As an undergraduate, she worked in a St. Paul, Minnesota, Planned Parenthood clinic where one day an envelope arrived containing white powder. That scare taught her what was at stake in helping women make their own reproductive decisions, but it also confirmed her choice about what to do with her life.

"Enjoy your time here," Lynne tells her. She turns to Gladys. "See you in Kampala." They have plans to meet at a fund-raiser that a mutual hero, Jane Goodall, is holding for Uganda's chimpanzees.

"Pray for the hippos," says Gladys.

———

Dr. Joy Naiga, senior national programme officer in Uganda's Population Secretariat, looks glum. She sits in the restaurant of the Sheraton Kampala in her slim black suit, having stopped for coffee between meetings. Beneath the table, her bare feet rest atop her high heels.

"It's the fiftieth anniversary of the birth control pill. I take the same pill my mother took. Women use the same IUDs. This is not new technology. And we still can't afford to have enough contraceptives in this country. I wish we could market them like mobile phones."

She likes the president. She has met with him and his first lady. She has tried to explain the math: even if Uganda suddenly strikes oil and annual GDP rises by 10 percent, they still can't become a middle-class country with a fertility rate of seven kids per woman. "Only when we reduce to 2.1 can we achieve that."

But the president still wants his country to be Africa's version of an Asian tiger, still insists that China and India's incipient superpower status results from their huge workforces. It's particularly frustrating for Naiga, because President Museveni responded so brilliantly to the AIDS epidemic with a ubiquitous nation-wide publicity campaign, led by his slogan of "zero grazing"—like goats that always find food close to home, men shouldn't stray. It was a smart strategy. Without moralizing, it simply told men to keep their sex life at home, however many wives that meant, and it worked: In less than a decade, Uganda's HIV infection rate dropped from 15 to 5 percent.

"If we could do that, we can do anything," says Naiga. Yet a national health sampling shows that 41 percent of women lack access to birth control. "And they just counted married women."

Her government, she admits, simply doesn't procure enough contraceptives. Most are donated through

UNFPA, the United Nations Population Fund, which has its own problems trying to meet needs. Uganda's contraceptive shortfall translates into at least a million unplanned pregnancies a year. A study concluded that three hundred thousand end in unsafe, illegal abortions. The ones that don't produce a surplus of unwanted children.

"Family planning is the most cost-effective way to get us out of poverty. It would buy us time to deal with our environmental ills. It would save women's lives. God help us if we don't slow down."

Outside, Kampala has transmogrified into another of the world's impossible cities, with incomprehensible traffic and tendrils of chemicalized air curling among withering jacaranda blossoms. Unbroken humanity stretches from Kampala's hills for thirty kilometers to Entebbe on the shores of Lake Victoria. Roads swarm with men doubled under loads of green bananas, mothers with armloads of infants, and throngs of children in a kaleidoscopic palette of school uniforms. At Lake Victoria, long, narrow pirogues, their gunwales nearly at the waterline, sputter up to jetties piled with teak and other hardwoods deforested from islands hours away, used for charcoal to smoke diminishing catches of tilapia and Nile perch. The world's second largest freshwater lake, Victoria, "the water tower of Africa," is both Kampala's water supply and the lowest point of its waste treatment chain. From the opaque green liquid lapping the greasy jetties, it's apparent which one is winning.

The oldest family planning NGO in Uganda is Pathfinder International, here since the 1950s, including through the Idi Amin nightmare. Its current director, Anne Fiedler, is one of twenty-seven children: her polygamist father, a school principal, had five wives. Upon entering university, she went to the infirmary and asked for a tubal ligation, saying that she didn't want kids: her parents had enough for her, too. She was told that she needed a signed consent from her husband or boyfriend or father. Even for contraceptives.

At the height of the AIDS epidemic, Anne Fiedler started Straight Talk, a radio program for teens. She now tries to tell her audience of sixteen-year-olds who are about to become mothers the difference between loving, feeding, and schooling two — or trying to do that for seven.

"After surviving Amin, and then HIV, everyone felt decimated and wanted to replenish our numbers," she says, pointing with her red-framed glasses. Even herself: she lost a sister to AIDS, contracted from a university colleague who, it turned out, had three other girlfriends, two already dead. "She was using pills. She didn't know she should be using a condom, too." Anne is now married, and has one child. Some of her other sisters who didn't get to college have six apiece.

"Population growth is outstripping our future. I'm not waiting for our leaders anymore, but we have to give families a reason to change behavior. Otherwise," she says, fingering an open ledger on her desk, "we're just peddling commodities: pills, condoms, injectables. But it's hard to tell someone in a village to have fewer because their whole country is at risk."

On the last Friday in July 2010, Lynne Gaffikin finishes her work and hurries to the Serena Hotel, Kampala's fanciest. It is twilight; army snipers that for the past week manned twenty-four-hour positions atop government buildings, embassies, and five-star hotels, including the Serena, have finally taken their AK-47s and left. The triple gauntlet that hotel guests had to cross is back to normal: one metal detector, not three, plus just a single X-ray following a hand search of luggage and purses.

The paranoiac security was for the fifteenth summit of African Union leaders. A week before it began, two bombs exploded simultaneously, one in a rugby club, the other in a restaurant. Each was packed with patrons watching a World Cup match between Spain and the Netherlands. Seventy-six died, including several foreign tourists. Things worsened with the arrival of Libyan dictator Muammar Gaddafi, the chief suspect behind the bombings. Gaddafi, in power for forty years, detested President Museveni—his junior, having led Uganda for only a quarter century—for opposing Gaddafi's calls for a United States of Africa. Under this plan, Africa would become a single nation; although Gaddafi claimed that it would create a strong economic front, Christian African nations such as Uganda smelled a scheme to entrench Islam. Suspicions were not alleviated when Gaddafi's three hundred bodyguards picked a fistfight with Museveni's presidential guard during the summit's opening ceremonies.

But the rest of the week passed uneventfully—as usual, the summit produced nothing of import—and now the Serena's pool terrace, lined with palms and artificial waterfalls, is the scene of the fund-raiser for Dr. Jane Goodall, founder of the institute that bears her name, dedicated to the survival of Africa's chimpanzees.

Waitresses bearing trays of wineglasses and flaked pastry hors d'oeuvres circulate among women professionals in silk blouses and tailored pants and men from the diplomatic corps in jackets and ties. The American ambassador and several staff are present, as are World Wildlife Fund, the Wildlife Conservation Society, and the Uganda Wildlife Association.

Lynne, in a black sweater and green slacks, finds Gladys, who's in sandals and a CTPH polo shirt. Her husband, Lawrence, the telecommunications specialist, wears a blazer. Lawrence had a polygamist great-uncle who sired one hundred children whose ages spanned generations, several younger than some of his grandchildren. Lawrence's grandfather, one of Uganda's first engineers, only had six, which bewildered his prolific brother. "Do we really need more?" he'd reply. The whole family had to help support his brother's offspring.

"We needed a private NGO just to take care of our relatives," Lawrence says. Lawrence was a rarity in Uganda — an only child, which was all his mother wanted until she married his stepfather and inherited six more. When relatives would ask if she and her new husband were having some together, she'd ask if they were offering to pay school fees.

A murmur on the patio as Jane Goodall joins the gathering: a thin, erect woman with long gray hair, wearing a deep orange shawl over a black turtleneck. She is immediately surrounded.

"With the right publicity," whispers Lawrence, "I think Gladys could be to gorillas what Jane Goodall is to chimps." The gorilla chair is vacant, sadly, because

Louis Leakey's other famous protégée, Dian Fossey, was murdered, likely with her own machete, either by the poachers she fought, or by enemies in the tourism industry, which she hated because she felt it needlessly exposed mountain gorillas to human diseases.

Fifty years have passed since Leakey sent Jane Goodall off to study chimpanzees in what is now Tanzania. She has come to Uganda to tell the African Union summit that when she started her life's work, there were 1½ million chimpanzees spread across twenty-one African countries. Today there are fewer than three hundred thousand. Uganda's small chimp population is in the Albertine Rift; some in the Bwindi Impenetrable Forest; but most of them north of Queen Elizabeth National Park.

And that is right where, it turns out, Uganda's fortunes have recently turned. The country has indeed struck oil.

President Museveni's visions for Uganda suddenly feel like more than dreams. Leases have been awarded. In fact, the event this evening is sponsored by a UK oil exploration firm that has the contract for the areas of the Albertine Rift with the greatest concentration of chimpanzees. A company executive is present, in an open-necked blue shirt.

"We're proud to be associated with chimpanzees," he tells the gathering. He describes the tree planting campaign they've begun where they are drilling. "The environment is close to our hearts. We have a responsibility to leave it better than we found it."

He does not mention the refinery they are also building there, and he doesn't say that they will stay for at most twenty years, the life expectancy of the oil field. The Ugandan deposits are estimated at 300 million barrels, what the United States consumes in about sixteen days.

After he speaks, he introduces and hugs Jane Goodall. She smiles. She then describes her first trip to the Rift, when it was unbroken chimpanzee habitat from north of the Burundi border all the way south into Zambia.

"You could climb to the escarpment and look east: chimp habitat as far as you could see, green rolling forest. Gradually those forests have disappeared." Tanzania's Gombe National Park, where her institute is based, is down to twenty square miles, and fewer than one hundred chimpanzees. Only on the steepest surrounding slopes, where farmers desperate to cultivate and women desperate for firewood can't reach, are there still trees.

She turns and glances at the oil executive. "And now," she says, "we're killing ourselves to try to save the Albertine Rift from the oil companies." Again, she smiles, exactly like before, and everyone laughs.

She does not mention that apart from global warming, the two biggest nonnuclear environmental disasters in history are ones that oil companies have left in the jungles of Nigeria and Ecuador.

She ends with a fund-raising appeal for Roots & Shoots, an international environmental education NGO she has founded for young people in 120 countries, lest they lose hope in the future.

"Let's help as many young people as we can grow up with the right values. And," she adds, "let's see if we can level out human population growth, to have optimization: the right number of people living in the right places."

An auction follows for a portrait of a chimpanzee with Jane Goodall, and for signed copies of her memoirs. The oil executive and his striking blond wife outbid everyone for the portrait, and Jane resurrects the smile once more as she poses for a photo with them.

Lynne Gaffikin wins one of the books. "It's for you," she tells Gladys, who goes to the podium, where Goodall inscribes it. The elegant, elder woman who has devoted fifty years to saving the world's chimpanzees, only to watch four-fifths of them disappear, hands her life's story to this young veterinarian who is trying her best for the world's last few hundred gorillas.

The smile of recognition they exchange is genuine.

CHAPTER 8

The Great Wall of People

i. By the Numbers

Lin Xia[1] had no idea, until her mother happened to mention it at dinner.

"I was still breast-feeding you," said her mother. "I hadn't had my IUD replaced yet, because my chance of conceiving was low."

She'd already returned to work, bookkeeping for a plant that serviced trucks. "Between my job and baby daughter," she said, smiling at Xia, "I was too busy for another child." Reaching for an apple chunk, Xia's father, a retired schoolteacher, nodded agreement.

Not just too busy. That was only three years after

---

1. Her name is changed by request.

China's one-child policy began. Although they lived in Anhui province, six hundred miles south of Beijing, there were no exceptions yet for rural families, and they knew the rules. After having a baby, if a woman tried for another, she could be sterilized. So Xia's mother dutifully informed her factory. In the inverse of maternity leave, she was given abortion leave, including a subsidy that paid for the procedure, her convalescence, and for replacement of her stainless-steel IUD ring. "They still give that today."

It was the first time Lin Xia knew of the sibling she never had. "Were you scared? Or sad?" she said, gazing softly at her youthful, round-faced mother, who could pass for her older sister. If they had sisters.

They were in Xia's Beijing apartment, on the eleventh floor in a complex of ten identical twenty-eight-story square towers. Her mother gathered Xia's orange cat into her lap. "It was like having a tumor," she said. "You have to get rid of it. I wasn't scared, just a little nervous. After you went away to school, I missed not having another. But not enough to break the law."

Breaking the law could mean a fine equal to more than a year's wages. It still does, the amount varying by province and by how close local population planning officials are to meeting monthly quotas: Like speeding tickets elsewhere, penalties for extra children have represented significant revenue in China. In Shanghai or wealthy Jiangsu province, this "social burden tax" might be US$30,000 for a second child, and more for a third. But a peasant may pay only the yuan equivalent of a few hundred dollars.

"Back then," said Xia's mother, "they mainly forced you to give up the pregnancy. If a woman ran away to avoid an abortion, they'd jail her family until she returned."

" 'We'll buy you a rope or a bottle of poison,' " quoted her father. "That was their slogan for women who said they'd rather kill themselves than abort. Today, peasants ignore authorities and have three or four until they get a boy. In 1980, they would have bulldozed their houses." He poured himself tea. "Those bad things were done by local officials. The central government's intentions were good. China had to control births."

Their own parents had suffered through history's worst famine, from 1958 through 1962. It was during Chairman Mao's Great Leap Forward, when private farms were collectivized and millions of peasants conscripted as industrial laborers. Grain was requisitioned for growing cities, even as yields plummeted under inept directives from distant Beijing. Nobody dared disobey. Nobody dared to report true figures from disastrous harvests in terror of being purged, which often meant execution. The shortfall was so grave that up to 40 million Chinese people perished — no one is exactly sure. Millions more were malnourished.

The memory of not enough food to sustain the population was seared into China's collective consciousness. "It was offensive to smash houses and confiscate people's appliances, or to jail a woman's parents until she got an abortion," said her father. "But we needed a government policy. There were just too many people."

China's contentious one-child policy, which in 2013 newly anointed President Xi Jinping signaled may be relaxed gradually during his incumbency, is already partly a misnomer. Some twenty-two legal exceptions have allowed 35 percent of families at least two; many Chinese refer to the "1½-child policy." Because Lin Xia's parents live in a rural region, they could have tried again for a son after six years — the required length of spacing also varies by province. Besides the rural allowance, since 2002 China's fifty-six ethnic minorities — anyone other than the 92 percent Han majority — have been permitted three, lest they shrink into cultural extinction. Exemptions were also granted for miners (because of high mortality), for the disabled, and for children born abroad.

In recent years, single children who marry each other may now also have two, although most couples willingly stop at one: the cost of kids gets daunting if two singles also are expected to help support four retired parents and up to eight grandparents. With China building more and bigger cities than the Earth has ever seen, and filling them as soon as the concrete dries, the newly urban occupants no longer need sons for farmhands. Instead, they need factory salaries to raise the one allotted to them. Only the luckiest who, through some entrepreneurial stroke, propel themselves up the upwardly mobile spiral, even think of more children.

Although bereft of siblings, Lin Xia also benefited from the one-child policy. Before, when sons had preference, just one-fourth of university students were female. Today, it's nearly half. After studying mechanical engineering and communications, she works as a science writer. Her magazine's office is in one of the dozens of skyscrapers built in the pre-2008 Olympics frenzy in Chaoyang, a bleak industrial warren that metamorphosed into Beijing's gleaming Central Business District. It's exciting to live in this incredible city and bigger-than-anything country.

But how big can China actually get?

It is now the world's biggest consumer of grain, meat, coal, and steel, and the biggest market for—

and maker of—automobiles. It's also the world's biggest emitter of carbon, with the soot and CO_2 to match. Although China contends that 40 percent of its smokestack emissions are from manufacturing goods for the United States, no one objects to the money, and they keep pumping out more.

There are now at least a hundred fifty Chinese cities with more than a million people; by 2025, there will be two hundred twenty. During the first quarter of this century, half the world's new buildings will be built in China. With half the Chinese now living in cities—compared to one-fifth in 1980—and three-fourths expected to be urban by 2030, the construction will only increase. Although China's fertility rate dipped to replacement within a decade of the one-child policy's enactment, sheer momentum means that its population will keep growing for another generation. In 2012, China was adding another million people about every seven weeks.

"I can't imagine 400 million more Chinese," Xia says—that being the difference the one-child policy is widely believed to have made. She's told her parents about her work, about seeing dried-up lakes around Beijing, the treeless dust bowl of Gansu province, the stinking Yellow River. And the dams: Half the world's forty-five thousand biggest dams are in China. Three Gorges Dam on the Yangtze, which displaced 1.3 million people, is the biggest, costliest construction in human history. It will soon be surpassed by the even costlier South-North Water Transfer Project, which will take a half-century to complete and will channel the equivalent of another Yellow River twelve hundred kilometers north from the Yangtze Delta to thirsty regions around Beijing.

For the South-North Water Transfer, which will tunnel under the Yellow River itself, water must be pumped uphill over more than half its distance. That is akin to tilting Asia to make water flow backward, frightening to Shanghai, whose Yangtze Delta water will be siphoned northward. Shanghai has already pumped so much water that it's sunk six feet. The South-North project assumes there will be higher rainfall in upper Yangtze basins as global temperatures rise. But so far, climate change instead has brought droughts so deep that coal barges can't navigate low river levels, causing power shortages and driving China to the brink of needing to import rice and wheat.

Lin Xia recalls another slogan, from the Chinese National Population and Family Planning Commission: "Mother Earth is too tired to sustain more children." She once heard a prominent Chinese demographer remark that 700 million would be the right population for China—just over half the current 1.3 billion. Given the dust storms the size of

Mongolia that she has seen, and smog blanketing four contiguous provinces, she would agree.

"Imagine," she says. "We wouldn't have to burn all that coal, or build more dams."

Seven hundred million was China's population in 1964. Just a half-century ago.

ii. Rocket Science

Around 2030, China's numbers should peak just below 1.5 billion — even an easing of China's child-birth rules isn't expected to change the modern preference for small families. Population will then drop dramatically as members of the transitional generation between high-fertility and low-fertility China pass away. After years of subreplacement fertility, there simply won't be as many births to replace them. By 2100, there will again be fewer than a billion Chinese. The problem, however, is what will happen between now and then.

That aging transitional generation is on Jiang Zhenghua's mind as he sits in the garden of the Red Wall Restaurant in a quiet alley in one of Beijing's few remaining old hutongs, a few blocks from the Forbidden City. He is waiting to dine with an American scientist interested in his role in developing

China's one-child policy, whose thirtieth anniversary, September 25, 2010, is three days away. He looks forward to meeting her. She has been honored with awards in Europe, Asia, and America for visionary work that calculates the cost-benefits to humans derived from preserving the environment, showing that it's in people's best interest not to dismantle the natural infrastructure from which humanity springs. She is also, he understands, a protégée of American population biologist Paul Ehrlich, whose work was noted with interest when China decided to rein in its population.

In China, she is collaborating with one of his own protégés, demographer Li Shuzhou, an expert in an unforeseen consequence of the one-child policy: millions of girls missing from the census roles. In 2000, Li Shuzhou cofounded Care for Girls, a program that counsels and provides loans to families that wanted sons but got daughters, and monitors the girls' upbringing. As for Jiang Zhenghua himself, now vice-chairman of the Central Committee of the Chinese Peasants and Workers Democratic Party, the government has called upon him to help solve a related challenge: how to care for the elderly, now that there are far fewer young people. It will be interesting to hear what the American scientist thinks about that.

* * *

"Professor Jiang, a pleasure," says Gretchen Daily. He beams at the trim, athletic woman with short fair hair and friendly light eyes. She smiles back at the professorial man in pin-striped suit and paisley tie. With his hair still dark and his posture erect, only Jiang's oversized rimless glasses suggest that he is in his mid-seventies. He introduces her to the woman who manages the restaurant, who dotes on him. He orders for them: duck, organic rice with braised sea cucumber, an Australian shiraz. He sits back, hands folded.

Jiang Zhenghua was born in one of China's loveliest cities, Hangzhou—but just barely. It was during the Sino-Japanese War, and Hangzhou had just been invaded. His parents were fleeing when his mother went into labor at the city gate, where she delivered him, so they stayed. His father taught primary school, history, and geography; his mother taught mathematics. When the war ended and the country adopted communism under Mao Zedong, his historian father gave him books explaining how, over hundreds of generations, Chinese came to believe in government as the authority destined to unite people for a better life.

By the late 1950s, after graduating in electrical engineering from Jiaotong University, Jiang was already hearing discussion of plans to stabilize

China's population somewhere between 700 and 800 million people, so that his country would have a healthier environment in which to develop.

"What were the concerns?" Gretchen asks. "Food and health care? Forests? Land degradation? What were people thinking then?"

"Economic development," he answers. "In the 1950s, Chinese people didn't know about environment. To the Chinese way of thinking, we are a huge country rich in resources, so we don't need to worry about that. Until, of course, 1958. The Great Leap Forward, you know. We did many silly things. We cut trees in the mountains until they were bald. We tried to smelt iron in poor ovens."

During Mao's Great Leap Forward, which jerked China from six thousand years of agrarian life into the industrial age, the air filled with oily smoke from hundreds of thousands of backyard brick furnaces that peasants were ordered to build to smelt scrap iron. To meet quotas, families melted down bicycles and their own pots and pans. Because the furnaces were fired mainly with green wood from millions of newly felled trees, the pig iron that resulted was mostly useless.

"Silly," Jiang repeats. "But at the time nobody thought it was unreasonable. In the 1950s, the government was highly respected. This was just after the Japanese War. People believed the Communist Party could do anything."

But the idea of restricting population growth was a radical departure from communism. Marx and Engels condemned Thomas Robert Malthus for suggesting that pressure of overpopulation on resources would limit production, when it was surely the opposite: population provides labor resources that enhance production. Malthus was considered a bourgeois apologist for the capitalist ruling class, who blamed the world's problems on the lowly and exploited. At first, that was also Party Chairman Mao Zedong's belief: population was strength, not a hindrance. But following the disaster of the Great Leap Forward, Mao and Premier Zhou Enlai drafted scientists to help stabilize their reeling nation.

The idea of population control had first emerged years earlier. A 1953 census had produced the surprising news that there were nearly 600 million Chinese. Distribution of condoms and cervical caps ensued, along with a policy of encouraging women to postpone early childbirth and to wait several years before having a second child. Chairman Mao, torn between anti-Malthusian Marxism and realization that numbers were getting out of hand, frequently switched between the two positions. During the Great Leap Forward, he first proposed state birth planning, then abandoned it and persecuted his demographers.

Mao's 1966 Cultural Revolution ultimately set the stage for the one-child policy, but in an unlikely way. "I was actually working in missile control," says Jiang Zhenghua, grinning. "And atomic reactor control."

"Amazing," says Gretchen.

Just before Jiang graduated in 1958, much of Jiaotong University, including engineering, had moved from coastal Shanghai thirteen hundred kilometers inland to the ancient Chinese capital of Xi'an, in Sichuan province. Officially, this was to spread higher learning throughout the country, but Jiang recalls frequent sorties over Shanghai by enemy planes from Taiwan. There were strategic reasons for protecting his department, where Jiang was asked to work in the new field of computer science. His assignment was to design automatic controls for guided missiles and nuclear reactors.

During the Great Leap Forward, China's nascent computational powers were squandered, he tells Gretchen, on trying to streamline steel production from backyard smelters. But following that debacle, for five years the work became very engrossing.

"We built rockets. We even made our own semiconductor chips."

"My husband works in laser physics," says Gretchen. "He gets all the chips from China."

Jiang beams again. But his pride dissolves in a sigh as he recalls what followed. "The Cultural Revolution: If not for that, China might have developed so much earlier."

Instead, in 1966 Mao began purging suspected bourgeois elements. That lasted until the mid-seventies, shortly before his death. No part of society, from agricultural collectives to the highest ranks of the Communist Party itself, was spared, and no sector more punished than China's universities. Student brigades called Red Guards, whipped into a froth by Mao, denounced college administrators and faculties as "capitalist roaders," counterrevolutionary intellectuals, and traitors. Professors were marched through the streets and beaten. Journal publication and contact with foreign colleagues ceased, and libraries were trashed. By 1967, most universities had closed, their faculties banished to remote regions for socialist reeducation by the proletariat peasantry, who handed them hoes. Many wouldn't return for more than a decade.

There were strategic exemptions, however, and Jiang Zhenghua, working with missile systems, was among them. Only computer technology deemed vital to national defense was still intact—which was how the odd circumstance of the world's most famous and severe birth control policy, something normally the purview of social scientists and demographers, ended up being designed by a pair of missile engineers.

Today, non-Chinese have difficulty understanding how the world's fastest-growing economy, whose breathtaking growth inspires awe and envy in capitalists, persists in calling itself *Communist*. This discrepancy traces back to the Cultural Revolution, a time when China was simultaneously expunging itself of external influence, even as it reengaged with the world. In 1971, the United Nations admitted the People's Republic of China as the legitimate government of China. Heretofore, that designation, and a seat on the UN Security Council, had been held by the Republic of China — Taiwan, whose population was one-sixtieth of Red China's.

China began inserting itself noisily into the planetary dialectic, which then consisted of a so-called First World — capitalist North America, western Europe, and Japan, Australia, and New Zealand — and a Second World of communist-bloc countries. Both were trying to win — or force — the allegiance of less-developed Third World countries. China's participation became especially pointed during the first UN

World Population Conference in Bucharest in 1974. During that gathering, its representative, Huang Shu-tse, ridiculed Western fears that a population explosion would soon overwhelm world agriculture and resources:

> The claim that over-population is the reason why the have-not countries are poor is a worn-out tune of the superpowers. What a mass of figures they have calculated in order to prove that population is too large, the food supply too small and natural resources insufficient! But they never calculate the amount of natural resources they have plundered, the social wealth they have grabbed and the super-profits they have extorted from Asia, Africa and Latin America. Should an account be made of their exploitation; the truth with regard to the population problem will at once be out.

As Harvard anthropologist Susan Greenhalgh writes in *Just One Child,* her sweeping twenty-year investigation of China's reproductive policy, those acid denunciations referred especially to a 1972 study prepared by three MIT systems modelers, Donella Meadows, Dennis Meadows, and Jørgen Randers. Their book-length report had been commissioned by an international think tank, the Club of Rome.

Titled *The Limits to Growth,* the report to the Club of Rome echoed the warnings four years earlier of Paul Ehrlich and of "the notorious Malthus," as the Chinese termed him. It predicted that swelling global populations and massive harvesting of resources were on a catastrophic collision course. Like Ehrlich's *The Population Bomb, The Limits to Growth* had sold millions of copies worldwide.

In 1974, China was having none of it. As Huang Shu-tse told the Bucharest conference:

Today, the world population has more than quadrupled that of Malthus' time, but there has been much greater increase in the material wealth of society, thanks to the efforts of the broad masses of the people in surmounting numerous obstacles. In the twenty-odd years since her founding, the People's Republic of China has increased her products many-fold. The creative power of the people is boundless, and so is man's ability to exploit and utilize natural resources. The pessimistic views spread by the superpowers are utterly groundless and are being propagated with ulterior motives.

What Huang didn't know was that back in China, his few compatriots with computer access, missile and defense experts, were modeling systems themselves. Because it was a national priority for scientists to keep up with their American, European, and Soviet counterparts, they enjoyed unique privileges, such as traveling to the West. In Western technical journals they read how systems engineering could be applied to anything from electrical circuitry to traffic control to social organization. They read *The Limits to Growth* and came to rather different conclusions than comrade Huang Shu-tse.

"These were very interesting ideas," Jiang Zhenghua explains to Gretchen Daily. China's leaders had asked him to model economic scenarios. "Economists in China were good in theory, but not mathematics. If we want faster economic development, what kind of input do we need? If we have limited resources, what is the maximum output we can get? They wanted to know the limitations of development, and how to allocate our resources. For the input-output model, we considered the balance among different economic factors, but also — I knew, because I had read the Club of Rome material — factors of the environment system."

"Fascinating," says Gretchen.

Besides Jiang Zhenghua's systems department in Xi'an Jiaotong University, China's other working computer complex was ensconced in Beijing's Seventh

Ministry of Machine Building, devoted to the space industry. The chief missile scientist there was a slight, mild-mannered man named Qian Xuesen. Qian graduated from Jiatong University in mechanical engineering in 1934, then earned a master's at MIT and a doctorate at Caltech, whose faculty he was invited to join. He was a founder of Caltech's Jet Propulsion Laboratory in Pasadena and, during World War II, designed missiles for the United States and was commissioned as an Air Force colonel. Nevertheless, during the McCarthy era he was purged as a suspected communist over the protests of American scientists and military officials, and held under house arrest until the mid-1950s, when he returned to China.

Driven by U.S. anti-communist zealots into the arms of the very communists they feared, with detailed knowledge of the U.S. missile technology he'd helped develop, Qian became Mao Zedong's and Zhou Enlai's science advisor and father of the Chinese missile program. His brightest protégé in the Seventh Ministry was a cybernetics engineer named Song Jian. Song had designed an elegant calculus theory to optimize efficiency in applications from mechanics to military strategy to social structures. In the Seventh Ministry, he worked on missile guidance systems.

During the Cultural Revolution, he was sheltered by his mentor Qian Xuesen's protection, and encouraged to apply his theory and the missile division's computational muscle to develop models for China's mounting social planning needs. Like Jiang Zhenghua, Song could travel and had access to scientific literature from the West. He recognized that quantifying fresh water, soils, and pollution as well as human demographics, and understanding how they interacted, was critical to guiding economic and social development. Both he and Jiang knew that American and European ecologists were alarmed that their populations were exceeding their carrying capacity. If so, what did that portend for high-fertility underdeveloped countries of the world, such as China?

Regardless of China's bluster in UN conferences about solidarity with Earth's downtrodden, the message these scientists heard from the leadership was not about pride in belonging to the Third World. The goal was parity, both scientific and economic, with First World powers. They were charged with applying cybernetic tools to determine how to achieve it.

Working independently in Xi'an and Beijing, Jiang Zhenghua and Song Jian focused on the ecosystem's most easily quantifiable parameter: human population. As Susan Greenhalgh notes in *Just One Child*, population science is the intersection between natural and social sciences. As Jiang and Song applied their skills, models, machines, and interdisciplinary breadth to determine how many humans were the right number for their country, they were the advance guards in the latest, perhaps most decisive chapter of a saga that has engaged—and enraged—religious authorities, philosophers, and scientists throughout history. It is a saga summed up in a single question: What are we?

Are *Homo sapiens* so highly evolved, or divinely imbued, that we transcend rules governing the rest of nature? Or are we simply a part—an undeniably compelling part—of the Earth's great living pageant, whose existence conforms to the same boundaries of everything else alive here?

Although the mandate from their leaders was economic—how many people can maximize our output, without requiring more inputs than we can provide?—the variables they had to consider were the same ones that concerned the authors of *The Limits to Growth*.

"We didn't have a very clear idea about the relationship between population, economic growth, and the environment," says Jiang, pouring more wine.

"It seems that we still don't," says Gretchen, taking a sip.

But they proceeded nonetheless, pooling data from ministries and feeding it to their computers, studying the works of demographers and economists back to Malthus, talking with biologists and agronomists. Depending on who is judging, humanity was either reduced to just another biological variable factored into their models, or it was precisely situated in its natural context.

In December 1979, Song and Jiang each presented their research at a National Symposium on Population Theory, held in Chengdu, the capital of Sichuan province. Its sponsors were the State Council on Birth Planning Office and the Chinese Academy of Sciences. Both had been ravaged during the Cultural Revolution, with top scientists exiled to farms and factories. But now China was poised to make one of history's most astonishing forward leaps. The "Great Helmsman," Mao Zedong, was dead. In his waning years, a power struggle ignited between Mao's fourth wife, a former movie actress named Jiang Qing, and a Zhou Enlai protégé named Deng Xiaoping, who was purged during the Cultural Revolution yet managed to resurrect himself. An advocate of market-based economic reforms, he was purged again by Madame Mao, but by 1979 her "Gang of Four" had been disgraced and deposed, and Deng was back, taking charge.

The population symposium was a convocation of social scientists: demographers, sociologists, humanists, and ethnographers, all finally reinstated as universities and institutes reopened. Nearly a hundred fifty presented papers, but for a decade they been under severe research constraints. The State Council on Birth Planning Office, an informant told Susan Greenhalgh, was making its projections with abacuses.

Into this gathering came Song and Jiang, the missile scientists, who had enjoyed the number crunching of cybernetic computation and access to world knowledge. "We presented two different papers. We didn't know what the other had been doing. He used different mathematics from mine. But there wasn't much difference in the process, or in the results."

That was far more mathematics than anyone else had. The charts, figures, and graphic simulations of different scenarios electrified interest well beyond the specialized audience. Calculating the carrying capacity of China involved countless variables, but they had focused on arable land, locally available raw resources, the cost of importing others, and the economic potential (and cost) of each added person. Referring to the Club of Rome report, Jiang had looked for parallels and found that, per capita, China had significantly fewer water, forest, and metals resources than much of the world. Song's group, concentrating on food capacity and ecological balance, had calculated, like Jiang, that the optimal population for China would be somewhere between 650 and 700 million people.

Yet China had already passed 900 million, and was growing fast. Song's presentation included a graph showing that if the current fertility rate of three children per woman continued, by 2075, China would have more than 4 billion people.

"Our conclusion," says Jiang, spreading his arms, "was that we had no chance of holding population below one billion by the year 2000—even if every family immediately started having only one child."

The demographers and social scientists knew that Deng Xiaoping believed that population must be checked before it became an economic impediment rather than an asset—he had once famously been banished for expressing such anti-Marxist blasphemy. To that end, they had prepared gradual plans involving incentives for voluntary limits, birth spacing, and postponed childbirth. They weren't expecting Song Jian's mathematical recommendations of one child per couple for the next few decades until a generation died off and the graph peaked at just over a billion Chinese—and then, as population momentum reversed and shrank back toward the optimum, people could gradually return to replacement-level reproduction.

They also weren't prepared for his highly irregular but effective strategy following the symposium, and neither was Jiang. "Song got his findings published in *People's Daily*," he recalls, shaking his head with admiration and a hint of envy.

Song had used his high connections to reach the most influential news medium in the country, the official paper of the Communist Party's central committee. Suddenly, the topic of population control burst from the obscurity of an academic conference and became national news. Publication in *People's Daily* was tantamount to the government's imprimatur. Accordingly, Song's paper was joined by a front-page editorial advocating a one-child policy to halt population growth.

Jiang Zhenghua's work, using different mathematics to arrive at the same conclusions, became an important corroboration of Song's hypothesis. Rebuttals by social scientists who'd been blindsided by the statistical barrage of these defense scientists were drowned out in the Deng Xiaoping government's clamor for a one-child policy, which, in 1980, became official.

Several of those rebuttals proved prescient, as in the coming years social problems materialized that the mathematical models missed, problems such as: What was the value of a child on a farm compared to a city? What was the traditional value of a son compared to a daughter, and how did those values change depending on class and setting? And while the current fertility rate of 3.0 was above replacement level, it had fallen from 5.0 within a generation. Couldn't China's population goals be met without such drastic measures?

Behind those questions lurked another, tricky to articulate in a country where the wrong word could get someone purged: Wasn't drawing upon mathematical tools to engineer human behavior dehumanizing? Didn't a policy that forbade humans to have the children they desired violate human nature?

"I didn't want to apply harsh rules to people," says Jiang Zhenghua. "But we were shocked by the numbers we saw. Numbers of resources, numbers of people. We knew what suffering would come." Removing his glasses, he rubs his eyes, a man who remembers the years of famine in his early twenties. "My hope was for a China in which everyone could prosper. Lowering fertility seemed the best way to achieve that. We're better off now for being fewer. But we have a long way to go before we reach an optimum level, so for a while this compulsory method has been necessary."

The idea of nearly a half-billion more Chinese needing jobs, water, fish, grains, appliances, cars, and housing chills him. Although fertility would have likely dropped anyway with China's astonishing modernization, as in western Europe, it is indisputable that it happened far more quickly by forced transition. But, Gretchen wonders, did the government consider the suffering that the policy would spawn? The late-term abortions dragooned by local officials obsessed with meeting quotas? The bulldozed houses and fines, the panicked hiding of children from surprise inspections by family-planning cadres, the institutionalized bribes to buy them off? And worst of all, the gendercide of infant girls drowned or left in the woods to die so that peasant parents could try for a boy to help work the farm?

"Did any of the models predict that?"

Jiang doesn't answer this question. "Actually," he says, "gender discrimination existed in China long before the one-child policy." Although the custom of binding women's feet had largely died out by the birth of the People's Republic of China, which outlawed it, a purpose of hobbling women was to make it impossible for them to do men's work, literally keeping them in their place. In the modern Chinese workplace, women's fortunes have greatly improved. "The number of women employed, the proportion in Congress and of women officials here is better than in many developed countries. But the gender imbalance we see today is still from sex preference."

The imbalance he means is an annual average of 118 male babies for every 100 girls. The natural birth ratio for *Homo sapiens* is about 105 male children per 100 females. The reasons for China's unnaturally lopsided ratio are well known; what has been disputed, and possibly distorted, is the relative significance of each of them.

Despite worldwide outrage over female infanticide in China, it is now considered rare, and may have been through most of the one-child policy, especially after the policy was relaxed to allow rural couples whose first child was a girl to try for a boy (and then further eased to simply allow two, regardless of sex). Long before China's mandatory birth control, in much of the world infanticide was a means of keeping families to a manageable size, dating back to our prehistoric ancestors. Reports of widespread slaughter of live baby girls under China's one-child policy may have been based on hasty assumptions derived from skewed sex ratios, due in part to archaic prejudices against what Westerners once blithely called "the heathen Chinese."

According to some anthropologists, two other causes may account for many, if not most, of the missing girls. The first — still repugnant — is prenatal sex screening followed by selective abortion. By coincidence, a year before its controversial birth policy, China began manufacturing ultrasound machines. Soon, in much of the country it wasn't hard for a woman to learn the sex of her fetus. Because rural parents have been allowed to try for two since 1984, they usually don't abort a first daughter. But the reported sex ratio for *second-borns* in rural regions runs as high as 160 boys to 100 girls.

Of course, many consider abortion to be no less murder than hurling a baby into the Yangtze River. The second, less violent reason that several researchers believe may account for much of the apparent surplus of Chinese boys is that girls' births aren't being reported. Both UN demographers and Chinese census takers have noticed that China's skewed sex ratios seem to narrow in primary school enrollments. Besides bribing local family-planning officials to undercount children, the surge of Chinese industrialism has made it easier to conceal extra daughters. With millions of western rural parents heading east to Chinese factories for much of the year, someone must care for their children left behind. In the fluid new social mechanics of urbanizing China, families that lived close together for thousands of years are now scattered across the map, and offspring are often sent across provincial lines to live with aunts and uncles. When these young internal migrants start school, local officials have little way of knowing whether the aunt has slipped in another girl or two of her own.

Other researchers contend that something completely legal accounts for significant numbers of the missing girls: adoption. Domestic adoption, whether by infertile parents or by those wishing to legally have more than one child, is rising along with Chinese affluence. And the phenomenon of international adoption is impossible to miss in the beautiful sprinkling of Chinese girls appearing in recent generations of North Americans, Europeans, and Australians — girls adopted and adored by couples who can't give birth, or who want their natural children to have siblings without risking another pregnancy or adding to the population.

Reports surface of officials confiscating female babies to sell to orphanages that are really baby farms for the adoption market. But the fact that discrimination against girls in China has also brought happiness to thousands of childless families may prove useful in a world that one day concludes that human populations must be managed. Whatever a country's family-planning policy or lack thereof, orphaned or abandoned children have never been a scare resource. In the event that humanity were to agree that on an overcrowded globe we have entered a time calling for reproductive restraint, adoption is an alternative for families that choose to embrace as many children as their households can hold.

Demographers are sometimes called accountants without a sense of humor, since the ciphers they're totaling aren't mere shekels, but us. In China, creative evasions of the fertility police have made their work even harder. China reportedly now has between 24 and 50 million more males than females, more than half of them "bare branches" — men of marrying age who can't find mates. Nobody really knows for sure how many. Few unequivocally trust the numbers, no matter how heroic the efforts of census takers. (China's most recent census, 2011, put the population at 1.34 billion. The United Nations expected at least 1.4 billion — a difference of 60 million people, which sounds hard to hide, except most Chinese can't name many of the biggest cities in their country, so dizzyingly fast do they materialize.)

Whatever the actual total of surplus Chinese males, it creates a tension that nature ultimately won't tolerate. So far, crimes of passion between jealous men fighting over the scarce supply of eligible females aren't epidemic. But single Chinese men now make marriage junkets to Vietnam, where, for upward of US$5,000, they can choose a wife from a lineup of poor village girls sold to a bridal broker by their parents. Like immigrant laborers in Europe, the cyber-and-jet-age version of mail-order brides is another way wealth gets redistributed in an inequitable world.

Sex-selective abortion following ultrasound became illegal in 1995, and many retired parents find that the most dependable single child to care for them—and up to four living grandparents—is a daughter. Infanticide may be rare, yet sensational press accounts still appear. Among the grisliest was a 2012 story from South Korea about seizures of thousands of smuggled capsules of an alleged health tonic. Citing the Korean Customs Service, the Associated Press reported that "the capsules were made in northeastern China from babies whose bodies were chopped into small pieces and dried on stoves before being turned into powder." No explanation was given as to how they knew the capsules came from China, nor whether the contents came from newborns or fetuses. But no denials were issued, and Chinese officials reportedly ordered an investigation.

If the value of an experiment is measured not only by whether it succeeds, but also by what it reveals, the Chinese one-child-per-family experiment, routinely denounced outside of China as horrific, has been eminently valuable. Without it, there would be hundreds of millions more Chinese today in a country where water, fish, and farmland are already growing scarce. But it has also revealed potential pitfalls of population control, such as the cruel and unexpected gender tilting of a generation that will take at least another generation to restore to equilibrium.

During the coming decades, the number of Chinese in their twenties will drop by nearly half, while the number above retirement age will rise even faster. "Life expectancy is rising insistently," says Jiang Zhenghua. "By the end of this century, in developed areas it could rise to ninety." That prospect has delayed Jiang's own retirement, as he was pressed into service to help his government devise plans for an elderly nation. Like Europe, China worries that there will be too few younger wage earners paying into pension funds to insure the social security of so many aged.

"We are considering communes of retired people, with younger ones caring for those that can no longer care for themselves." With fewer young people, some schools and campuses might house elderly enclaves. A pilot project already under way in some rural areas is known as the "old people's bank"—a labor bank in which younger elderly donate hours or money to help older elderly, understanding that when *they* get old, they'll be helped in return.

More unpredicted challenges will emerge as this

becomes China's broad reality, Jiang knows. Yet he has no qualms about the decisions they made.

"Our conclusion was that 1.6 billion people is the maximum size China can support. But that is not the optimum size. The optimum would be 700 million to no more than a billion, considering the pressure on resources, the limits of technology, and how much burden we can reasonably bear."

"What do you feel the optimum size is now, with our new understanding about climate?" Gretchen asks as they make ready to leave.

He settles back in his chair, considering. "We should not take risks that harm the whole human race." He studies his empty wineglass against the candlelight. "In ancient China, there was a philosophical argument about the nature of people at birth. One school said that people are born evil — that is our nature. The other said that we are born good and kind. My view is that both are incorrect. I think that people's nature is always to want a better life. So from that, we should not expect human beings to behave for benefit of the rest of nature — of the environment. You can only expect people to help the environment out of their own interest."

"I can see that —"

He lifts a hand, indicating there is more.

"This is why policy makers must decide. Because

people cannot see it until the danger is already upon them. In 1958, the highest level of China's central government was already discussing the need to control population. But the discussion was useless. Mao Zedong said we don't have the means, and other party leaders wanted more people, not less. So nothing happened. Only when the population reached 800 million did they finally see the problem. And they were shocked by its size."

iii. Sloping Land

After a twisting two-hour drive, Gretchen Daily alights with relief from the gray Buick minivan to relish the Sichuan landscape for a few minutes before the last thirty kilometers to Baoxing County. Before her stretches a mosaic of fields rippling up and down hillsides, covered with rows of green and yellow beans, sweet potato, cabbage, and bamboo. Scattered among the patchwork are conical sheaves of dried cornstalks for mulching.

"This is one of first times I've stood on actual soil in China," she tells Ouyang Zhiyun, who heads the Research Center for Eco-environmental Sciences at the Chinese Academy of Sciences, and Wang Yukuan of the Academy's Institute of Mountain Hazards and

Fields, Baoxing County, Sichuan, China

Environment. All around her, white, blue, black, and orange butterflies swirl on the warm breeze. Four of the five major families, Gretchen notes, are present: *Pieridae, Lycaenid, Nymphalid,* and a lot of *Papilionidae* swallowtails. Huge bees bumble among the sweet potato blossoms.

For much of the past week, she, Ouyang, Wang, and several colleagues have been inside buildings in Beijing and Xi'an, exchanging their latest research. The closest Gretchen got to nature was the grounds of Beijing's Fragrant Hill Hotel, where she was grateful to encounter a healthy flock of sparrows. During the Great Leap Forward, Chairman Mao declared war on China's ubiquitous Eurasian tree sparrow, because it ate grain. For four years, people hunted sparrows with slingshots, tore down their nests, and banged pots and pans whenever they alighted to scare them back into the sky, until they finally fell dead from exhaustion. Only after millions were exterminated and the species reached the brink of extinction did anyone connect the swarms of locusts devouring the country's rice to the missing sparrows. Eurasian tree sparrows, it turned out, were the locusts' principal natural predator.

The years in which the sparrows were absent from the Chinese ecosystem, not surprisingly, were also the years of the Great Famine that killed 30 to 40 million people. Gretchen hopes the sparrows she saw—descendants of the survivors of genocide perpetrated by human beings against a fellow species—were a good portent for the reason she is in China.

She and her Chinese hosts are colleagues in the Natural Capital Project, an international collaboration to keep ecosystems and people whose lives depend on them—meaning everybody—in healthy equilibrium with each other. That means focusing on three areas that literally cover everything under the sun—land and sea use, climate stability, and human demographics and economics—to determine how we can make sure we lose nothing essential, like those sparrows, to keep the planet supporting human life. (Or, conversely, to ask how much human activity a land- or seascape can sustain before it is too exhausted to sustain any at all.)

Since beginning in 2006, the Natural Capital team now operates on four continents and several archipelagos across the world's oceans. They have developed powerful software available for free to anyone,[2] to help people decide what to preserve or restore by calculating the potential return from services nature provides, such as water retention, pollination, and

2. At www.naturalcapitalproject.org/InVEST.html. The Natural Capital Project is a partnership of Stanford University, The Nature Conservancy, World Wildlife Fund, and the University of Minnesota.

soil conservation. But the program's strength depends on the depth of data available to plug into land-use scenarios. On this trip, Gretchen is awed by the vast raw knowledge her Chinese colleagues possess. Ouyang Zhiyun's presentation was a boggling compendium of forests, wetlands, soils, nutrient cycles, erosion indexes, carbon storage, and above all, water resources: nobody anywhere else has such complete water data.

China is the scene of the biggest interaction between people and the rest of nature in human history, with available manpower to accumulate a million data points to learn what touched off a flood a thousand miles downstream, or why there is a grain shortage someplace that someone had to hike for a day to see. Gretchen was trained by Paul Ehrlich and John Holdren to consider what every little thing does, so she has her grad students sifting bat poop in coffee plantations and documenting the role of individual trees. But the ecosystem is immense and their readings are incomplete, so it's often unclear how to interpret the flutter in gauge needles. Yet here is Ouyang with breathtaking quantities of information—to Gretchen it is like being in front of an entire instrument panel where you could plug in values, get answers, and see where to go. There might be only a few levers to pull, but the Chinese were willing to try pulling them if it seemed like a good thing—to ask, for example, an entire generation to make a sacrifice, if it seemed necessary.

If some kind of workable equilibrium could be forged here, conceivably it could happen anywhere. The landscape where they stand is an example. Brushing back his wispy hair, Ouyang points to fuzzy mountain ridges beyond the gentle cultivated hills. "All that forest back there was farmland ten years ago. You're looking at Grain to Green. Some trees were planted. Some came back naturally."

Grain to Green is part of the most ambitious — and expensive — environmental project any government has attempted: China's Sloping Land Conversion Program. Thirty million people were paid annual subsidies averaging ¥8,000 (yuan)[3] in cash or rice for ten years to leave their farms in the country's most mountainous regions — wherever the land sloped more than twenty-five degrees — and relocate to new villages. All their land would be replanted in native trees and grasses, in hopes of reversing the calendar to 1950, when China was still covered with virgin forests.

The combined losses of foodstuffs and lumber come to billions of dollars, and the program itself will cost upward of US$40 billion. But the Sloping

—————————

3. About US$1,260.

Land Conversion Program should save China from much greater losses. China has learned the hard way that these were lands that humans should never have colonized. The lesson began in 1997, with droughts that might never have turned so disastrous had trees been left in place so that their roots could hold water in the soil. Instead, the lower Yellow River dried up for 267 days, imperiling water supplies throughout northern China. The next year brought the opposite problem when the Yangtze in central China overflowed its basin, where one of every ten humans on Earth lives, inundating forty thousand square miles and carrying off 2 billion tons of topsoil. Thousands died, and millions of houses and the yuan equivalent of billions of dollars were lost. For both the drought and floods, deforested slopes were the main culprits.

The Qingyi River, a Yangtze tributary that the Natural Capital scientists have been following south from Sichuan's capital, Chengdu, has some of the steepest, and therefore most intact, stretches remaining in the watershed. The forests rising above the river valley are why southwestern China's mountains form one of the world's twenty-five greatest biodiversity hot spots, with more endemic temperate flora than anywhere, according to Conservation International. Sichuan has fir, spruce, cypress, pine, larch, bamboo, and broadleaf sassafras and maples that turn the slopes gold and crimson in autumn: many endemic only to western China. Because these heights are among the Earth's landmasses that have gone longest in geologic history without being inundated by inland seas, these are some of our planet's most ancient forests. Here grow cathayas, the Earth's oldest fir species, whose fossils account for much of Europe's brown coal; metasequoia redwoods that haven't changed in 65 million years; and wild ginkgo biloba, a living fossil dating to the early Jurassic when it covered much of the world, but now confined to this one small spot in China.

As China's population climbed toward a billion and beyond, people began invading and clearing even its most inaccessible terrain. Since the founding of the People's Republic in 1949, Sichuan has lost an estimated two-thirds of its original forests, habitat to snow and clouded leopards, but best known for the largest surviving population of giant pandas.

Of about eighteen hundred pandas left in the wild, a thousand are here. The only ones Gretchen will see on this trip are at a Chengdu breeding center, where wildlife biologists are trying to coax ninety-seven captive pandas to reproduce. Reintroducing pandas born in captivity to nature has proved challenging; after the first ones were killed by their wild cousins, researchers began wearing panda suits

and spraying themselves with animal scent to deha-
bituate the human-bred pandas.

Along with jungle smarts, the pandas need habitat to survive; the Sloping Land Conversion Program
hopes to provide that by planting giant sponges called
forests. But moving 30 million people off their farms
into urban occupations means somehow growing—
or buying—food elsewhere to feed them. "These
lands where the slope is not great are intensely cultivated now," says Ouyang, pointing around him. "The
population is very dense."

"We can't support all the people," says Wang
Yukuan, turning away from a black and white *nymphalid* the size of a small bat. "We have to import to
feed our country."

China's strategy has been to follow industrialized
Japan and South Korea, favoring factories over fields
and buying more food from the rest of the world.
But so great are the numbers it must feed that it isn't
merely purchasing commodities on the world market, but buying up chunks of the world itself—
investing in agricultural satellite lands in Africa, Brazil,
and the Philippines—all which also must feed their
own people.

The second goal of Sloping Land Conversion was
to lift the peasantry from poverty. Some whose farms
were returned to forest were allowed to start orchards

or grow spices where level land was available. But most, China hoped, would go to cities, get jobs, and send money to their families in their new relocation villages. They would join an immense contingent: 99 percent of China's construction workers are internal migrants. Combined with factory, domestic, and custodial workers, their numbers nearly equal the population of the United States. That is like taking an agrarian nation the size of the world's third-biggest country out of food production and transplanting it to cities that its population then must build. Small wonder that China wants all the raw building materials the world can provide.

Amid such tectonic demographic shifting, the Chinese Academy of Sciences and China's Ministry of Environmental Protection have been trying to shore up the nation's sagging ecosystem, by creating EFCAs: Ecosystem Function Conservation Areas. Spanning nearly a quarter of China's land area, "the EFCAs," explains Ouyang back in the minivan, "are designed to secure biodiversity, soils, and water, to store carbon, and to prevent sandstorms." All the landscape on this increasingly sinuous drive into an ever-tightening valley is an EFCA. Eventually, Ouyang says, they hope to preserve 60 percent of China, and to help alleviate poverty in the remaining 40 percent.

This combination—conservation of nature and

humanity—is why Gretchen Daily has hooked up with these Chinese scientists. The connection was Li Shuzhou, the protégé of missile engineer-turned-demographer Jiang Zhenghua and director of population studies at Xi'an Jiaotong University, whom she met through a Stanford colleague. On Gretchen's first trip to China, Li took her for a four-hour massage administered by three migrant workers retrained as massage therapists: one at her feet, another on her back and shoulders, and the third delicately cleaning her ears with bamboo swabs. For Gretchen, it was an irresistible beginning to a professional relationship.

Although his mentor was a co-architect of the one-child policy, Li Shuzhou was among a contingent of social scientists arguing that it be relaxed, or even scrapped. It had once seemed sensible for a poor country growing faster than its economy, he explained: decrease the numbers, and you increase wealth per capita. But the alarming sex-ratio imbalance meant structural trouble for Chinese society: "That and our aging population. By 2040, China will have more than 100 million eighty-year-olds."

Besides, he said, population would have come down regardless.

"We have four control areas where the one-child policy wasn't implemented, totaling about eight million people in four provinces. Since the mid-1980s, they were allowed two children. In each, population growth is under control, aging is controlled, and the sex ratio is normal."

Gretchen was amazed at a country big enough and willing to experiment with an 8-million-person sample. "Just to say, okay, we'll take four provinces and try this: The United States would never do that."

In Li's surveys, most Chinese couples want only one child, even if permitted another. "So I think a universal two-child policy would be better."

Italy, Spain, Hong Kong, Macau, Singapore, Japan, and Taiwan all have fertility rates lower than China's, and none has a one-child policy. Nevertheless, even though it was intended to last only thirty years to get China over a demographic hump so the economy could catch up, leaders have announced that it will continue. Unlike those other countries, China still has many rural poor, and fears a spontaneous birth spurt if the one-child policy were suddenly rescinded. Another reason is that with a half-million employees, the National Population and Family Planning Commission is too powerful a bureaucracy to dismantle. Yet when the government recently merged the commission with the Ministry of Health, it was interpreted by many not as a streamlining measure, but as a cue that the policy might finally change. Whether that happens may depend on who is loudest: government economists who predict labor shortages if it doesn't, or government scientists who warn of food and water shortages and more death by air pollution if it does.

For the Natural Capital Project, Li Shuzhou has been assessing how people fare as their ecosystem is patched back together. On this trip are two women economists from his team. So far, findings from their house-to-house surveys are mixed. Due to the one-child policy, the country is aging and labor is getting tight. But having four grandparents available to care for one child frees up parents to migrate from resettlement villages to the cities for work, easing the labor shortage.

One thing is certain: the need to migrate to earn a living is making people think hard about having children.

The landscape turns schizophrenic, as farmland abruptly gives way to rows of residential high-rises along the winding highway—which just as suddenly drops into a stunning canyon filled with a bamboo forest. Although giant pandas are omnivores, bamboo is their favorite food; this forest, Wang says, contains forty different species of the giant grass, and pandas eat them all. Baoxing County is also home to the seldom-glimpsed red panda—which is actually not a bear, but related to raccoons—as well as wild boars, black bears, wild yak, the endangered golden snub-nosed monkey, and the Chinese monal, a spectacular iridescent pheasant whose numbers are declining.

The canyon tightens further, buildings resume, and they arrive in the town of Ling'guan. Except for the white powder that coats windows, cars, and the leaves of trees lining the river, this could be Switzerland, with the Jiajin Mountains rising vertically on all sides. The powder isn't snow, but dust that emanates from more than a hundred marble-cutting factories: directly behind Ling'guan is one of China's most unique natural resources, an entire mountain of white marble.

The scientists spend an hour at a state-of-the-art plant, where a machine slices ten-ton marble blocks into slabs as though they were loaves of bread. This factory captures its dust with water, drying the resulting slurry to a paste that can be used for wall plaster, plaster bandages, or in cosmetics. They hope to convince all the smaller factories belching clouds of marble dust to consolidate, says Wang Yukuan, so that they can afford similar equipment. "This is an ecologically important, beautiful area. It can be perfect for tourism if we can keep it clean."

A small forest park on the edge of town, accessed

through a wooden archway carved with the motto "Place Where God Comes to Play," is an initial attempt at that. The scientists take a walk that ascends above the dust layer into an aromatic stand of long-needled, endemic Sikang pines. No other visitors are around: Baoxing's most famed natural attraction, the giant panda, is a furtive, camera-shy creature that doesn't lend itself to tourism. They return to the minivan and start to climb. The driver honks on every curve, as from the opposite direction stake-bed cargo trucks stacked with ten-ton blocks of white marble come hurtling toward them. After a half-hour, the road levels as they reach a plateau, and Gretchen relaxes her grip on the safety handle.

A cluster of red-tiled rooftops appears on a promontory: a Tibetan monastery. A little farther, past peach, pear, and apple orchards, they arrive at Qiaoqi, a village below a snowcapped limestone uplift called Jiajinshan Mountain. Sichuan is where China's Han majority begins to give way to ethnic Tibetans. Five thousand live here, in white houses with ornately trimmed windows and elaborate wooden balconies connected by strings of colored prayer flags. Wearing brilliant fabrics with elaborate embroidery and beribboned headwear, bearing trays of yak milk and cups of honey wine, the Tibetans greet the visitors.

Since 2008, explains a blue-robed village elder named An Lixing, they are no longer allowed to cut timber or graze cattle. Instead, the government sent him to learn about ecotourism. They have trained men as guides to explain the scenery and the area's heritage—Tibetan culture; the Long March of Chairman Mao's Red Army, which passed through here in 1935—and to take people to see golden monkeys, deer, and wild oxen. Depending on the season, they might even spot a giant panda, although that's more likely right here in the village, where pandas steal drying corn and sausages.

He preempts Gretchen's question. "We don't believe in the Dalai Lama. He doesn't support us; the Chinese government does. We believe in the Communist Party." They are happy to be Chinese, An says, and to speak Sichuanese Mandarin, not the Tibetan dialect. "As an ethnic minority, we Tibetans are allowed to practice Buddhism, and to have three children." As a result, Tibet has the fastest-growing population in China.

Two days earlier, the scientists had visited Feng Qian, a sloping land resettlement village outside Xi'an in Shaanxi province, near where China's massive South-North Water Transfer Project was being constructed. To reach it, they'd driven a new multilane highway that passed through the longest tunnel in

Asia. It had taken engineers just two years to bore eighteen kilometers through the Qinling Mountains, testament to China's ability to tunnel under the Yellow River to bring Yangtze water to the new cities encircling Beijing.

Feng Qian was more typical of where the 30 million displaced peasants had landed: About three hundred households were ensconced in stuccoed multifamily dwellings just off the new highway. Nobody complained, however, about trading mud huts in the forest for brick dwellings with electricity, TV, and toilets, and getting a subsidy as well. More than two hundred men and women were off working in eastern China factories or construction, earning ¥10,000[4] annually, returning home once a year. Yet many still resisted giving up farming. Most of them, overwhelmingly male and single, now tended mulberry trees for silkworm food.

Throughout China are troubling messes born of the one-child policy: single men in factory cities, squandering their hard-earned yuan on prostitutes. Vietnamese women running away when they realize they married a guy who saved for ten years to buy a bride but who now can't afford a house — practically oblig-

---

4. US$1,575.

atory now for Chinese men to attract a wife. Single women abandoning rural life for cities where men with money compete for wives. Kidnapping rings stealing wives from one province—or from North Korea, or Myanmar—and selling them to women-starved men in the next. Rising divorce rates as marriages last mere weeks, because of spoiled single children who quit before compromising.

Even on this trip, one of the economists casually mentions doing her doctoral work in Japan so she could have two extra children without penalty. Do people inevitably violate a draconian, unnatural law? Would China indeed have been better off without its one-child mandate?

"Without it we'd be heading over 2 billion," says Ouyang as they drive back to Chengdu. "Good-bye food and water, good-bye ecosystem." He has five brothers and sisters. "My wife's family is even bigger. Her father was one of ten. She has 53 cousins. My son is one of 57 grandchildren."

Had his son been born into the same arithmetic expansion, rather than post-one-child policy, he would have been one of at least 270 in his generation. Most Chinese, Ouyang says, see the need for the policy. It would be hard to find a Chinese ecologist who disagreed. "In 1979," Ouyang says, "in my hometown in Hunan province there was a tiger. A farmer shot him. I ate a piece of the meat, my first and last time. Since then, tigers have disappeared."

Wang winces. "You know how people always ask us what difference will it make to our lives if there are no pandas someday? Or no tigers?"

Ouyang and Gretchen nod in unison.

"I tell them that without pandas, then without tigers, next it will be fish that disappear. Then crops. Then everything. Then people."

———

On the final day, the scientists take Gretchen to China's smallest and southernmost province. About the size of Taiwan, Hainan Island sits nineteen miles off the mainland in the South China Sea. As the only part of China that dips into the tropics, over the past two decades Hainan has been discovered by luxury hotel chains and developers, who are converting its southern shore into China's Oahu, with Manhattan prices.

Their destination is the central highlands, where the number of rubber plantations has doubled due to China's explosive growth of automobile ownership and demand for tires, threatening the rainforests of one of Asia's biologically richest islands. With much of the lowlands in rice, cassava, sugarcane, and pepper plantations, the forests are not only Hainan's last stand of biodiversity, but also its bulwark against flooding and soil loss.

They drive to Five Finger Mountain in the center of the island, passing thousands of pepper tree vines tended by men in straw coolie hats, each vine supported by poles hand-hewn from granite that won't decay in the rain, but which cost unimaginable numbers of man-hours to fashion. Several cloudbursts slow their journey, and they pause at a restaurant beside a small pond filled with Muscovy ducks, which are featured on the menu. As usual, they count the number of species on the plates, and look for locally endemic spices and vegetables. Besides the rice and soy, which could be from anywhere, they count nineteen, including sautéed mountain ferns. Nothing on this trip has topped the vegetarian banquet in a Chengdu Buddhist temple two nights before, with at least thirty.

They reach the slopes of the third of the mountain's five peaks. In a hardening drizzle, they tramp around a steep rubber plantation with Chen Haizhong, a square-faced farmer in plastic thongs and calf-length khakis. Like most farmers here, he used his sloping land conversion subsidy to plant rubber trees, which was permitted because these latex-producing crops, native to the Amazon, are good at holding water and soil. Chen has also intercropped a medicinal herb for stomach ailments, and betel nuts. The polyculture is mutually beneficial, but rubber depends on synthetic fertilizer and pesticide protection. Ouyang's resident Hainan Island team hopes to encourage a shift to more sustainable native trees by proposing that sloping land subsidies for rubber be eliminated.

"It's a perfect opportunity," he tells Gretchen, "to use the InVEST software to assess if Sloping Land Conversion has caused more damage than benefit here by treating rubber as if it were a natural forest. We can use an alternative economic scenario to change people's behavior." With the simple graphical interface, he says, they can show policy makers what will happen if they do A or B instead of C, and let them make the obvious sensible choice.

Assuming policy makers ever did things that way. "Can you really get your government to listen to you?" she asks Ouyang.

"We try. We tell them that native forests and plants are strategic reserves for the future. When the high-yield rice was developed in China, it used genetic material from native Hainan Island rice. That got the government's attention. It helped to make them believe."

The drizzle has turned to squalls, and the horn blares on every curve as they press on over new concrete highways choked with motorized rickshaws, cars, and taxis. They stop at a forest preserve on the north face of Five Finger Mountain's first peak. Fifty years earlier, the 230-foot parashorea trees here were filled with an abundant endemic primate, the Hainan black-crested gibbon. It is now the world's rarest ape. Only twenty remain.

"People killed them for medicinal purposes," says Ouyang. "Their powdered bones are supposed to make people strong." He tilts his head to look up through the car window. "The gibbons normally never came down from the canopy. But hunters knew that if one died, the others would gather around to cry. So they would shoot one and wait until the rest came down."

"Is there any economic scenario we can use to change the desire for endangered species bones?" asks Gretchen.

"For some things. People now know they can be healthy without tiger bones. With aphrodisiacs, it's harder. Men and women will do anything if they think it will make them more virile and beautiful."

A waterfall and a river are cascading into a series of deep, transparent pools. It is raining hard, but nothing will stop Gretchen from seeing this old forest, so the rest follow her up the mountain trail. An hour later they are back, drenched but exhilarated. Even the tiny leeches they must pick out of each other's hair can't diminish the thrill of seeing so much crystalline water and smelling the world as if it were created yesterday.

But as they exit the preserve and descend, pristine clarity vanishes. All the rivers are running bloodred with eroded soil. Sheets of mud pouring through the rubber and pepper plantations wash across the highway. When they finally reach the airport on the island's northern shore, Hainan's rivers have burst their banks and the South China Sea is filling with red silt. They're able to fly out, but the following day, a typhoon that has already cost defoliated Vietnam millions of tons of topsoil hits Hainan full force. Before it passes, 135,000 people have to be evacuated.

On Hainan Island, or anywhere else, for that matter, the three axes on which the InVest program turns—land and sea use, climate, and demography—may ultimately hinge on the third. Decisions can be made about how to manage land. Climate change is already under way and will have to be accommodated. But moving people from wherever their overwhelming presence threatens existence means they must go somewhere. In China, that somewhere is cities, more and more of them.

But at a certain point, there will be no more room—or concrete, or pipes or asphalt—for more cities. Short of war to seize other lands, the remaining option may be some humane version of what China has attempted for the past thirty years.

PART THREE

CHAPTER 9

The Sea

i. Pamparegla

Living in Malabon, the most crowded of sixteen towns composing one of the world's most densely populated urban areas, metropolitan Manila, Roland[1] doesn't think much about nature, or even see it—except for the rain. Because flooding now regularly turns streets into canals, Malabon's nickname is "Venice," and Roland has grown resigned to wading to work. Rain is increasing, storms are strengthening, and supposedly their sinking town will one day slip beneath Manila Bay, preceded by Manila itself. The Dutch ambassador has already advised the Philippines to dike the bay, the finest

---

1: His name is changed.

harbor in Southeast Asia. But where will money come from for that?

The typhoon that drowned China's Hainan Island has moved east across the South China Sea: weaker but still plenty wet, it's overhead, soaking Luzon, the Philippines' biggest island. Beneath Roland's second-story window, the street is a swirling gray backwater. Beyond it, traffic in this megalopolis of 25.5 million[2] flows imperceptibly, like a species of tropical glacier. Occasionally, chunks break free and surge forward, then jam into other chunks and stop in axle-high water.

Roland, a slight, reserved man of thirty-nine, doesn't dwell on the climatic chaos erupting outside, as he is preoccupied with a more immediate question:

What is the carrying capacity of a woman?

Every day, Roland meets women who have answered that question for themselves, an answer that would not please many powers-that-be in his country. They want two or less. Or no more than what they already have. So they come to him. What they seek might be easily arranged elsewhere without the intervention of someone like Roland. But not in the Philippines.

---

2. This 2007 census figure is for "Greater Manila," which includes urban areas contiguous to the sixteen towns officially called "Metro Manila."

*   *   *

Philippine history is sometimes described as three hundred years in a Spanish convent, followed by fifty years in Hollywood. Few Spaniards today care that the Philippines was a part of their long-vanquished empire. Few Americans even know that, after posing as a liberator during the Spanish-American War of 1898, the United States decided to keep the Philippines for itself, as it did with Puerto Rico. That meant managing the archipelago's affairs, coining its money, imposing English on the Philippines' other 165 languages, and killing at least a quarter-million Filipinos who objected to becoming U.S. colonials. Only after World War II did the United States finally relinquish it.

When those Hollywood years began, the Philippines had just 7 million inhabitants, so a quarter-million Filipino deaths in the three-year Philippine-American War was not insignificant—except, perhaps, to the United States, where the only Americans who've even heard of that guerrilla conflict are usually of Filipino descent. (A pity, because it so much resembled the later U.S.-Vietnam War that, were its history better known, a disaster might have been averted.)

When the Republic of the Philippines became independent in 1946, there were 18 million Filipinos.

Today, there are nearly 100 million: as the rest of the planet's population quadrupled in a century, the head count here *quintupled* in half that time.

A big reason why is that today's Philippines — an archipelago of 7,100 islands facing Communist China, Muslim Indonesia, and Buddhist Southeast Asia — is the most Catholic country in Asia and, some say, the last bastion of the Vatican's theocratic empire.

Catholic Spain's government may hand out free condoms, and abortion may be legal in Catholic Italy, but in the Philippines, the Church never surrendered. In 2010, newly elected president Benigno ("PNoy") Aquino III, son of former president Corazon Aquino, who died in office the year before, inadvertently incurred Rome's wrath even before he was inaugurated. During a postelection visit to the United States, he was asked by some San Francisco Filipinos if he favored a reproductive health bill. Such bills, which would make family planning the business of the national government, including distribution of free contraception and maternity care for the poor, had been introduced regularly in the Philippine congress for forty years, and regularly shot down.

Under Aquino's deeply religious mother, whose own election over dictator Ferdinand Marcos was hailed as a divine miracle, there was no chance for such sacrilege to become law. Beloved for her courage after her senator husband was assassinated, Cory Aquino was cherished most of all by the Church, whose interests she literally held sacred. Following her funeral at Manila Cathedral, a campaign commenced for her beatification. But any assumptions that her equally popular son shared his mother's piety were dashed by his response in San Francisco. He was president of all Filipinos, PNoy replied, not just the 80 percent who are Catholic. He believed that couples knew best how many children they wanted, and that government should make appropriate services available.

His remarks made the headlines back home. The Catholic Bishops' Conference accused the United States of meddling in Philippine affairs, and hinted that Aquino was brainwashed while on U.S. soil. Manila's archbishop promised civil disobedience and mass demonstrations, which did not materialize, and threatened the president with excommunication. Aquino, in turn, invited the bishops to lunch at Malacañang Palace to talk, making their belligerence look foolish. He would not back down from supporting any of six reproductive health bills relentlessly presented by one side and parried by the other. About the only agreement between the two was that legalized abortion was not on the table. One thing at a time.

Which is why Roland will continue in his current employ for the foreseeable future. It wasn't what he had planned. He went to college to become a registered nurse. In the Philippines, nursing is not just a job or a calling: it is a ticket. In a country now far too populous to employ and feed its people, people themselves have become the Philippines' chief export—acknowledged by the existence of a government agency, the Philippine Overseas Employment Administration, to assist OFWs: Overseas Filipino Workers.

At any given moment, over 10 percent of Filipinos are working somewhere else. Men mostly get "3-D" jobs—dirty, difficult, dangerous—in construction, stoop farm labor, or as seamen. Women are mainly maids, more than 2 million in the Middle East alone. In Saudi Arabia, Filipinas are practically essential domestic appliances. Roland was headed to Jeddah, where a nurse makes more in a day than in a month back home. There is a serious doctor shortage in the Philippines, because they can earn far more working on other continents as nurses.

But Roland's infirm mother needed care, and his father was already working in Riyadh most of the year. So he answered an ad for a community outreach nurse in a charitable clinic providing obstetric and gynecological care for women who couldn't oth-

Manila, Philippines

erwise afford it. He liked the work. Many patients came from a shantytown he passed every day near Manila Bay, a former garbage dump where thousands of cannery workers tiptoed over rusting steel I-beams laid across plastic-choked drainage ditches, hoping to avoid infection from leptospira, a meningitis-causing bacterium spread through rat urine. There was no way to avoid dengue.

Roland believed that Jesus wanted him to help the poor. He belonged to the Legion of Mary, a lay devotional organization, and attended Mass daily with his fellow Legionnaires. Every week, he carried a statue of Mary to a different house and taught a family how to pray the Rosary. But he found himself in a dilemma when his job began to conflict with his Legion service.

No one had tried to hide anything from him. At his hiring interview, he was asked how he felt about contraception. Like nearly everyone he knew who wasn't a priest, he felt it was a couple's decision.[3] As a nurse, he knew that spacing children was wise.

He learned that the letters "MR" on a patient's chart stood for "menstrual regulation," a euphemism for adjusting a woman's cycle with birth control pills. Although the Philippines had no national family-planning program, regions and municipalities could pass their own rules. In Malabon, contraceptives were legal, though often scarce; in Manila proper, seat of the archdiocese, they were banned, so it was wise not to advertise that they were being administered.

But what did "VA" on a woman's chart mean? After his probationary period ended, he found out one night while on duty at the clinic's minisurgery. Even when asked to assist, at first he wasn't exactly sure what he was seeing.

"It's nothing like what pro-life groups or the Church claim. They say you see a small fetus. It's nothing scary,

---

3. Polls show that around nine of every ten Filipinos favor government-funded contraception.

just blood and some tissue. It's a medical procedure. And it does regulate a woman's menstruation."

"MR," he now realized, also referred to the two-part procedure that uses mifepristone, or RU-486, to loosen the placenta from the endometrium, soften the cervix, and begin contractions, followed by miso-prostol for final contractions to pass the material from the uterus. The procedure Roland saw that night was a "VA"—a manual vacuum aspiration: a method of abortion requiring no sharp implements, just a spec-ulum, a clamp, a thin plastic tube, and a large-barreled syringe. As he came to understand, many preferred the two-step chemical solution because it was non-surgical. But mifepristone and misoprostol needed to be smuggled into the country. Vacuum aspiration was a sure bet.

"VA" could also stand for *vehicular accident,* should authorities unexpectedly appear, demanding to see charts. Clinics like his have endured police raids, and stings by phony patients bearing marked bills and hidden cameras. They now take only confirmed refer-rals from friends or former clients, and operate behind double-locked doors.

Fear of the law was nothing compared to fear for his mortal soul, which Roland did for the first few days afterward. He knelt and asked forgiveness, but for reasons he can't explain, he never went to confession.

Instead, he entered "a reflection on my personal relationship with our Creator, my profession as a nurse, and my work providing compassion to women, especially to the poorest of the poor."

He'd seen mothers of five, torn between buying pills or food for their children. There were women whose OFW husbands—home for their annual visit from Russian oil drill ships, Singapore restaurants, or Texas airline maintenance crews—stayed long enough to impregnate them for a seventh time. Or women accidentally pregnant just as their own OFW jobs finally came through, such as a frantic nursing instructor friend who was headed to Chicago.

And pregnant rape victims. Such women would go to the street market outside Manila's Black Nazarene basilica where, amid rosary beads and pirated DVDs, herbalists sold 200-peso bottles of *pamparegla* and ulcer tablets from China. Roland sometimes had to clean up the frightening results.

Fifteen years after being trained to perform abortions himself, he now does five to ten a month under sanitary hospital conditions, unlike most of the estimated 750,000 annual illegal abortions in the Philippines. The majority involve catheters threaded into the uterus, or to induce contractions, herbal potions like *pamparegla* or makabuhay vine extract (also used as a pesticide), or overdoses of ulcer medicine. Or women find a *hilot*—a Filipino combination of masseuse and chiropractor—who looks for an abdominal mass and crushes it with her hands. The procedure, repeated until bleeding commences, requires women to bite on a blanket to avoid screaming.

To avoid a conflict that might bother his conscience, Roland quit the Legion of Mary. He still attends Mass sometimes, but he has never returned to confession and doubts he will.

"To confess what? That I'm helping women in need? This is between me and God now. This doesn't go through priests."

ii. Passage and Reef

Luzon is the largest, longest, and northernmost of the major Philippine islands. At its southern shore, sixty-five miles below Manila, men with paddles strapped to their feet shuffle through muck laden with heavy metals in the tidal flats of the Calumpang River for clams. To the east, the shoreline rises into bluffs topped by flaring stacks and cylindrical tanks of oil refineries. A concrete pier large enough to receive petroleum tankers juts into the water, pointing into the Verde Island Passage that separates Luzon from the thousands of Philippine islands below.

Only fifteen miles across, the Verde Island Passage is narrow enough that several of those islands are visible on the horizon. It is also a bottleneck through which tropical marine species pass between the South China Sea and the Pacific—a bottleneck with a coral net to catch them. A UN Food and Agriculture Organization study of the Coral Triangle—the region bordered by the Philippines, Malaysia, Indonesia, Papua New Guinea, East Timor, and the Solomon Islands, known as the center of Earth's marine biodiversity—determined that "the center of the center" is the Philippines, with 5,000 species of mollusks, 488 corals, five of the world's seven sea turtle species, 2,824 fish species, and thousands of other aquatic organisms. The richest concentration of all—more than half the species found in the entire study—is Verde Island Passage, making it the planet's most biologically diverse body of water.

Verde Island itself is a green dot, three miles by four, its profile like a brontosaurus lying low in the water, with a thousand-foot hump on its eastern end and a long neck that stretches west, ending in a small hump. Reached by outrigger ferry, it lies midway between Luzon and Mindoro, an island dominated by mile-high mountains. Other tiny outriggers roam the passage, piloted by solo fishermen. Except for nylon cord used to lash their bamboo struts, the technology is little changed from that used by humans who left these islands to discover Polynesia and Hawaii.

A fishing village, San Agapito, one of six packed onto Verde Island, hugs a turquoise inlet on its southeastern shore. Behind a beach of light brown sand, coconut palms rise above a row of neat houses of bamboo and basket-weave thatch. A path lined with multicolored painted stones, barely wide enough for a three-wheeled cargo bike, is the only road. In the yards grow yellow orchids, hibiscus, anthuriums, and jasmine. The village is spotless—the road is swept daily—and quiet: the only electricity is from a diesel generator that runs after sunset for four hours. There's a whitewashed Catholic church with a blue tin roof, and a one-bed maternity ward and immunization clinic.

Romeo Gonzalez, in a straw hat and patched red bathing trunks, sits on a bench in a thatched, open-air hut, teasing knots from a nylon seine. His family has lived on Verde Island since people arrived in the Philippines, he says. A widower in his forties—his wife died young, of a heart attack—he has always fished: for grouper, octopus, fusilier, moonfish, humpbacked wrasse, gizzard shad, Indian halibut, and skipjack tuna. At low tide, he goes for oysters, lobster, and baby white shark. Mostly, he nets; for squid and cuttlefish, which range up to four kilos, he jigs at night with a lamp and a hook.

The problem is that over the past decade, there are far fewer fish.

"Too many people using cyanide," he says, a technique for stunning coral reef fish that is often lethal to the coral. "Too many people, period."

At least no one here uses dynamite, the other illegal way of scooping up many fish quickly. You need a compressor, he says, to dive deep and spray cyanide, and he doesn't have one. He also doesn't have many children. "Just three. We were one of the first couples to use family planning." But there were supposed to be only two. The method they used, withdrawal, surprised them with a third.

"Today there are pills, condoms, shots that last three months. That's good. Otherwise, families would have eight. Eleven, even. There are thirteen hundred people in this village, and four hundred of them are fishermen." With the other villages, he adds, waving his cigarette at the rest of the island, there are at least fifteen hundred fishing boats. "Plus the ones who invade from Mindoro."

"Hi, Romeo."

Shading his eyes, he sees it's Jemalyn Rayos, her pink cooler hanging from a shoulder strap. From it he selects a melon-flavored fruit ice; she, her seven children, and her eight siblings make and sell them around the island. Jemalyn, in her late thirties, is also San Agapito's midwife, and recently became a family-planning peer educator, which generated much kidding. "I know, I know," she says. "Only before, I didn't." She advises her own seven kids, and everyone else, to stop at two.

Her employer is Poverty-Population-Environment, the continuation of an internationally funded program that ended in 2008 called IPOPCORM, a digestible acronym for a serious mouthful: Integrated Population and Coastal Resource Management, an idea that makes sense in a country with one of the world's longest coastlines. It is also where, IPOPCORM's founders realized, the highest human fertility rates occur in the areas of highest biodiversity—a logical outcome of bountiful fecundity, but one approaching a classic tipping point. Filipinos get 80 percent of their protein from seafood, and their numbers had grown beyond the capacity to feed them all. The country's richest seas were being devoured, and among the imperiled species was the one doing the devouring. At the epicenter of the Coral Triangle, the Philippines was the marine equivalent of Uganda with its gorillas—only here, people weren't gobbling habitat: they were eating the wildlife itself.

The organization that connected the dots between

rising population and diminishing fish catches was a Philippine NGO born of the AIDS crisis. Its director, Dr. Joan Castro, grew up in an Igorot family in indigenous northern Luzon, so deep in the mountains that she'd never tasted shrimp or crab until she traveled seven hours to Manila to study medicine. Her mother was one of seven, her father one of eleven. When they married, boar, deer, and river eel were already growing scarce, so they held themselves to four and taught their children why.

Castro planned to study obstetrics, but in the 1990s, growing numbers of OFWs were returning infected with HIV — especially Filipino sailors, working the flagships of practically every maritime nation. After graduating, she ran an AIDS counseling hotline, phones being the safest way in a homophobic Catholic country for a frightened person to approach a doctor about sexually transmitted disease. The program was underwritten by USAID, and young Joan Castro caught the eye of Leona D'Agnes, an American public health specialist. After years in Thailand and Indonesia, D'Agnes had come to the Philippines to begin a branch of PATH,[4] an international family-planning foundation. Traveling through this impoverished country with such spectacular marine fauna

---

4. Program for Appropriate Technology in Health.

had given her an idea, and Joan Castro seemed just the doctor to help implement it.

To finance the program they dubbed IPOPCORM, they approached environmental agencies, arguing that the best way to preserve the Philippines' matchless aquatic environment was through reproductive management in the communities that depended on it. To family-planning funders such as USAID and the David and Lucile Packard Foundation, they argued the converse: that by helping fisherfolk create marine reserves to save their livelihoods, they could persuade them to produce fewer children. Armed with a species map from Conservation International, and with data mined from the national census and thousands of municipal records, they identified the thirty-five areas of highest marine biodiversity cross-referenced by population density, and then focused on the twelve most imperiled of these hot spots.

Over eight years, IPOPCORM spread to 1,091 coastal communities in eight Philippine provinces, and its successor program now focuses on the most impoverished, such as this one. Romeo points with his fruit ice to the fish sanctuary, where no one is allowed to dive. Sixteen more similar sanctuaries ring the island. Each village has coastal resource managers, who patrol and go door-to-door, talking conservation. Enforcement is a communal effort. It largely works, says Romeo, though he admits that there's a lot of diving around sanctuary edges. Jemalyn is one of four volunteer health workers who also go house to house, teaching women and schoolgirls about family planning, receiving the peso equivalent of US$28 each month as honoraria.

Since the PATH Foundation came in 2009, she gets enough pills to give out. "Most women want them: if they get pregnant, they can't migrate to get a job. Some are scared of side effects. We tell them it's a lot safer than drinking boiled makabuhay vine to get rid of an unwanted pregnancy. The population here is still growing. But slower."

"We hope the fish population is growing, but faster," says Romeo.

———————

The next-to-smallest primate[5] on Earth, the tarsier, has huge eyes that, apart from its bat-like ears, make it resemble E.T., the Extra-Terrestrial — that is, if E.T. could fit in the palm of a human hand. The tiny tarsiers are also the oldest existing primate; the family *Tarsiidae* predates our own, *Hominidae,* by at least 40 million years.

———————

5. Our smallest fellow primate is Madagascar's Berthe's mouse lemur, weighing just over an ounce.

After dark, in a remnant stand of teak and mahogany on the island of Bohol in the Philippine archipelago's midriff, five hundred kilometers southeast of Manila, tarsiers crawl over tree trunks on their chameleon-like, spaded toes, hunting crickets. Nocturnal insectivores, their big ears and eyes—plus a neck that rotates 180 degrees—allow them to pounce on the bugs that compose their diet in the few remaining Southeast Asian islands where there's still enough standing hardwood to support them.

With intense biodiversity and equally intense humanity, Bohol became a pilot region for the IPOPCORM project. A lopsided oval, Bohol is about the size of Rhode Island in the United States and, with 1.3 million people, has nearly the same population. But few Rhode Islanders catch or grow all their food, while nearly everyone on Bohol feeds themselves directly from the land and surrounding seas.

Under a tin sky, Geri Miasco, a stocky woman of thirty-five, drives along Bohol's northern coastal road in late October 2010, watching the weather. A former kindergarten teacher, she was recruited by the PATH Foundation in 2004. She is one of nine children, and several of her fisherman uncles and cousins here have lost boats, limbs, eyes, or their lives when the dynamite they were using exploded too fast.

Tarsier, Bohol Island, Philippines
PHOTOGRAPH BY JASPER GREEK LAO GOLANGCO

A practicing Catholic, she dismisses the idea of any conflict between her faith and family planning. "Population goes up, resources come down. If population goes too high, they're gone—and then, so are we. God doesn't want us to kill ourselves." So while her husband goes to sea to fish, she works on land to ensure there will still be something to catch.

On her way to lunch with the mayor of the coastal town of Ubay, Geri stops by a "Pop Shop"—one of several family-planning convenience stores that PATH opened around the island. By its entrance is a white-board listing the local women expecting babies, their number of pregnancies and living children, and their due date. One is on her fourth pregnancy, but the others range from zero to two.

Inside are cheerful displays of pills, injectables, and condoms (in plain, banana, or strawberry) with a wood carving of an erect, circumcised penis to demonstrate proper application. A box of three rubbers costs the peso equivalent of 45 US cents; a month's supply of pills varies from 50-cent Yellow Ladies to 83-cent Altheas and 90-cent Trusts, the more expensive ones containing acne suppressants and supposedly causing fewer side effects. After IPOPCORM ended, the community took over the project, which the PATH Foundation continues to monitor and the Pop Shops help to finance. No one's need goes unmet: subsidies for whoever can't afford birth control are in the municipal budget. At first, women were told in church that pills and Depo-Provera provoke abortion at the instant of insemination. After Geri explained a few times how the chemistry simply prevents insemination in the first place, word spread and a daily stream of women commenced.

A slim young woman enters. She is from Mindanao, the southernmost Philippine island, home to a large Muslim minority already present when the Spanish arrived, and in nearly constant rebellion against the ruling Catholic majority ever since. Her husband, a soldier, is now stationed in Bohol, she says, sounding relieved. She explains that she had her first child, a son, two months earlier, earning praise from the midwife who runs the shop for her impressive recovery. She smiles, saying that they want to plan now until they're ready for another, if ever. The midwife weighs her, checks her blood pressure, and hands her a questionnaire that they fill out together. The new mother works for a community lending agency, and can afford the Trust pills she decides to try.

More clients arrive, so Geri goes on to Ubay, one of the first towns to sign onto IPOPCORM after the disappearance of sailfish and black marlin here got everyone's attention. She has a working lunch of broiled snapper, squid cooked in their ink, and a pile of blue crabs with Mayor Eutiquio Bernales and Ubay's coastal resource manager, Alpios Delima. The trick, says Delima, is balancing the amount of fish, squid, and crabs they sell to Hong Kong and Japan; how much they keep to eat themselves; and how much stays in the water to maintain the stock.

"The only way we can do that is by controlling the number of people doing the selling and eating," says Bernales. "It just makes sense. If you like mangoes, don't cut the tree: gather the fruit."

He's even gotten Ubay's priest on board. "He realized that it wasn't in his best interest for his congregation to starve. We'll make a deal, I told him. You take care of the spirit and I'll take care of the bodies."

Bernales, now seventy-five, grew up fishing with dynamite. They'd toss in a bundle of two or three sticks; the shock waves would stun big groupers and snappers, and kill the smaller ones by bursting their internal organs. He would have to dive to twelve fathoms to collect the ones with ruptured swim bladders before they sank out of sight.

"It was quick, cheap, and dangerous." A well-placed charge could yield ten tons of fish, which were so abundant back then that people could afford to send their kids to college. "Me included — to medical school."

"Today it's all high-tech," grumbles Delima. "They have air compressors and go down twenty fathoms. They use depth charges with remote detonators, so we don't hear the explosion or see the geyser. They use sinkers and waterproof plastic mining fuses that get smuggled in. For inspection, we have to do fish forensics: slash them open to see if the intestines are blown apart."

But most of the dynamiters are now from somewhere else: along with family planning, IPOPCORM blitzed the island with advertising about what dynamite does to the reef that supports them. Delima's men patrol round-the-clock, but it's hard when illegal fishermen use cyanide—which, being volatile, is usually impossible to detect by the time they get to the lab. Lately people are dipping bait in Zonrox, a chlorine-based bathroom cleaner that's far cheaper and just as toxic, squirting it on the reef with baby bottles, then scooping up fish that float up.

"Or they set mist nets that catch everything, including juveniles before they've had a chance to reproduce. Or they mix ammonium nitrate fertilizer with gasoline in bottles filled with enough sand to sink, topped with blasting caps."

"Filipino ingenuity," laughs Bernales. "But we're staying ahead of them. Young fishermen and their wives all understand now."

They see the numbers of kids dropping. They see people looking for alternatives to fishing: sweet potato farming, seaweed farming, catfish and tilapia ranching, oyster culture—they're even trying to grow one of their money species, milkfish, in cages. Filipino ingenuity works to their advantage, but the thread binding the socio-econ-eco web here is family planning. With no national program, that has always depended on foundation money and USAID for condoms and contraceptives. They saw what happened when things began drying up during the George W. Bush presidency, how PATH had to scramble for grants, and it's scary to think of what they'll do if that ever happens again, and how much of their fate hangs on politics halfway around the globe.

Bernales and Delima take Geri for a spin in their patrol boat to see one of Ubay's two off-limits fish reserves. It's a fifty-foot outrigger painted battleship gray, powered by a cast-iron diesel engine cannibalized from a dump truck, its cooling system converted to seawater. With a carpet of four kinds of sea grass, the transparent bay is a shimmering green. By night, it sparkles with luminescence. This was once habitat to a delicious, abalone-like conch that they hope will return. They hope their reef hangs on: the dreaded climate-driven bleaching has reduced parts of many reefs to coral skeletons in the Philippines, but a few actually show signs of growth. They're hoping, too, that the shoreline's thin border of mangroves, remnants of a forest ripped out decades earlier for an ill-conceived tiger shrimp farm, will spread anew. But mangrove makes good firewood, burning hot and steady like coal, so it's hard to stay ahead of the poachers.

In Talibon, Bohol's northernmost town, Geri meets with the municipal health officer, Dr. Frank Lobo. He's just been with a United Nations official who was following up on a UNFPA program that built women's health and birthing centers in the poorest towns in the Philippines, leveraged with funds from USAID. "In a country where eleven women die in childbirth daily, one of the riskiest things a woman can do is get pregnant. Our goal," Lobo says, "is to lower maternal and infant deaths through clinic deliveries, and to reduce the population 35 percent. It's working: Mothers are surviving; so are their babies. We're down to three hundred deliveries a year from eighteen hundred. We've gone from zero to two hundred vasectomies."

Reducing population pressure here is urgent, he says, because one of only six double barrier reefs on Earth lies just offshore, encrusted with an extravagant array of sponges, soft corals, brain corals, and encrusting, branching, and table corals.

"It is priceless," says Lobo, "and it is our life. We have one fish stock, and ten thousand fishermen that want to catch it. The number of fish directly depends on the number of humans. We don't talk about population explosion here. We talk about jobs—one job, ten thousand applicants. That's the way to get people to appreciate the environment."

With the UNFPA project over, and with USAID funding always teetering on the vagaries of American politics, the Philippines must finally pass a reproductive health bill, he adds. At least they've disarmed the local church. "All of us in family planning are its most faithful donors. They don't want to alienate us."

It's only ten minutes by outrigger out to the double reef and to tiny, triangular Guindacpan Island, its sides just a quarter-mile long. Once covered by mangroves, they're long gone. A small stand of coconut palms remains amid the 432 houses of Guindacpan's fisherfolk.

Zephyrs from another typhoon to the north are bending the palms. Arriving in blowing rain, Geri is met by Estrella Torrevillas, the public health nurse here for twenty-five years. Her green khaki pants are rolled above her calves, and it's immediately clear why.

Except in a few high spots near the palms, much of the island is under water. They slosh down narrow, sandy lanes, joined by the village nutritionist, Perla Pañares, whose blue jeans are soaked halfway to her knees. People with brooms are pushing water out the doorways of bamboo houses. Their seawater toilets, says Estrella, aren't flushing well anymore. "So people are using the shore."

They pass the island's single well, its water now too saline to drink. Houses have rain catches, says Perla. "But it's never enough with this many people. The ones who can afford it are buying bottled water."

"Bad," Geri says. "What about food?"

"It's lucky we like fish," says Perla. The reef and sea grass have always provided crab, shrimp, black-lipped oysters, squid, anchovies, and sea cucumbers. People jig from the docks with drop lines for rabbit-fish, garfish, and cardinalfish. They gather flower crabs, mud crabs, and Venus clams. "But for how long?" she wonders. The fish are getting smaller and fewer. "The big problem is vegetables: We have to buy them on Bohol. Now that salt water covers everything at high tide, nothing grows in the gardens. Except for seaweed."

Plastic windowsill pots filled with soil brought from Bohol grow onions, tomatoes, peppers, and spices. They come to a cement basketball court, where shirtless children splash barefoot, trying to dribble a blue basketball over a skin of water. Perla frowns, hearing three of them coughing. Fruit is scarcest of all. Many children only get it at Christmas.

"None of these kids gets enough vitamin C." She has four herself; Estrella has three. "That's low: most families range from five to nine." Perla has recently weighed every child five years old and under—a quarter of Guindacpan's population—and noticed that the ten most severely malnourished kids all have either six or seven siblings.

"Contraception used to be free here. Then UNFPA put in birthing clinics that charge."

Except, Estrella reminds her, it wasn't really free—a donation was always required, however small. The real problem is that family-planning supplies run thin in remote places like this. Even PATH has been able to reach only half the people in the country's extremely imperiled marine hot spots. Estrella distributes whatever she can get. "But it's never enough."

iii. Inland

Should seas continue to rise and cover the world's lowest islands, family planning on Guindacpan may become a moot issue. But higher elevations aren't exempt from changes that will affect their carrying capacity for human beings.

A day later, back on Luzon, the typhoon has passed, leaving a deep blue sky laced with wispy cirrus veils. Sunshine is welcome at the International Rice Research Institute, halfway between Verde Island Passage and Manila, where concern is mounting over one particular variable in the longest-running rice experiment in the world. In 1963, when IRRI was founded by the Rockefeller and Ford Foundations, scientists set aside a one-hectare test plot to see how long rice can grow continuously on the same piece of land. One hundred forty crops later—their hybrids get three harvests per year—the results are encouraging. Even in areas with no nitrogen application, they get production. The goal now is to bring production up and artificial nitrogen down to meet at an optimum level.

They can manipulate fertilizer inputs and crop breeds. They've already cut back to just 2 percent of the insecticides they used fifteen years ago: egrets and plovers now root for snails and frogs in their test paddies; flycatchers hunt above them for buzzing insects missing from silent, pesticide-drenched fields elsewhere. But what they can't control is the heat. For years, they've been charting yields against climate data. Since 2000, there is more cloudiness, less solar radiation, and rising nighttime temperatures. The higher the temperature at night, the more energy a plant burns to convert sugars — energy it otherwise would apply to growth. This has coincided with a 15 percent average drop in yields of IRRI's "miracle rice" variety, IR8, that helped avert famine in Asia during the 1960s.

If the warming trend continues, at this point there's not much more rice breeders can do. Current hybrids were developed to maximize fertilizer uptake, resist pests and disease, grow faster (and as with daffodil-gene-manipulated golden rice, deliver extra vitamins). But temperature tolerance was never an issue — that is, until now.

IRRI is the tropical analog of CIMMYT, Mexico's wheat and maize improvement center — but hybridizing rice proved tricky. Rice, whose florets are hermaphrodites, pollinates itself. It was impossible to breed high-yield rice strains until, in 1970, a Hunan agronomist named Yuan Longping found a wild rice mutation on Hainan Island whose male half was sterile. That meant that its fertile female side could be crossed with male pollen from another variety, producing a hybrid with the best qualities of both. His discovery changed the world just in time: production from previous improvements — semidwarf, high-yield Green Revolution strains — had plateaued, just as the population of Asia, where half the planet's people grow 90 percent of the world's rice, was making a quantum leap upward. Today, China's entire hybrid rice industry is based on those wild rice genes.

But the more successful a rice variety, the more vulnerable it is. After arriving at a desired hybrid, the subsequent self-pollinating crops, like clones, can all catch the same flu. A disease infecting one plant will roar like wildfire through the whole lot. It's a precarious base on which to balance humanity's most widely consumed foodstuff. IRRI scientists have learned to chemically force male sterility, allowing them to crossbreed new strains to keep pace with new diseases. But today's best hybrids for today's climate, diseases, and pests won't be tomorrow's, because everything constantly changes.

In a world where massive monocultures of the most profitable strains replace natural crop diversity, old strains must be preserved so that agronomists will always have something with which to crossbreed. Outside the refrigerated vault of IRRI's gene bank, women sit at a long table in an air-conditioned room lined with hundreds of green file drawers, sorting through piles of seeds from hybrids and their wild relatives, selecting the healthiest kernels to preserve. After pausing to examine a new batch of Bangladeshi rice the women have just received, Ruaraidh Sackville Hamilton, a sandy-haired, Cambridge-trained evolutionary ecologist who heads IRRI's Genetic Resources Center, enters the gene bank.

It's a 3,650-square-foot, two-story refrigerator, furnished in tall brushed-stainless-steel racks and movable shelves. The active collection is stored in sealed aluminum foil packets at +2°C (35.6°F). It contains seeds from 117,000 known strains, which are given to any grower who asks, ten grams at a time. Belowdecks, an identical "base" collection is kept at −20°C—frigid enough to preserve seeds stored in vacuum-sealed aluminum cans for at least a century, assuming the electricity stays on or backup generators don't run out of diesel.

"These are for our great-grandchildren," says Sackville Hamilton. As with CIMMYT's maize and wheat, there's an additional set of IRRI's collection at the U.S. Department of Agriculture's National Center for Genetic Resources Preservation at Fort Collins, Colorado. Yet another is buried in the Svalbard Global Seed "Doomsday" Vault in the Norwegian Arctic.

This facility is flood-proof, typhoon-proof, and earthquake-proof up to 4.7 on the Richter scale. However, should one of Luzon's nearby active volcanoes awaken and cover them with lava, "We wouldn't survive," Hamilton acknowledges.

As steward of this anthropocentric botany

collection, Sackville Hamilton doesn't see the human-cultivated varieties as unnatural, but rather as part of evolution in which *Homo sapiens* are players, rearranging nature to improve our chances at survival, just as beavers do with riverbanks. He agrees that placing our bets on vast monocultures is something that nature shows us repeatedly not to do: they lack all the robustness of diverse ecosystems. So why do we do it?

"Because of cost. It's more profitable for seed companies to market one variety over a large area. The more hectares sown to your variety, the more successful a breeder you are, which is the opposite of promoting diversity. Also, we simply don't know how to build productive diverse systems. How can you harvest a mixture with a combine? We know we need diversity, but to develop large-scale diverse farming—we're not there. That's why we need this gene bank, because diversity is not out in the fields, although that's where we need it to be."

So they forge on, trying new tricks to improve on the natural order of things. IRRI's biggest quest now is to increase the photosynthetic efficiency of rice by 50 percent, to give it enough solar energy to produce more grains and to fix its own nitrogen. The resulting "C4" rice would greatly increase yields and even be able to create its own fertilizer—the potential cited by the Vatican as how to feed a world that keeps adding more people.

But that will require reconfiguring the very cell structure of rice leaves. To find a winning combination of genes and crosses amid all these varieties is, at minimum, a twenty- to twenty-five-year project. Even their funding from the Bill and Melinda Gates Foundation can't force that schedule. By then, world population may nullify the gains, even as a renegade climate shrinks the amount of arable land, fresh water grows scarcer, and soil degrades further.

C4 rice would be one of history's major transformations of agriculture. But it, or any other improvement, can only do so much, says Sackville Hamilton.

"In this gene bank we can deal with nearly any future challenge the world throws at us, except for one: increasing population. Because we cannot indefinitely increase the amount of food we grow."

He pulls a ten-gram foil seed packet from a shelf, scans the label, and replaces it. "We can respond to new diseases," he says. "Even, I think, to climate changes. We can improve technology: Last year I saw a Japanese farm trying to grow commercial rice hydroponically. An ideal variety for hydroponics would have a different root structure from one grown in the field. That presents a new breeding challenge, but we could address that challenge from this collection."

He hugs himself against the chill. "We can handle anything. Except indefinitely increasing population."

———

Up in Manila, the chances for reversing the Philippine fecundity that surrounds IRRI were not looking promising. Despite newly elected President Aquino's professed interest in a national reproductive health plan, as 2010 dragged into 2011 and then 2012, the Catholic Church maintained a steady frontal assault on congressmen who dared broach such an abomination. For decades, the Church had quashed every proposed bill for universal access to family-planning information, free contraception for the poor, and mandatory sex education for secondary school children. The Catholic Bishops' Conference of the Philippines wasn't about to let any president overturn that record.

"Contraception is corruption," declared one archbishop.

"Sex must never be taught separate from God and isolated from marriage," decreed another.

"Don't fool with the Church. Because she will bury you," warned a third. As debate on the latest bill alternately waxed and wilted in Congress, Filipino bishops bused thousands of Catholic school students into Manila for traffic-stopping prayer rallies and blanketed vehicles with smiley-face "Gospel of Life" bumper stickers. In every sermon, they admonished their flock that contraception is just one more form of abortion, which is outlawed by the Philippine constitution.

In the Manila suburb of Alabang, they muscled through an ordinance making the purchase of condoms without a doctor's prescription punishable by six months' imprisonment—a measure "more Catholic than the Pope," pundits noted, as Benedict XVI acknowledged that condoms help prevent AIDS. In Congress, pro-Church forces piled the reproductive health bill high with amendments—thirty-five proposed by one anticontraceptive congressman in one day alone—and otherwise exploited parliamentary procedure to keep proceedings safe from closure. One night in November 2012, when it seemed like the bill—favored by 70 percent of Filipinos—might actually come to a vote, so many cowed legislators stayed away that the House of Representatives couldn't muster a quorum. Championing the Church's intractable position was the most famous Filipino of all, congressman and boxing legend Manny Pacquiao. The fourth of six siblings himself, Pacquiao reminded everyone that he would never have won world titles in eight weight divisions if his parents had used birth control.

Yet again, the reproductive health bill seemed still-born. But then, on December 8, 2012, in the sixth round of a welterweight bout in Las Vegas, the seemingly invincible Pacquiao collided with an unexpected right to the head by his arch-rival, Mexican Juan Manuel Márquez, knocking him out so thoroughly that for minutes fans thought he was dead. Although after just three days Pacquiao was back, fighting the reproductive health bill in Congress by claiming that his survival only deepened his belief in the sanctity of life, his ignoble defeat proved a portent of surprise outcomes.

Ten days later, President Aquino orchestrated his own creative ploy with Robert's Rules of Order, forcing a vote on the bill before anyone could abscond by declaring it a presidential priority. His country, despite headquartering the International Rice Research Institute, had grown so far beyond its carrying capacity that it was now the world's biggest importer of that grain. Worse still, the world was also now on track to warm more than 2°C—at which point coral reefs, home to the main protein source in the Philippines, aren't expected to survive. President Aquino's even more popular than his sainted mother, Cory, and his refusal to let the population double again and risk starvation finally carried the day in the Philippine House and Senate.

In a conciliatory move, he waited until Christmas to quietly sign the Reproductive Health Bill into law, with no fanfare. Nevertheless, Philippine bishops vowed to defeat every apostate legislator in the next election, to fire all faculty at Catholic universities believed to favor the bill, and to appeal to the Supreme Court to declare it unconstitutional.

Should they fail, there will be only country left on Earth where political decisions on reproductive health are still controlled by the Roman Catholic Church. Unlike the Philippines, which adds 2 million more people each year, that tiny country suffers no population crisis, because its citizens include virtually no women, and are mainly—at least theoretically—celibate men.

What they do within Vatican walls is their own business; the fact that they can no longer sway any other country may prove timely on an Earth that, in every sense including biblical, humans have now filled.

CHAPTER 10

The Bottom

i. Sahel

Libya is that rarity, a sparsely populated country. The reason is simple: Although it has valuable natural resources, they're inedible. The world's seventeenth largest nation by area but 103rd by population, it has just 6 million people, 90 percent living in a tight band hugging its northern coast, where its Mediterranean ports were once its greatest assets. Today, oil is number one; another commodity, however, may irrevocably limit Libya's population to its present size, or possibly fewer. That is water.

Because Libya's northern wells are depleted or fouled by seawater, drinking water for that 90 percent now comes via Muammar Gaddafi's magnum opus, the "Great Man-Made River"—the world's biggest network of pipes, connected to more than a thousand wells drilled half a kilometer into a sandstone aquifer in the south. The water they tap accumulated when the Sahara abounded with plant and animal life, a wet period that ended about six thousand years ago when the Earth's axis wobbled slightly—just as growing populations and their flocks and crops were demanding more water than ever. The unfortunate collision of those events altered northern Africa profoundly. Estimates for when the Libyan aquifer will be pumped dry range from sixty to a thousand years, the high figure possibly more attributable to Gaddafi than hydrology. Whenever it happens, one thing is almost certain: nothing will replenish it anytime soon—neither in human nor geologic time.

The Sahara is as monochromatic and vast as the Arctic—except that the Arctic is shrinking and the Sahara is growing, southward into the semiarid transitional belt known as the Sahel that separates the desert from central Africa's tropical savannas. Cinched around the upper body of the African continent, the Sahel is six hundred miles thick at its widest point—at least, for now.

In the West African nation of Niger, due south of Libya, Al-Haji Rabo Mamane knows a lot about the Sahel, but he isn't sure how many children he has, so he reaches for his prayer beads and starts counting.

"Seventeen," he presently says. Mamane is the chief of Bargaja, a Sahel village of two thousand, twenty kilometers north of the border with Nigeria. He sits on a blue and green woven cotton mat under a thatched awning in front of his mud-plastered home, surrounded by the men of his village. A white-goateed man of seventy, he adjusts his sky-blue djal-abiya around his bare ankles, straightens his round embroidered blue prayer cap, and then adds: "Seventeen who are still alive. I've lost at least that many."

The past years have been hard. In 2010, few crops in Niger made it to maturity. Millet, the staple cereal, dried and died on the stalk, as the great heat came early. Same with the groundnuts. Sorghum, usually drought-tolerant, grew but produced no seed. The cattle lacked grass.

"So our children began to die." The World Food Programme tried to airlift in emergency food for 5 million desperate people, but Mamane still lost three—even though, as chief, he was able to send a wife to the health center run by French doctors in Maradi, the region's capital. There she watched them die of malnutrition, one after another.

She is his youngest wife. "I married her when she

was twelve, when she was fresh. All her babies have died; one was three years, one was two. One died after just a week."

In 2011, he lost two more. Two of his other wives had been nursing; malnourished, they grew anemic and their breast milk faltered. The babies died of anemia and opportunistic malaria. "My youngest wife was still so upset that I considered divorcing her to give her another chance with another man. But fortunately, she is pregnant again."

A murmur of approval from the men seated around him.

He doesn't have a sure count of wives, either. Although the Qur'an allows him up to four as long as he can responsibly care for them, over the years some wives have stayed, some have left. "Some of them died, too." One, he knows, has three children still living. Three out of nine births.

His oldest son, Inoussa, squatting at the edge of his father's mat in a dark blue flowing djalabiya and purple prayer cap, adds some figures in the dirt with his finger. "Last year, this village lost a hundred eighty children." Inoussa, forty-two, has three wives who have borne him eleven children, six still alive. He is considered rich because he farms an entire hectare himself. Fifty years ago, everyone had two hectares, but the land has been so partitioned among multiple sons that the two hectares that once supported a family of twenty now must support sixty or seventy.

"We have these problems we don't know how to solve," says his father.

"We have too many people," Inoussa replies. Frowning eyes turn to him. "Yes," he says. "We are weeping because we are being crushed by our own children."

All his life, he's heard that every birth is a blessing. God provides, although God also takes away. Two years before, after he and his wives stopped working for three days to pray for the soul of the latest child to die, they made a decision. They went to the clinic in Maradi. With his consent, all three wives began to take family-planning pills. Inoussa didn't try to hide it in the village, and the other men didn't hide their discomfort over what he'd done. He hasn't tried to convince them: "Their eyes can see the results. My wives were so thin, but now they've gained weight. No one has gotten pregnant for two years. It's good, because having eleven is a big test of their strength."

As he explains this, the other men look baffled. In Niger, every woman averages between seven and eight — the highest human fertility rate on Earth. His wives should have borne at least twenty-one among them, but they stopped at barely half that.

In a room a few feet from where the men are talking, two of the chief's wives sit on the dirt floor near the doorway, listening. Neither weighs more than ninety pounds. In rural Niger, the best food, like eggs, goes to the men. Next the children are fed. In lean times, women barely eat at all. Hassana, the taller, older wife, is nursing a son named Chafiou, four months old. She has two others, a boy and a girl. But a mother keeps score of her losses, too, and she's behind, four to three.

"The first, a boy, died at four years. The second, a girl, at a year and seven months." Three and four lived. "The fifth died at age three. The sixth at one year. Those two were also girls." She sets Chafiou in her lap and wipes an eye with the hem of her flowered hijab. The baby's own eyes widen as he looks up at her.

She pulls him back to her breast. "It is such darkness to have and lose a child. God gives life, then takes it back. But I can't go against God's wishes. Because I know that God can also take my life anytime He wants." She's heard about family planning before. It doesn't interest her. "When a food crisis hits and sweet children die, you have to keep having them while you can. If I stopped, what if the ones I already have don't survive? I'll have nothing."

But wouldn't only three have a better chance, because there would be more for them to eat?

Chief's wives, Bargaja, Niger

"If we could guarantee enough food so I wouldn't have to always have one in my womb and another one on my back, then yes. But this guarantee doesn't exist." She glances at her cowife, Jaimila, huddled in the opposite corner, a blue khimar over a batik skirt hiding her pregnancy. "Besides, if there are fewer children and more food, husbands will just race to get more wives, and wives will compete with each other to have more children. Then there won't be enough food again."

She married late, at sixteen. Not so Jaimila, who was twelve when she married the chief, and whose three babies have all died. Does she regret not taking the opportunity to find a younger husband, rather than bearing the child of a seventy-year-old man?

"But he is the chief," she replies, puzzled by the question.

There is a saying in Niger: *An old man with money is a young man.* Other men's wives lose even more babies, and faster, because the chief has the most land and animals. Though these days, no one has much. "If I still had my three, or if God gives me three more after this one, maybe I could stop someday. But I would have to go all the way to Maradi for the pills. And he will be old soon, and won't want to. So I abandon the idea."

Landlocked Niger is slightly larger than France, Germany, and Poland combined. Directly below Libya and Algeria, the northern four-fifths of the country is mostly uninhabitable desert. Most Nigeriens live farther down in the Sahel, which many still remember as covered with acacia forests, grasslands, and baobab trees. Today, as vegetation shrivels and temperatures average 1.5 to 2°C higher than during the 1990s, they fear it will increasingly resemble the Sahara.

In far southwest Niger, the Niger River, Africa's third longest after the Nile and the Congo, enters the country for the middle of its 2,600-mile journey. One hundred sixty miles after passing through the capital, Niamey, it reaches Nigeria, whose fertility, averaging slightly under five children per female, isn't quite as alarming as its neighbor's. But with ten times the number of people—166 million to Niger's 16.6 million—Nigeria has the highest population in Africa, more than twice that of second-place Ethiopia. By 2040, Nigeria is expected to double to 333 million, a number that will so far transcend its agricultural capacity—and the continent's—that no one has any idea what will happen.

In his palace in Maradi, Sultan Al-Haji Ali Zaki is not worrying about Nigeria or 2040, because he has enough trouble here and now. Despite its tragic infant mortality rate, his region also has the highest population growth rate in Niger, which has the highest in the world.

The reason is a Niger River tributary, the Goulbi de Maradi, one of Niger's most important seasonal wadis—"hands of the river" in the Hausa language. The greenest part of its country, Maradi is considered a breadbasket, but its villages, such as Bargaja, are full of dying children. It is Friday; religious leaders gathered here earlier to discuss the crisis, and now village leaders have assembled.

Ignoring his carved throne, the sultan sits in a comfortable stuffed chair, in a gold-embroidered white robe and caftan, white silk turban, and a white lace scarf around his neck. He is elderly but thickset, with

large, red-rimmed glasses perched on a broad triangular nose. He is the only man in the room wearing
shoes: white leather with golden buckles. Everyone
else sits on the thin red carpet, except the four orange-
turbaned guards standing nearby in green, white, and
ochre robes, with daggers and cudgels ready. The
sultan's right wrist is wrapped in prayer beads. On
his left is a stainless-steel Rolex.

"Last year we suffered much hardship," he says.
"Drought killed our cattle. Thousands simply dropped.
People starved. Luckily, we were helped by the government and international donors and NGOs. They did
their best, but their statisticians can't predict our needs,
because they can't keep up with our numbers. Nobody
can anymore. But we thank them for trying."

One of the guards shouts his praise of the
government.

"And now we are again facing poor rains," the
sultan continues. "The government and the NGOs
will again miscalculate the provisions we will need."

Recently he traveled to northern Maradi, where
the Sahel is fast fading to desert. A few areas received
a bit more rain this year, but most villages were like
one he visited, Mailafia, a silent town with soil baked
yellow-white, its women gaunt and leathery, its children sullen, its goats stunted. The big trees were gone,
as were the cattle. Their sole concrete-lined well, dug

by a French NGO after the 2005 famine, wasn't enough to water livestock and the people, too.

"In my youth," said a forty-five-year-old man named Issa Ousmane, after they'd knelt in the sand for prayers, "you wouldn't have been able to see those houses and granaries, because the trees were so thick. You would need someone to lead you by the hand. There was grass as high as a standing man. Rabbits, deer, guinea fowl, antelope. Now all you see are our poor buildings. The sand is nude."

The palms, tamarinds, and baobabs were there until more people needed wood than the forest had to give. The few remaining acacia grow poorly, because of the lack of rain and a hotter sun. They were used to drought arriving every ten years. But then it was every five years.

"Then every three. And now last year's hasn't ended. We still have no production. We are surviving on the sale of our cattle."

Four of his nine sons have taken his animals south to sell, including his breeding stock. "Soon, cattle herding will disappear. This is like a disease without a medicine. And it will end our lives."

"There is no longer enough milk to make porridge," a mother of eight had added, pounding millet in a wooden churn. "All we want is food so we can produce children."

Earlier today, the sultan now tells the men gathered before him, he asked the imams about family planning.

"We marry to harvest children," objects a man in a white djalabiya. "What is life's purpose other than leaving heirs?"

"My father and grandfather had many wives and many children," replies the sultan. "I have just seven. My sons have two, three, and four. We are of different generations, and as we become educated, we learn that feeding children is a big burden. We hope for cooperation from the mosques to teach people that it is unhealthy to repeat pregnancies quickly. To leave space between births, for the safety of the mother and the child."

The men stare at the floor. No one shouts praise.

The sultan leans forward, forearms on his knees. "Allah does not want us to have children we cannot feed or care for."

"What Allah wants," says Imam Raidoune Issaka in his study, "is for us to have bigger families, not to bend to any pressure to reduce their size."

Imam Issaka is thirty-five and smooth-cheeked, with a scrabble of beard below his chin. His djalabiya is gray with silver stripes, his prayer cap white with black embroidery. He is one of thirteen children. The young man in a tall red cap and gold-stitched caftan he addresses is an aide to the sultan.

The imam is seated in a green upholstered chair by a sagging bookcase containing leather-bound commentaries on the Qur'an and loose pages of notes for his sermons. He raises his palm toward these. "The teachings of Islam allow us to space deliveries of children only if there is a known health risk to the mother. To reduce or stop producing children on the pretext of difficulties feeding them goes against a pact between Muslims and God. Allah has promised to provide for all the children."

He takes a sip of tea from a cup on the leather hassock by his feet. "He will provide for all their needs, *provided that they respect all His rules.* But if they go astray from the way that God has drawn for them, they will face His punishment. It will not be a happy result."

But how have little children sinned? Why should they suffer and die?

"God's teaching refers to parents who have committed lewd acts and sinned. It is a call to them to return to the path, if they wish their future to be bright."

The sultan's man, seated by a small black table that holds a portable radio, does not reply. "Of course it pains us all," continues the imam. "That is why in the mosque we call on the community to assist the needy."

He acknowledges that the population is five times what it was when his father before him was the imam of Maradi. The very room in which they sit was once a horse stable outside the town that now surrounds it. "In one sense, this is a symbol of development and advancement. But in another, it is nothing to cheer about. People are not acting to safeguard nature. Our farmlands and pastures are being destroyed."

Is there no connection between that and soaring population? What will this come to, if this continues?

"Our doom," he says matter-of-factly. The sultan's man straightens in his chair as the imam settles back in his, nodding.

"We know the future is alarming. But man cannot hold back doomsday. The Prophet says that God has preordained its time."

Several dusty blocks away, another imam, Chafiou Issaka, sits on a straight-backed metal chair in the middle of a small, roofless alcove attached to his home. Except for a low wooden bench where the sultan's aide awaits, it is otherwise completely bare, its mud-brick walls unplastered. The imam wears sunglasses against the glare reflecting off his crisp white djalabiya.

"The Holy Qur'an," he says, "states that your family's needs are under God's control. But it also suggests that there should be a space of two years or more between children, because of the health of the mother *and* of the children. Look at the problems for the family when a child appears on Earth and the last child is not even weaned. There is no conflict over that."

Then why do so many families have a mother exhausted and hungry children dying?

"Because people do not respect what the Qur'an says. Allah does not impose on us anything beyond our capacity to support. But men only hear the part about being allowed four wives. Then they can't afford it, and they get into trouble."

To have properly spaced children, are women allowed artificial contraceptives?

"We have been campaigning in sermons and on the radio about the need for these methods."

Maradi now has many mosques; his, with two short minarets, is just across the unpaved street from this house in which he and Imam Raidoune Issaka, who is his younger brother, were raised. In Islam, there is no central authority, as in the Catholic Church, to dictate dogma. Yet how is it that these two brother imams disagree on something so fundamental?

"There are many divisions in religion," says Imam Issaka the elder. "There are now many people, with many values and with scientific knowledge that is constantly expanding. This brings many conflicting visions."

Only one-fourth of Niger's people can read, and just 15 percent of the women. He has seen the NGOs' studies: less than 1 percent of girls complete primary school, but the few who reach secondary school will usually only have two or three children. Healthy children.

"With education, Niger need not just depend on crops and cattle. It has uranium and petroleum. There is iron. In Maradi, there is even gold."

Yes, but the sultan's aide knows what is happening to those resources in his illiterate country. The French take all the uranium. The Chinese are coming for the oil. No one has yet bid to exploit the iron. The gold is mined by some Canadians, with the cooperation of a few rich chiefs. It gets loaded onto helicopters that head straight for the airport in the capital. No one knows what Niger's share is.

The imam meets with his brother and with other imams to talk about such things, and about what their suffering people need. "And we all seem to understand each other. And yet, after meetings, some decide to not agree with what we all said."

The sultan's aide looks perplexed.

The imam raises a hand. "Muhammad, peace be

unto His soul, foresaw many branches of Islam, but said that only the right one will be the path to paradise. Of course," he adds, "every branch thinks it is the right path."

The east-west road that passes through Maradi is Niger's main—and nearly only—paved highway. It passes through the comparatively greenest part of the country, home to 85 percent of Niger's population, but much of it is a bedraggled land of desiccated sticks hung with shreds of black plastic snagged from the wind. Trucks piled twice their height with bundles of corn and rice barrel past camel trains and donkey carts, but most of that food is not destined to stay here. In crowded Nigeria to the south, security has grown so precarious that to avoid bandits and hijackers, grain shippers from Vietnam now use the neighboring port at Cotonou, Benin, instead of Lagos, the coastal Nigerian megalopolis. Trucking their cargo up through Benin to Niger, they let Nigerian[1] buyers meet them here.

This close to Niger's southern border, many cars have license plates from Nigeria. The reason is that Niger, while nearly entirely Muslim, is not a theocracy. Its secular constitution is copied from France,

---

1. Nigerian: person from Nigeria. Nigerien: person from Niger.

the colonial power here until 1960. Therefore, shariah law is not enforced here, as in Muslim northern Nigeria, so Nigerian men stream north for liquor and prostitutes. This reverses a trend of the 1990s, when international NGOs distributed condoms in Niger to counter HIV. Nigerien women would give them to their truck driver husbands heading to Nigeria so they wouldn't get infected.

Along the highway, many of the men in ragged linens driving flocks of dromedaries are slaves. Slavery is even more common in Niger's north, where nomad chieftains live in luxury tents equipped with satellite phones, but it exists throughout the country. According to one of Niger's most prominent scholars, Dr. Galy Kadir Abdelkader, up to 10 percent of the country is in bondage, even though slavery has been outlawed since 2003.

"Islam says that no man should be anybody's slave, and the Prophet encouraged people to free slaves. Our religion is protected with ignorance of itself," says Dr. Abdelkader. "Slaves are told that they must accept fate, that as God is the supreme owner of Paradise, the master is the owner of the slave. Whoever wants to live in paradise someday must respect the will of God, which is reflected through the master whose purposes they serve."

Among those purposes is producing more slaves,

an economic driver that helps to maintain Niger's unrelenting fertility rates. Children of slaves are also slaves, so masters breed them, frequently to their own siblings or even their daughters. Although slave markets have disappeared since the 2003 prohibition, particularly beautiful slave girls command high bride-prices, should a wealthy men desire to marry one. Or if a man can't afford to buy and free a woman, he can still enjoy her flesh by marrying her for less than full price, but without releasing her from bondage. Under this arrangement, a pre-agreed number of her children are returned to her original master as slaves.

In every village, women churn out babies, trying to stay ahead of death. The only thing that checks Niger's world-highest fertility is its fifty-year life expectancy. In the town of Madaoua in Tahoua region, between Maradi and Niger's capital, Niamey, gray-bearded elders in loose turbans and sweat-stained prayer caps gather under a thatched portico. It is the first meeting with their new mayor, who wears a tall white prayer cap embroidered with a pattern of diamonds. The sultan of Tahoua, resplendent in white and gold, is also present. At a respectful distance behind the men stand women in a rainbow of headscarves.

They are discussing the drought that now never seems to end.

"Forty years ago," says the sultan, "it rained here five months a year. But since 2000, the climate change caused by Western countries has dried our rains. Children, cattle, even goats have died. People are fleeing to Nigeria, refugees from a war against the Sahel with no enemy to strike back at. What can be done?"

Even in the West, there is no technology to tame the unleashed climate. Have they considered family planning, to reduce the numbers that the lands must sustain?

The men explode with laughter. "Everyone here has more than one wife," says the sultan, who has four.

"You can't ask a father to stop having children without a solution for who will work on his farm," protests a white-turbaned elder.

"If you have children, God answers to their needs," says the new mayor. "I myself have thirty-three."

His potency is well known, and admired. But the meeting falls silent, as if it penetrates that this is no longer the land these men grew up in. In the past, there was room and grass aplenty for all the children a man could have. Then, in just twenty years, the trees are gone and only people are left.

"We have entered different times," says the sultan. "Maybe we have to think differently."

ii. Post-Colonial Hangover

The traffic in Niamey is sparse: some transport trucks, taxis, oxcarts stacked with yellow plastic jerry cans, and occasional white SUVs bearing the logos of UNICEF, the Red Cross, the EU, and FAO, bristling with satellite phone antennae. The dust hanging over the capital mixes with haze rising off the Niger River, so thick that the sun here resembles the pallid disk above China's manufacturing cities. But here, there are no factories.

On the walls of her ground-floor office in the Niamey building that the UN shares with foreign gold and uranium mining companies, Mme. Martine Camacho has hung posters from projects in all the African countries where she's worked for UNFPA, the United Nations Population Fund. "Equilibre Familial," one reads. "Had I Known, I Would Have Waited to Finish My Education," says another. Mme. Martine is French; her current assignment began in 2007, when Niger was pressed by the UN to establish a real population policy after being cited for the world's highest growth rates. The government appealed to the World Bank, which contracted with UNFPA to do something. Previous programs had been conducted by bureaucrats with anatomical flip charts and videos of people having sex, which they showed to rural Nigeriens who had never seen such a thing displayed publicly. When nurses began demonstrating how to roll a condom onto wooden penises, onlookers would flee.

Until 2007, just 5 percent of Nigerien women used contraceptives, she says. There is still tremendous resistance; women—or their husbands—often believe that birth control and child immunizations are a secret foreign plot to sterilize them and seize their lands when they become too few to defend them. Some women who were interested in spacing births would only use leather talismans containing herbs around their waists, or drink potions pounded from tree roots and drunk from wooden bowls inscribed with Qur'anic verses.

Here in the capital, Mme. Martine has heard educated men ask why having the highest rate of population growth is a problem. Just 15 million people in 1,267,000 square kilometers—Niger is the world's twenty-second largest country—leaves a lot of land to host more Nigeriens. One study suggested that most people actually wanted *more* children, not fewer: eight to nine for women, and twelve to thirteen for their husbands.

Contraceptive acceptance is now up to 16 percent, pills being most common, followed by Depo injections. "So we've gained 10 percent. The easiest 10 percent. I figure another four hundred years, and we'll have everyone wanting birth control."

Unfortunately, the money for this program, called PRODEM, runs out in 2013. Meanwhile, she worries, Muslim extremism here is rising and seems better funded. Yet two of the world's best family-planning programs, she says, are in Muslim countries, Tunisia and Iran, which are both below replacement rate.

"Tunisia and Iran don't force twelve-year-old girls to marry." Lest a girl be raped or grow ripe with desire, Nigerien parents often betroth daughters before they begin to menstruate. "In Tunisia and Iran, they send them to school. Everyone there reads. Most people here can't."

Yet HIV has declined, and in a country where female circumcision is still practiced, there is an encouraging project to abolish female genital mutilation by paying the mutilators to put down their knives. Instead of earning the equivalent of US$10 in West African francs—or a goat, or some chickens—for removing a girl's clitoris and, depending on the skill of the mutilator, slicing off vaginal labia, they're being given a hundred dollars to set up businesses selling peanuts or livestock. Others are being retrained as midwives. But as for family planning, Mme. Camacho is not very optimistic.

"In all the places I've worked — here, Ivory Coast, Rwanda, Burundi, Comoros — I've never seen a country ask for this. It's always initiated by the UN or some Bretton Woods lending institution. They're not conscious of the threat — only the West is. In Niger, they've designed a family-planning program, but deep in their hearts, they feel it's not their problem. They've adopted it without owning it."

When she arrived, the population director in Niger was a man with three wives and twenty children. "I'd talk to him about it. What kind of message was he giving to people? *Faites ce que je dis, mais ne faites pas ce que je fais,*[2] he'd reply. It would make me furious, but then I'd think of what we Westerners have done in Africa: pollute, pillage, and teach them to consume. We're hardly an inspiring model."

Fifty kilometers southeast of Niamey, the last small herd of a unique subspecies, the West African giraffe, clings to life in a hard yellow desert. As long as the rangers who guard them keep planting the acacia seedlings the giraffes eat in soil they bring from the Niger River's banks, they may survive, as they have no natural predators left other than humans. In the

---

2. Do as I say, not as I do.

mid-nineteenth century, Niger still teemed with lions, cape buffalo, monkeys, rhinoceros, and antelope, and all of West Africa was giraffe habitat. When the French colonial period came, so did firearms, and the poaching commenced. Giraffes were killed for meat and leather, and their tongues and genitals were harvested for talismans. Boiled giraffe bones were rendered into a paste to combat fatigue. Girls who reached twenty-five without marrying put giraffe tails in their bathwater to attract lovers.

Only 120 giraffes were left in Niger in 1993, when an NGO program to sustainably market deadwood from the surrounding savanna backfired, as people cut thousands of live trees and let them die before selling them. With this loss of food, Niger's giraffe population dwindled to 50. A French ethologist studying the herd began a campaign to save them; wood cutting was banned, and the Niger herd was also replenished by giraffe refugees fleeing Mali and Nigeria. Today, with tigerbush and acacias slowly recovering, there are now about 250 West African giraffes in Niger. They must coexist, however, with the flocks of goats swarming around them. Once giraffes retreated here because this savanna was uninhabited; today, there is nowhere that their eyes, nearly twenty feet above ground, can scan without seeing thatch huts.

Thirty kilometers south of the giraffe refuge is a

five-hundred-hectare experimental farm begun in 1989 by ICRISAT, the International Crops Research Institute for the Semi-Arid Tropics. After millions of square kilometers of desolation, to enter ICRISAT's leafy orchards and fields is a photosynthetic shock.

Along with programs to improve millet and peanut production, ICRISAT-Niger is growing drought-tolerant jujube trees from India that bear a small fruit called Sahel apple, as well as Sudanese tamarinds and Ethiopian moringas—whose leaves, boiled with peanuts, provide ten times the calcium of milk and more vitamin A than most vegetables. Under tents of shade cloth, okra, hibiscus, sesame, and heat-tolerant tomatoes spring from the tan Sahel sands, along with heat-resistant lettuce from Israel. Nearby grow papaya and Israeli mangoes. (ICRISAT-Niger's Israeli director believes that if food can grow in the Israeli Negev, it can grow in Niger.) As proof, they've resurrected a delicious native onion that was developed by the French, but lost after colonization ended. There are also cowpeas, oranges, pomelos, tangelos, and stands of *Jatropha curcas,* a Central American shrub whose oily seeds can be pressed for biodiesel. Lining the paths are Indian neem trees—a source of natural antiseptics and bug repellant.

Under development are desert-adapted grapes and figs. ICRISAT has created this nutritious oasis with minimal insecticide and with only microdoses of fertilizers, injecting directly to the roots of each plant just one-fifth of a typical field's normal application of nitrogen, phosphorus, and potassium. It also has fifteen scientists, one hundred field technicians and support staff, and three hundred laborers. And something else, rare in Niger's poor croplands: deep wells.

As in the Negev, all you have to do to grow food in a desert is add technical know-how, hard labor, and water. Except the rains have all but stopped, or they now fall at the wrong times. After three years, the 2010 drought is being called the one that never ends.

"True," says ICRISAT hydrologist Navid Dejwakh. "But the western Sahel is on top of an ocean of water."

There is an immense hydrological potential just below the surface, he says—in some places, barely three meters down. Much is so shallow that the energy of a solar panel is all that's needed to extract it. "Or a hand shovel. It's so counterintuitive—you can't see it based on vegetation, because so many trees have been cut."

Almost two-thirds of the country would be suitable for producing food, his colleagues believe. In fact, NGOs in parts of southern Niger have tapped this water since the early 1990s to plant some 200 million trees. Although one in five is killed by the rising heat, and this regreening still covers only a tiny percentage of the land, it is proof that the water is there.

This subterranean ocean, says Dejwakh, is from ancient rainfall and from the underground alluvial flow of the Niger River. "It is contained by a sand layer, with very little slope. It's perfect for filtering rainwater. It is rather amazing to think that there is all this water waiting for these people. They don't have to starve."

Dejwakh and everyone at ICRISAT, which is part of the international agricultural research consortium that includes both CIMMYT and IRRI, are certain that, given financing, there is enough water just below Niger's surface to grow plenty of food for everyone in the country. "Absolutely."

Everyone—meaning all 16.6 million current Nigeriens?

"Right."

And in thirty years, when, at the present growth rate, there are 50 million of them?

Dejwakh's smile vanishes. "Fifty million?"

Right.

"Fifty million," he answers slowly. "Less rainfall, too." He purses his lips. "Even with this ocean of water, 50 million people will have serious problems."

CHAPTER 11

The World Unraveling

i. Sin

The road to the naval colony in Karachi, Pakistan, passes a fifty-acre field so lifeless that its soil is bleached white. This is Moach Goth, a cemetery for the unknown. The tens of thousands interred here are found in the streets, the dumps, or in the mangroves along the harbor: addicts, unclaimed bombing fatalities, terror victims, the homeless. Their graves are marked with plywood triangles bearing fading numbers and sometimes a date. Across the road, two other equally large fields, already full, are disappearing under weeds and mesquite scrub.

In the farthest row, a man in a loose white turban, his nose gullied with lesions, sinks a spade into the white dust. His name is Khair Mohammad; all morning he has been digging little rectangles, three feet long. Each will be headed by a small blank hunk of stone, because they are for children who never lived long enough to be named, or who were never born at all. No one will visit them. Mohammad has buried thousands.

Once a week, they are brought in ambulances by Pakistan's Edhi Foundation, one of the world's largest social welfare NGOs, each wrapped in white cloth. Mohammad has received them for twenty-three years; the caretaker before him, his father, recalled them arriving in wooden carts pulled by men. Some are found in the garbage, some are left in front of mosques. If an infant is still alive, the Edhi Foundation gives it a home. If not, they come here.

"God knows who they are. God knows who is the father. The mothers are sinners: they sin, then throw their baby away."

The majority are girls. Some are full term, some fit in the palm of his hand. Sometimes he and his son Nadeem, who assists him, can't tell if it was male or female. God would also know how many were unrecognizable lumps of tissue that never made it here, or were never seen in the trash. An estimated 890,000 abortions occur in Pakistan each year, though

Grave digger, Moach Goth Cemetery, Karachi, Pakistan

no one really knows. Women of means use abortion as stop-gap birth control. Mothers who can't afford more children often get rid of new babies.

"Unmarried pregnant women," explains Karachi gynecologist Nikhat Saeed Khan, "have no place to go, because premarital sex doesn't exist in our culture, of course. So they endanger their own lives with untrained midwives or abortionists, or find some misoprostol to take." The same, she says, goes for adulterers and for women claiming rape who can't produce witnesses: their "crimes" risk punishment by death.

Nadeem arrives, carrying a jerry can of water. He's

the fifth youngest of Mohammad's four sons and six daughters. He wears a white tunic, his head uncovered despite the sun. Nadeem's job is to wash each baby, then offer prayers over them as his father buries them.

"They are innocent of sin, so they will go to God," he says. "And God will ask their parents why they aborted or abandoned them."

"This is our sad job,' says his father. "I believe God will reward us."

In the white sky overhead is a swirling funnel of hundreds of black kites—the bird that circles Karachi garbage heaps and docks when fishing boats discard offal. Their long shadows speed across the tiny nameless graves.

Could all this be avoided? What if the mothers could choose when to conceive a child, and when not to?

"Ask God," says Nadeem.

ii. Shakiness

"It happened so fast," says Tanveer Arif.

Although he's talking about 1995, he still sounds stunned. That was when the wells went dry in Gadap Town. Only two decades earlier, the lands here were among the most productive wheat and cornfields on Earth. There were guava and coconut orchards, and 5,000 farms that provided all the vegetables for nearby Karachi.

Most of those farms are now overgrown with invasive mesquite, and used only as picnic grounds for weekend outings. A few rent horses, or have private zoos stocked with the black bucks, wild ass, and blue bulls that were here when Pakistan was carved out of India in 1947 and was still one-third forest. Today, Pakistan's forest cover is barely 4 percent, a figure that includes lands designated as forest where little or nothing is actually covered.

Arif sits on the crumbling porch of a brick farmhouse belonging to a friend who no longer comes here. There's only one employee left, a caretaker with a curly beard named Soomar, who's worked here forty years, since he was five. "The well then was only 25 feet deep," Soomar says. "Fifteen years ago we had to go to 200 feet. Then 250. Then completely dry." They dug another, a foot-wide bore hole he keeps covered with two mud bricks. After 350 feet, still nothing.

"So we quit," he says, spitting out a wad of betel leaf.

A third hole, at the same depth but 2,000 feet away, still delivers, but its pressure is falling. Soomar pipes its flow down shallow ditches to fields whose soil is now just powder, and farms at a very modest scale—just enough to keep himself employed, Arif suspects. He harvested 40 kilograms of wheat this year. They used to get 150 kilos.

"This is a man-made environmental disaster," says Arif, mopping his skull with his shirtsleeve. Gadap Town was a Green Revolution zone, planted in dwarf hybrids that yielded incredible harvests: just add water. So everyone stuck straws in the ground, and when the flow slowed, they stuck in more, and deeper. Now that has failed, with no alternatives in place, such as catchment dams in dry riverbeds to capture monsoon runoff.

"Instead," says Arif, "they mine them all the way down to bedrock for sand to build more Karachi, so the soil can't replenish." Where trees once lined Karachi's rivers are now mounds of sand and gravel that go on for miles. As does Karachi.

Arif, a biologist, directs the Karachi-based Society for Conservation and Protection of Environment. Running an environmental NGO in Pakistan practically redefines the word *defeat*, but Arif soldiers on. His efforts to save the Houbara bustard, a game fowl favored by Dubai oil sheiks who jet over on weekends with permits allowing them one hundred birds apiece, elicit phone warnings that his legs will be broken. All the good trees around—especially guggal, the local myrrh species—were cut by men with political connections and weapons, or by politicians themselves, who then brought in Texas mesquite to control erosion, which instead ran amuck in the fields. People try burning it, but it just comes back faster. Then they brought Australian eucalyptus, whose thirsty roots broke up pipes all over town. Arif led the campaign to have guggal declared endangered, but thugs hassled the Green Guard youth brigades he organized to protect the remaining stands. East of Karachi, in forests along the Indus River, the timber exploiters are often members of parliament who can quickly relieve a protesting ranger of his job. Up north, the Taliban does the same.

Until quite recently, Pakistan brimmed with fecundity. A major cradle of human civilization arose along its great Indus River, which carried nutrients down from the Roof of the World, the Tibetan Plateau, and deposited some of the richest soil in Asia over its enormous flood plain. Pakistan's current water crisis and dwindling crop fertility are, as Tanveer Arif states, a man-made disaster. There are multiple causes of this; all stem from packing 185 million people into a country not much bigger than Texas, which has 26 million.

Within the next two decades, Pakistan, one of

the fastest-growing countries on Earth, will surpass Indonesia as the most populous Muslim nation. Indonesia has 248 million, but it also has one of the developing world's better family-planning programs; still, it will add 40 million by 2030. Pakistan, however, currently with three-fourths of Indonesia's population, will add double that amount. By mid-century, if its growth continues apace, Pakistan will far outnumber today's United States, with a projected 395 million people — all in a land the size of Texas.

Along with India, Pakistan is where the Green Revolution was first implemented. Starvation was averted, and millions lived to beget millions more. Today, 60 percent of those Pakistani millions are under thirty. The wells and rivers that watered the Green Revolution and gave them life are now giving out, leaving one-third of Pakistani children chronically malnourished. Unemployment, in double digits, grows along with the population, and the percentage of those underemployed is even higher.

Unemployed young men grow frustrated, and angry. A nation filled with angry young males is not a stable place, especially when they are tempted with paid opportunities to commit mayhem, including international mayhem.

A shaky nation with too many people running out of water and driven to mayhem becomes an entire planet's concern. Especially when that nation happens to be a nuclear power.

Yet again, the explosions have subsided in Lyari Town. The streets here, the oldest part of Karachi, are once more mobbed with cars, motorbikes, horse-drawn wagons, motorized rickshaws, carts of watermelon and betel leaf vendors, and the fabulously painted transport trucks that have become Pakistan's greatest indigenous art form, whose extravagant adornment often costs a trucker more than his house. Everyone is back: men in white kurtis and prayer caps; hijab'd women brilliant as tropical birdlife, wrapped in multihued loose pants and tunics called salwar kameez; other women in black chadors, even transvestites in chadors, all threading their way through the stalled traffic, buying provisions and tea.

Since 10:00 a.m., that traffic has gone from mere paralysis to pandemonium, as Lyari's stoplights are out for the next three hours. All but the most privileged parts of Karachi are subject to load-shedding — daily rolling blackouts — because the city can't possibly keep up with demand. There were fewer than a half-million people here in 1947. Today's 21 million is a forty-two-fold increase.

No one could have prepared for this.

Three days earlier, when the grenade attacks began, everyone stayed hidden until long after the explosions ended. Thankfully, only two deaths this time. At the Civil Hospital, Pakistan's biggest, which has a police station at its front entrance, eleven wounded were brought into emergency. That was far better than the attacks two weeks earlier, when the grenades were rocket-propelled, with forty wounded and eighteen dead—an overload for the fourteen tables in the surgical theater, where armed guards are posted lest warfare erupt in the triage units. To handle Karachi's literally exploding population, a fourteen-story trauma unit is under construction.

This latest salvo was over an unpaid loan. Everyone knows who owed whom, but as usual, no arrests. Newspapers reported it as yet another episode in "the ongoing gang wars" and life resumed. Lyari's balconies are hung anew with laundry that is grimy again even before it has a chance to dry. Billboard-sized posters of smiling gangsters—urban Robin Hoods who provide most of Lyari's jobs—continue to festoon exterior walls everywhere, except on mosques.

Many of these urban warlords descend from the original farming families when Lyari was a village, long before Britain decided to build a major warm-water port on the Arabian Sea near a small fishing enclave called Kolachi, in what was then part of India. As the two villages grew and merged, farmers opened shops, consolidated, became community fixers, made land deals, and became powerful in a city where laws were scorned under colonial rule, and now exist mainly on paper.

British rule in India ended in 1947, a triumph for Mahatma Gandhi's gentle civil disobedience. But Muslims who feared living under a Hindu majority demanded independence, and Pakistan was born in two Muslim majority regions cleaved from eastern and western India. With its two halves separated by a thousand miles, governance in Pakistan was weakened from the start, and the division couldn't last. In 1971, East Pakistan finally bolted. Following a civil war in which by some estimates 3 million died, it became Bangladesh.

Although beset with its own problems — along with tiny Pacific atoll nations, it is the country most imperiled by sea level rise, lying almost entirely in the Ganges Delta — Bangladesh is comparatively stable, in part because since the 1980s it has made family planning a national priority. In Pakistan, however, the precedent of weak government was never really reversed, even under periodic military dictatorships. Even in cities, tribal allegiances still trump all others.

In a room whose door opens directly onto a rubbled Lyari street where a dozen goats hug a strip of shade along a wall, ten women sit on the concrete floor where they waited out the grenade bombardment, embroidering salwar kameez for a dowry. The betrothed, a slender, pink-clad woman named Rashida,[1] is one of eight people who currently live in this room. The goats are hers; she grazes them every day along the dry Lyari River, an hour's walk away. She has three sisters and five brothers, all without work. Her father staples papers and serves tea in a bank. Rashida is lucky: her fiancé drives trucks. "Most men just roam around," she says. "They're mad because there's nothing to do."

"And take out their tempers on us," says orange-clad Shehzadi, who housekeeps for a politician.

The mud-plastered room is stuffy and dim, as the power is still off. Rashida takes the turquoise kameez she's beading with burgundy thread over to the doorway and holds it up to approving murmurs. Every woman is beading a different-colored set of salwar kameez for her; Rashida's truck-driver husband-to-be is helping to pay. By the wedding, she'll have twenty-five or thirty sets. The outfits will cost around four thousand rupees[2] apiece. Because the garments are loose-fitting and so well crafted, she

---

1. Names in this family have been changed.

2. About US$43.

expects to wear them all her life. "Before, women would have eighty or ninety sets. But everything's so expensive now!"

Especially children: "Who today could possibly want a lot? I only want two girls and two boys. No more." The other women smile and keep sewing, knowing better. They all said that once. And look what happened.

All these women wrapped in beautifully appointed cottons, their multiple earrings dangling beneath long dupattas, are Balochs. Their fathers brought their families to Karachi, in Sindh province, from the western desert province of Balochistan, where there is even less work than here. Rashida, born here, dreamed of being a doctor when she was in school, but school ended after eighth grade. The schools are often closed because there's no water or electricity. To protect all the children wandering the streets, the government builds extra-high speed bumps to slow traffic. Rashida's sixteen-year-old sister Nasreen, sullen because the power failed during the soap opera she was watching while she embroidered, hasn't studied at all.

"I hope my own children have more to do than housework and embroidery," Nasreen says, without much conviction. She's working on a yellow tunic, triple-stitching the long reinforced pocket that women use to thwart pickpockets. "It doesn't always help, because they just cut the bottom." They know, because they have brothers who are pickpockets.

Zeynep, a woman in green with a furrowed brow, finishes the eggshell-blue kameez she's embellished with tiny red diamonds and struggles to her feet, pausing to collect two pails she left by the door. "I've aged before my time," she declares, "staying up all night waiting for water to appear in the tap." She's given up on ever having it in her house again, and now walks five blocks to fill pails for her six kids from a public spigot. After her last three pregnancies ended in miscarriages, she took a daring step and got sterilized. To her surprised relief, her husband didn't object. Balochi relatives in Iran helped her with money from their government pension. "It was a nice hospital," she says wistfully.

As she leaves, two young men enter, Rashida's brother Nawab and his cousin Shahid. Both are dressed in white, with short-cropped hair and beards. "*Assalam-o-alaikum,* Auntie," they greet Zeynep as she passes. Everyone on this street is related.

The men sit on the floor. With fabric scraps, Shahid begins to clean a pistol. "We aren't criminals," he says. He looked for a job last week, but no luck. "They don't hire Balochs. Jobs come easier to other sects." Meanwhile, one of the local strongmen pays them a thousand rupees a day to guard the community. "The

guns are to protect our neighborhood from outsiders—
you can't depend on the police."

One political party recently promised two hundred construction jobs in exchange for their votes,
says his cousin, but they didn't materialize. "All we
get from them are free body bags."

These men are uneducated and unemployed, working as armed goons for their street. Their city has
plunged into havoc, yet in this room all seems calm.
Women fuss over a girl's trousseau, men polish weapons, and life proceeds.

"We don't think about the future," Nawab says.
"It's up to God."

But where is God amid all this killing and rage?

"We don't all shoot each other in streets," he says.
"We take out our anger at home."

The women's eyes stay averted.

In a provincial family-planning clinic a mile away,
the benches are jammed.

"Always," says Asma Tabassum, one of Pakistan's
ninety thousand LHWs—Lady Health Workers.
"The only time it eases up is when a bomb goes off."

Now that tensions from the last grenade battle
have eased, a rainbow of women wrapped in yards of
colored fabric has landed in her office all at once.
Usually she gets from fifteen to twenty a day, but by

10:30 a.m. she'd already seen that many. With a stethoscope dangling beneath her pink hijab, she checks blood pressure and gives prescriptions for progestin contraceptives: monthly injections of Norgestrel or oral packets of lo-femenal and ferrous fumarate tablets. Women can also request IUDs, longer-term Depo-Provera shots, condoms for their husbands, or tubal ligation, but shorter-term birth control methods are preferred here. The goal of most Pakistani women is birth spacing, which husbands are more willing to accept. Anything beyond monthly medication prompts fears of unintended sterilization.

The women in her windowless office, fanning themselves with pamphlets describing Bayer progesterone, represent several Pakistani ethnicities. Some have arrived in Karachi seeking work; others came as refugees from the Federally Administered Tribal Areas in northern Pakistan along the Afghan border, including one woman whose chador resembles camouflage fabric. As Asma takes her pulse, she confesses that for the past three days she has been self-medicating, because she has irregular periods. Now her head hurts; she thinks she made a mistake by experimenting with two pills a day. Asma tells her not to worry since it was just three days, and recommends regular injections so she won't accidentally overdose again. But the woman declines and leaves.

The next chador is black, trimmed in fine gold thread. Asma checks the woman's pulse; she is in her thirties and diabetic, so she should avoid anything hormonal. They discuss an IUD, but the negligible chance of infection is magnified because of her condition. "Your husband should use condoms," Asma tells her. They cost two for one rupee here: about a U.S. penny. Everything else, including an IUD, costs three rupees. Logos on a wall poster above Asma's head indicate that contraceptive funding comes from USAID and the Population Council, an NGO founded by John D. Rockefeller III.

The woman says she'll try to ask her husband, but she doesn't see him often. She is the second wife of a man who was her brother-in-law until her husband died in a bombing. In northern Pakistan, a man will often support a brother's widow by marrying her. He has six children with his first wife, and three with her. She wants to keep pleasing him so he'll be attentive. Alma takes her hand. "But in your condition, more pregnancies are a risk."

The overhead fan quits and the deadened air is immediately stifling. The women exchange worried glances, because load-shedding was over for the day, and unexpected blackouts often signal yet a new civil disturbance. Asma pulls a flashlight from her desk drawer and motions for the next client. An entire bench stands and approaches: five women in white burqas bordered with lace, their dark eyes peering through woven lattice grills in their face hoods. They are Pashto speakers from Pakistan's own version of Switzerland, the Swat Valley in Khyber Pakhtunkhwa: a sublimely beautiful region wedged between Afghanistan and Kashmir in far northern Pakistan. As one woman sits and gingerly lifts her veil, revealing a round, anxious face with a triangular nose ring, her companions stand protectively around her. The other clients titter at these monochromatic women, calling them cabbages and shuttlecocks—the term that colonizing British coined to describe their full burqas.

These women are rarely seen here, and birth control isn't this patient's agenda: in fifteen years, she's been unable to conceive. She's endured many treatments in villages and is tired of trying, but she really wants a child. This is her third visit, and Asma has test results for her. "You're fine," she tells her, her own diamond nose stud glinting as her penlight illuminates the page. The answer came in the semen test: "The problem isn't yours. It's your husband's."

The woman's reaction is a confusion of relief and trouble. She retreats behind her veil. "If a man can't conceive, he gets by," says Asma as the Pashtun contingent files out. "If a woman can't, she gets left. Or he gets a second wife."

The hot afternoon crawls on, the line of colorful women advances. Without asking, Asma knows which are housewives, because they want help with birth spacing. Nearly anyone who works, usually either a schoolteacher or an LHW like herself, wants to stop after two. When one housewife pleads that she wants to wait after her second child is weaned before starting on her next, Asma asks how many she wants to have.

"My husband wants at least six."

"And you?"

Shyly, she raises two fingers. The other women in the room are watching. They nod.

"You're wise," Asma assures her. "We'll never be healthy and have enough schools if our population keeps growing." More nods.

A middle-aged woman named Nazaqat in a full black chador and rectangular wire-rimmed glasses appears. She is today's vaccination technician on duty, responsible for seeing that pregnant women have their tetanus and polio shots, but she won't give a contraceptive injection that Asma has just prescribed.

"I don't believe we should practice family planning. Our community should increase in number." Asma gazes at the ceiling. "It's not for me to question why," Nazaqat continues. "It's God's will. He determines destiny."

She would have had as many as possible, she says, had she ever married. Yes, she knows, it's a problem that kids roam the streets because there aren't enough schools. And yes, it's heartbreaking to watch women try to feed eight children. And yes, her own work is made harder by men who forbid women to take polio vaccine, because they suspect it's really birth control.

"But every country has problems," she says. "Ours is overpopulation."

iii. Coeducate

Because schools, although constitutionally guaranteed, are so often scarce, and population grows so fast, a Pakistani child is less likely to get educated than a sub-Saharan African child. One summer night in 1995, six Karachi businessmen found themselves at dinner, whining again over their country's dismal descent. Especially infuriating, they concurred, were teachers who collected government salaries but showed up only once or twice a month. That night, they decided to take matters into their own hands. When they announced plans to start 1,000 private schools in the poorest parts of Pakistan, friends asked if they'd gone crazy.

"An insane country needs crazy solutions," they'd reply.

Eighteen years later, TCF—The Citizens Foundation—is up to 830 schools. One of the first was in a ramshackle colony near Karachi's harbor, whose name, Machar, means "mosquito," being Karachi's epicenter of malaria and dengue, as well as leprosy. Unlike its surroundings, TCF's Vohra School has solid whitewashed walls and a pleasant brick courtyard filled with ornamental plants. There are classrooms for kindergarten through fifth grade and, rare in Machar, electricity and plumbing. A nearby TCF secondary school also has science labs with microscopes and dissecting tables equipped with sinks, and a computer room.

Vohra School's upper windows look out on a jumble of unplastered walls and corrugated roofs held in place by stones, and columns of smoke rising from cooking braziers sliced from fifty-five-gallon oil drums. With eight hundred thousand residents, Machar is called the biggest illegal squatter community in Asia, although there are many contenders. Few streets are wide enough for vehicles, which navigate with their horns through the cows and goats. Most are lined with ditches filled with plastic debris and a scum of shrimp shells. Women and children sit in doorways, peeling shrimp that arrive in port around 3:00 a.m., an event so critical that it's announced by the mosques, like a muezzin call. It is the sole source of local employment, but only for woman and children, whose small fingers are fastest.

The children peel from 5:00 a.m. to 8:00 a.m., then change into tan shirts and slacks for boys, tan salwar kameez and white hijabs for girls, and head to school. Their first stop is the washroom, where they soap their hands with filtered water and get Vaseline to treat the cuts on their fingers. Most have stomach and eye problems from the water at home. When her parents first visited the school, says a fourth grader, "I brought them here because the bathroom smells so beautiful." Her mother inquired why, and took home a bottle of disinfectant.

The businessmen founders decided that to foster responsibility, everyone must pay something. Sliding monthly tuition ranges from 10 to 200 rupees (10¢ to US$2.00); the school subsidizes half the cost of the 300-rupee uniforms, purchased in installments. Half the students are girls, and classes are coed so that boys learn respect for the opposite sex. All fifty-four hundred TCF teachers are female, because most parents won't send girls to male teachers, nor allow daughters to teach where men are on the staff. Although the monthly salary — the rupee equivalent of about US$200 — is below the government rate, they get many applicants, because it is considered safe: a fleet of minivans, small enough to negotiate the warren maze of Machar streets, transports teachers daily to and from home. They get full support from mosques, says Afshan Tabassum, the school principal. "Some TCF schools are inside madrassas. They want kids in religious class in the morning and in our school the second half."

Although their per-school budget is half that of government schools, 95 percent of The Citizens Foundation students pass national exams, versus the 55 percent national average. The minuscule dropout rate—under 1 percent—is partly because Tabassum and other principals constantly visit students' homes, coaxing parents not to take their daughters out of school to marry them off.

"That's the key. When a girl receives an education, she educates the entire family." They started with 60 students, and now have 410 (TCF student enrollment nationwide is 115,000) in double-shift classes taught in Urdu, 30 students per class. There is a waiting list of 250. Because they take siblings, the size of families is a huge burden. Machar has nearly doubled since Tabassum came nine years earlier.

"Every family has six or seven, and is expecting another." There are so many kids that people sleep on roofs. She's had success with hygiene and literacy classes for mothers, but talking to parents about family planning usually doesn't work. "The more kids in a family, the more pails of shrimp the Karachi Port Trust will bring them to peel."

But the girls enrolled here figure out family planning for themselves. By eighth grade, along with math, science, social studies, geography, and English, they enter a mentoring program that pairs them with professionals in fields they'd like to pursue. If they complete school and find work, most, like their role models, have no more than two children.

"I want to be a doctor, and help heal and feed people," says Rubina, braids bouncing under her hijab.

"I want to be an air hostess and travel on airplanes," says Nimra.

"A teacher, like you," Naeema tells Principal Tabassum. "You are always in my heart."

The boys want science and engineering, or to be pilots in the Pakistani Air Force. But in Vorha School it is clear that in the coming years Pakistan will be blessed with many women doctors and educators.

"Which is how we'll change Pakistan," says Citizens Foundation vice president Ahson Rabbani. He's proud that this has been a success, that they've raised more than $100 million to build these bright, well-equipped schools, and 95 percent of that money comes from Pakistan. But the most important measure, he agrees, is the number of girls they've reached.

"In northern Pakistan, they blew up two hundred

fifty schools because they were teaching girls. In the entire Swat Valley, girls stopped going to school. When we get threats from the Taliban, we tell them: Blow up one school, and we'll build five more."

———

The dirt-scrabble of Machar ends at a wide mudflat of green mangroves separating it from Karachi Harbor to the south. As the community's population expands, more rubble foundations push into this natural area, even though cutting mangroves is prohibited. A timber mafia pays squatters to down more trees, and pays police to overlook the plunder clearly visible from the school's roof.

Past the harbor, the mangroves resume on a thickly forested 400-hectare sand-spit that protects the city from typhoons. Endangered green turtles nest on the Arabian Sea beach where fisherfolk, as they are known, launch dinghies to catch mackerel, kingfish, and grouper. When they realized that city effluent was poisoning the mangrove lagoon where they catch crabs, prawns, shrimp, and cuttlefish, they contacted the United Nations Development Programme and World Wildlife Fund. Eventually, a wetlands center was built, and both organizations gave grants to two adjacent fisherfolk communities to help to protect the mangroves and plant more.

One community used the money to start an eco-tourism project, with lagoon boat cruises. It was soon attracting 250 people on the weekends. Visitors marveled at this placid oasis, filled with flamingos and frogs, that most never knew was at the edge of their churning city.

But the other group began cutting mangroves and selling the wood. They divided protected land into lots to sell to Saudi and Dubai sheiks for beach and harbor view vacation homes. The first group filed complaints. One night in January 2011, their computers were smashed, life jackets were shredded, and their office was riddled with bullets. They reported it to the police, who never responded. A lawyer advised them to forget it.

They moved to another office. On May 5, a grenade blew off its roof, bending the steel I-beams into parabolas. Two tour boats and the jetty that UNDP built were burned. Men parked outside the house of the ecotourism project founder, Abdul Ghani, and fired guns into the air. The fisherfolk fled into the mangroves. At 3:00 a.m., they returned, except for Ghani and a colleague, Haji Abu Bakar. The next day, they found them floating in the lagoon. Bakar's hands were tied behind his back, and his neck was broken. Ghani was mauled and strangled.

Two days later, Ghani's three brothers, his nephews,

and his twin twelve-year-old sons sit barefoot on the flat green carpet, looking at photographs of the dead leader and at an entry in his journal, signed in blue ink, written after the January attack. "I had spoken against the destruction of the forest, and [X] became my enemy. He and his men threatened my life. If anything happens to me, they are responsible."

The mattresses they hid behind that night still block the windows. Ghani's wife, daughters, and sisters weep in the next room. Over and over, the men watch on a Nokia mobile phone the video of his body being hoisted from the lagoon. The man he named, a well-known local strongman, is said to be hiding in Karachi. The UN and WWF staff came by; they took the names of the twins, their four sisters, and their eight-month-old brother, and promised to provide for them. No one has come from the government. The police van and unmarked gray sedan with a blue light slapped on its roof outside are supposedly for their protection, but everyone knows who pays them. Twenty-five witnesses, no arrests.

"All we tried to do was save trees and the lagoon," says Ghani's brother Mohammad Harun, a thin, deeply bronzed fisherman in a crumpled knit prayer cap. "All is now madness."

iv. The Indus

East of Karachi, the road to the Indus River delta is lined with tents of refugees from floods that, three summers in a row, have scoured entire villages from the land. Stagnant lakes fill what were once fields.

In the village of Haji Qasim, fifty kilometers north of the seacoast, people are leaving for the opposite reason: because the water has left them. Since the dawn of human civilization, the great serpentine Indus, one of the world's biggest rivers, brought snowmelt from the Tibetan plateau down through the fertile Punjab of India and Pakistan, then ended its journey here in Sindh province, where it gushed freshwater and sediments a hundred miles into the Arabian Sea. That silt gave Sindh province some of the richest farmlands in Pakistan, famous for the rice and tea they supplied to all Asia. Now the flow of water is reversing: first India, then Pakistan built dams and barrages across the Indus, trapping the water in the Punjab, stranding the blind Indus River dolphins that had evolved to be sightless in the river's nutrient-rich silt load. Since powerful Punjabi farmers no longer send enough water to allow the Indus to reach the sea, the sea is creeping up its delta.

In Haji Qasim, a mud-and-thatch village now devoid of foliage, men still make their living from the irrigation canal, but by fishing, not farming. At noon, they come out of the sun to drink tea steeped in buffalo milk in a communal room alongside the wide canal. A wall is lined with yellow jerry cans filled with drinking water they bring in by donkey cart. The only fresh water that reaches here now is during floods, which, strangely, are caused in part by drought: as dry riverbeds fill with windblown sand, they flatten and can't control the flow during the monsoon. When the floods subside, seawater intrudes, and mangroves at the river's mouth die.

"Without the mangroves, the wind has changed," says Shafit Mohammad, a cotton farmer who now fishes for mullet. "Long before this happened, our elders had a premonition that the sea was coming, from the wind. People below had to cut the trees, because salt water killed them."

He wipes buffalo milk from his moustache. "It was beautiful here. There were so many trees that children couldn't go in alone, because of boars and wolves. As the sea approached, first our crops were ruined. Then our date palms and forest."

Now the sea is rising in the canal. "Every fifteen days, it comes up at night. It has taken boats and flooded our houses." The floor of this room is a raised wooden platform. Shafit points out the doorway at the yellow hardpan, where rice and wheat once grew. Now, only salt-scrub, and dead palm stumps. "The water is now like cancer to the land."

They have built mud berms to hold the rising waters back, but most of the thousand people who lived here have left. "When a man dies, we have to go to Thatta for sweet water to clean his body, it's so scarce. Three more years, and there will be no more village." They will have to move to where water is still fresh. Again.

The elders who read the wind predicted that the Arabian Sea would one day reach Thatta, a town fifty kilometers to the north. No one believed them. But in Ahmed Jat, ten kilometers farther upstream, they are beginning to believe. To the families left in Haji Qasim, visiting Ahmed Jat is like time-traveling to their own village just a decade earlier. Orchards of date palms, filled with mynah birds. Neem trees, figs, mangos, and almonds. A network of trickling irrigation channels bringing transparent water to cotton, sugarcane, rice, wheat, tomatoes, squash, and okra. Hand pumps and solar panels. Goats and water buffalo.

"Everyone here is related by blood to a single couple who founded this village sixty years ago,"[3] says

---

3. In Sindh province, marriage between cousins is common.

Shafi Mohammad Jat, a wiry man in a long orange kameez with a thicket of black hair, his cheek full of betel leaves. Today, Ahmed Jat has 270 families, most with seven or eight children. God has blessed them with a good life, Jat says, even though the last drought killed sixty goats, and even though they are so remote that the Green Revolution never came here.

"We never got those fancy fertilizers." Plus, the nearest clinic is thirty kilometers away. Eight women have died in childbirth trying to reach it in the rains.

"But we do well," he says, showing off crops grown with buffalo manure, and a bamboo-shaded longhouse filled with poles of healthy betel vines. "Except—"

Except another of their wells has just turned too brackish to drink. "We can still use it for most crops," he says. So they're digging more wells, this time a thousand feet from the village. "But we know what's going to happen." Seawater is moving north, a kilometer a year. "Maybe we have ten more years. Or less."

And then?

He points north. "We move to Thatta."

In a room on the outskirts of Thatta, a man with a fan-shaped moustache named Shaikh Tanveer Ahmed quotes from Qur'anic verse 2:233, the Surah Al-Baqara:

"Mothers shall suckle their children for two whole years."

His audience, four young bearded imams, quotes with him in unison. The surah has become Ahmed's mantra. It is the key that opens a tightly shut door. He has debated many religious leaders who oppose family planning, but he always wins, because it is incontestably clear that the Prophet intended for women to nurse babies thoroughly, thus spacing their births.

Ahmed directs HANDS, the Health and Nutrition Development Society, a Pakistani NGO that gently presses the government to deliver services it promises. He is under no illusion about what his country faces. During the 2010 floods, caused by ferocious monsoons, 175,000 people—70 percent of the district of Thatta's population—fled one night when a levee broke. During the 2011 floods, one-fifth of the country was under water, and again in 2012. Now the sea is advancing, pushing millions of people into less and less space.

Reducing population pressure is critical, he says. "But you can't say 'family planning.' You must say 'birth spacing.' If it's about health, they accept. Numbers, they resist."

In every district, they identify the four most important leaders, such as these white-clad mullahs. "We send them to Islamabad, to meet with high religious leaders who have been trained by the Population Council. They learn that to have healthy nursing mothers means dealing with the fact that half of Pakistani girls are malnourished. That means changing the custom of women getting what's left over after men have their fill. They learn that this submissiveness can't be overcome if there are ten times as many schools for boys as for girls."

"In the 1960s," says Qari Abdul Basid, imam of Thatta's Shah Gehan Mosque, "the government didn't consult the imams. The proper way was ignored. So people refused family planning." Now, in Friday prayers, they teach that Islam professes health and nutrition, and they repeat the directive in Surah Al-Baqara that a child has a right to two years of mother's milk.

They prefer nursing to avoid conception, but they accept pills and condoms. Much of the birth control comes from USAID, a delicate point with Pakistani mullahs; the pamphlets they share in meetings with extremist religious leaders omit the USAID logo and its accompanying motto, "From the American people."

"Acceptance is growing," says Imam Basid. "People space births, and instead of seven or eight, they have four or five. That is important: without birth spacing, our resources will be finished."

A prayer chimes: it's the ring-tone of his mobile phone. He begs his leave. The four imams file out, leaving Ahmed at a table surrounded by a new USAID shipment of midwifery instruments.

In the village of Ahmed Khan Zour, fifty kilometers farther north, a HANDS theater troupe is giving its 640th performance. More than one hundred women in bright salwar kameez and sparkling nose rings, surrounded by daughters with henna-painted arms and even some fathers, crowd under a portico to watch. The performers begin with a song that equates happiness with health, and health with a two-year gap. A male actor explains that the drama will reveal what that means, and invites them to fig-ure out what's wrong with the picture they're about to see.

It begins with a marriage ceremony; the bride is very young. The scene shifts to a bedroom. The wife lies against a pillow, trying to comfort an unhappy infant.

"What's wrong?" asks her husband.

"He's sick," she says.

"Fix him!"

"What can I do? I'm sick myself. I'm pregnant again," she sobs.

The next day, a neighbor comes by and finds her

sicker and weaker. "Why don't you space your births?" she asks. "My husband and I do."

The whole family gathers. "You're not sick, you lazy liar," declares her mother-in-law. "You just don't want to give my son children. You only worry about yourself!"

By now, the audience is murmuring, and the action stops. "What's wrong here? And why has it happened?" the actor playing the husband asks.

Hands raise; opinions are voiced. The wife wasn't even sixteen; she wasn't ready to have children. Her parents should have taught her about waiting between children. Most comments, though, blame the mother-in-law: "They want us to have as many children as they had to have," says a woman in a black hijab, to applause.

The woman playing the mother-in-law turns out to be a doctor. Out come the pills, the injectables, the T-shaped copper IUDs, the foil-wrapped con-doms. She explains each, and explains which ones require a visit to the clinic.

"We have to go all the way to Thatta," a woman says.

"Not today," says the doctor. Walking to stage left, she pulls back a sheet, revealing the ambulatory clinic they've brought along. She steps inside. "I'm here all day," she says. And the line forms.

*   *   *

When Pakistan developed a nuclear bomb, USAID cut off funding family planning here for six years. Funds for the roving theater performances run out in 2013. "We tell USAID," says HANDS director Shaikh Tanveer Ahmed, "that without continued support, Pakistan will probably produce more of the kind of people that the USA fears."

Only about 13 million of Pakistan's 90 million females have access to contraceptives, he reminds them. "They understand. But sometimes politics in Washington make them reluctant."

Even if they do continue providing, he knows that a two-year gap resulting in four or five children per family will not add up to population stability.

"No. We're really afraid we can't cope with the growing population. We are a crowded, underdeveloped nation — more a crowd than a nation. So we'll have more illiterates, more youths without productive jobs, and more chaos."

He makes some marks on a pad. "If we can't keep providing contraceptives or encourage their use, by 2050 we'll be approaching three times the number we're at today."

He tosses his pad down. "We're praying that Pakistan only doubles."

CHAPTER 12

The Ayatollah Giveth and Taketh Away

i. Horses

When Hourieh Shamshiri Milani entered medical school in 1974, just thirteen of seventy students in her class at the National University of Iran were women. "And of those thirteen, only two of us wore the scarf."

During the reign of Mohammad Rezā Shāh Pahlavī, the final Shah of Iran, head covering was rare among educated women. In 1936, seeking to modernize the country, his father, Rezā Shāh Pahlavi, had decreed that all Iranian women be unveiled. When Rezā Shāh was forced to abdicate in 1941 by the invading British because of his cordial ties with Germany,[1] the rule was relaxed, and hijab became a matter of personal choice. In Shamshiri's family, they chose to wear it. She would choose to do so still, although now there is no choice.

In the alcohol-free piano bar of the Espinas Hotel in central Tehran, her hair concealed under flowered silk, Dr. Shamshiri is a handsome woman with striking eyebrows. She was born in Tabriz in northwest Iran, near the border with what was then the Soviet Union. In that region known as Iranian Azerbaijan, a woman felt naked in public with her head uncovered. Her family was devout, but her father was also a high school teacher who gave his blessing to her desire for education. "Although," she remembers, "he did not want people to know that his daughter was attending university."

During her fourth year of studies in Tehran, the utterly unexpected happened. Like his father before him, the Shah of Iran had grown more despised over time. His loss of public trust began with a 1953 coup

---

1. A claim popularized in Rezā Shāh's time was that *Iran* and *Aryan* were essentially the same word. His courtship of Germany was partly strategic, to counter British and Soviet designs on the Iranian petroleum that each hoped to control. Although friendly with Hitler, he also personally guaranteed the rights of Iranian Jews, whose synagogues he would visit.

that deposed a popular prime minister who had dared to nationalize Iran's oil industry, because 80 percent of profits went to the drilling company known today as BP, née British Petroleum. With Shah Pahlavī's cooperation, the coup was engineered by Britain's M16 and the CIA (the United States having assumed, erroneously, that the prime minister was a communist).

In the mid-1970s, the Shah, ostensibly a constitutional monarch, abolished every political party except his own, which incited spontaneous strikes. A high-ranking Shi'a cleric named Ruhollah Khomeini, exiled for denouncing the Shah's lavish rule from the Peacock Throne and his coziness with the West, became a symbol of defiance in absentia. The strikes intensified and organized, until millions filled the streets. Suddenly to everyone's shock, in January 1979 the Shah fled to Egypt. A year later he died from lymphoma.

The bloodless revolution that toppled him had been joined across the country's political spectrum, from orthodox mullahs to intellectuals. When the triumphant Ayatollah Khomeini returned from exile in France, even soldiers in the Shah's army celebrated. A referendum on whether the monarchy should be abolished in favor of Islamic government won 98 percent approval.

The victorious citizenry widely believed that in newly liberated Iran, both secular and religious would live and worship as they liked, with Ayatollah Khomeini as the country's guiding spirit. Soon, however, Iranians learned that Khomeini's idea of spiritual leadership was not mere guidance, but theocracy. Although the revolutionary constitution had established a democracy, Khomeini anointed himself Supreme Leader, with a Guardian Council of religious clerics holding veto power over parliament, president, and prime minister. Among his first edicts was reinstatement of the compulsory hijab. Women's heads must be covered, and their bodies cloaked in chadors or long, loose-fitting garments.

Secular Iranians felt betrayed. But as Hourieh Shamshiri entered her specialized studies in gynecology, her divided country suddenly united behind the Ayatollah, because Iran was attacked. Shortly after the Ayatollah Khomeini's ascension, across Iran's western border Saddam Hussein had assumed the presidency of Iraq. For thirteen years, Khomeini had lived there in exile, stirring revolutionary fervor among Iraqi Shi'ite Muslims until Hussein, a nominal Sunni and Iraq's military strongman, finally pushed him out of the country. A year later, as Iran was still reorganizing after centuries of dynastic rule, Hussein seized the chance to invade his weakened, distracted neighbor, whose oil-rich Khuzestan province he coveted.

A decade later Saddam would try the same thing

in Kuwait, and the United States would respond by invading to protect international petroleum interests. But no such help was forthcoming to Iran. During the chaotic infancy of Iran's Islamic Republic, a group of students, incensed that the Shah was receiving treatment for his declining health in Texas, stormed the U.S. Embassy. For 444 days, they held fifty-two embassy staffers hostage. Among the upshots of that crisis was American backing for Saddam's Iraq, in what became the twentieth-century's longest war between conventional armies.

Iraq struck with ground forces, missiles, and mustard gas. It had the support of both the USSR and NATO, which supplied its armaments, including feedstock for nerve gas. Iran, with more than three times the population, responded with repeated waves of soldiers. Within two years, it suffered tremendous human casualties but regained the ground lost to Saddam's initial incursions. The two countries then dug in for six more years of entrenched warfare, during which hundreds of thousands of Iranians died.

Before its Islamic Revolution, Iran had begun a family-planning program, following a 1966 census that showed a startling increase over the previous decade. In 1956, Iran had 18.9 million people, but Iranian women were averaging 7.7 children apiece. In only ten years, they added 6 million more. The health ministry began distributing birth control, but with only modest success: the 1976 census still showed fertility rates of 6.3 children per woman. The top-down program was training medical personnel, but failing to explain to parents why they might want to limit the size of their families.

By the time of the 1979 revolution, there were 37 million Iranians. Although many mullahs extolled traditional virtues of early marriage and large families, the Ministry of Health was able to keep its family-planning program. The Supreme Leader himself clarified religious questions about artificial birth control with a fatwa stating that it was permitted. But war with Iraq changed everything. The Population and Family Planning office closed. In its place was a campaign for every fertile Iranian woman to help build Iran a "Twenty Million Man Army."

The legal marrying age for girls dropped from eighteen to thirteen. To encourage women to bear many children, ration cards were issued on a per capita basis, including newborns. According to Iranian demographer-historian Mohammad Jalal Abbasi-Shavazi, rationing covered not only foodstuffs, but "consumer goods like television sets, refrigerators, carpets and even cars." Because nursing children used little of their allotment, a black market in extra food and appliances became a key source of family income.

As war with Iraq dragged on, the birth rate surpassed Khomeini's demographic dreams. Although a million Iranian fighters, including mere boys, were martyred by inhaling poison gas, clearing land mines, or charging in human waves into artillery barrages, the 1986 census counted nearly 50 million Iranians: a doubling in two decades. By some estimates, the growth rate peaked at 4.2 percent, near the biological limits for fertile women and the highest rate of population increase the world had ever seen.

Tehran, an inland city, grew prosperous and populous because of plentiful springs in the Alborz Mountains, which form its snowy backdrop to the north — a vista that, smog permitting, includes 18,000-foot Mt. Damavand, the highest volcano in Asia. From north Tehran's posh foothills, the city descends two thousand feet through a broad middle-class swathe, dropping into an arid plain filled with working-class neighborhoods that end in south Tehran's fringe of hovels. Down there, females are invariably enveloped in black fabric, but through much of Tehran, women perform daily fashion miracles, defying the intent of modesty laws by making what is barely hidden all the more alluring. Obligatory long manteaus tighten at the hips and bodices of shoppers in tailored jeans and spiky heels. By sheer numbers, women contriving to conceal the least amount of hair under gauzy hijabs overwhelm morality police trying to enforce shariah dress code. They are further undermined by hundreds of stores selling hair extensions, makeup, wigs, hair clasps, and lingerie—the latter is even sold in the gift shop at the Ayatollah Khomeini's tomb. Smuggling networks widely assumed to be run by the Ayatollah's Revolutionary Guards help keep stores stocked with European and New York haute couture—sluiced, like the BMWs and Lamborghinis of north Tehran, through portals like Dubai.

Even during sanctions, Tehran, like Havana, thrums with energy. But it lives on time borrowed from mountain springs recharged by rain. In 1900, they easily supported the 150,000 Tehranis. Counting the 3 million workers who commute here daily, 15 million drain that water today, a hundred-fold increase in just over a century. Khomeini's divine mandate to build not just an army, but an Islamic generation with no memory of the Shah, spawned as breathtaking a demographic leap as the world had ever seen—which made what came next all the more astonishing.

In 1987, Dr. Hourieh Shamshiri Milani finished her obstetrics and gynecology residency in Tehran. During the war, her specialty had become politicized, as demographics became the most potent weapon in Iran's arsenal. With the stunning 1986 census figures, Iran's prime minister declared their new huge population "God-sent." But others—especially the director of Iran's planning and budget office—were plain frightened. As the stalemated war headed to a UN-brokered ceasefire, his office calculated the numbers that their shattered economy might reasonably support. All those males born to man the Twenty Million Man Army would need jobs, and chances for providing them shrank with each new birth.

Secret meetings commenced with the Supreme Leader to discuss the population blessing that was now a population crisis. Years later, demographer and population historian Abbasi-Shavazi would interview the 1987 planning and budget director, and learn that he had met with the president's cabinet and explained what excessive human numbers portended for the nation's future. To feed, educate, house, and employ everyone would far outstrip their capacity, as Iran was exhausted and nearly bankrupt. There were so many children that primary schools had to move from double to triple shifts. The planning and budget director and the minister of health presented an initiative to reverse demographic course and institute a nationwide family-planning campaign. It was approved by a single vote.

A month after the August 1988 ceasefire finally

ended the war, Iran's religious leaders, demographers, budget experts, and health minister gathered for a summit conference on population in the eastern city of Mashhad, one of holiest cities for the world's Shi'ite Muslims, whose name means "place of martyrdom." The weighty symbolism was clear.

"The report of the demographers and budget officers was given to Khomeini," Dr. Shamshiri recalls. The economic prognosis for their overpopulated nation must have been very dire, given the Ayatollah's contempt for economists, whom he often referred to as donkeys.

"After he heard it, he said, 'Do what is necessary.'"

It meant convincing 50 million Iranians of the opposite of what they'd heard for the past eight years: that their patriotic duty was to be forcibly fruitful. Now, a new slogan was strung from banners, repeated on billboards, plastered on walls, broadcast on television, and preached at Friday prayers by the same mullahs who once enjoined them to produce a great Islamic generation by making more babies:

One is good. Two is enough.

The next year, 1989, Imam Khomeini died. The same prime minister who had hailed fertility rates approaching nine children per woman as God-sent now launched a new national family-planning program. Unlike China, the decision of how many was left to the parents. No law forbade them from having ten if they chose. But no one did. Instead, what happened next was the most stunning reversal of population growth in human history. Twelve years later, the Iranian minister of health would accept the United Nations Population Award for the most enlightened and successful approach to family planning the world had ever seen.

If it all was voluntary, how did Iran do it?

Nodding to the Persian music issuing from the piano, Dr. Shamshiri smiles, remembering. "We used horses. Doctors and surgeons, teams from universities, carrying our equipment on horseback to every little village."

The horseback brigades that Dr. Hourieh Shamshiri and her fellow OB-GYNs accompanied to the farthest reaches of the country made any kind of birth control—from condoms and pills to surgery—available to every Iranian, for free. Because Ayatollah Khomeini's original contraception fatwa emphasized that neither mother nor child should be harmed, it was assumed to exclude both abortion and operations. But his successor, Ayatollah Ali Khamenei, issued a fatwa of his own—"When wisdom dictates that you do not need more children, a vasectomy is permissible"— that was interpreted to include tubal ligations for women.

The program's initial goals were modest. According to Mohammad Abbasi-Shavazi, they hoped to reduce the average fertility rate of Iranian women to four children by 2011, and eventually drop the population growth rate from its astronomical levels during the war to slightly above replacement rate. But Iranian families were just as broke and fatigued as the nation, and they leaped at the chance for fewer children. Within two years, Iran's demographers were disbelieving their own numbers.

The horseback doctors had planned to encourage women — who were not required to seek husbands' approval for birth control — to space pregnancies three to four years. They were to advise them to bear children only between ages eighteen and thirty-five, and to suggest stopping with three children. "But every woman who already had children wanted an operation," says Dr. Shamshiri. "More than a hundred thousand women of that generation were sterilized. All the younger ones told me they only wanted two, one of each if they could. I'd ask them why. 'The cost of rearing children,' was the first thing they said. So I'd ask them to imagine that tomorrow their economic problems had been solved, how many children would they want. Again, they answered, 'Two, because of education. We should send our daughters to university.'"

They were seeing modern women on television—including herself, as she and other gynecologists were now frequently on Iranian TV programs. "Families would find my telephone number. They'd ask, 'How did you get this degree? How can we educate our daughters like you?'"

Increasingly, the answer was easy. All the accolades that Iran's family-planning program received in forthcoming years cited one indispensable factor: female education. Not just primary and secondary, but university. In 1975, barely a third of Iranian women could read. In 2012, more than 60 percent of Iranian university students were female. The literacy rate for females twenty-six and under was 96 percent. Giving women control over their wombs and their education made it increasingly hard to deny them the workplace. By 2012, one-third of government employees in Iran were women. As Dr. Shamshiri recalls her horseback missions, two taxis arrive at the Espinas Hotel driven by female cabbies, while just beyond, women police officers cruise Keshavarz Avenue.

At one point during the push to a Twenty Million Man Army, the marriage age for girls dropped again, to nine—the "official age of puberty." With the family-planning program, that was repealed, and the average age of a bride soon rose to twenty-two, as women postponed marriage and childbearing until they finished school. By the 1994 World Population Conference in Cairo, the numbers from Iran were so astounding that UNFPA sent its demographers to check the figures that Abbasi-Shavazi and his colleagues were collecting—and got the same results. Dr. Hourieh Shamshiri, by then a deputy in Iran's Ministry of Health, was a delegate, and was besieged with questions. Everyone wanted to know how such a thing could happen in a Muslim nation—and with a voluntary program, no less.

There was no covert coercion, she'd explain. The sole requirement was that all couples attend premarital classes, held in mosques or in health centers where couples went for prenuptial blood tests. The classes taught contraception and sex education, and stressed the advantages of having fewer children to feed, clothe, and school. The only governmental disincentive was elimination of the individual subsidy for food, electricity, telephone, and appliances for any child after the first three.

By 2000, Iran's total fertility rate reached replacement level, 2.1 children per woman, a year faster than China's compulsory one-child policy. In 2012, it was 1.7.

———

"Iran's family-planning program succeeded," says Mohammad Jalal Abbasi-Shavazi, "thanks to the Islamic revolution. There was a national commitment to reduce the gaps from the Shah's time between rich and poor, urban and rural."

Under the Shah, agriculture ministers rarely left Tehran. Now water, sanitation, agriculture, energy, and finance officers arrived in the remotest villages, extending technical help during planting, installing toilets, launching literacy programs. "Most important was building a health network that reached the farthest outposts of the country."

Every hamlet in Iran today has a "health house," staffed by two *behvarz* selected by the village. Usually a man and a woman, they receive two years of training in family medicine, including prenatal and postnatal care, contraception, and immunization. For illness, there is a rural clinic for every five health houses, staffed by doctors, who also visit each health house twice a week.

The *behvarz* maintain birth, death, and vaccination records for each person. In Iranian cities, teams of women volunteers go door-to-door, doing the same. With such oversight, the spread of diseases like tuberculosis was checked, and Iran's infant mortality rate dropped to western European levels, further convincing parents to limit family size.

It was to these health houses that Hourieh Shamshiri, her fellow OB-GYNs, and horseback mobile surgical teams would arrive. As Iran's postwar economy improved, horses gave way to four-wheel-drive vehicles and even helicopters. Iran pioneered "no-scalpel" vasectomies, ten-minute procedures involving just a tiny puncture in the abdomen. During the early years of the revolution, contraceptives were often hard to find. Now Iran became one of the world's biggest producers of condoms. Several months' worth of contraceptive supplies were stockpiled to assure that shortages didn't occur. And everything—condoms, pills, IUDs, injections, vasectomies, and tubal ligations—remained free.

Nevertheless, demographers report, the preferred method of contraception in Iranian cities remains coitus interruptus. One reason may be that the cautionary tale in Genesis of Onan, whom God kills for disobeying his father by spilling his seed on the ground, has no equivalent in Islam: according to Hadith commentaries to the Qur'an, the Prophet Muhammad did not forbid withdrawal, known as *al-azl*.

According to Dr. Shamshiri, the truth is more mundane. "It's the usual fear of side effects, and dislike of using condoms. Which is why sterilization and vasectomies are so popular, once people have the children they desire."

One other country where reliance on withdrawal is similarly high is Italy, which also has low fertility rates and, coincidentally, is also home to a theocracy—albeit a theocracy reduced to 110 acres in which no females reside. Outside the Vatican walls, abortion is legal during the first trimester. In Iran, however, abortion is prohibited, despite suggestions in the Qur'an that the soul does not enter a fetus until the fourth month of pregnancy.

"Abortion is still illegal," says Dr. Shamshiri, now a professor at Tehran's Shahid Beheshti University of Medical Science. "A few years ago, Parliament expanded a rule about saving a mother's life to include therapeutic abortion. It took hard work to pass this."

In the halls of Parliament, religious authorities had confronted her. "Abortion is killing. Why do you write papers supporting it?" the mullahs demanded.

"You asked today if a fetus is a person or not," she replied. "Because, you said, if a fetus is a person, you can't kill it."

They nodded.

"It's worth discussing. But first, I hope you agree that a woman is a person."

On religious grounds, it is difficult for her. "As a matter of women's rights, I support abortion. But personally, I don't agree. I won't do abortions myself. If I have a patient with breast cancer who needs a therapeutic abortion, I refer her. But women should use family planning if they don't want pregnancy. If they do, the need for abortion becomes very rare."

Rare, but never zero. Condoms can break. Antibiotics can lower the effectiveness of pills. And *al-azl* has a notable failure rate. In Iran, as everywhere, women find ways to have an abortion. In wealthy North Tehran, where women see private doctors, it is not hard to find physicians to perform safe abortions. Dr. Shamshiri's concern is for poor women whose contraceptives fail. "We have a street in Tehran where illegal drugs are sold, including abortive drugs. People go there and buy suppositories. That is not safe. That's why it is important to provide women this service."

In 2005, Mahmoud Ahmadinejad, a conservative ex-mayor of Tehran popular among the working class, was elected president of Iran. In 2006, he proclaimed that Iran's family-planning program was un-Islamic. He called for women sixteen or older to leave the universities, get married, and get pregnant. Iran's 70 million population, he said, needed to add 50 million more. His pronouncement helped spur Iranian women to collect a million signatures demanding repeal of all laws that denied them equality, a campaign that won many international women's rights awards.

In June 2009, in what was overwhelmingly believed a rigged result, Ahmadinejad was reelected over a moderate reform candidate. The streets of Iranian cities filled with hundreds of thousands protesters, the majority female. When a philosophy student named Nedā Āghā-Solta⁻n was shot by a member of the Ayatollah's paramilitary volunteer militia, her death, captured on video, was seen by millions around the world.

Iran's so-called Green Revolution, named for the moderate opposition leader's campaign color, became an inspiration for the Arab Spring uprisings. But the regime's brutish response — at least seventy slain, and hundreds more imprisoned — sapped its energy. The massive street gatherings are gone, but as one anonymous participant says, "This revealed how corrupt the Revolution has become. The love we feel for Islam has been undermined by our contempt for the mullahs who mix mosque and state, and are destroying both in the process."

The newly reelected President Ahmadinejad reiterated his call to nearly double the population, which was denounced in Parliament, in the Ministry of Health, and even by some clerics. His offer of 10 million rials—about US$1,000—for every new baby backfired when the math of population increase was explained to him and he realized that his goal, 1.35 million new children per year, would cost more than a billion dollars annually. His modification—the money would be held in trust, and given to the child at age eighteen—earned even more derision, and women ignored it.

"The preference for one or two children, or even none, is now woven into the cultural fabric of the nation," said demographer Abbasi-Shavazi in 2011. "What will happen is what women want. And they don't want three."

"I once read," says Hourieh Shamshiri, "that you save women so that women will save the world. My Muslim religion is a pure one in which woman is as human as man, and their rights are equal. We have a sentence in the Holy Qur'an that means 'We created you from the same soul.' Different shapes, but the same soul."

ii. Carpets

For centuries, the cultural fabric of Iran has been woven by Persian carpet makers. In Turkish rugs, each strand of yarn is knotted around two warp strands, but Persian rugs, with one weft per each warp, are twice as tight. The tightest still made today, in Iranian cities such as Esfahan, have 144 knots per square centimeter. A rug like that, of wool from the bellies of spring lambs, can take two people eight years to finish. In Tehran's Carpet Museum hang old masterpieces created for royal families with 160 knots per centimeter, woven by girls with sharp eyes and tiny fingers. One fabulously complex floral pattern that measures 320 square feet took three people working ten hours day eighteen years to complete— the principal weaver was seventeen when she started, and thirty-five when it was finished.

As a biology student in the 1960s, Esmail Kahrom would stare at rugs in the museum, such as one completed in 1416 that depicts the Tree of Life, a Zoroastrian symbol that predates Islam. Among its branches he recognized turkeys, bustards, vultures, mynahs, owls, doves, thrushes, hoopoes, flamingoes, swallows, quail, parrots, ostriches, and partridges. Around the trunk crawled bears, turtles, alligators, beetles, centipedes, lions, and leopards.

The depictions were so detailed that zoologists could determine each species. He was looking, Kahrom understood, at creatures now extinct in his land. The eyes of ancient carpet weavers are how Iranian biologists today know what once lived here.

Esmail Kahrom was the son of an air force pilot who, like his mother, was one of twelve children. As a boy, his father would take him riding in Khosh Yelagh, a wildlife refuge whose name means good summer pasture, in the eastern Alborz Mountains watershed, just south of the Caspian Sea. The grass there grew so tall that he would lose sight of the park ranger guide and have to stand on his horse's back to see where the stalks were moving, to know which way to go. Khosh Yelagh was then home to the largest population of cheetahs in Iran. The sight of the fleet creatures thrilled him, and he resolved to become a naturalist.

After graduating from the University of Shiraz, he became a field ornithologist with the Department of the Environment, and traveled to every ecosystem in Iran. Eventually he was appointed director of the Bureau of Wildlife, and began a weekly television program that introduced viewers to the natural wonders of their country. The government sent him to England for graduate studies. After receiving his doctorate at the University of Wales, he returned to Iran to teach ecology, both in college and through the media.

His TV documentaries made Esmail Kahrom Iran's best-known naturalist. He took viewers to places like Miankaleh, a forty-eight-kilometer sandy peninsula that is the last stretch of natural shoreline along Iran's eight-hundred-kilometer Caspian seacoast, where half of Iran's 504 bird species are found. In the early seventeenth century, Shah Abbas of Persia's Safavid dynasty once killed 90 leopards and 30 tigers there. In 1830, Naser al-Din Shah of the Qajar dynasty, who had eighty-five wives, wrote that early one spring morning he watched millions of migrating birds darken the skies for four hours. Fifty years later, one of his many sons would take a group of friends to Miankaleh. With newly invented high-powered rifles, they shot 6,000 pheasants, 150 deer, 63 buffaloes, 18 leopards, and 35 tigers.

That same prince later described an area outside the southern city of Shiraz where hundreds of men hunted day and night. "The mountain is so rich in wildlife," he wrote in his memoirs, "that if the numbers of hunters were ten times over, there would still be enough game animals for everybody. We stayed here for two months and when we were leaving, the number of animals was still the same."

"Statements like these," Kahrom told his audiences, "prove that the Qajar hunters never set out to eradicate entire species of wild animals. In fact, they hoped to hunt forever. They considered natural resources such as wildlife and forests to be renewable resources that simply could not be exterminated by man. But all the species they prized are now rare, or threatened, or extinct: the mighty lion, the Caspian tiger, the Iranian wild ass, gazelles, big-horned mountain sheep, leopards, and the cheetah."

"Yes, the cheetah," he says, passing a plate of figs. The walls of his home near Tehran's Islamic Azad University, where he teaches, are trimmed with ornate molding and hung with brass wall sconces and chandeliers. Small Persian rugs cover the hardwood floors. The brick fireplace is flanked by paintings of migrating cranes and the endangered red-breasted goose that winters in Miankaleh. Above the mantle, a nineteenth-century Tabriz tapestry declares in graceful Farsi calligraphy that God is the greatest protector of all.

Whenever Kahrom, a dapper man with a sandy moustache who favors ascots, is confronted by someone demanding to know whether it really matters if cheetahs disappear from the face of the Earth, or if tigers go extinct, he tells them about one particular cheetah.

It was where he'd least expected to encounter one. It was January 2003, and he was visiting America for the first time. A cousin in San Diego had married a schoolteacher, who invited him to observe a sixth-grade class. He was charmed that the teacher had brought an Iranian flag and Iranian coins to show the students. When she next unrolled an exquisite crimson rug, his eyes widened. The rug, he knew immediately, was a pure silk paisley pattern from the holy city of Qom, worth thousands.

"Our guest is an ecologist," she told her students. Ecology, she explained, is the science of how everything on Earth—people, plants, animals, fungi, microbes, rocks, soil, water, and air—is connected. "All over the world, there are people who protect animals and plants so that the connections don't break. Dr. Kahrom is one of them."

There was a knock on the classroom door, and Kahrom gasped along with the sixth-graders as another teacher entered, accompanied by a curator from the San Diego Zoo. The leash he held was attached to a muzzled cheetah.

"There are two populations of cheetahs," said the teacher, "one in Africa, the other in Asia. The Asiatic cheetah today lives only in Iran." Kahrom was amazed that this American woman knew something he wished his own people comprehended.

"What do you think would happen," she asked, "if Asiatic cheetahs disappear from the Earth? Would it be a disaster? Would we be in trouble? Would you still be able to go to school? Will there still be gasoline for your father's car? Will we have electricity and water? Should we be concerned?"

The students agreed that this elegant creature, silent

on its haunches before them, deserved to live. But none thought that their world would come crashing down along with the cheetah's, in the event it didn't.

The teacher turned to the glowing silk Qom rug, draped on an easel. "This beautiful Persian carpet belongs to an Iranian who lives in San Diego. It's made with more than one-and-a-half million knots. It took women years to do that. Now, suppose some boy with a pair of scissors cuts a few knots from its edge. What will happen? Nothing. You will not even notice it.

"Now, suppose that he returns and makes two hundred knots disappear. Probably you still wouldn't notice it among the one-and-a-half million. But what if he keeps doing it? Soon you'll have a small hole. Then it will get bigger, and bigger. Eventually, nothing will be left of this carpet."

Extending her arms, she pointed at the La Jolla foliage outside and at the cheetah that was watching her as raptly as her students and Kahrom. "All this is the carpet of life. You are sitting on it. Each of those knots represents one plant or animal. They, and the air we breathe, the water we drink, and our groceries are not manufactured. They are produced by what we call nature. This rug represents that nature. If something happens in Asia or Africa and a cheetah disappears, that is one knot from the carpet. If you understand that, you'll realize that we are living on a very limited number of species and resources, on which our life depends."

In the Miankaleh Wildlife Refuge, park director Ali Abutalibi has watched the knots unravel all his life. His father, a shepherd in the nearby hills, had to guard his flocks from leopards and wolves. Now maybe ten wolves remain. The last leopard here was killed by a hunter in 2001; four years later, the last tiger; a year after that, the last elk. Without the top predators, the jackals and wild boars exploded. Feral horses and cows roam the preserve, decimating the grasses and berries.

During Abutalibi's boyhood, migrating wetland birds overhead still numbered in thousands. "Swans, geese, pelicans, flamingoes, spoonbills, ducks. Also pheasants, bustards, francolins. We would hunt on horseback. You could kill two hundred birds in ten minutes." Embarrassed, his fingers work his white prayer beads. "That was before I became an environmentalist."

The park, whose willows, alders, and wild pomegranates were once part of a forest that spanned the entire coastline, is now abutted by soy, cotton, rice, and watermelon fields heavily dosed with agrochemicals. An adjacent wetland to the west disappeared under a port facility, where lights that blaze all night chased off thirty thousand nesting shorebirds. An invasion of jellyfish via a shipping canal that connects the Black Sea to the Volga River, which then flows to the Caspian, has devoured 75 percent of the zooplankton. Caught between algae blooms, the fouling from off-shore drilling rigs, and poaching, the 200-million-year-old Caspian sturgeon, source of the world's black caviar, is nearly extinct.

"So many fish are gone," says Abutalibi, looking over the pale green sea. And the creatures that eat them: he now sees a Caspian seal only every few months. He lets local shepherds fish for shad and white trout, limiting them to two apiece, but the poachers who sneak in know no limits.

"There used to be forty hunters here — now there are three hundred," he says, running fingers through thinning curls. "God told the Prophet Nuh[2] to save all the animals because the life of man depends on them. Without them, what will we do? If we kill everything except for cows and chickens, can we live in a world without birds that sing?"

West of the Miankaleh refuge is the city of Ramsar, where in 1971, eighteen nations signed one of the most important global environmental treaties: the

---

2. Noah.

Ramsar Convention on Wetlands of International Importance. Today, there are 164 signatories. Ramsar's own wetlands, however, have all but vanished beneath roads, tea plantations, hotels, and the villas of wealthy Tehranis.

To the east of Miankaleh lies Golestan National Park, Iran's oldest and biggest. Its name means *rose garden*, for its fragrant native flower. In Golestan, mountains are still thick with cypress, cedar, and Persian juniper. This is the largest remnant of Iran's great Hirkani Forest, a relic that escaped freezing during the Ice Ages. Below the conifers are stands of oak, maple, wild cherry, and barberry, and valleys filled with wild saffron. Beyond them are the steppes where, in wetter times, Esmail Kahrom rode through grasslands taller than his mount. Most of the riding here now is done by car: Despite the pleading of every ecologist in Iran, an east-west expressway completed over the last decade now bisects the park.

"This road is our biggest sorrow," says head Golestan environmentalist Jabad Selvari. His clean-shaven cheeks burn when he thinks how easily the highway could have been routed a few miles south. They didn't even build underpasses for the animals. Now, oil tankers from Iraq and buses from Turkey bore through, their diesel roar filling Golestan's canyons and waterfalls. The highway divides breeding populations of gazelles, endangered ibex, elk, roe deer, curly-horned urial sheep, three species of wildcat, and leopards. And it makes it nearly impossible to stop poaching, especially the trapping of sparrow hawks and red kites for the falconry market.

"Rich Arabs and Turks pay up to $60,000 US for these birds," says park superintendant Mohammad Rezah Mullah Abbasi. Smugglers, he says, can hide three falcons, their talons and wings bound, inside hollow truck doors. "We are fanatics like Taliban to preserve nature," he jokes, "if we inspect and find blood or feathers."

But it's no joke to them. The shoulder patches on their khaki uniforms show a leopard and the words *Environmental Guard* in Farsi and English. The leopard is the symbol of their park; every year, they find the skinned bodies.

"In the seventies, when Iran had half our current population," Selvari says, watching a golden eagle swoop over the rippling saffron, "there were still tigers and lions here."

iii. The Missing River

In Iran today, highways are built mainly by companies owned by the Ayatollah's Revolutionary Guards.

After the Iraq war ended, this elite branch of Iran's military began forming corporations to create jobs for itself. Over three decades, it became Iran's biggest conglomerate, with interests in both legitimate business and black-market smuggling, including alcohol, drugs, and allegedly even prostitutes, channeling Iranian girls to Dubai. As the protector of the ruling ayatollahs, it gets first choice of public works contracts.

Most lucrative are dams: Iran is the third biggest dam builder in the world, with six hundred completed and hundreds more under way. "Think of the Revolutionary Guards," says an Iranian scientist who studied in the United States, "as a combination of the U.S. Army Corps of Engineers and the Mafia." Many Iranian dams are built mainly for the huge construction contracts, he says, with little regard for how much water they can actually impound or the damage they wreak. Northwest Iran's Lake Urmia, the world's third largest saltwater lake and both a UNESCO Biosphere Reserve and a Ramsar wetland site, is now half its former size and may disappear altogether, because thirty-five dams have been built on rivers that feed it. When the Ministry of Energy consulted with Esmail Kahrom about the Urmia situation, he warned them that the homes of 14 million people were in danger of being lost to blowing salt, not to mention the habitat of 210 water-fowl species.

Kahrom advised them to stop building ten dams already under way, and release 20 percent of the water behind the others to resuscitate Lake Urmia until rains replenish it and the reservoirs.

"We don't have any water behind the dams," he was told.

"If you don't have any water, then why did you build thirty-five dams? And why you are planning a total of seventy-seven?"

Nevertheless, in 2011 Iran's parliament rejected a motion to increase inflows to Lake Urmia, the biggest lake in the Middle East, to save it from extinction. Should it dry completely, scientists fear that it could release 8 billion tons of windblown salt storms over cities in Iran, Iraq, Turkey, and Azerbaijan.

In the central Iranian city of Esfahan, three environmental scientists gather in a house on Abbas Abad Street to discuss a tragedy even more imminent and possibly greater than Urmia. Abbas Abad, lined with plane trees that form a magnificent arch, is often called the most beautiful street in one of the world's most beautiful cities. The seat of Persian government during the sixteenth-century Safavid dynasty, Esfahan is a marvel of Islamic architecture. The overpowering

Shah Mosque in Naghsh-e Jahan Square, the world's second biggest after Beijing's Tiananmen, is an astonishment in blue mosaic. But even more than its domes and minarets, the loveliness of Esfahan derives from five covered stone bridges over the Zāyanderūd, a river that flows across the city.

Along the Zāyanderūd's banks, girls in black headscarves glide on Rollerblades over paths that wind through a green belt of plane trees, weeping willows, and topiary shrubbery. The paths lead to the bridges, such as double-decked Khaju, with its cool arcade where picnickers take tea on broad stone benches and watch the sunset framed through the bridge's arches. Built in 1560, the arches were engineered acoustically so that when Sufi poetry is recited or music played on summer evenings, it can be heard along the bridge's entire length.

A mile farther downstream, it is believed impossible for a couple strolling by night on the Si-o-se Po Bridge, its thirty-three arches reflected on the Zāyanderūd's water, not to fall in love. Except since 2008, there has been no water. The riverbed is now dry sand, where men cross on bicycles and boys play soccer.

"For a few weeks during winter they open the sluice gates on the dams to keep the foundations of the bridges wet, or they'll crumble."

Khaju Bridge, Esfahan, Iran

Mehdi Basiri, a retired professor of environmental science at the Esfahan University of Technology, is meeting with Ahmad Khatoonabadi, who teaches sustainable development, and plant geneticist Aghafakhr Mirlohi. The three have formed Green Message, an environmental NGO whose mission is to get through to decision makers. They haven't had much luck.

"In any ecosystem," says Basiri, "the limiting factor is water. But the government never thinks about it. In 1966, Esfahan had two hundred thousand people. Today, 3.5 million. There is huge pressure on the aquifers and river. But what do they do? They build steel mills, aircraft plants, stonecutting and brickmaking plants, all demanding water."

"They plant rice, a crop that doesn't belong here, which evaporates more water," says Khatoonabadi.

Worst, they built pipelines north and east, to carry Zāyanderūd water to the desert cities of Qom and Yazd. "It's just like Lake Urmia," says Basiri. "They build forty dams, dry it up, then ask the government for money to build a two-hundred-kilometer pipeline from somewhere else to bring in water to refill it." On the outskirts of Qom and Yadz, well-connected landowners are irrigating new pistachio groves. "And now they're building steel mills and tile factories there, too."

"They convert rangeland to orchards, leaving no water for native plants," says Mirlohi. "The water table drops, the land settles. The Si-o-se Po Bridge is damaged. The historical buildings are in danger."

But it's not just about buildings and bridges, he says. "I think we have only a few years to survive."

Basiri's living room grows quiet as the men sip chai. They have a petition with the signatures of thousands of people brave enough to demand that water be returned to the river that defines their city. "But a third of the national budget is now used for building dams. When so much money is involved, you can't stop it."

A mile away, in an echoey, fluorescent-lit community house basement, four women are trying, regardless. The leader of the group is a middle-aged, self-described nature lover; one is a dentist; another is a hydrologist; the other a recent graduate in ecology. They are with the Esfahan chapter of one of Iran's fiercest NGOs, the Women's Society Against Environmental Pollution. It was founded by Mahlagha Mallah, a University of Tehran librarian who, in 1973, was puzzled by a book on an unfamiliar topic: environmental pollution. Not knowing where to catalog it, she ended up reading it cover to cover. A granddaughter of Iran's first feminist writer, Bibi Khanoom Astarabadi, Mallah became a pioneer in the Iranian environmental movement. Revolution and war with Iraq interrupted her efforts, but during the 1990s, at age seventy-four, she began traveling around Iran to organize chapters of her new NGO.

"Women," she told recruits, "are instinctive teachers. We're also the world's main consumers: most advertisements try to attract us. We produce the most household waste. But just as population control rests with us, we can cure our shopping disease and our polluting, and educate our children to care for the environment."

Still vigorous at ninety-four, she is heroic inspiration to these women who meet monthly to plot how to save their country from itself. They sit in a circle of white plastic chairs, wearing sandals, light manteaux, and colored hijabs, joined by two men in polo shirts: an architect and the dentist's student son. Usually, about forty appear for meetings; tonight is a special session, because on top of their other travails, there is something new to discuss.

Before the Ahmadinejad years, Iran finally seemed to be relaxing its grip on its own people. A reformist president, Mohammad Khatami, was even broaching rapprochement with the West. New voices flourished, and dozens of environmental groups formed. In a 2001 eco-convention attended by hundreds, the Esfahan women heard geologists explain that their river was heading for disaster. They began holding demonstrations and Earth Day events in schools to warn people about the threat to the Zāyanderūd.

Then, in 2008, the river actually dried up. Dazed, they stood on the lovely bridges at night and saw no reflection, only darkness. This, they figured, would finally mobilize people. Except, like the scientists' group, Green Message, they found their NGO accused of being Western spies. News columnists called them hoodlums for wanting to steal water from thirsty people in Qom and Yadz.

"We have an address where people can electronically sign the petition to save the Zāyanderūd, but now they block any e-mail that has the word *petition* in it," says the nature lover.

"School principals now say we need authorization from the Ministry of Education in Tehran to talk to children about the environment," says the dentist.

"When we hand out our magazine, *Cry of the Earth*, we get hassled by men demanding to know who we are," says the hydrologist. She stands and paces. "We get hauled into police headquarters and grilled about our environmental pamphlets. We say: 'We're glad you asked. They're about recycling, tree-planting, water conservation, and solar energy. Very dangerous.' We tell them that their city, the most beautiful in Iran and one of most beautiful in the world, is now one of the most polluted. And that their river is dying and the climate is changing and WHAT DO THEY INTEND TO DO ABOUT IT?" She sits down, reddening.

"Even in Pakistan NGOs can freely contact people," says the dentist.

They fear that their country has become unhinged. "A new subway is tunneling under Esfahan's most gorgeous historical buildings. We keep telling them the vibrations will crack, or even collapse the monuments," says the architect. "But their ears do not hear."

The one thing that Iran's authorities have done right, all here agree, is to create the health care and family-planning system. Of course population must be controlled—the land is bursting. Except for the group leader, who is the oldest present and mother of three, the others have two or fewer. "But we're not allowed to do anything else useful without their permission."

And now, even permission to control their bodies and decide reproductive matters for themselves is suddenly in doubt.

Just recently, rumor has it, the Ayatollah Khamenei said that people shouldn't worry about a population crisis until Iran has 120 million people, or 150 million. Maybe then, he added, it will be time to think about the consequences.

"What?" exclaims the dentist. "He's the one who

issued a fatwa about tubal ligations and vasectomies! During my rural service, one day I saw fifteen women get their tubes tied. This is the mentality that Ahmadinejad has put in his head. Can't anyone see what the pressure of all these people is doing?"

"This is the countdown for the Iranian environment," says the group's leader, her fingers twisting the ends of her pale green hijab. "Once again, women will have to pay."

When the Esfahan women met that night in 2011, Ramadan had just ended. Life in Iran resumed, only with more difficulty: the West, pressured by Israeli and impending American electoral politics, applied ever harsher economic sanctions to try to dissuade the Islamic Republic from developing a nuclear program. Outside the country, it was believed that Iran was building atomic bombs; although the International Atomic Energy Association had found no evidence of attempts to develop nuclear weaponry since 2003, Iran resisted giving inspectors full access to military facilities for verification. Within the country, however, where dying rivers were dammed to squeeze every kilowatt from diminished rainfall, the nuclear program seemed to be about what Iran insisted it was: making energy.

Although Iran had designed the world's most enlightened and effective family-planning program, it still had decades to wait until the immense baby boom generation of the Iraq war years began to die off and numbers returned to sustainable levels. In the meantime, its 75 million people and its industries demanded electricity, and Israeli rhetoric was goading Iranian hawks to call for nuclear arms as well as power plants. A breathless world wondered if these two enemies would spark a firestorm worse than even the heat of the unmoored climate.

Another Ramadan came, and the Supreme Leader made the rumor official. The family-planning policy, declared Ayatollah Khamenei, "made sense twenty years ago. But its continuation in later years was wrong."

"Population control programs belonged to the past," the health minister told the press. Effective immediately, funding for family planning was removed from the national budget, and applied to encouraging larger families. The Ayatollah's new goal for Iran was 150 to 200 million people. A bill was introduced in Parliament to return the legal marriage age for girls to nine.

Speculation over what changed his mind included fear of another war requiring a mighty army, this time with Israel or even America. Some guessed it was a signal to the West that Iran wasn't bothered by its sanctions, but rather was abundantly prepared— for abundance. But the Ayatollah himself gave a more prosaic and parsimonious explanation: Demographers, he said, calculated that if the birth rate stayed the same, by 2032 Iran would face a declining, aging population. That would mean more medical and social security costs for seniors, and fewer productive younger people to pay for them. After twenty-plus years of birth control, it was time for a new policy for the next twenty.

President Ahmadinejad's earlier calls for women to be more fruitful had been fruitless, and many doubted that the new policy would have any abrupt effect. With unemployment and inflation soaring under the West's sanctions, income was down and couples were even postponing marriage, let alone children. Besides, even if birth control were outlawed, the Revolutionary Guards' smuggling apparatus would doubtless leap into the breach. The Guards and the Ayatollahs were locked into a symbiosis that neither could easily break: the clerics' increasingly unpopular regime depended on the Guards' protection, and purchased their loyalty by turning a blind eye to their limitless enrichment.

What would not continue, however, would be premarital classes, or teams of surgeons flying into the hinterlands to perform free contraceptive surgery for millions of Iranians who otherwise couldn't afford it. No more free IUDs, pills, or injections.

After years of being able to decide how many children to have, the vast majority of Iranian couples had determined they wanted no more than two. But that was no longer convenient for Iran's military-industrial theocracy.

And if Iranian women wouldn't choose to have more children, the regime, by withholding the means, would henceforth be making that decision for them.

[Author's note: "Use our names!" members of the Women's Society against Environmental Pollution insisted when I met with them in Esfahan. Later, however, circumstances in Iran deteriorated, especially with regards to the national family-planning program they cherished, so I've withheld their identities. This is entirely my decision, and neither a reflection on them nor on their courage. —AW]

PART FOUR

CHAPTER 13

Shrink and Prosper

i. Contraction

"I will do my best," promises the little white bear. "I will carry you," it continues in the politest Japanese, "as though you were a princess."

The bear's sex is unclear, its voice falling in the range that overlaps tenor and contralto. From its gracefully tapered waist, suggestive of a female nurse, it bends forward over a man—far from a princess—who lies on a hospital bed in a large windowless room. The bright green floor is polished so highly that it reflects the bear's round ears, big black eyes, crinkly smile, and smooth white skin.

It extends two slim paws. One forearm slides under the patient's knees, while the other reaches under his back. Behind it, Susumu Sato, a young engineer with an unruly crew cut and black-rimmed glasses, reaches to touch a spot on the polar bear's left triceps, and it moves closer. Three men who are watching audibly inhale. Gently, the bear lifts and straightens until the patient is suspended over the floor, cradled in its arms.

"Is it all right?" asks Sato. A silver ballpoint protrudes from a penholder on his left sleeve.

"Quite comfortable," the man replies. To be snug against the bear's well-padded chest is, in fact, oddly comforting.

The bear's name is Riba II, meaning Robot for Interactive Body Assistance, Second Edition. Accord-

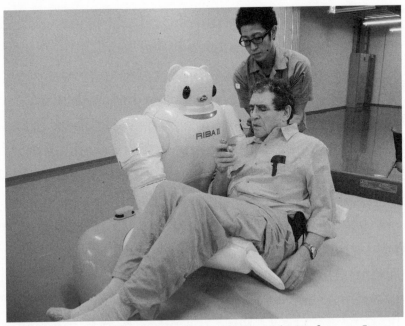

Riba II and author, Nagoya Science Park, Aichi Prefecture, Japan
PHOTOGRAPH BY JUNKO TAKAHASHI

ing to its inventors, it is the world's first robot that can lift a human in its arms. Now it pivots on rollers concealed in its wheeled base—no rear paws—and glides soundlessly over the shiny green floor to a waiting wheelchair. On its shoulders are tiny blinking green lights. "They're just decorative," says chief engineer Shijie Guo, who follows anxiously behind, his hair falling onto his forehead. Now comes the hard part, but RIBA II is the least nervous creature in the room—and it actually does seem like a creature, and not just in the Shinto sense that everything contains a spirit. Almost tenderly, the bear sets its human cargo onto the chair. Its right arm carefully lowers his legs, then slides away. Sato presses a rubber sensor on its left forearm. The bear straightens up.

"I'm finished," it announces.

Everybody in the room exhales and claps. They are in the Nagoya Science Park, where RIBA II was built jointly by RIKEN, Japan's oldest scientific research and development firm, and Tokai Rubber Industries. Since 1929, Tokai Rubber has mainly made automotive parts, such as hoses and wiper blades. But Japan is the first country to be facing the inevitable fate of other developed nations, and its industries are shifting accordingly. Already, more than 60 percent of the world's industrial assembly robots are from Japan, and the reason is no accident.

*　·　*　　*

What the Ayatollah Khamenei fears for Iran is already happening in Japan: a country with below-replacement growth is now reaching the end of the momentum that kept its numbers rising for two generations after its fertility plummeted. In Japan's case, however, there was no intentional program to curb runaway population growth. Like Iran, it had just suffered through a terrible war, albeit one of its own making.

In 1931, Japan, a mountainous country with only 15 percent of its land suitable for agriculture, found itself in an unprecedented situation: Its population had grown to 65 million, far more than it could feed. It was already importing soybeans from Manchuria, the Chinese region bordering Korea, which also had iron and coal that resource-poor Japan needed. With China weakened by internal strife during the early Mao years, the temptation to invade was irresistible.

As Germany would soon similarly conclude about its neighbor Poland, Japan saw thinly settled Manchuria as a place to move surplus population. But one invasion led to another, and by 1937, Japanese expansionism had pushed deeper into China. In 1941, bent on controlling the entire Asian Pacific, it attacked the United States at Pearl Harbor.

Four years later, Japan's dreams of empire were dead. Its defeated soldiers returned to their wives, and predictably, a baby boom followed. Unlike the victorious United States, whose armaments industry had pulled it out of the Depression, Japan's economy was wrecked. Nevertheless, over the next five years its wartime population of 72 million spurted to 83 million.

The country that couldn't feed itself two decades earlier now had millions on the verge of starvation. By the late 1940s, hundreds of thousands of Japanese mothers desperate to feed their children were seeking illegal abortions, with the usual percentage of unfortunate outcomes. Until then, legal abortions involved a complicated process to verify an emergency. Now, faced with a nationwide emergency, in 1948 Japan passed the Eugenic Protection Law, legalizing contraception, abortion, and sterilization for health reasons.

A year later, with the crisis unabated, the law was extended to permit abortions and family planning for economic reasons. Thus, Japan cut off its postwar baby boom. Birth rates soon hovered near replacement. The country's economy struggled back. In the 1950s, the phrase "Made in Japan" was mocked by the victors across the Pacific as synonymous with *cheap,* but the victors kept buying. Gradually, Japan's humble industries evolved into electronics and automobile manufacturing that earned billions and restored its respect. Wealth financed education, including for women, and fertility rates dropped further, to under 1.4 children per female.

Which is why RIKEN and Tokai Rubber are making robots—specifically, a nice white teddy bear robot that can carefully cradle elderly people in its padded arms, soothe them with courtesy and a secure embrace, and move them from bed to chair and ultimately to the most critical challenge: the bathroom.

"We have to do this," says chief engineer Guo, "because there is a double problem to solve: Soon Japan will have many more old people who have trouble moving by themselves, and many fewer young people available to help them. There is already a shortage of geriatric nurses. It is hard to lift people forty times a day while working two shifts in twenty-four hours. Half of elderly caregivers complain of back pain. We'll need robots for all the jobs people don't want to do, because there will not be enough workers."

So far, Riba II takes a minute and a half to pick people up from bed and deposit them in the wheelchair. "A human usually takes ten seconds. We have to get under a minute to be acceptable." After lifting, nurses say that dealing with adult diapers is their hardest task. Guo took a class in how to clean up geriatric patients. "It's a tough one," he admits. Then there's communication: much R&D has gone into what the robot should say to people. "It has to talk, to make the patient feel safe. This one can identify voices, but only recognizes some simple words. But we plan for it to greet people, to do therapeutic massage, even to sing to lonely old people."

Whether technology can meet such human psychological needs remains to be seen, but something has to deal with the larger demographic dilemma that Riba II was invented to help solve. Western Europe is watching closely to see what will happen here, because Japan is the first to reach the end of its demographic transition—when high mortality and high birthrates both turn to low. Japan's first shrunken generation—born in the late forties and early fifties, when Japanese severely curtailed their reproduction—is now entering retirement, and members of the generation before them are entering their final years.

With nearly the world's highest life expectancy—until the March 2011 earthquake and tsunami that hit Fukushima and surrounding prefectures killed twenty thousand people in one day, it was *the* highest—its elderly population will continue to boom. (Japan's 79.4 years for men and 85.9 years for women is only slightly behind Hong Kong.) The U.S. Census Bureau projects that by 2040 there will one Japanese centenarian for every new Japanese baby. But long before that, as the large generation that preceded the demographic downsizing passes on, Japan's numbers will suddenly plunge.

This demographic destiny cannot be reversed, and has already begun. In 2006, for the first time since World War II, Japan recorded more deaths than births. Its population peaked at just over 128 million. Since then, it has fallen each year; by 2012, it was at 126.5 million and dropping. Before 2060, even if life expectancy continues to rise, Japan will be back to around 86 million, which was its population in 1950.

There is a quick fix to looming labor problems like Japan's, one that another country whose population is already declining—Cuba—is contemplating. Cuba's 11 million are diminishing due both to emigration and to low fertility rates resulting from a high percentage of female university graduates, plus decades of economic difficulty, universal health coverage, and legal abortion to back up family planning. To shore up its contracting labor force, Cuba is considering wooing immigrants from nations with even less favorable economics, such as Haiti.

Likewise, immigrants should fill Europe's labor breach in coming decades. Despite below-replacement birthrates, in 2012 Germany's population actually grew by nine hundred thousand, mainly due to immigration from eastern Europe made possible by EU membership. But Germany's first wave of immigrant labor—thousands of Turks, imported after the Berlin Wall cut off the supply of East German migrants—has been less easy to absorb. Today, there are 4 million Turks in Germany, a source of unresolved cultural tension and tightened immigration policies. In 2010, German chancellor Angela Merkel told a meeting of Christian Democratic Union Party youth, "At the start of the '60s we invited the guest-workers to Germany. We kidded ourselves for a while that they wouldn't stay, that one day they'd go home. That isn't what happened. And of course the tendency was to say: let's be *multikulti* and live next to each other and enjoy being together, [but] this concept has failed, failed utterly."[1]

The Cold War that cleaved Germany shortened its postwar baby boom, and the advent of birth control pills nearly halved birthrates on both sides of the Iron Curtain. Reunification of East and West Germany in 1990 only seemed to further depress fertility. Even tempting couples with €2,000 a year for having a second child hasn't made a difference. German working mothers complain that with inadequate day care, school days that end as early as 1:00 p.m.

---

1. Source of English translation: Connolly, Kate. "Angela Merkel Declares Death of German Multiculturalism." *The Guardian* (UK), October 17, 2010.

make it even more complicated to have children. The result is rock-bottom birthrates, and a population aging as fast as Japan's.

Should the rise of xenophobic political parties continue, European immigration rates could lower. But immigration so far has never been an option for Japan, which deeply values its largely homogeneous population: fewer than 2 percent of Japanese residents are foreign-born. One rationale offered for robot nurses is that they aren't burdened with cultural differences or unpleasant wartime histories that elderly Japanese might associate with East Asian health-care workers. Although some Japanese accuse their country of racism, most agree that shared cultural values are why Japanese society functions so smoothly, why its cities are so orderly, and why crime in Japan is so low.

And now it will have a low population to match, making it a laboratory for the question we all will face if we decide — or if nature decides for us — that to reduce human impact for our safety and survival, we must reduce the number of people on the planet. If we were any other species, as long as our numbers didn't drop low enough to endanger our gene pool, bringing our population into a more compatible balance with the rest of nature would be sufficient. But we are more complicated than that. We gather into societies, some as small as our own families, some as large as nations or multinational corporations, that thrive by trading with each other. Unlike nesting birds or pods of dolphins, however, we are not content with merely thriving. We always want more.

The measure of nearly every economy that humans have designed has been defined by whether or not it grows. The exceptions—potlatch societies of the Pacific Northwest; co-op communities—may have much to teach us, but they are so rare as to prove the rule. The business news judges how healthy the economy is by whether housing starts rose or fell this month: Never mind that each new house pushes sprawl ever farther, chews up landscape, and requires more resources to provide plumbing, sewers, electricity, and roads. That house represents profit for developers and real estate brokers, and jobs for carpenters, masons, plumbers, electricians, painters, carpet layers, landscapers, paving crews, and furnishers. Maintenance during its lifespan will create even more jobs. And the economy will grow on.

So what happens if there are fewer of us, needing fewer homes and fewer things? What happens during the transition to a smaller society, with fewer consumers every year—and fewer laborers paying into welfare coffers to support a surplus of unproductive, needy elderly people?

And what happens if we actually reach some optimum number of humans who can harvest and recycle resources at a replenishable pace, so that we achieve equilibrium with the planet that supports us? To maintain such an ideal level would mean never growing beyond it.

Can we do that? Can we have prosperity without growth?

Japan has no choice but to become the first modern society to try.

———

"Paradoxically," says Akihiko Matsutani, "our shrinking situation could end up being beneficial. We have to change our business model. That usually takes a long time, but we can't wait. This is the moment we have to change."

Matsutani, professor emeritus at one of Japan's premier economics schools, the National Graduate Institute for Policy Studies, has been saying things like this for years. Until recently, he's gotten scant attention: No one has wanted to hear that Japan's economy was demographically doomed to downsize. But now, events 180 miles north of his Tokyo institute have abruptly forced the entire nation to reconsider living beyond its means.

The moment Matsutani refers to is the aftermath

of a 9.0-magnitude earthquake on March 11, 2011, off the Tohoku Peninsula in northeastern Japan, which pushed a tidal wave over the sea barriers at the Fukushima Daiichi Nuclear Power Plant. Three reactors exploded and melted down, and everyone living in a fifty-mile radius of the damaged facility had to evacuate.

That fifty-mile radius included some of Japan's richest farmland: until the disaster, Fukushima was known as the Kingdom of Fruits. A bunch of Fukushima grapes would sell for ¥2,500—over US$30— that is, until they vanished from the market because no one would buy them. The same for its sweet akatsuki peaches and its apples, cucumbers, and turnips.

The tragedy also caused Japanese to ask if it was wise to build nuclear plants near seismic faults and coastlines—a description that applied to most of the fifty-four atomic reactors that provided nearly one-third of Japan's electricity. In the building where Matsutani has his office, months later elevators were still off because of post-Fukushima energy restrictions, as were the air-conditioning and the electric toilet seats with their heated bidets, so beloved in Japan.

Akihiko Matsutani is shocked by the terrible losses his country has sustained, but not surprised. "People who keep saying that Japan should be like France, which gets most of its power from nuclear energy, forget that France isn't in an earthquake zone. But now that this accident has happened, we have an opportunity to do something positive." That something is learning to live within its limits, which both Fukushima and the shrinking Japanese population are forcing them to do. "This will actually be good for Japan," he insists.

Matsutani is the author of a book whose title makes progrowth economists shudder: *Shrinking-Population Economics: Lessons from Japan,* a copy of which sits on his uncluttered desk. On a blank piece of paper he sketches the iconic symbol of demography: a pyramid, which he divides into three sections. "In most countries, the tip of the pyramid represents the elderly. The middle"—he shades this portion with his pen—"is the active portion of the population, the labor force. The base, the biggest portion, is the young people. Babies, children, students."

Then he flips the drawing upside down. "This is Japan. Fewer children. Lots of elderly." He points to the shaded middle zone. "As more of these move up, we'll have fewer workers to replace them."

Recently, a research group at Tohoku University warned that in a thousand years, Japan's childbearing will cease—statistically anyway. They posted a simulated "Child Population Web Clock" showing that every one hundred seconds, the number of Japanese children drops by one—they're not dying, but growing up, and fewer babies are replacing them. At that rate, they conclude, "Japan would have only one child in May 3011. By the next year, therefore, there would be no children in Japan."

These kinds of horror stories about Japan's subreplacement fertility are nonsense, says Matsutani. Japan is certainly top-heavy with old people, and becoming more so. But once the age bubble bursts with the old, high-fertility generations dying off, subsequent generations will even out, and the pyramid will become a cube as the number of children will be closer to the numbers who are passing on. People won't stop having babies, and if fertility readjusts toward two children per couple—a reasonable outcome in a less-crowded world—population would stabilize.

However, he warns, reshaping demographic geometry from triangular to rectangular in a country with such long life spans takes at least a century. Either way, stable or shrinking, the population would not be growing, which raises a big question:

What happens to the economy?

Traditional economics preaches perpetual growth as a self-evident truth, even though nothing, save God or the universe, can possibly be perpetual—and there's some doubt about the universe. But assuming an ever-expanding economy were possible, there are only two ways to achieve it: keep inventing more new products (or new versions of old ones) and keep finding new consumers.

Being endlessly creative is hard. Being endlessly competitive to win all the customers works only as long as there are still more customers left—unless, of course, a growing population keeps giving birth to more new consumers. This is one of two reasons why most economists traditionally favor population growth. The other is bigger labor pools: the more workers competing for jobs, the less companies have to pay them.

Unfortunately for those economists—and for us, as long as the system works their way—on a finite planet, an economy dependent on constant growth is no more perpetual than a chain letter or pyramid scheme, which always needs more people buying in. Eventually, there aren't any more, and everything collapses. Or the raw stuff to make whatever's being sold grows scarce, and the substitutes aren't as good, or they run out, too.

Akihiko Matsutani is convinced that his shrinking country can and will have a viable economy, because Japan has no other choice. But it isn't as simple as fewer people needing fewer things. Although Matsutani agrees that a smaller population means less pressure on resources and land, he cautions that the transition to fewer people will place different strains on the environment.

"Suppose you have a sewage treatment plant for a million people," he says. It's an example he knows well; along with his economics degrees, he has a doctorate in civil engineering. "Then suppose the population drops to nine hundred thousand. You can't just remove 10 percent of the pipes. Even if population drops by half, you still have to maintain 100 percent of the infrastructure. That won't be easy when we have fewer laborers."

An economical alternative might be to abandon huge treatment facilities in favor of individual purification tanks for each house. "Centralized sewage treatment is probably better for the environment, but it will be impossible to maintain. So we may have to revise our standards, and accept a dirtier environment."

But he's encouraged that personal lifestyles need not suffer in a Japan with fewer people. A leaner economy, he says, will bring its own advantages.

"In the beginning, companies will try to save by cutting wages or workers, but they'll soon realize that laborers will have become more valuable, and they'll want to keep the ones they have. So lowering wages won't work. What will work instead is higher pay, but fewer hours. Right now, we work long hours for lower pay. Laborers will be pleased to have more leisure time. Since World War II ended, we've been obsessed with gross domestic product. But GDP has no direct bearing on living standards in a shrinking population economy."

The hope he sees is the chance to define prosperity by people's quality of life rather than what money can buy. In this paradoxical nation, where the world's most populous metropolitan area—Greater Tokyo, with 35 million people—coexists with the fastest-shrinking population, he sees a perfect opportunity for the country to decentralize.

"We'll have to think in terms of smaller systems, not a big government taking care of everything with big infrastructure. Smaller cities will make more sense. When population grows, prosperity means going to Disneyland once a month, and buying too much and throwing away too much. When population shrinks, prosperity is going on picnics, or taking your children camping. You don't throw things away—your values change from constant new things to things that last."

What will inspire investors in a shrinking world? Before he started teaching, Matsutani spent twenty-seven years in Japan's Finance Ministry. "Just like sewers, finance will get worse until we learn to adjust to a smaller scale. We will go to perpetual bonds — in a sense, we're already doing it. Japan's debt is trillions of yen. It's impossible to repay, so we just pay the interest. Perpetual bonds would work like that. We won't be as wealthy as when population was growing, but that doesn't mean we can't have profit. Total productivity will be less with fewer workers, but per-capita productivity won't change. The number of workers drops 10 percent, so do sales, and so do profits. But per person, it all remains the same."

In fact, something that traditional economists have ignored — especially those in Europe wringing their hands over declining populations — is that both Japan's and Germany's economies began recovering from a decade of slump and recession in the early years of the new millennium, at the same time their populations began to contract. By 2010, Germany had record economic growth, more than twice the rest of the European Union.

In Russia, precipitously dropping numbers predating even Japan's have panicked economic advisors to the Kremlin. Russia's birthrate began its descent with the 1991 collapse of communism and the loss of the Soviet Union's cradle-to-grave assurances of work, education, and shelter. Add to that Russia's high divorce rate, and since the USSR dissolved, Russia's population has dropped by 5 million. But even more significant than low fertility is the grim state of Russian health. Russia's incidence of syphilis is several hundred times higher than in western Europe. Its HIV rates are the world's fastest growing; by 2020, up to 10 percent of the population could be infected. Cardiovascular deaths are at epidemic levels, and the incidence of mortal violence and accidents is a dozen times higher than Britain's. Both heart disease and fatal injuries are linked to the Russian addiction to vodka, a national rate of alcoholism unmatched anywhere, which has only worsened since communism ended. Russia's life expectancy is about the same as Pakistan's, which is lower than most of Africa's.

At the same time, Russia's economy, fueled by its vast oil and gas reserves, has grown vigorously in the new millennium, resulting in the curious anomaly of Moscow, capital of the country with, until recently, the world's fastest-falling population, having the world's highest population of billionaires.[2]

Such numbers confound the conventional wisdom

---

2. In 2009, the population of Russia rose for the first time in fifteen years, and has increased by a few thousand per year since then. The growth is due not to rising birth rates, but to immigrants from other former Soviet republics.

that having fewer people spells doom for robust economies. Nevertheless, Akihiko Matsutani's book about how shrinking Japan can remain prosperous has attracted scant attention from his country's financial circles and other economists.

"They'd rather translate American and European books about how to generate growth. They talk about rebuilding the fishing ports destroyed in the typhoon—except it will take up to twenty years to do that, and in twenty years only a quarter of the fishermen will still be alive, so three-fourths of the port facilities won't be necessary. Such simple discussion isn't taking place. People don't want to accept that things they know have changed. Some will say, okay, we can let more immigrant labor in. But at this point, we would need 24 million immigrants by 2030 to maintain our workforce at today's size. That won't happen."

What *will* happen, he says, is what's already happening. Not just to Japan, but to the world. "World population is still growing, but agricultural output isn't. Output from the seas is shrinking. Add those two together, and we get famines."

He looks at his glass-fronted bookshelves, filled with copies of his book. "In the animal world, when population exceeds its limits, species start reducing. Probably that is what will happen to us humans.

Maybe we're lucky here in Japan, because we're not waiting until disaster reduces our population."

———

In the island city-state of Singapore, one of the world's most developed nations with one of the world's lowest birthrates — 1.1 children per fertile woman — August 9 is celebrated as National Day, marking independence. In 2012, Mentos Singapore, a division of the multinational mint manufacturer, launched a promotion declaring the evening of August 9 to be "National Night" — during which, televised commercials urged, men should "raise the flag" and married couples should "go all the way for Singapore." Singapore had already sweetened this call to patriotic pillow duty with the world's most lavish baby bonuses: $4,000 apiece for a couple's first two children, and $6,000 each for the third and fourth. The government also matches, dollar for dollar, parental contributions to a child's savings account, up to $6,000 apiece for the first and second child, $12,000 for the third and fourth child, and $18,000[3] for each child thereafter.

During the 1970s, Singapore's government, fearing that the city-state would become overcrowded,

———

3. 1 Singapore dollar is approximately US80¢.

had tried to convince everyone to "Stop at Two." That succeeded so well that by the mid-1980s they were trying to reverse it, and have been ever since. But to no avail: not even the extravagant baby bribes have tempted Singaporeans to have more children.

The Mentos campaign, set to a rap song—"it's National Night, so let's make fireworks ignite, let's make Singapore's birthrate right"—would have had even less chance in Japan. Each year, not only the number of babies but the number of Japanese marriages drops, further depressing childbirth in a culture where having a child out of wedlock is almost unknown. The falling marriage rates are often attributed to the disappearance of assured lifetime employment, once a staple with Japanese corporations. Without that security, fewer are willing to risk starting a family. Government projections now assume that 36 percent of the current generation of young Japanese women will never have children.

On the eighth floor of an apartment tower in Takanawa, a posh central Tokyo neighborhood, Keiko, a thirty-five-year-old mother of a two-year-old daughter, greets her visitors. Two are friends who have brought their own daughters for a playdate; the third, who is unmarried, is a Spanish-language court interpreter (the accused are mainly Latin American drug mules). Keiko, round-faced with short dark hair, wears a gray T-shirt, capri pants, and a platinum wedding ring; Nanako, her daughter, is a miniature of her mother.

It is a Monday afternoon; Keiko's husband, an investment counselor at a finance company, left at 7:00 a.m. and won't return until 10:00 p.m. Keiko also used to work there. They had been married ten years when Nanako was born. "We didn't think we needed a child. We were having fun. Raising a kid is so much work, and none of my friends wanted the responsibility. But we decided to give our aging parents a grandchild."

They have no regrets—nor any intention of having more, she says, hugging Nanako, who's joined her on the charcoal gray couch. The apartment they own has maple floors and white shag rugs, but just two rooms, plus a compact kitchen. "It's hard enough with three of us. The size of a house pretty much limits the number of children." Most of her friends have just one. "A few have two. But more have none."

She hands Nanako a rice ball from a bowl on the granite coffee table, sends her back to her playmates, and confesses the extreme form of birth control she and her husband use to assure that they don't have another:

"Not having sex."

It's not as radical as it sounds, she says. "Frankly, Japanese people don't have sex much anymore."

That would definitely guarantee population decline. But surely there are other ways in Japan to prevent conception? "Of course," says Junko, the court interpreter. "But not having sex is the most common. Women here don't like Western medicine—I would never take pills, because of the side effects. And many women believe that an operation changes their hormones. Some use condoms, but young people don't like to. So either they abort, or do without sex."

"It's more than that," says Keiko. "Sex isn't how to prove affection in a marriage. When we were dating, we needed to do it to confirm our love. But when people are married and become a family, they affirm their love just by living in the same house, eating the same food."

All these women—young, healthy, and quite lovely—nod in agreement. "Westerners can't believe it," says Keiko. "My German girlfriend keeps asking how is it conceivable that we don't have sex? But I don't miss it. I don't feel dried up, but I also don't feel that desire when I see my husband or any other attractive man. I'm very satisfied with my life. It's enough just for us to sleep together."

Again, no one argues. "My male friends say sex is just a form of recreation," says Junko. "Like going to a baseball game or the movies—in this case, to a bordello. Once a guy has a family, he doesn't see his wife as a woman anymore. She's family, like his mother or sister. Guys don't have sex with them, either."

A 2011 Japanese government survey showed that 36 percent of Japanese males aged sixteen to nineteen were either not interested in, or actually "despised," sex. A term for young men more enamored of animated video games than live female humans is "herbivores" — the implication being that, by comparison, dynamic Japanese career women are "carnivores."

"Japanese men are getting weak," says Junko. She glances out the picture window, where Japan's most blatant phallic symbol, the Eiffel-shaped Tokyo Tower, is spewing potent radio and TV signals. "And women don't have as many needs as men." More nods.

She laughs. "Our German girlfriend wouldn't agree."

ii. Growth-free Prosperity

Environmentally attuned Western economists have been mulling an economy of prosperity without growth for decades, especially since publication of *The Limits to Growth* and Paul and Anne Ehrlich's work. To the University of Maryland's Herman Daly, the dean of steady-state economists, it's simply the law of diminishing returns: produce too many goods, and they're not so good anymore.

"We then have uneconomic growth, producing 'bads' faster than goods—making us poorer, not richer," Daly, a former senior economist at the World Bank, has written. "Once we pass the optimal scale, growth becomes stupid in the short run and impossible to maintain in the long run."

Long before him, Thomas Robert Malthus, John Stuart Mill, and Adam Smith warned that economic growth, like everything else on Earth, was subject to resource limits. But identifying what doesn't work is one thing; figuring out what will, and how to transition to it, is another.

There's already an excellent model for the steady-state economy that Daly and his ecological economist colleagues have long espoused: the Earth itself. "Neither the surface nor the mass of the Earth is growing," Daly continually reminds people. On Earth, inputs and outputs have always cycled and recycled ad infinitum, transforming one into the other. Things only got out of whack when one species—ours—started demanding more stuff than ever before, requiring more concentrated energy for that stuff's manufacture than nature had ever accommodated all at once.

We're not the first instance of that happening in

the planet's history. From time to time, there have been other exaggerated inputs—like the asteroid strike that knocked off the dinosaurs and nearly two-thirds of everything else alive. It took several million years for Earth to absorb its dust and spawn a new cast of characters to be fruitful and multiply. To avoid bringing something comparably drastic upon ourselves, the ecological economists propose we rethink the way we provision civilization—starting now.

It's a big job. Today's globalized economy literally means an economy the size of our planet—but as Daly points out, that also means there's no more room to expand. The addition of more fuel reserves than we once thought we had—in the form of gas we free by shattering bedrock, oil we wring from sand and shale, and newly ice-free Arctic deposits—seems impressive from a short-term perspective, such as an election cycle. But the math reveals that they'll buy us relatively little extra time, and may cost much more than they give. The techniques to harvest them make alarming messes, and burning them turns the skies even more uncontrollable and the oceans increasingly corrosive.

"The closer the economy approaches the scale of the Earth," Daly told the UK's Sustainable Development Commission in 2008, "the more it will have to conform to the physical behavior of the Earth." In a steady-state economy, we wouldn't be seeking more and dirtier ways to fuel the engine of growth, because we'd live within our planet's means. But if an economy permanently stopped expanding, wouldn't that mean it has failed?

No more, said Daly, than it means that the Earth is static—"a great deal of qualitative change can happen inside a steady state, and certainly has happened on Earth." In a steady-state economy, the population would stay more or less constant at a livable, optimal level, and so would the consumer base. Same with the labor pool, which would make just enough stuff for the consumers to consume. Manufacturing wastes, and products that had passed their useful life, would be continually recycled. Like a terrarium, everything would be in balance...

...which is easier said than done. The transition alone will be daunting, because throughout human history, we've been doing exactly the opposite, and nearly everyone alive knows no other way. What worked fine for our ancestors—run out of game, pick up and move to new hunting grounds—doesn't work when there's nowhere else to go that we haven't already picked over. But it's hard for most of us to see that, because, like Alberta tar sands, we keep squeezing more out of soil and water. The fact that they give steadily less is mainly apparent to a growing fringe at the bottom of the human tapestry: more hungry people than the population of the entire human race before industrialization began blowing the lid off our numbers.

So how do we get those of us at the top of the food chain to comprehend, lest we join their ranks?

The 2008 global financial crisis created a whole new batch of recruits to the world's chronic have-nots: growing numbers of underemployed and job-less, as the traditional economy fails them. University of Vermont economist Joshua Farley, coauthor of the 2010 book *Ecological Economics* with Herman Daly, has spent much time since that avalanche began think-ing about something that few of us understand: mon-etary policy.

"That's the problem: Most people don't know where money comes from, nor how it's created."

Which, he believes, is the reason why our econ-omy today resembles a chain letter based on the fic-tion of an infinite number of recipients, instead of a terrarium—such as *Terra,* the Earth itself. Farley, whose boyish looks are belied only by his shock of gray hair, has become adept at explaining it to policy makers who should already know it but don't, and to college undergraduates.

"Take the United States. There are about 800 bil-lion dollars in actual bills, but that's a tiny fraction of the actual money we use." The rest is money that banks magically create whenever checks are written, because a bank only has to keep a fraction—usually around one-fifth—of actual deposits at any time, based on the usually reliable assumption that its customers aren't all going to simultaneously withdraw their savings.

This is the easy part: If a bank need only keep 20 percent of deposits on hand, it can lend out five times the amount of actual money it has. Which it does. Each time this happens, Farley explains, the economy has just grown again. "Banks virtually loan money into existence—and at interest." Of the interest it earns, four-fifths gets loaned out again.

Now comes the hard part: "So when I went to the bank and took out a mortgage for $100,000," says Farley, "the bank wrote me a check that essentially created that amount. As long as I haven't paid it back, that money circulates through our economy and lubricates the whole economic process. Except it isn't really money based on anything of value, except my promise to pay it back. It's debt that they've created. All the money in our country right now is debt: about $50 trillion in total interest-bearing debt in the United States alone."

In the days when money was backed by its face value in silver or gold, there were limits to how much wealth could flow around the world. Today, it's virtual money that the bank lends into existence on a computer screen. "And unless the economy continually expands, there is no new flow of money to pay back that money, plus interest." Hence the chain letter.

"As it stands now, if banks start loaning money more slowly than they collect debts, the quantity of money in the economy goes down, and it's impossible to pay back debts. So we get defaults on houses, defaults on mortgages, defaults on loans. We get collapsing businesses. Our economy plunges into misery and unemployment. Under our current monetary system, the only alternative to that is endless growth. So one absolute thing we have to change is the whole nature of the monetary system."

So how might we do that?

"It's fairly simple. It's a change that's been proposed by economists for centuries. We deny banks the right to create money."

Instead, Farley says, money creation would go back to where it used to be. "We restore that right to the government. It can spend money into existence on public goods, like rebuilding our infrastructure, our education systems, our sewage systems, and restoring our watersheds and forests. Or it can loan money into existence to state governments and local governments or to central industries, like renewable energy systems—but at zero interest. At zero percent interest, when it's paid back, the money's destroyed. So there's no continual increase in the money supply."

There's a challenge with that solution, he admits. "You're trying to take the right to create wealth away from some of the wealthiest people on the planet."

That does present an obstacle. And it's not simply confiscating Goldman Sachs's or HSBC's legal magic wands that allow them to conjure substance out of thin air by only maintaining fractional deposits: It also deprives them of vast interest income. The government would no longer have to borrow money, because it would literally create it by spending it on public goods and works. That also means no more needing to raise taxes in order to pay borrowed money back, plus interest.

The wealthiest 10 percent would appreciate the reduced tax part, but they wouldn't much like the loss of interest. "Since the top 10 percent of the economy is who receives interest payments, and the bottom 90 percent pays them, interest payments today essentially redistribute wealth from the bottom 90 percent to the top 10 percent."

In a steady-state economy, Farley says, the opposite would happen: Government would spend for things that benefit 100 percent of the people, creating jobs to build and maintain them, and redistributing money more equally throughout society. Taken globally, a fairer redistribution of wealth plus population reduction—either because we gracefully nudge our numbers toward some ecological balance, or because some unpleasant act of nature abruptly jerks us in that direction—are the inseparable sides of the new coin the human race must spend to afford the future.

It all makes sense, and sounds highly unlikely. Picture a world where economic decisions are made not to benefit the cleverest financial whizzes, nor the brawniest companies, nor the most powerful nations, but according to what's best for the most people and for the planet that sustains us all. Lovely, right?

Now, picture all the interested parties letting it happen. Not so pretty.

The switch to a sustainable economy, wrote Herman Daly in *Scientific American* in 2005, "would entail an enormous change of mind and heart by economists, politicians, and voters. One might well be tempted to declare that such a project would be impossible. But the alternative to a sustainable economy—an ever-growing economy—is biophysically impossible. In choosing between tackling a political impossibility and a biophysical impossibility, I would judge the latter to be the more impossible, and take my chances with the former."

*　　*　　*

To have a world where the majority enjoyed a life that most of us would accept—something like a European lifestyle: less consumptive and energy-intensive than in the United States or China; more secure than in Africa—would require fewer people dividing up the world's goods, and leaving enough for nature to thrive. "Usually," says Jon Erickson, Farley's University of Vermont ecological economist colleague, "people presume that when economists talk about raising everyone's material standard of living—be it to a European, Japanese, or American standard—they mean for all seven or nine billion people. But mathematically, that clearly won't work. If we want a more affluent world, we have to drop population size. They go hand in hand."

The world's current, chronic economic crisis springs from everyone—from homeowners to entire nations—getting into more debt than we can possibly pay back. The idea of the whole world incurring even more debt just to pay off debts that can't be met is Ponzi financing in the extreme. That's where national economies—and even international, such as the European Union's—approach the brink of collapse. Yet thus far, says Erickson, it's the only kind of financing we've tried.

"We take on more debt, over and over again,

assuming we'll simply grow more in the future and pay it off later. The only way we can possibly pay down that debt without growing is by consuming less."

There are only two ways to do that. "Either everybody on the average consumes less, or we have fewer people consuming."

Or both. Getting people to want less sounds tough, though from Farley's and Erickson's vantage point, perhaps not impossible. The Gund Institute for Ecological Economics, where they teach, which began at Herman Daly's school, the University of Maryland, moved to Vermont because, says Erickson, "at Maryland, it was like an outcast institute. Here, it's more central to what this university, Burlington, and Vermont are about: a transition to a reasonable economy."

Burlington, Vermont: whose last three mayors described themselves as either socialist or progressive, rather than Democrat or Republican. A city with a community land trust featuring a "ladder of affordability" for housing, offering everything from single rooms to co-op rentals, home ownership, and cohousing. A Lake Champlain waterfront converted mostly to public space. A supermarket-sized, city co-op grocery. Citywide composting. An electric utility that produces fifty megawatts from waste wood products.

Hard to get much more livable, boast patriotic

residents. And yet, Erickson says, neither Burlington nor steady-state economics are radical. "It's good old Vermont conservatism"—and quite similar, he adds, to Akihiko Matsutani's prescription for Japan, which turns out to be very appealing for fiscal conservatives: If deficit spending is necessary to a growing society, in a shrinking society what's needed is exactly the opposite. As populations start shrinking—"as they must," Jon Erickson tells his students, "either by design or by default"—we will have to learn to live with balanced budgets.

Which, whether it likes it or not, Japan is en route to doing.

———

Yoshimi Kashitani, his khaki cargo pants tucked into black rubber boots, sloshes through the cold water cascading down his terraced wasabi patch. Bending, he inspects some one-year-old plants. "They are doing very well," he tells Yoshio Takeya, his new helper, who's watching closely from the next tier up.

Kashitani is a healthy, wiry man of eighty-three. He has been doing this right here all his life, as did his father before him. His wasabi grows high up a steep canyon above the village of Nosegawa in mountainous Nara Prefecture on south Honshu Island. Takeya, fifty years younger, is from Osaka, part of

Japan's Keihanshin metropolitan area that includes Kyoto and Kobe, together home to 18 million people.

Nosegawa has five hundred people and counting—down. In 1975, twenty-three hundred lived here, working in forestry, growing wasabi and shiitake mushrooms, making chopsticks, and hatching amago trout. But mechanization and reusable plastic killed their hand-carved chopstick industry, which employed dozens who scraped and planed standard chopsticks from sugi cedar and fancy chopsticks from hinoki cypress. Mostly, though, the numbers withered away as older generations died off and fewer young people took their place. Nearly half of Nosegawa's residents are now over sixty-five.

It's the same throughout the Japanese country-side: fields and farmhouses vacant, elementary and middle schools down to handfuls of students, and elderly farmers still working the land because there's nobody else to do it. "Once we were fourteen wasabi farmers here," says Yoshimi Kashitani, rain dripping from the bill of his cap. "Now just five of us are left." He has three daughters, born right after World War II before the short-lived baby boom abruptly ended. They now live in Yokahama and Osaka, and aren't coming back to grow wasabi. Only one of the five growers had a son, and he, too, left for the city. "So this young man is our only hope."

In a town where young means fifty years old, Takeya, who's dressed like his mentor except his rubber boots are white, is truly youthful at only thirty-three. After graduating from Osaka University in agriculture, he found few jobs awaiting in the dying countryside. But wasabi interested him. Despite all its soba and sushi eaters, Japan now mainly imports it from China, where, he says, the mass-produced, pesticided field wasabi barely resembles the native wasabi horseradish grown chemical-free in rivers like Mr. Kashitani's. Takeya found this place on the Internet: the prefecture's website described how the

Wasabi growers, Nosegawa, Nara Prefecture, Japan

Nosegawans were using indigenous heirloom stock, hand gathering and nurturing their own seed. No one else he knew of still did that.

All around them, springs and waterfalls gush from the canyon walls. The mountain stream where Kashitani built sixteen stone terraces is lined with maple, beech, and Japanese oak, which retain water far better than the cypress and cedar that have replaced much of the native hardwoods in the mountains surrounding Nosegawa. Hinoki cypress and sugi cedar are also native, but in the postwar years the balance of Japan's deciduous-conifer forests began to tip, as much of its hardwoods were clear-cut by the government to make way for faster-growing cypress and cedar for the construction and furniture industries.

The result is a national ecological snafu. As each of those species matures, it emits increasing amounts of pollen. By 2000, more than a quarter of the Japanese people were itching and sneezing from a hay fever pandemic, due to all the cypress and cedars their government had planted. Each year, with the trees' advancing age, more eyes redden and more sinuses burn. During the peak month of April, half the country is wearing face masks — and complaining.

But in this cool canyon, too steep for timbering, the air is bracing and fragrant. Leaf detritus and droppings of bears, boar, deer, fox, and monkeys that drink here provide the nutrients for the shiny, heart-shaped wasabi leaves poking up from the terraced stream-bed. As the rain eases, morning clears the mountain-top fog. The trills of Japanese bush warblers echo off the bedrock, as overhead, a Japanese mountain hawk-eagle, whose own population fell along with the hard-woods that once supported its massive nests, circles on barred wings.

Nevertheless, as the number of people here declines, the numbers of animals have increased. Villagers must fence off potato and cucumber gardens from bears, and hang netting over the stacks of oak logs injected with shiitake mushroom spores to protect them from herons and macaques. To young Yoshio Takeya, his bowl-cut hair rain-plastered to his forehead, it only makes his future more beautiful. He and his girlfriend from agriculture school will soon take over one of Nosegawa's abandoned wasabi patches for themselves.

As he sloshes his way to the next tier, a cloud of white butterflies circles his head. Their larvae eat wasabi leaves, but he doesn't mind: the presence of insects is proof that the ton of wasabi this mountain produces each year is unadulterated and organic. His girlfriend is a bit concerned that this isolated village has no supermarket, but here they can have something of their own, and be able to marry and have a child.

Kashitani approves of his protégé's plans: he and his colleagues, now in their eighties, are still strong enough to keep working for a while. "The air and water are so pure and good, we live longer here." Yet his own wife's recent death marked the first of their generation to go, and talk in the village has turned to wondering who will maintain their ancestors' tombs for them when they're all gone. For a while, their children will come back during the summer Obon festival to venerate them, but—"Unless more young people arrive, this village will disappear." He nods at young Takeya. "Maybe now they will come."

"They should," says Takeya. "Most of our classmates couldn't get jobs, because they wanted to stay near the cities, in agribusiness. They should spread out. This," he says, indicating the river plunging through the green terraces, "is real."

Which is exactly what economist Akihiko Matsutani, who sees prosperity in population reduction, expects more young people to realize. Right now, metro areas like Greater Tokyo and Osaka-Kyoto-Kobe are magnets for young people. But as today's workforce ages and becomes less productive, the megalopoli themselves will age. A smaller workforce will be employed in fewer heavy Japanese industries requiring coastal harbors for imported raw materials. By 2030, Matsutani calculates, shrinking Tokyo would need more than 6 million immigrants from elsewhere in Japan to maintain today's labor levels — an impossibility because, if for no other reason, they couldn't afford the real estate.

Instead of laborers seeking heavy industries, more nimble industries making lighter consumer goods will go where laborers are, spreading opportunity more equitably across the land. Smaller, more localized markets will take on new appeal, and as prosperity is redefined around shorter working weeks and quality of life rather than relentless accumulation, the hinterlands will be ever more attractive places to live.

The transition to a smaller population with, at least for a while, a higher proportion of older people — a completely new experience in human history — won't be painless.

"I wish we were wise enough to downsize gracefully and intelligently," says Matsutani. "The longer people fail to face what is happening, the harsher the adjustment will be." The part that makes most economists shiver is pensions, which have always been a way to share the fruits of economic growth across generations — "only fair," Matsutani writes, "since the previous generation laid the economic foundation for the affluence of the following generation." But in a shrinking, aging economy, when affluence is no longer growing, and with fewer workers paying into pension plans for all those long-lived seniors, people will have to save more for their own retirements, and make do on reduced income.

.Like China's Jiang Zhenghua, now charged with planning how his country will deal with its own aging populace, Akihiko Matsutani sees those savings helping to finance communal public housing, parks, and cultural facilities that seniors will need. He's heard the scary rhetoric in Europe about how high payroll taxes must soar to meet the pension shortfall if populations fall, and how everyone should pump out more babies, lest their economies crumple beneath a mass of unproductive, gray-haired retirees. In reply, Matsutani reminds people that children, too, can be considered a burden on society, since they don't work and require their own infrastructure. Smaller populations won't need as many schools or subsidies for public and private universities. The size of government, too, will shrink along with the body politic: all representing savings that can be reallocated where they're needed.

"It's a more peaceful society when a large part of the population is aged," observes Japanese senator Kuniko Inoguchi, who is also a demographer. "The aged won't sacrifice health care for guns. Because of the graying populations in most democracies," she says, "in the twenty-first century there's hope for us to find a geriatric peace."

And with less dependence on foreign imports to sustain frenetic levels of production, a country might be less inclined to spend billions defending access to resources overseas, as the United States has done at such great financial and human cost. Without resource wars, there would be that much more available for caring for the elderly, until ages come back into balance, leveling out with each passing generation to a smaller, leaner population, with more breathing room to savor life.

iii. Satoyama

As a boy in the city of Matsumoto in central Japan, Keibo Oiwa would accompany his mother to Genchi no Ido, an artesian well in the middle of town that's been used for thousands of years. He now teaches anthropology at Meiji Gakuin University in Yokohama, but following a Zen purification retreat in Matsumoto, he's returned to the old wooden portico that shelters the well. Thirst quenched and ablutions completed, he bows before a statue of a standing Buddha holding an infant, with two other babies tugging at his robes. "Buddha as compassionate mother," notes Oiwa.

Few Japanese mothers have three children anymore, but Oiwa's actually headed to see one: his former student Mari Tokuhisa. Oiwa, lean and denim-clad, is the founder of The Sloth Club, a group that promotes the sustainable life he envisioned in his popular book *Slow Is Beautiful*. His friends Mari and her husband, Kin, recently found an old house in Shiga, a nearby farming village, where, like most of rural Japan, the median age is in the seventies and empty houses rent cheaply—in this case, for ¥10,000 a month, about US$130.

The half-hour drive there climbs through a cypress forest still ribboned with oak, beech, and camellia. Descending, the road crosses a narrow valley of terraced rice paddies, bisected by a small river. On the opposite side, Shiga's wooden houses fill a mountain pass lined with red pines.

It is very quiet, because few live here now. Mari, in a peasant blouse and long skirt, and her three small boys, Kyusen, Gennosuke, and Yosei, await in front of their new home, the former village chief's house. The town is now so small that legally it no longer exists.

"It's beautiful here," Oiwa says, greeting Mari with a hug.

"Hai." With the same haircut as her sons, they resemble a family of pixies. The house, about a hundred years old, has curved Japanese eaves. Its interior, carpeted in woven straw mats, has a reed ceiling and window shades. Shoji screens that divide the large space into rooms are open so that afternoon light fills the house. A brick chimney is retrofitted with an iron woodstove made by Mari's husband, who's off building stage sets for a theater company. They met as students; disillusioned with the shaky Japanese job market after their first son was born, they escaped to Amami Oshima, a tiny island near Okinawa at the Japanese archipelago's southern tip, to practice permaculture. So far from the big crowded islands, life there turns around families, which tend to be larger than the rest of Japan, and they soon had two more. "I still want more. My friend just had her fifth."

Before becoming a mother, she worked in one of the slow food cafés that Keibo Oiwa has sponsored around Japan, which feature local ingredients prepared from scratch. When they decided to return to Honshu, they were committed to becoming as self-sufficient as possible, a decision underscored by the Fukushima earthquake-tsunami-nuclear disaster of March 11, 2011 — known evermore in Japan as 3/11.

"Our life here is simple. We grow our food and make our furniture. Our sons' nursery school meets outdoors. But if we're not free from nuclear power, it's not enough. So since 3/11, we're heating our bathwater with firewood."

Yes, it takes more time, she says. "But it's also more fun. When we had a modern life in Yokohama, we would waste time. Now, by putting effort into making things, it's like we're regaining time."

"Hai," says Oiwa. "Exactly. That is the slow life. People think environmental living means being ascetic. But every culture has a huge storage of fun. Sure, there's fun technology. But today we see so many sick, unhappy, empty people. Before 3/11, people gave thanks to nuclear power for allowing us to have our lives. But now, post-3/11, we realize that we all die. We who survived aren't immortal; we're in the palm of Buddha. Knowing that we die is the first wisdom of human beings, the beginning of philosophy. Every day I wake up still alive, that is happiness."

They're having tea around a table hewn by Mari's husband from cypress slabs. "We humans have a proper speed, and when society speeds beyond our limit, we get social problems," Oiwa says. "Psychological problems. Things break down. We've now contaminated much of this island, but they still say we need economic growth. They act like we'll live forever. But if we can face the wisdom that everyone dies, we'll see that we live not because of nuclear power, but because of the sun and the air. Once we realize that, maybe we can turn this around."

They go next door to see Mari's seventy-year-old neighbor, Michiko Takizawa. A widow early in life, she raised her two children by growing vegetables and rice and keeping cows, angora rabbits, and silk-worms. With pleasure, Oiwa inspects her two-hundred-year-old house: traditional post-and-beam, strong enough to sustain a second story of thick, earthen walls. The main beam, fully a half-meter wide, is from a single Japanese red pine.

They kneel at a low round table, where Michiko-san sets bowls of sliced eggplant, zucchini, green beans, and plums she pickles in sugar and vinegar. "Take," she says, handing a plum to Mari's oldest, whose second-grade classroom has just four other students. "And that's after they combined two schools. After we die"—other than Mari's family, Michiko's youngest neighbor is fifty-five—"all these houses will be empty." Her unmarried son, who works construction, still lives nearby. "But women don't want to marry men here. Women today would rather have a job than get married." One man brought a Filipina bride, she says, "But she left. The culture was too different. She said she didn't like wasabi."

"Aren't more city people moving here?" Keibo asks.

"More are still leaving than coming." She looks

sadly at Mari, who just smiles at her until she has to smile back.

"You will see," Mari tells her. She and her husband have rented one of Michiko-san's rice paddies, which they will cultivate organically. A discussion ensues about how to keep water in the paddy all winter, despite the snow, to control weeds.

Afterward, they end up in Michiko's cornucopial vegetable patch. On her hands and knees, she harvests sweet peppers, eggplants, okra, and soybeans for her guests. Oiwa gazes raptly at her bountiful garden, bordered by lilies and filled with dusky blue butterflies. Beyond it are rice paddies latticed with channels of water borrowed from the river, the brilliant green stalks heavy with grains about to turn golden. Past them is a perfect triangular wedge of mountain covered with mixed forest—and farther, more cool mountains dissolving into fog.

This, Oiwa knows, is a blessed remnant of *satoyama*, the harmonious marriage of human and natural landscapes that for thousands of years defined the Japanese countryside. In these tranquil mosaics of cultivated lands, wildflower meadows, ponds, streams, orchards, and forests, Japanese culture was born. On islands where, since ancient times, humans have shaped and manicured all but the craggiest terrain, *satoyama* has been the salvation of Japanese biodiversity. For millennia, people dwelling in *satoyama* landscapes harvested firewood and charcoal, pastured animals, and grew crops with an aesthetic that invited and nurtured fish, frogs, dragonflies, butterflies, fireflies, grasshoppers, songbirds, ducks, storks, and falcons.

But in the 1960s, farmhouse chimneys gave way to oil burners. As synthetic fertilizer took over the fields, coppiced woodlands that once provided warmth, fodder, and leaf mulch for rice paddies were no longer visited daily. Pesticides banished the grasshoppers and caterpillars, and the herons, egrets, and majestic Oriental white storks that fed on them failed to return. Concrete lining for ditches to drain fields wiped out tadpoles, snails, and sludge worms. As cows and beef cattle switched from pasture to imported corn and soy feed, grasslands and meadows that once surrounded Japanese cities disappeared beneath housing developments and golf courses.

Within a half-century, Japan no longer resembled a timeless ink-on-silk painting. But as numbers recede, and as a smaller younger generation seeks alternatives to the corporate soldiering that came to define Japanese work, there is a chance for a slower life to return, along with landscapes to sustain it.

*   *   *

The last wild Oriental white stork in Japan was seen in 1971. In 1989, a stork hatchery at Toyooka, an hour from Kyoto in Hyogo Prefecture, successfully produced offspring using breeding pairs from Russia. But the local rice fields, soaked annually with organo-mercury pesticides, proved too toxic for the fledgling birds to be released. In 2004, a ten-year-old schoolgirl named Yuka Okada learned that storks like the caged birds in Toyooka's now crowded hatchery had once filled the skies and nested on every chimney. After learning why they no longer did, she went to the mayor and demanded that Toyooka serve organic rice for school lunches.

To do that meant eliminating mercury, inviting back grasshoppers but also making the rice paddies safe for storks. The mayor, hearing the simple truth from a ten-year-old, could only agree. His city's slogan became "An environment good for storks must be good for humans, too." The next plantings were pesticide-free. A year later, the first stork was released, and today, wherever they nest, the rice is twice as valuable because the presence of storks guarantees its purity. An economy that had bottomed was rejuvenated, and today tourists flock to Toyooka to watch hundreds of storks do the same.

The value to be reaped from tourists and fancy

organic rice is easy to quantify. Harder, but most critical, is calculating the value of nature—what conservation ecologists call *natural capital.* How much is a grasshopper worth, anyway, if nature always provided them for free? Trees in forests were free. Rivers and the atmosphere were free places to toss wastes. Free, but ultimately costly, when they vanish or can hold no more.

The accounting of nature's capital has never been included in corporate balance sheets, but every prechemical farmer knew it well. In a Japan with far fewer Japanese, as Japan will inevitably become this century, there is a chance for natural capital to replenish, and for people to enjoy healthier, even happier lives.

The rice fields may yield less, if humans must share the grains with grasshoppers—but with fewer humans, that won't be such a problem.

CHAPTER 14

Tomorrow

i. Pantheon

Caring for the elderly during the transition as the world comes back down to size will be tricky, Shubash Lohani agrees. And he's not even talking about people.

Lohani, deputy director of World Wildlife Fund's Eastern Himalaya Ecoregion Program, is in Lalmatiya, a town in southwestern Nepal just above the Indian border, visiting an old age home — for cows.

Lalmatiya is in Nepal's Terai, a narrow strip of bottomland at the base of the world's highest mountains and Lohani's birthplace. Until the 1950s, the Terai was completely forested. It was also infested with malaria. The only inhabitants, the ethnic Tharu tribe, had an unexplained malaria tolerance —

because, some believed, Tharu were direct descendants of Gautama Buddha, who was also born in Terai. In the 1950s, with help from the United States, the entire Terai was sprayed with DDT. As malaria was eradicated from successive areas, they were opened to settlement. Anyone who wanted could clear and claim land for free. Millions did, shearing most of the Terai's trees, which mostly ended up as railroad ties in India.

Besides children—until recently, Nepalese families averaged seven—Terai settlers brought nearly one cow per human. This was a problem, and not just locally. The multi-chambered digestion of ruminants like cows and sheep involves much belching and flatulence. As the numbers of domestic animals worldwide, like our own, reached into the billions, their burps and farts account for around a quarter of human-related emissions of methane, a gas that traps twenty-one times more heat than CO_2.

In Nepal and neighboring India, it's even worse, because cows are considered sacred, and killing them is taboo. (Like India, Nepal is predominately Hindu. After Gautama Buddha's birth gave rise to his eponymous religion, Nepalese have commonly observed both.) In the Terai, when cows get too old to give milk—the generous gift for which they are revered—owners release them in the forest. There they browse on saplings, their hooves compacting the soil so that little else grows. For World Wildlife Fund, this is serious: tigers, rhinos, and elephants are native to the Terai, as well as leopards, peacocks, macaques, and langurs, and what's left of the forest is where they live.

There are also seven endangered species of vultures here — red-headed, white-rumped, cinereous, bearded, and Egyptian, as well as both Eurasian and Himalayan griffons — which led WWF to an imaginative solution to the cattle crisis. "We realized," Lohani explains, "that they all were being poisoned by feeding on the carcasses of old bovines." It turned out that farmers kept their aging cattle working by applying diclofenac, a painkilling ointment, that proved fatally toxic to the kidneys of carrion eaters. "So we donated ten thousand dollars to set this up."

The sign reads, "Old Age Home for Livestock and Vulture Conservation Centre." Behind it, several senescent, skinny cattle roam peaceably around a former eucalyptus plantation overlooking a dry riverbed. Here, before they get so arthritic that owners must slather them with diclofenac, cows are retired, fed, and finally given a respectful funeral with chanting, flowers, and incense on a ceremonial platform — which also serves as a dinner table for vultures. Because vultures are also venerated in the Hindu pantheon as nature's cleaner, people here felt doubly blessed when six of the seven vulture and griffon species began showing up for meals.

Lohani, a stocky man in his mid-thirties with a green bill cap and shirt bearing the WWF panda logo, follows Moti Adhikiri, the elderly Centre director, down to the bombax trees growing along the riverbed. Three years earlier, there were just two vulture nests. Now there are 61. Besides four roosting griffons, Lohani also sees hornbills, drongos, pheasants, and red-vented bulbuls. Adhikiri has seen spotted deer, wild boar, blue bulls, Himalayan black bear, and—"For the first time in forty years, elephants and leopards are here!"

Lohani congratulates him and heads west, driving past miles of mud huts down Nepal's two-lane Highway 1, weaving around throngs of people, goats, water buffalo, men on motor scooters with sari-clad wives riding sidesaddle, streams of bicycles, and thousands of cows. He is on a tour of slender landscape corridors that connect protected areas in Nepal and India that are home to Asian one-horned rhinos, Indian elephants, and the world's highest concentration of Bengal tigers. Two hours later, he is standing in a rosewood thicket in what he calls one of the eleven lifelines keeping these animals alive. This one, the Khata corridor, links Nepal's Bardia National Park with India's Katarniaghat Wildlife Sanctuary. *Lifeline* is not a casual metaphor: In places, the Khata corridor is only five hundred meters wide, and never more than two kilometers. Yet camera traps show elephants, tigers, and rhinoceros passing here between the two countries.

Keeping these corridors intact isn't easy. "A few years ago there were twenty-three hundred illegal squatter households here," says Lohani, leaning against a chipped concrete boundary marker, one foot in Nepal and the other in Uttar Pradesh. Saving nature in the Terai requires wrangling 5 million cattle, untold numbers of goats and buffalo, and 7 million settlers.

They've nurtured community forests around every settlement to replace trees that ended up as charcoal, rail ties, or roof beams. To dampen fuel wood demand, WWF has brought in solar panels, LED lighting, induction stoves, and biogenerators that yield cooking gas from vats of cow dung slurry and people's privies. In an inspired stroke, they realized that this qualified for carbon offset credits that they could sell in international investment markets to finance more conservation. They've taught people to grow and press chamomile, citronella, mint, and lemongrass into marketable oils. They've negotiated tourism revenue sharing for people who live alongside wildlife preserves, such as the hundred thousand around the edges of Bardia National Park.

And they've brought family planning, no simple task in a country where a common wedding blessing goes, "May your children and theirs cover the hills." World Wildlife Foundation isn't a family-planning organization, but saving wildlife is pointless if humans then push them off the land. So they joined with government and NGO health partners to get funding from USAID and corporations like Johnson & Johnson for programs that help all creatures, human and otherwise. USAID, which had once soaked the Terai with DDT, was persuaded. In less than a decade, average family size in the area dropped from 8.5 children to 2.5.

Yet more arrive weekly, especially refugees from mountain communities washed away by melting glaciers. "We can't eliminate overpopulation anytime soon, any more than we can get rid of greenhouse gases tomorrow," says Lohani. "Both have been growing for a long time, and we're bound to add more before we finally stop."

Especially since, for all that they might accomplish in Nepal, they really have no control over the fate of this land. That resides at the other end of these corridors: in the country that in the next decade will surpass China as the world's most populous.

Lohani peers into India. Lately, its far northern reach is filling with Bangladeshis, whose own land is disappearing under rising waters. The refugees tell him they've come to this periphery to clear some forest and make a life.

"My dream," he says, "is to have a landscape like in the Buddha's time, when people and wildlife lived in harmony."

In Nepal alone, that would be a challenge. But ecosystems know no borders, and what happens south of this boundary, Lohani knows, will determine Nepal's future—and quite likely, the world's.

ii. Celphos

Dr. G. S. Kalkat was speaking at Guru Nanak Dev University in the Indian state of Punjab when a student asked, "What do you consider the three biggest problems facing India?"

"Population, population, and population," he replied.

Yet that would not have been the answer given by the worried people who, five years earlier, brought him back from retirement after a distinguished career at the World Bank and as a university administrator, to chair the Punjab State Farm Commission—exactly where he'd begun in 1949. To them, Problem No. 1 was what hydrologists were saying: that the water table below Punjab's central wheat and basmati rice area in places was dropping ten feet per year. Wells that were 100 feet deep in 1970 had been rebored to 300 feet, then to 500 feet. New ones were going more than 1,000 feet down.

Monsoons that once lasted thirty days or more were down to ten or fifteen. Soils were turning saline. Although Punjab, the size of Vermont and New Hampshire combined, makes up just 1.5 percent of India's total land area, it is the nation's pantry, growing 60 percent of its wheat and 50 percent of its rice. "We're desperate," say the three farmers in Dr. Kalkat's office, two in purple turbans, one in yellow. What are they going to do?

They are going to do what their fathers did, he tells them: diversify their crops. Before 1970, in summer farmers grew corn, peanuts, a little cotton, some rice. In winter, wheat, legumes, and chickpeas. Back then, however, the population of India was less than half what it is now: 500 million, versus today's 1.1 billion. Even then, many Indians were starving: they had exceeded the land's carrying capacity. Kalkat was then Punjab's deputy director of agriculture, having returned in 1964 after a doctorate at Ohio State, courtesy of a Rockefeller Foundation scholarship. That was just before Rockefeller scientists arrived here from their wheat improvement center in Mexico with new high-yield seeds.

They were calling the project, of which Kalkat became joint director, a "green revolution."

"Our first crop season with the new wheat was 1968. We planted 1.6 million hectares. In 1969 came what IRRI called Miracle Rice. Before, we would get a ton of rice and 1.2 tons of wheat per hectare. Suddenly, our harvests were 4 tons of rice and 4.5 tons wheat. The only thing needed was irrigation. We sunk wells, because it was much faster than putting in dams and digging canals, which take ten to fifteen years. We could dig wells in one week. And that's what we did, from 1968 to 1970. We still do."

His voice grows softer as he reflects on what resulted from perforating the Punjab with 1.2 million wells. "We have 2.6 million hectares in rice. With the water table dropping so fast, we calculate that we must move a million hectares of rice into low-water crops: maize, pulses, and oil seeds like soy. Soy isn't as high-yielding, but it's priced higher. With luck, the farmers will be compensated. India is short of edible oils for cooking."

His gaze rises toward his pale blue turban, as if to retrieve a thought.

"Stabilizing the water balance, so that what we

use equals the annual recharge from rainfall, will take ten or fifteen years. But if we don't also control population and bring ourselves into balance with natural resources, we'll have a serious problem. Farmers will suffer. We'll have social upheaval. Our immediate concern is water. But unless we do something in the next decade about population, we will have decided, en masse, to commit hydrological suicide."

Sheela Kaur, her blue batik chunni framing a face hard as a mask, knows about hydrological suicide. Her husband, Prakash Singh, was only twenty-seven when he walked into their wheat field and opened a new can of Celphos. When he failed to return for lunch, his brother went to look and found his body.

Celphos is a trade name for aluminum phosphide, a fumigant for grains that is lethal to insects and rodents. It comes in powder or tablets; when exposed to moisture or humidity, it releases a colorless gas that smells like garlic. If that release occurs inside someone's stomach, within minutes most internal organs fail. No one witnessed how much Sheela's husband took, but four tablets is the customary dose in Punjab, where, according to Bharatiya Kisan Sangh, the Indian farmers' union, forty to fifty thousand have similarly taken their lives in the past two decades. (Nationwide, reports India's National Crime Records

Bureau, 270,000 Indian farmers have committed suicide since 1995.)

"It is common," Sheela says tonelessly, slumped on her woven cot, turquoise paint peeling from the walls around her. In her village, Kurail, some of her neighbors' husbands have flung themselves in front of trains or off roofs, but ingesting pesticide is the symbolic death of choice here.

His watch hangs from her left wrist. The photograph she holds shows a slim, smiling youth standing by a river, wearing jeans and a jacket over a red shirt. Like many Punjab farmers, Prakash Singh had gotten into debt. Sheela had seen him grow worried as loans he took deepened along with the well he was digging. He had calculated costs for a 300-foot well, never dreaming that he would need to go 500 feet. Back in his father's time, 45 feet would have been plenty.

Soon the moneylender, who charged 24 percent, was showing up early each morning to humiliate him in front of his family. He intercepted their three children on the way to school and asked for money. Another loan, with a bank, was secured by property Prakash owned with his brother, but men still came demanding payment, sometimes three times a day. Prakash promised to pay everyone when the wheat was in. But the harvest was disappointing.

"I never knew how much the well cost—men usually don't tell women," says Sheela. "Or they say it's less than it really is. When he said that the only way out was to drink something and die, I told him that his mother and sisters and brother would stand by him. But they had their own debts, he knew. By the time he did it, I expected it. When someone gets like this, nothing can be done."

She told her children that their father had an accident. Now her eldest son says he wants to farm. But with Prakash gone, he will have to marry off his sisters, so the debts will go on. Although dowries now are outlawed, every groom's family still expects one.

Suicide-by-pesticide widow, Punjab, India

At the very least, some gold and a vehicle. Then there are clothes and jewelry for the bride, and a feast for a hundred neighbors. The fact that daughters are so expensive in northern India is one reason why, like India's population growth, illegal ultrasounds and aborted baby girl embryos are surpassing rates in China. In the neighboring state of Haryana, the ratio in one town was down to 590 girls per 1,000 boys.

In a way, says Biku Singh, it was easy to get farmers like himself indebted to the Green Revolution, because Punjabis already had a tradition of social debt. But going into hock for a few years to marry off a daughter was nothing like this.

"The price of everything is now ten times what it was, while the amount of water is ten times less." By everything, he means labor, seed, pesticide, and fertilizer. Fertilizer keeps going up because the land needs more all the time; pesticide because insects develop resistance, so farmers must buy new kinds.

"And electricity: the deeper the water, the more you need to pump. It used to cost 200 rupees per acre. Today it's 2,000.[1] So you need a twenty-horsepower pump instead of ten. Half our people are sick from pesticides: heart attacks, high blood pres-

---

. 1. About US$40.

sure, cancer. Our kids have skin diseases and bad eyesight. No matter how much they eat, they're anemic. Their teachers call them slow learners. And their fathers, all of them two hundred thousand rupees in debt on every acre, are all suicides-in-waiting. We're all on each other's suicide watch."

It is late May, a week shy of the monsoon that so far shows no sign of arriving. Biku, who has a dark, shaggy beard, is driving a dirt road along an irrigation canal choked with brown phosphate foam. Next to him is Labh Singh, a generation his senior. Both wear long white kurtas and billowing white pants. Biku's turban is orange; Labh's is smoky blue. They stop to inspect a field of sorghum fodder; the other fields are bare, their winter wheat harvested a month earlier. The 2011 yield was decent, but not enough to make up for a terrible 2010, when it was too warm. Now they await the rains to plant the flat, dusty land in rice.

There are no birds nor insects. In the corners of fields are mud-plastered cone-shaped silos for storing cow dung, which is used for fuel: there isn't enough manure to fertilize all the crops they must grow to be Green Revolution farmers.

"Before the Green Revolution," says Labh, "when we depended on nature for everything, we were more prosperous. Since the introduction of petrol and pesticides, our fortunes have fallen. In our subdivision, we have eighty villages, and we've had seven hundred suicides."

As more farmers abandon their farms by abandoning their lives, land is being converted to housing, as ever more populous villages spread and merge with each other. Per capita alcohol consumption is among the world's highest. By many accounts, the most lucrative business here is no longer agriculture but heroin grown in Afghanistan and smuggled over the border with Pakistan's Punjab. When recent state government studies declared that nearly 75 percent of Punjabi youth were addicted, no one challenged them.

The Green Revolution made Punjab one of the wealthiest states in what is set to become one of the world's wealthiest countries. But its legendary grain-based bounty, extolled in Bollywood the way cattle ranching was mythologized in Hollywood, is now collapsing. In a given year, harvests may still even set records. But every year, the water is farther away, and few are changing to heat-tolerant, low-water crops. "Nothing else pays enough," says Biku.

"We're stuck," says Labh. "The more we have produced, the more our debt has risen. Our expenses are higher than our returns. And we're all poisoned."

The Green Revolution was never for farmers, they

believe: it was for the rest of the country. Until the water started to vanish and accumulated chemicals and debts overwhelmed them, they were proud to be feeding their nation.

"Not just India: we fed the world," says Labh. "Forty trains a day left Punjab carrying thousands of tons of grain. We grew enough to feed everybody. But now there are so many. And every year, we will be able to feed fewer."

———

The neighboring state of Haryana was once part of Punjab. Just as the original Punjab was cleaved in two in 1947 when Muslim Pakistan broke from India's western flank, in 1966 it divided yet again along sectarian lines, leaving Punjab populated mostly by Punjabi-speaking Sikhs, and Haryana mostly by Hindi-speaking Hindus. Yet another reason for the preternaturally skewed sex ratios in Haryana is a widespread belief among Hindus that passage to heaven depends on having a son to light his parents' funeral pyres. Since the invention of ultrasound imaging, that has translated into vans equipped with portable machines driving from village to village in Haryana, and a robust trade in illicit abortions.

Although abortion has been legal in India since 1971, sex-selective abortion is punishable by both jail and fines. Enforcement, however, is so lax that by 2030, India could have 20 percent more men than women—a deadly prescription for, among other problems, jealousy-fueled violence and escalating rape. Although abortion preempts the killing or abandonment of unwanted baby daughters, mortality statistics reveal indirect infanticide through neglect: According to the United Nations, Indian girls are 75 percent more likely to die before their fifth birthday than boys, suggesting that they're fed what's left after their brothers have eaten.

Fertility has dropped in India in the new millennium, but Haryana is among ten of twenty-eight Indian states that remain well above replacement level. Unfortunately, those ten states contain half of India's population. Another baby is born every two seconds in India, more than forty-three thousand a day, and more than 15 million a year: nearly two more New York Cities. Recently, government demographers revised their prediction that India would achieve stable population in 2045, with 1.45 billion people. They now say that population will keep growing until 2060, peaking at 1.65 billion. Given growth rates that even government cash incentives for delaying childbirth have failed to stem, few are convinced that this prediction will hold any more than the last one.

One simple thing might make a difference, however. Indian women who make it to secondary school average 1.9 children apiece. For those who graduate, it's 1.6. The fertility rate among women with no education is 6.0.

And for decades, India needed to look no farther than its own southern tip for a remarkable example of how education and equality for females can change everything.

iii. Seducing Utopia

The Indian state of Kerala has been lauded internationally for showing how a poor society can nevertheless enjoy a high standard of living, if the standard is not wealth but quality of life. No child marriages, feticide, or gender imbalance here: Kerala actually has slightly more women than men, which is natural for our species. Since the 1970s, it also has the lowest fertility rate in India—a stunning reversal from 1947, when its population growth was the highest in newly independent India.

Yet today, Kerala is also a cautionary example of how tangled human ecology is in the twenty-first century, and of what we must avoid if we ever want to achieve a lasting peace—or to at least to strike a truce—with our own planet.

*   *   *

"If you look at tomorrow, your heart will break," says Sugathakumari.

A revered Indian poet who writes in Malayalam, the language of her native Kerala, as she approaches eighty, Sugathakumari is not happy with our species.

"Animals, birds, bees, and flowers obey nature's laws. Only one creature has broken them. I almost feel that the world would be a better place without us."

Even Kerala? Where, despite incomes averaging only a few hundred dollars a year, in the 1990s they achieved 100 percent literacy? Kerala, which has India's highest life expectancy, nearly that of the United States? And universal health care, equal status for the sexes, and schooling for all? And tropical wilderness where tigers and elephants still roam the steep forests of the Western Ghats, including the fabulous Silent Valley, a national park that Sugathakumari herself saved from government dam builders? Kerala, where a man who marries goes to live with his wife's family, not vice versa?

"I don't know what happened to Kerala," she moans, her ceiling fan stirring her long, silver hair. "I don't know what happened to Kerala's women. I'm disgusted."

The Kerala where she was born in 1934 contained what might have spelled trouble elsewhere in India:

a 60 percent Hindu majority, with the balance equally divided between Muslims and Christians—mostly Catholic or Syrian Orthodox. (The latter claim to be descendants of Brahmins evangelized in Christianity's early days, when the doubting apostle Thomas came to Kerala and founded seven churches.) But rather than ethnic strife, Kerala's multiple religions dwelt in harmony. During the nineteenth century, a rare alliance among enlightened British missionaries, a benevolent young queen, a charismatic outcaste Hindu swami reformer, and several respected Muslim leaders had resulted in state-mandated schools for everyone, regardless of gender, creed, or caste—including slaves and untouchables.

In 1956, India's former principalities of Hindu maharajas and Muslim Nawaabs were reorganized into linguistic states, including Malayam-speaking Kerala. In 1957, its pro-education caste reformists formed the world's first democratically elected communist government. Since then, communists have held power frequently in Kerala, winning praise and votes for their commitment to public health and schooling.

Their success was due in part to realizing by the 1960s that Kerala had the fastest population growth in the country, an unintended consequence of improved medical care that slashed infant mortality and boosted longevity. A family-planning program began distributing newly available pills for free, emphasizing that fewer children are easier to educate. Modest payments were offered to whoever volunteered for vasectomies or tubal ligations. Compliance with family planning tracked directly with female literacy, allowing Kerala to escape Sanjay Gandhi's "emergency" forcible sterilizations in the mid-1970s of more than 8 million Indian men and women—a barbarity that toppled the presidency of his mother, Indira Gandhi.

By the end of the 1990s, Kerala became the first place in India—and in all south Asia—to achieve replacement rate fertility. It was another social success for which democratic communism was credited, even as it was blamed for the state's general economic shambles.

"Cashews, rubber, coir"—coconut fiber—"and agriculture: we had everything," recalls Sugathakumari, who has no political affiliation, but whose campaigns for women's and environmental rights flourished under the leftist governments. But the communists' effectiveness at defending workers ultimately backfired. "They didn't teach our laborers the prestige of doing their duty. They taught them to demand more and more wages, and to limit their workday. The laborers became very proud, very strong, very powerful. Their unions dictated terms to the people hiring them. And one by one, the factories closed."

In 1957, Kerala's first communist government capped the amount of land that citizens could own, redistributing holdings of important families among poor farm laborers. "On the one hand," says Sugath-akumari, "that was good for poor laborers. But our agriculture suffered. If you grow rice, you need big fields. As they were partitioned into smaller ones, the laborers lost interest. So they sold the land, and agriculture dwindled into something weak. It's a sad thing to say."

Outside the mental health shelter for women that she founded in 1985, a leaden sky signals the gathering monsoon. The storm that Sugathakumari fears, however, is one that has rained in from the Persian Gulf, flooding the streets of Thiruvananthapuram, Kerala's capital—with capital. This once-serene city that Mahatma Gandhi praised for its jungle-like lushness is now a cacophony of relentless commerce, much of it involving jewelry and surprising numbers of expensive cars.

It began with Kerala's Muslims, once its poorest community. The decay of Kerala's economy coincided with the rise of Dubai, Abu Dhabi, Doha, and the other Arab petro-capitals. As those cities grew—and grew more lavish—plentiful construction work was just a hop across the Arabian Sea, and soon Kerala's Muslims were returning no longer poor: they were driving foreign cars and wearing enough gold that Kerala's highly educated Hindus couldn't help noticing.

Migrating for work was nothing new: Most of Kerala's stars — India's first female supreme court justice, first female surgeon general, first female head of its stock market, and international literary figures such as novelist Arundhati Roy — made their careers outside the state. Because of their excellent schooling, employees from Kerala are prized; in Mumbai and New Delhi, companies routinely advertise for applicants from Kerala, especially independent women with no qualms about working in distant cities.

But now Keralites were bypassing professional careers in India, because even menial jobs in the opulent Arab Gulf paid better. It was said that Kerala had finally built its economy — but in the Gulf. However, the money that migrants brought back also changed the face of Kerala.

"All spent on gold, fancy boats, and luxury cars," mourned Sugathakumari, as Kerala became India's biggest market for Audi, Mercedes, and BMW. "So many shops, resorts, theaters, and hotels. Hundreds of new mosques built by wealth, looking like the Taj Mahal. More roads, more electricity, more river sand for cement, more land for even more buildings. More, more, more. That's the slogan of today: 'We want more.'"

Never had she seen so much gold jewelry. That was something she'd expect in northern India, where people compete to have the biggest weddings, the biggest jeweled necklaces and rings, the biggest dowries. And something else: "We've always had fathers, mothers, uncles, sisters, and grandparents living together, all sharing the family wealth. Now everyone wants separate homes, and freedom from family responsibilities."

The deluge of materialism confounded the image of Keralans enjoying dignified lives on very low incomes. Kerala's progressive social development and miraculously low fertility had been frequently extolled by Nobel laureate economist Amartya Sen. In the 1990s, the "Kerala Model" became an inspiration for the UN's Human Development Index that Sen developed with Pakistani economist Mahbub ul Haq—an alternative to GDP as the measure of healthy development. Kerala was cited repeatedly during formulation of the UN's current Millennium Development Goals as a world-class example of gender equality, women's empowerment, reduced maternal and child mortality, and universal health care and education.

Now, even the admiring Amartya Sen publicly worries about Kerala's failure to develop a domestic economy to staunch the draining of its most highly educated brains to other parts of India and south Asia. "And when oil runs out in the Gulf," wonders Sugathakumari, "what will happen to these people? If they come back, how can Kerala contain them all?"

They had done so much so well, she says. Not only could everyone read, but they did: Kerala is said to have the world's highest per capita newspaper readership. They had the highest number of hospital beds per capita in India. They'd effectively mobilized against Coca-Cola's overexploitation of groundwater, and led—and won!—the world's battle to ban the endocrine-disrupting pesticide Endosulfan. They preserved enough forests that tigers, elephants, leopards, deer, Indian goats, four species of civet, wild boar, porcupines, pythons, and hairy-footed gerbils still shared Kerala with *Homo sapiens.*

On Sugathakumari's desk is a photograph of herself surrounded by ferns in the Silent Valley they saved, singing one of her poems that inspired thousands to defend their natural heritage.

We bow to the trees with their sacred dreadlocks;
the forest gives us our life-breath

like Lord Shiva, who swallowed the poison
that would otherwise destroy the Earth…

"But then the money poured in like poison." She shakes her head: all their achievements, undermined by temptation.

"We don't know what will happen to Kerala now. As Gandhi said, there is enough for everyone's need—but not for everyone's greed."

iv. The World to Come

If Kerala—or Kerala before it was seduced by lucre—can't be the future, then is it Mumbai? Is the densest mass of humanity in what soon will be the most populous country a glimpse of what's next, if we don't guide our demographic destiny?

Rukmini[2] is used to the police. "Namaste—I salute the God within you," she greets Inspector Sudhakar, her palms pressed together, fingers pointed heavenward.

In her gold-trimmed, shimmering red sari, Rukmini strikes an artful balance between demure and

---

2. Her name is changed at her request.

dazzling. Her long dark hair is tied with a deep red ribbon, which is also the color of the powdered part in her hair. On her forehead's third eye chakra is a black bindi. This is a cryptic message: a vermilion head stripe is a bride's symbol, while a black bindi is worn by widows or unmarried girls. Rukmini doesn't know if she's a widow, because her husband in Calcutta left after she bore her second child, yet another daughter. She managed a clothing store there to feed her two girls, but when they entered secondary school, she needed more money. A friend gave her the name of someone in Mumbai who needed a manager.

It wasn't what she'd expected, but it's worked out. She redid the interior of this tiled, British-era building—it was a brothel in colonial times, too— and made it a proper house, not like the dens of tiny cribs up and down the adjacent streets. She added faux marble flooring and paneling in the parlor, and installed wide plywood beds. In the street-level doorway where she waits every night, inviting and approving clients, is a shrine to the deities Lakshmi, Ganesha, and—because she's from Kolkata—Kali. At the top of the staircase, there's another.

Five of her thirteen girls are paraded out for the inspector and his two constables. The premium trade she caters to demands young girls, and they're dressed accordingly. Only one wears a sari; the rest are in short skirts or diaphanous blouses with skin-tight pants. One wears a T-shirt that says "Human Being" in white letters stretched across a taut bosom. They sit on plastic chairs across from the sofa and smile at the officers through carmine lips. The officers stroke their moustaches, surveying the goods by the glow of standing lamps and an illuminated aquarium over-filled with goldfish.

"So little business tonight?" Inspector Sudhakar asks.

Rukmini indicates the hallway. "Only one. The rain keeps them away." Outside, for the second night, the monsoon is pounding. On a normal evening, they'd have twenty clients. But life's getting harder here in the red-light district of Siddharthnagar, a central Mumbai slum. Fears of HIV have cut into this historic business, but there's no shortage of girls for the work: there's a steady surplus of neglected unwanted daughters of Hindus who keep having babies until they get a son to light their funeral pyres. They come from the most populous states, where procurers prowl crowded villages, promising illiterate girls a chance to make money in Mumbai, possibly by getting bit parts in Bollywood films. Or husbands.

By the time Rukmini meets them, they've learned otherwise. "When they come crying," she says, "I tell them not to get into this life. I tell them if they do, then earn your money fast and go back to your village, live with your parents, think about your children."

The girls, all in their teens, glance at each other and titter. Things could be much worse for them. Nobody beats them here, like in Siddharthnagar's cheap cages. Rukmini makes clients wear condoms. She takes her girls for medical checkups. Because she charges more than anyone on this street—350 rupees, about US$6.35—they don't have to go with unbathed men who live under tarps. They're fed. They can go shopping by themselves, or pray in the temple or church or mosque. And they're free to leave when they choose. So far, these girls aren't going anywhere. Most wouldn't be welcome back home anyway, although the money they send is. And the ones from Nepal and Bangladesh—in high demand for their beauty—don't ever want to leave Mumbai, where there is actually money to make.

Prostitution is illegal, but Rukmini and the police have an understanding. "If these girls couldn't work, there would be a terrible increase of rape in this city. Most of the men we get have left their families to work in Mumbai. They're away from their wives for so long, and like everyone, they need sex. If these women weren't here, this city would go insane."

An hour later, as the police make ready to leave, a young john emerges from a back room, a Nepali girl in a black sari behind him, carrying the sheets. He stops when he sees constables in black caps and gold braid with truncheons, but they wink and wave him off. Usually Rukmini locks the door when the law visits, but this one was already here. She accompanies Inspector Sudhakar and his constables downstairs. As they leave, several drenched men who've been waiting outside rush in.

Rukmini greets them and leads them up, pausing to pluck a spent lily from the pile of blossoms at the Lakshmi icon's feet. Morning, evening, and midnight she performs puja, showering these deities with fresh flowers and prostrating before them.

"My girls and I know we're guilty of a mistake," she says. "I admit that, and pray for their blessed forgiveness."

Back in their mobile unit, a Mahindra jeep, the three policemen crawl through the Siddharthnagar streets. Things are improved since Mumbai brought in paving stones; before, the narrow lanes turned to soup during monsoon. But pavement hasn't sped up traffic, because the roads are also used by pedestrians, as sidewalks have been usurped by blue, yellow, and red tarps, under which everyone is either cooking something, repairing something, or just living, often with goats.

With the downpour now a drizzle, swarms of men

in rolled-up pants, and women hiking their saris with one hand as they clutch babies with the other, negotiate the puddles. The police's windshield is screened with heavy mesh against stone pelting, but what they really need is a cowcatcher to deflect humans. Earlier, at noon, several solid blocks here were filled with rows of kneeling Muslim men in prayer caps, overflowing the red-light district's forty-eight mosques. Most are still here, among the throngs of resident SC/STs—"scheduled caste/scheduled tribes," bureaucratese for *untouchable*—whose Hindu temples are equally numerous. Thousands cluster around tarps, where people make chapatis, stir dhal, fix computers, mend clothing, hawk electronics, cobble shoes, and milk goats. Yet for being stupefyingly jammed, Siddharthnagar is surprisingly congenial.

"God's gift to Mumbai," says Inspector Sudhakar, "is that people are mostly respectful. It comes from the dharmas, which tells us to be compassionate and understanding." In all his years, he has used his .38 revolver only once, during the 1993 sectarian riots that killed nearly a thousand, mostly Muslims. That ended with thirteen bombings across the city on a single March day, widely believed to have been masterminded by the don of Indian organized crime, Dawood Ibrahim, who operated from a Siddharthnagar tailor shop, encoding secret messages in his stitching. Today, the worst problems involve not violence, but the stresses of infrastructure whose limits have been sensationally exceeded.

"There's no place to park, so people leave autos on the street. The whole city is like a used car lot. We're lucky that only fifty a day get stolen."

But other than an occasional terrorist attack from Pakistanis next door, things are amazingly calm. "That is fortunate, because our manpower is stretched as these mobs keep getting bigger. At least we're not Karachi. The difference is because here," says Inspector Sudhakar, "everyone works. When everyone has employment, no one has the time or need to break the law. Mumbai is a lot safer than New York."

———

Has Mumbai, née Bombay, somehow suspended the laws of physics? It is swollen beyond anyone's comprehension. Traffic is beyond berserk. Lanes are ignored or nonexistent, horns insistent, construction cranes omnipresent. Everywhere are legions of humanity, picking their way over eternal building rubble, weaving between stalled cars, or leaping sidewalks and road dividers in motorized rickshaws. Greater Mumbai, population 21 million though nobody really knows, is the archetypal new megalopolis. When India becomes the most populous country, metro Mumbai will be closing fast on shrinking Tokyo for the dubious distinction of being the world's largest city.

The difference, however, is that Tokyo is in hyperdeveloped Japan, while half of India is still in mud huts or under tarps. Yet this city, its biggest human crucible, somehow works—because everyone here is working. Anybody in India who wants a job can come to Mumbai and either find or make one. And they do, about a thousand more each day. With its deepwater harbor, Mumbai is India's principal port and its financial, business, and entertainment capital. Forty percent of the country's tax revenues come from this humongous city. With its Bollywood and coastal real estate, it would be south Asia's Los Angeles—if Los Angeles were this solvent.

There is so much work here because of the perpetual construction, regardless of diluvial monsoons and temperatures that even in winter can approach 100°F. Just before June rains, 107–110°F is not unknown. To see Mumbai enter a monsoon is like watching a stew come to full boil. The atmosphere jells, heat waves ripple from pavement, asphalt perspires shiny beads of tar. But nothing stops. If anything, Mumbai accelerates, as construction turns feverish ahead of ruinous downpours, and colored tarpaulins are rigged over the gaps between soaring new properties-in-progress.

It is a city devoid of vacant lots. Between every pair of new skyscrapers are more ubiquitous tarps, with people who arrived yesterday living under them. Beneath affluent high-rises along the waterfront, people dwell in drainage pipes. Wherever there's a wall, bridge, or abutment, tents are strung by migrants. They come willing to work any job, high on a bridge or deep down a hole. First the laborer arrives, then his brothers, then an entire generation of relatives accompanying his wife, then they have kids. When they've worked long enough to amass scraps of metal or loose concrete chunks, walls slowly rise to meet the oilcloth roof, and then there's another slum.

Nobody chases them away, because they're productive. Over past decades, it's been China with the huge young labor force. But with China now aging, it's India's turn for what demographers call the population dividend, and a cornucopia of labor runneth over in Mumbai. Even the richest man in town, Mukesh Ambani, chairman of the energy and materials conglomerate Reliance Industries, who's built a twenty-seven-floor, four-hundred-thousand-square-foot home for his family, doesn't run off the neighbors living in the cracks between the surrounding buildings, because his mansion needs a staff of six hundred.

Mumbai is one of the few places on Earth where

there is 100 percent employment, where literally any-body can find work—unlike its gloomy megacity alter-ego five hundred miles up the Arabian seacoast, Karachi. Mumbai may lack Karachi's menace—but what will happen when it's all built?

Building is what Krishna Pujari is worried about—not that they'll stop, but that Dharavi, where he lives and makes his living, is where the developers have fixed their crosshairs next, and they're going to build him out of business. Until recently, Dharavi claimed to be the biggest, most densely agglomerated slum in Asia. By 2011, however, the *Times of India* reported that Dharavi had been surpassed by four others—all of them also in Mumbai.

Still, Krishna declares, none has the sheer pres-ence of Dharavi, an expanse of tarps and tin roofs reaching the horizon, so close together that when seen from the tracks above—Dharavi is wedged between two commuter rail lines—it seems possible to stroll across them and never touch ground. And they are seen from those tracks by millions daily, because Dharavi is practically in the middle of Mumbai's financial district, on sublimely valuable real estate that has developers drooling and scheming.

In the seventeenth century, before the British East India Company appeared, Mumbai was a clutch of fishing villages on seven islands. The British built causeways to connect them, encircling what became Bombay Harbor. By the nineteenth century, the gaps between the islands had been filled. Where Dharavi sits today was once under water—its name means "waves"—and frequently is again when monsoons engulf the open sewers.

In Dharavi's dark passageways, most barely broad enough for two adults to pass, a million people work in ten thousand small industries, under conditions that would burst dials off occupational health and safety meters, if such things existed. In warehouses with scorched asbestos walls, blackened men melt scrap aluminum soda cans into ingots. Nearby, other men salvage empty five-gallon vegetable-oil tins by immersing them in cauldrons of water heated over indoor bonfires to boil away the residues. Alongside them, women scrape off loosened labels while mopping their faces with limp cotton saris. Above, smoke gathers like a low-hanging thundercloud as it slowly bleeds through a hole in the ceiling. The room clangs like a giant bell as more men flatten tins too damaged for reuse.

Two streets over, Krishna Pujari greets by name every man who, for a stretch of several blocks, recycles cardboard—saving what can be stamped with a fresh logo, shredding the rest to mulch into new cardboard. He pops his head into rooms where flocks of children salt cowhides headed to China for tanning, a business employing forty thousand Dharavi citizens. He proceeds to Kumbharwada, a ten-acre sector where twenty-two hundred families—mothers, fathers, swarming kids—turn truckloads of clay hauled from rice paddies north of Mumbai into ornamental ceramic pots. These are some of Dharavi's original tenants; their pottery works are licensed cottage industries, which Gandhi promoted. On homemade wheels, they throw thousands of flowerpots, wrapping each in clothing scraps that burn off as they're fired in hundreds of mudbrick ovens.

This was one of Dharavi's more benign industries, until cotton clothing gave way to polyester.

"I warn them," Krishna says, "that fumes from melting nylon are toxic. 'We have to work,' they say. 'Show us a better way, and we'll use it.'"

Krishna Pujari's own way is entrepreneurial. A whiplike, smiling man in jeans, polo shirt, and gold chain, he was thirteen when he came in 1993 from a farming village near Mangalore, the second oldest of nine children. He put himself through secondary school carrying tea to office workers, and when more of his brothers arrived, they started servicing cafeterias. Waiting tables one day, he learned from a British expat that tourists in Brazil actually hire guides to show them dirt-poor favelas above Rio de Janeiro. Since 2006, he's run Reality Tours & Travel, offering guided trips through Mumbai slums to around twenty tourists a day who pay to see abject poverty.

Recently, he's begun bicycle tours that begin at dawn at Dhobi Ghat, the vast outdoor laundry where linens from Mumbai's hospitals and hotels are scrubbed and hung to dry. He's done well enough to bring a wife from his village, a marriage his parents arranged. His latest venture is the computer class he started in a long, dark room whose floor is lined with a dozen old terminals. In front of each sits an intent barefoot child, half of them girls, including three in headscarves. "We're teaching them skills of the future," Krishna says proudly.

He continues on, dodging barefoot children retrieving balls from open drains that froth with gray bubbles, past doorways emitting the sharp tang of lye, where men and women carve three-foot-high brown blocks of the laundry soap they make into bars. Above their heads hang plastic bottles of colored liquids, each a different scent for the dish detergents they also make. Farther above, beyond the ceiling, is where they live. Nearly all of Dharavi's people live above their workplaces, but it's too tight here for staircases, so sleeping quarters are accessed by ladders clamped to exterior walls.

Krishna climbs one that leads to a roof—which,

like every other rooftop in sight, is covered with kaleidoscopic piles of crushed plastic that's been washed and spread on tarps to dry. Plastic is the biggest Dharavi industry of all. It arrives by truck in huge sacks from around the world: salvaged water bottles, plastic cutlery, hospital waste, cruise ship waste, spent plastic bags, and mountains of synthetic-fiber clothing. Dharavi plastic pickers have contracts with hotel chains and entire airlines for their disposable cups, knives, forks, spoons, and coffee stirrers. "What looks like garbage to others, to us is gold," Krishna says.

In an alleyway below, women separate all this scrap plastic by color into dozens of milk crates, while a girl in a paisley hijab serves them tea. From here it is bagged and hauled farther up the alley to cast-iron grinding machines built from retrofitted truck flywheels, which spit sparks and billowing plastic dust. The pulverized results are dunked and doused in a succession of fifty-five-gallon drums, then taken up top to dry. Finally, they're rendered in vast vats into molten polymer soup, whose acrylic stench suffuses the alleys where more women are sorting used swizzle sticks and stacks of lipstick-stained plastic airline cups, and men strip insulation from enormous tangles of copper wire.

The plastic gets poured into molds, producing pellet-sized nurdles to be shipped and remelted into consumer goods: so-called "added value" whose profit margins Dharavi never sees, except for what gets molded right here into miniature temples, plastic deities, cruciforms, and other trinkets. The curios of the world are no longer confected by the world's artisans, but mass-crafted by its slum dwellers.

A few blocks later, Dharavi's acrid aromatics dissolve into something actually inviting. Krishna drops into a basement bakery, one of hundreds here that make cakes, biscuits, bread, and savory curry-flavored pastries. He accepts a piece of a wheel of pappadam, stretched to dry across a straw basket.

"Few people realize that tons of food that Mumbai eats daily is made here—the labels don't say where." Neither do many know that Dharavi's combined annual income is an estimated $665 million. Mumbai's financial rajahs have other plans for this prime location: a contentious Dharavi Redevelopment Project involving blocks of high-rise apartments, offices, hospitals, shopping malls, and multiplexes is scheduled to begin momentarily. Everything else will be demolished.

"Everybody's fighting it. But the government says whether you agree or not, we'll do it, because we own the land." And if they're all kicked out?

"We'll go farther north. And build many more Dharavis."

Human-rights advocates often argue that the world's poor are unfairly targeted for population control, because collectively they leave a much smaller footprint on the planet than the overprivileged few. That was surely true a half-century ago, when two-thirds of the world's humans were peasants. Today most are urban — and most of them are urban poor. However ragged they may be, Dharavi's rabble increasingly carry mobile phones; the electricity they use to charge them may be pirated, but generating it produces carbon nonetheless. The stupendous Mumbai traffic grew even more demented with the introduction of Tata Motors' Nano, powered with a rickshaw engine and designed to sell for US$2,000 so that everyone might afford one. Most Dharavi dwellers probably can't — but their children, already learning to colonize the twenty-first-century cyberscape, probably will. With the roads and rail tracks of Mumbai lined by more multistory housing for miles in all directions except seaward, their cumulative demand will broaden that footprint across what was once farmland and home to myriad tropical fauna.

The ancient Hindus saw those fauna not as creatures beneath ourselves, but as manifestations of the many faces of God. The first four avatars, or incarnations, of the life-affirming deity Vishnu weren't humans, but animals: a fish, a tortoise, a boar, a lion. Hanuman, the great warrior deity of the *Ramayana,* is depicted as a monkey. And one of the most venerated aspects of God in the entire Hindu pantheon is Ganesha, the elephant-headed overcomer of obstacles.

At Mumbai's Siddhivinayak Temple, which is dedicated to Lord Ganesha, the usual multitude has gathered despite the afternoon's wall of rain. It is Tuesday, the most auspicious day for Ganesha worship according to Hindu astrology. Bearing bouquets of marigolds and hibiscus, five hundred thousand people shuffle barefoot in snaking lines past several metal detectors, toward an elephant-headed effigy seated in half-lotus on a gilded throne draped with garlands of flowers. According to legend, the two-and-a-half-foot-tall icon, carved from a single chunk of black slate, was discovered buried in a field. Today it is coated with red lacquer and encrusted with diamonds. Ganesha wears a gold crown and rings on his four hands. His trunk swings to the right, signifying that he fulfills all desires. The pilgrims who leave flowers, sweets, and fresh fruit by the carved wooden image of Kroncha, Ganesha's pet mouse, come to beg the deity's protection for their marriages, their newborns, their new homes. For those far in back, a Sony monitor overhead shows the devotional puja service, where, to the echo of kettledrums, the choicest of these gifts are laid directly at Ganesha's holy feet.

"The elephant is huge, strong, and intelligent," says pandit Gajanan Modak, Siddhivinayak Temple's head priest, a thickset man in a gold-trimmed white dhoti. "Like humans, elephants have religious rituals. They mourn their dead, and bury them with branches and leaves. They have sharp eyes, and deep emotions."

But unlike humans, India's elephants are now endangered, and humans are outnumbering and imperiling all the animal aspects of God in the pantheon. In Mumbai, the Parsi Zoroastrians, who believe that burial and cremation contaminate the Earth with impurities, have always left their dead atop holy towers for vultures to consume. But now the birds have disappeared, felled by the same cattle ointment that devastated Nepal's carrion-eating birds. The Parsis are left to try decomposing bodies with solar concentrators.

When Mumbai's vultures disappeared, feral dogs and cats proliferated, causing a rabies epidemic. "We humans are a problem," Modak says. "When we perform puja, afterward we pour the rice and flowers into the river as offerings for the fish. But nowadays people stuff them into plastic bags that end up in the sea." There is a need, he says, to measure the number of people this world can contain. In Hinduism, there is no proscription against using any means available to do that. "Hindus have always planned their lives. Modern life requires modern planning."

But is there not a need to bear children until a son is born to light his parents' way into heaven?

"A myth. I have two daughters. They are as capable as any man to light our funeral pyres."

He serves prasad—yogurt and honey, blessed during puja—to his guests. "We are bringing the Kali Yuga upon ourselves," he says. "That is when we destroy our environment and kill ourselves. Even the smallest insect has a reason to be in this world. We are all creatures connected with each other. Lord Ganesha has his mouse, to whom we bow and ask permission to venerate our lord. Lord Krishna has his divine cow, Saraswati her swan, Lakshmi her owl. Hindus accept that we can't live without animals. If they survive, we survive."

Along with his sacred cow, the blue avatar Lord Krishna is always shown with his beautiful lover, the supreme goddess Radha.

"She is nature, the mother of us all. Krishna, like Jesus and Buddha, is the incarnation of God in human form. He represents the human population. They are the ideal couple we must strive to be: humanity and nature, in perfect balance. In perfect harmony. In perfect love."

CHAPTER 15

Safe Sex

i. Rubber

Thirty kilometers below Bangkok, where the Chao Phraya River meets the Gulf of Thailand, stands a remnant mangrove forest. In the early twentieth century, several monks retreated here from the city to practice the oldest form of Buddhism, known as Theravāda, or the Forest Tradition. They named the temple they founded Wat Asokaram, the Monastery of No Sorrow.

In the twenty-first century, the estuary surrounding Wat Asokaram is no longer a forest wilderness. To one side are shrimp farms; on the other, a beach resort. The temple itself is now a Buddhist tourist attraction: a three-tiered, white wedding cake with thirteen spires. At one end of its ample parking lot, a path leads into what is left of the mangroves. Along raised walkways amid the trees are the monks' kutis: clapboard cottages on pilings above tidal mud flats, shaded by curtains of hanging aerial roots.

The throb of urban Thailand fades here beneath the chitter of curlews and the splash of crabs and mud skippers. "In a city," says Ajaan Boonku, a monk here for more than half a century, "you can study to control the mind. But it is difficult to achieve tranquility. In a forest, it is much easier to not think."

At eighty-three, Ajaan Boonku is mostly sinew and bone. Wrapped in a brown muslin sanghati, he sits cross-legged atop a prayer rug on his covered porch. A bench against the wooden porch rail holds offerings from pilgrims who come seeking peace and guidance: shampoo, bars of soap, mouthwash, toothbrushes, Sensodyne toothpaste, and boxes of tissues.

To Buddhists, attachment to material things, even to the world itself, is a trap, because nothing is permanent. Is there no obligation, then, for a Buddhist to try to conserve the world, such as these mangroves and their fragile fauna?

"A humble Buddhist cannot strive to control the world," he whispers in a voice like rustling leaves. "But balance cannot be achieved without nature. We monks of the forest try to preserve nature, as examples for others to follow."

Ajaan Boonku, Theravāda Buddhist monk, Wat Asokaram
Monastery, Thailand

And if the entire human race falls out of balance because there are more of us than nature can accommodate, does Buddhism permit us to control our reproduction?

"If more people means more problems, they can adjust by any means. In Buddhism, we don't prevent birth control. People with good morals know to have the right-size family."

But to those who lack a monk's discipline, the means to act on those morals were long unavailable, and human numbers grew overwhelming, undoing much of nature. Has an onrush of humanity possibly hastened its own demise? Ajaan Boonku shuts his eyes and leans on one thin forearm atop his thigh. Minutes pass. Then he straightens.

"We don't know if the end for humans nears. We know it may come, so the mind must be ready. Overuse of this world by people brings disaster — floods, global warming. But it's not the end of the Earth, even if it is our own. Nature will move onward, beyond us. But for now," he says, "it is a good idea for us to save trees. It helps."

Across the mouth of the Chao Phraya, another Buddhist temple, Wat Khun Samut Trawat, has been severed from the mainland by the rising Gulf of Thailand. Perched now atop a rocky islet, surrounded by half-drowned utility poles where there once was a village, the temple's floor has been raised several feet, but the water keeps coming.

In 2011, a monsoon bearing 345 percent more rain than normal submerged much of Thailand, including half of Bangkok, a metropolitan area of 14 million people.

To the Western world, it would have been yet one more flood in a low-lying south Asian country, except that this one inundated Bangkok factories that assemble much of the world's computer hard drives and semiconductor chips, as well as Japanese and American automobiles. The toll in Thailand approached $50 billion, and supply delays amplified those losses throughout the world. Damages would have been even higher, but a decision was made to open floodgates to divert the floodwaters into millions of hectares of rice paddies upstream of the city, to spare Bangkok's downtown.

That included Sukhumvit Soi 12—a narrow four-block spur off Sukhumvit Road, a Bangkok thoroughfare lined with Sheratons, Westins, and a high-rise fashion mall. Along Soi 12's length, food stalls sell skewers of fried fish, pad Thai, oyster omelets, and sizzling chicken. Every few steps is a parlor offering variants of massage: herbal, oil, aroma, or soapy; facial, foot, head, or full-body—the last sometimes featuring Thailand's euphemistic "happy ending."

Halfway down Sukhumvit Soi 12, just past a miniature Buddhist shrine atop a white marble pedestal, a brick path lit by bamboo lanterns leads through a garden of banyans and palms, to a restaurant. According to guidebooks, it is one of Bangkok's best. Inside, the lanterns give way to yellow, orange, green, and red fixtures shaped like globes, bouquets, and giant strawberries. On closer inspection, their designs turn out to be glowing collages—of multicolored condoms. A step farther, and condoms are covering everything, including several life-sized mannequins. Here's Santa Condom, his suit, beard, and curly hair entirely confected of red and white rubbers. Same with the dress of the Thai princess at his side. A bride's traditional white wedding gown and her tiara: all condoms. Ditto for bikini'd beachgoers, a bowing Chinese couple, assorted superheroes (including one named Captain Condom), and even Tiger Woods, the shaft of his putter a long stack of rolled condoms, next to a sign asking if he remembered to use them.

In addition to condoms, a gift shop sells coasters that read, "No Glove, No Love"; long-stem condom flowers; condom brooches; condom-shaped USB drives; 100 percent Thai silk neckties bearing a Gumby-like happy condom; condom key-chains that read, "In Rubber We Trust"; and T-shirts printed with ditties such as "Weapons of Mass Protection"—and:

"We took off our clothes, I got on top of you. How long before it starts feeling good?"

"I don't know, but I've got a headache already."

Above the bar, near a portrait of a sly Mona Lisa dangling a pair of rubbers, is a model of the *Mayflower*, its hull, sails, and riggings crafted of condoms. In the restaurant's courtyard, where the haute prophylactic décor continues, menus reassure that "Our food is guaranteed not to cause pregnancy." In lieu of after-dinner mints, the check arrives with flavored condoms.

The name of this discombobulating place is Cabbages & Condoms. Although its history is peripherally meshed with that of Thailand's legendary sex industry, which crescendoed when fifty thousand U.S. troops were stationed here during the Vietnam War, the impetus behind Cabbages & Condoms goes far deeper. Quirky as it seems, it is part of what many call a miracle that changed all of Thailand—and continues to do so.

"Foreign assistance," Mechai Viravaidya once told a visiting delegation of U.S. congressmen, "is like an erection. It's nice while you have it, but it doesn't last forever."

That exchange took place in 1976. At the time, Mechai was in charge of something for which his economics and commerce degree from Melbourne University had absolutely not prepared him. Upon graduating, he had taken a post with Thailand's economic development agency, traveling to evaluate infrastructure projects. Until then, he knew little of his country outside of Bangkok, where his parents were doctors.

The job was a chance to learn about transportation, energy, irrigation, schools, and telecommunications. But as Mechai's biographer, Thomas D'Agnes, recounts in his book *From Condoms to Cabbages,* wherever he went, the same thing repeatedly grabbed his attention: astonishing numbers of children.

"In every village I asked women how many," he recalls over coffee at the conference table he moved into the Cabbages & Condoms bar, which is much more fun than his office upstairs. "Seven to ten was typical." He would look at the hordes of kids, then at mothers nursing one while pregnant with another, then at the prospectus for the project he was evaluating. Nothing added up.

"When I studied economics, they taught us not to worry about the number of people, because we can always expand food production. No problem." Except there were plenty of problems. Mechai hadn't studied demography, but he'd learned accounting. The numbers he ran told him that at a certain point there wouldn't be any more places to put more rice paddies. And not just food. Every child ratcheted up demand for housing, clothing, schooling, and jobs. Add things like plumbing, water purification, and health services, then multiply them by the multiplying little bodies that surrounded his government jeep in every village he visited, and he concluded that his agency's goals were futile.

There was no way that Thailand could go forward with so many people. On the contrary, they were doomed to fall farther back with each new, bigger generation. What were developmental economists possibly thinking?

With his agency reports vanishing into the bureaucratic maw, Mechai Viravaidya began moonlighting, writing folksy newspaper columns about economics under the pseudonym "GNP." They earned him another extracurricular job as a radio commentator under yet another pseudonym, as he was still working for the government. But then radio led to television: A tall and handsome former national tennis champion, Mechai soon became a highly recognizable soap opera star and stage actor.

But he was still an economist, and he was thinking hard about how to leverage his media skills to

Cabbages & Condoms, Bangkok, Thailand

that end. A column he wrote in 1968, extolling family-planning workers as unsung heroes of development, caught the eye of a Thai government advisor from a U.S.-based NGO, The Population Council. Their ensuing friendship led him to a position with the newly created Planned Parenthood Association of Thailand.

He didn't stay long. His director proved to be squeamish when talking about sex: a bit of an occupational challenge under the circumstances. She was especially mortified by Mechai's public presentations.

"I would start out with a box of pills, and people would just look at it. Then I'd show an IUD and get blank stares." One day, while showing a condom at a training session for schoolteachers, without thinking he unwrapped its foil pouch.

Immediately, people started giggling. *"Aha,* I thought."

So he unfurled it. Women shrieked. Now he definitely had their attention. Improvising, he explained that condoms were all-purpose tools that could be used as tourniquets, hair bands, wineskins ("or," he adds today, "as waterproof protectors for mobile phones"). Then he did what boys everywhere have done, but not before an auditorium filled with two thousand teachers: He blew it up. Now even the shriekers were laughing. Condoms were distributed, and Mechai enlisted the whole room in an inflating contest, with a year's free supply for the biggest balloon.

Soon thereafter, he persuaded some key people at the International Planned Parenthood Foundation to fund an experiment in family planning, separate from Thailand's staid Planned Parenthood affiliate. It was an idea he'd gotten from women with big families in tiny villages.

"You have seven?" he'd ask. "You must be really smart. My mother is smart, but she never could have handled that many."

Almost invariably, that provoked a sighing admission that they'd never wanted all those kids. There was a way to control such things, he'd explain, handing them a box of pills. "These are family-welfare vitamins. You take them for the welfare of your family. They make you stronger, by giving your body a rest. If you decide you want to get pregnant again, you just stop."

Letting women choose proved far more effective than making them feel stupid or guilty for having so many children. Everyone wanted the pills—which led to the next problem: Until then, only medical clinics dispensed them, but just 20 percent of the population lived in easy reach of one. Even if they did, many found medical centers intimidating.

"In business school, we're taught to get to know our customers. So we'd ask local women who they trusted the most. Often, it was the local shopkeeper." That was perfect. He'd put up a sign reading, "Contraceptives Available Here" right next to the Coca-Cola sign.

"We had the same customer base as Coke, so we used the same vendor. And our product was far less bulky."

Letting communities distribute their own contraceptives was the idea he'd pitched to International Planned Parenthood, and he used his showmanship to leverage a $250,000 grant, far beyond expectations. It soon seemed like Mechai Viravaidya was everywhere in Thailand, passing out T-shirts that read, "A Condom a Day Keeps the Doctor Away," getting taxi drivers and traffic cops—his "Cops and Rubbers" brigade—to hand out condoms, and passing them out himself at state dinners to foreign dignitaries. Along Thailand's rivers and coasts, where shopkeepers were usually fisherfolk plying their catch, floating markets sold fish and contraceptives. Throughout the country, condoms became known as "Mechais."

When the inevitable question arose about whether birth control might be sinful, he consulted Buddhist scholars for scriptural guidance. The closest anyone could find was a reference in Theravāda Buddhism's Pāli Canon, stating that birth causes suffering.

"From your own teachings," Mechai wrote to every temple in Thailand, "we can conclude that to prevent birth prevents suffering." He enclosed a photograph of an abbot from a Bangkok temple sprinkling holy water on pills and condoms. It was soon published by newspapers throughout the country.

"No wonder there's no side effects from the pills," women told him. "They've been blessed."

Within five years, Mechai Viravaidya's organization—known today as PDA, the Population and Community Development Association—trained three hundred twenty thousand teachers to educate students about family planning. "We have to win over kids," Mechai told his staff, "because the most important thing to customers is their children." Besides the ever-popular condom balloon contests, he had Thai kids playing his version of Chutes and Ladders: Mother takes a pill or Uncle buys a condom: move one square ahead. Uncle gets drunk and doesn't use condom: fall back five squares, etc.

One day a village woman told him, "It's true that many children make you poor. But fewer children don't make you rich, either."

"You're right," he agreed. So he raised more money

to fund an idea that began to pay back almost immediately: nonpregnancy agriculture credits. Villagers would elect a group of trusted women to stake other women with starter loans. "If you're not pregnant for a year," they'd explain, "you can borrow money to raise two pigs. If you're not pregnant for two years, you can get money for four pigs. Not pregnant for three years, you get six pigs."

Women soon realized that when they weren't pregnant, they were making money. The nonpregnancy credits soon led from pigs to mushrooms, crabs, vegetables, edible crickets, and fruit trees. Finally, Mechai was fulfilling his real goal: making his country viable. His training was in economics, not family planning. Contraception, he argued, was a means for people to have a chance at prosperity, and for Thailand to have a future.

"The only way out of poverty is through business and enterprise. Access to credit must be a human right." Years later, when his PDA won the Bill and Melinda Gates Foundation's 2007 Award for Global Health, he used part of the $1 million prize to take his "barefoot entrepreneurs" model even further, by establishing Thailand's Global Warming Foundation. The idea was to give poor people a way to help themselves and to help meet a global emergency. Over the years, their lending had expanded to small businesses ranging from embroidered silks to ice cream to raising off-season organic limes and cantaloupes that earned several times their normal price. Now, partnering with sponsoring Thai companies, they could finance these micro-loans by planting trees. Under the plan, companies pay elderly villagers to sprout seedlings that younger villagers plant. Each is valued at US$1.25, so a village that plants twenty-five thousand trees earns $30,000 for its development fund.

"This way," says Mechai, "they feel ownership of their lending banks, and of their planet's future."

In 1970, the United States invaded Cambodia, a country it was already bombing in hapless pursuit of North Vietnamese forces. The invasion had the unintended consequence of unleashing Cambodia's Khmer Rouge, a communist force previously under the disciplined rule of North Vietnam. Its genocidal leader, Pol Pot, soon launched his own equally disastrous version of China's Cultural Revolution. After U.S. troops left, the Vietnamese finally routed the Khmer Rouge in 1979. Under its reign, entire harvests had been destroyed, a fifth of Cambodians had perished, and famine had struck. Nearly a million Cambodian refugees, many starving, were either in Thailand or packed into refugee camps along its border.

They needed to eat, even as Thailand was trying

to feed its own exploding numbers. By then, Mechai Viravaidya's PDA, working with the Ministry of Public Health, had helped to cut Thailand's stratospheric fertility rates by nearly half in just six years. The toll of women dying from illegal abortions that commonly involved bamboo slivers had slowed after PDA established a clinic for legal terminations to protect the health of the mother, which became the model for clinics throughout the country. It was no surprise to Mechai when they were asked to help with the Cambodian crisis.

His prescription for the refugee camps was what PDA was already doing in Thai villages: First, empower families that could ill afford more hungry children with the means to control pregnancies if they chose. Second, give them a chance to provide their own relief, rather than depend indefinitely on donations. They organized family-planning clinics in the camps, run by the refugees themselves. Other refugees were soon in charge of sanitation and waste removal. To counter animosity from locals, they channeled relief funds to purchase food directly from a network of small farmers that they started, cutting out middlemen.

That program worked so well that surplus cabbages, garlic, squash, and other produce began to accumulate at PDA headquarters in Bangkok, so

Mechai opened a vegetable stand with profits going toward the refugee fund. As he still reflexively disbursed condoms—Thailand today is the world's biggest producer—its sign read, "Cabbages & Condoms." The vegetable stand prospered, and became a restaurant. Then six restaurants.

In the 1980s, Mechai was tapped more for public service, as head of Thailand's public water authority and as Deputy Minister of Industry. Then came another national crisis. When AIDS first appeared, he tried to convince the prime minister how serious it was. The prime minister feared that declaring a national emergency over a sexually transmitted disease would be disastrous for Thai tourism, of which the sex industry had become a pillar. Not waiting for things to deteriorate enough to change his mind, Mechai approached the military, which happened to own 326 Thai radio stations. The generals, understanding the threat of their troops becoming infected, gave him carte blanche access to their airwaves.

Having the world's foremost condom expert running a national AIDS program, as eventually occurred, proved fortuitous. Presently, Captain Condom was dispensing samples in the nation's schools and reminding business leaders that "dead customers don't buy." After Mechai was named Minister of Tourism, resorts held Miss Condom pageants and hotel minibars were stocked with prophylactics. It became mandatory to use a condom in a Thai brothel. Because prostitution is not just a tourist attraction but considered routine recreation by Thai men, the United Nations calculated that 7.7 million Thais were prevented from getting infected with HIV.

By the new millennium, HIV infection rates in the country were down by 90 percent. And Thailand's fertility rate, 7.5 children per woman in 1975, had fallen to 1.5, where it remains today.

ii. Bamboo

In the rural province of Buriram five hours northeast of Bangkok, ten kilometers from one of the two Cabbages & Condoms vacation resorts PDA operates to finance its projects, is a large geodesic dome made of bamboo. It is the auditorium for the campus of the Mechai Pattana School, where carbon-absorbent, fast-growing renewable bamboo is the chief construction material. Since 2009, ninety local children in grades seven to nine attend; a high school opened in 2012. Each classroom has two teachers, a 1:5 teacher-student ratio. Students have classes in math, Thai, English, science, history, art, social studies, and environmental studies. They also help to screen and select applicants for incoming classes. (To avoid nepotism, siblings are automatically accepted; since even rural women now average two at most, there are plenty of places left over.) Students also participate in interviewing and hiring prospective teachers, and serve with parents and teachers on the school board.

Rather than textbook-based lessons, the curriculum is woven into study projects that students propose, based on whatever piques their curiosity. Emphasis is on original thinking, not rote learning. "The school's two goals," says its founder, "are to turn students into social entrepreneurs and philanthropists."

Meaning: helping their villages become places they don't have to leave in order to earn a living, instead of going to Bangkok factories or Israeli date plantations, or becoming sex workers. While attending "the bamboo school," they teach younger children to use computers, elderly villagers to read, and their own parents to design household budgets. Students start and run their own businesses, raising specialty fruits, recycling plastic, selling duck eggs, making jewelry, sprouting beans, and preparing baked goods, all financed by a student-run bank. Half the profits underwrite scholarships for needy primary school students they identify in their villages; the rest is reinvested in their fledgling enterprises. During tenth grade, students spend a year helping to run Birds & Bees, PDA's resort in a famous

Thai beach destination, Pattaya, where they learn the hospitality business.

In lieu of tuition, students and parents plant four hundred trees and contribute four hundred hours of community service, tutoring and keeping their village and temples clean. "Our school is not just for students," Mechai tells parents. "We guarantee that every family living near the poverty line will be out of it in nine months." Parents are automatically eligible for micro-loans and for occupational training. In sixteen surrounding villages, students' families are running cricket farms, purifying and selling water, cultivating mushrooms, making paper-flower wedding and funeral wreaths, and raising pigs.

Mechai Viravaidya stands on a thatch-and-bamboo-covered bridge built on multicolored struts that leads across a lotus-filled lagoon to his school. From the water's surface, haze and a frog chorus rise along with the temperature into the bright morning. Mild-mannered, in his usual bow tie, at seventy Mechai is slowed a bit by diabetes but still athletically fit and unremittingly engaged. He proceeds to the campus side, where the bridge's rainbow scheme continues in dozens of painted planters cut from sections of discarded drainage pipe. Here, students grow asparagus, chilies, basil, eggplant, assorted edible greens, and lime trees, which, through clever pruning and watering schedules, they coax to fruit just when limes are out of season and scarce. Mechai watches girls and boys in uniforms they designed themselves—dark skirts and trousers, white shirts and blouses with plaid collars—water a living sculpture of discarded soda cans filled with soil and nailed to colored posts, from which sprout herbs and chives. Lettuce grows in suspended tiers of discarded PVC pipe, slit lengthwise and drip-irrigated by discarded intravenous feeding tubes connected to plastic bags that once held saline solution. Even discarded sneakers and irrigation boots have been converted to planters.

Mango, coconut palm, banana, custard apple, and rose apple trees are spread among bamboo classrooms, where students at computer screens learn to graph growing cycles. There's a library with bamboo furniture the students built themselves, and a toy lending library for village children, stocked with playthings that students have collected. Surrounding the campus are rice paddies, which grow an organic cash crop that pays for teacher salaries and the school's operating budget.

A motto embroidered on the students' sleeves reads, "The more you give, the more you get." Mechai sits among them in the spacious, open-sided cafeteria, kept spotless with homegrown, chemical-free cleansers made from neem tree oils and lemon grass, where students earn their meals by planting more trees. "No free lunches," he reminds them.

As long as they waste no food, students may eat all they want. It will take half a generation to see if these rural children—who, but for this school, might otherwise have grown up illiterate, undernourished, and impoverished—turn into the entrepreneurs and philanthropists Mechai hopes. More than half are girls, and one thing he is confident of is that they are destined, if not for careers of their own making, at least not to be sex workers—and not mothers to more children than they, their village, and their country can afford.

"In Thailand," says the man who got his whole country laughing by blowing up condoms, and then got everyone to use them, "we should train leaders of tomorrow, not followers of yesterday. Yesterday, we had too many births. Today, we have a more manageable number to feed and educate. With that, and with people benefiting by helping each other, there can be plenty for everybody."

PART FIVE

CHAPTER 16

Parkland Earth

i. The Oxymoron

In his teens, Theodore Roosevelt read Charles Darwin's *Origin of the Species* and decided to become a wildlife biologist. At Harvard, his career in natural science gave way to political science, but Roosevelt would eventually have an impact on biology that, at least quantitatively, approached Darwin's epic qualitative contribution. Between 1903 and 1909, President Theodore Roosevelt created 150 national forests in the United States, including 93 in a single day, preserving an area roughly equal to France, Belgium, The Netherlands, and Luxembourg combined. He also doubled the number of American national parks (to 10; there are now 59).

By doing so, he helped expand the concept of

wildlife biology to include an applied field, which Darwin might have termed an oxymoron: wildlife management. The idea that something can be both wild and managed epitomizes our complicated human identity—suspended, as French philosopher Blaise Pascal described us, somewhere between angels and animals. Nevertheless, the fate of many species beyond our own now depends on the skills of human stewards to finesse a delicate equilibrium among prey, predators, plants, and ourselves.

This is not easy. Consider one of the most famous episodes in the annals of wildlife management, the mule deer of Arizona's Kaibab Plateau, north of the Grand Canyon. In 1906, President Roosevelt created the Grand Canyon National Game Preserve to protect deer that browse on the Kaibab Plateau's spruce, aspen, oak, ponderosa pine, piñon, and juniper. At the time, there were an estimated four thousand deer there. The new game preserve enhanced their survival by banishing the sheep and cattle that competed for their forage, and by offering bounties on the mountain lions, wolves, bobcats, and coyotes that preyed on them. Over the ensuing decades, thousands of predators were killed—so many that the wolves were effectively exterminated.

In 1913, when Roosevelt arrived there to hunt lions, there were so many deer that he wondered if hunting should be permitted to control their numbers. But he was no longer president, and laws he'd created prohibited harvesting the species they were designed to protect. By 1922, between fifty thousand and one hundred thousand mule deer were gobbling all the available berries, acorns, seedlings, and forage, and Forest Service personnel feared that their population was headed for a crash. Biologists and wildlife managers met to discuss taking action. Among the options were relocating some deer elsewhere, culling the herd by legalizing hunting, or doing nothing.

But science was complicated by politics. The Kaibab Plateau was divided between two federal jurisdictions: the national game preserve, and the newly created Grand Canyon National Park. Each had different management goals—as did the young state of Arizona, which declared that keeping tourists from the Grand Canyon's North Rim just so men with noisy guns could slaughter big-antlered tourist attractions was not going to happen.

The surging deer population had been helped by a dozen exceptionally wet winters before 1918, which had produced bumper crops of succulents and nutritious forage like deer vetch and cliffrose that allowed does to produce plenty of milk for their fawns. Some years of normal rainfall followed—until 1924, which was particularly dry. Spring forage was way down, and low-hanging tree branches that does could reach were quickly overbrowsed.

That autumn, defying both the National Park Service and the state of Arizona, Forest Service wildlife managers enlisted horseback cowboys in an attempt to herd thousands of mule deer off the North Rim, down into the Grand Canyon, and up the other side. Except for providing bestseller material for western writer Zane Grey, who participated, the great Grand Canyon deer drive was a grand fiasco. All it accomplished was to confirm that wild creatures do not behave like docile, domesticated cattle. Next, the Forest Service opened the game preserve to hunters, several of whom Arizona arrested. That was followed by a severe winter, and the crash that everyone feared commenced. An estimated 70 percent of Kaibab Plateau mule deer starved to death in the North Rim snows.

Two of the twentieth century's foremost ecologists, Aldo Leopold and Rachel Carson, would later cite the tragedy of Kaibab Plateau mule deer as an object lesson in why predators are necessary to nature's plan. Without such a natural check, a species is doomed to overpopulate its range until it eats itself out of its natural home.

Biologist David Brown, professor of wildlife management at Arizona State University, does not disagree—except, he adds, "To say it's just predators is an oversimplification. The controls that kept lions in check didn't so much reduce them as prevent them from expanding with the deer during the wet years. When deer declined after 1924, that's when we started moving toward population stability. There was enough food to maintain a population, but not enough nutritional forage for it to increase."

By 1940, the Kaibab Plateau's mule deer population finally stabilized around an estimated ten thousand, where it has since been maintained by both predators and controlled hunting. "The lesson," says Brown, "was to harvest enough so that the population wouldn't crash again in the future."

But to maintain stability, at times wildlife managers also boost populations, by seeding plots with a species' favorite kinds of vegetation, or with nutritional plant mixes of fats, carbohydrates, and protein. Sometimes they artificially fertilize existing forage, or remove competing plants with herbicide or controlled burns. If they're managing a game species, in the spring they count nibbled twigs on winter forage plants to determine how many hunting permits to issue in the fall. In low rainfall, they provide access to water with troughs or tanks, or they dam creeks or even pump to create ponds.

David Brown, whose ruddy complexion reveals a

man who's spent more than four decades helping U.S. Fish and Wildlife manage bighorn sheep, elk, and pronghorns, disapproves of such water management, because, he maintains, desert-adapted ungulates handle drought much better than their predators. What concerns him more are diseases for which wild animals never evolved defenses. "It's like Indians who didn't have antibodies against European smallpox. Trophy hunters don't extinguish bighorn sheep: domestic sheep diseases do." The solution is to keep livestock away from wildlife, which has never been simple. "We don't even know all the vectors: Prairie dogs die of plague that probably didn't show up in this country until the 1930s. Ferrets die of canine distemper. It's probably more of a factor than we realize."

With trade and transport now erasing ocean barriers that once separated human populations, we may be even more susceptible than wildlife. Nervously, epidemiologists try to stay a step ahead of the latest Ebola, SARS, and bird flu virus mutations, lest they leap continents as easily as they jump from animal species to our own. Are there lessons from wildlife management that might help humans plan our own future?

"Absolutely none," says Brown. "The reason we can do it with animals is that we have the massive superiority of one species managing another. That does not apply to managing ourselves. We've proven ourselves to be fully incapable of that."

He remembers being in eighth grade, seeing 1940 census figures in a textbook. "There were 120 million Americans then. It was a good number. Economists weren't happy—we were still in the tail end of the Depression—but we had zero population growth without any battle with religion. Economics did it. It was basically a comfortable situation: few immigrants, because there were no jobs for them, and limited average family size."

Then came World War II. "Like with deer management, there's always something to upset the applecart. The war ended, and the first thing we did was try to repopulate. And we didn't want just a sustaining economy: we wanted growth. It's in our DNA to want to grow. That's true with Kaibab mule deer herds, or with wolves in Yellowstone. It's part of the biological process. It would be nice to get to just the right carrying capacity of humans and maintain that number. But who's going to do that?"

In 1924, he says, Kaibab deer were down to skin and bones. Fawns were dying or stillborn, or does weren't conceiving. It was tragic, but they had to die to restore a livable balance. Imagine, though, if we tried that with people.

"It's totally counterintuitive if you want to manage people. If you go to Darfur and see people starving, you bring them food, and their reproductive rate goes back up. Haiti has an earthquake, you bring in food and relief, and their reproduction rebounds." He shakes his head at the irony: by replenishing the population, the suffering inevitably recurs.

"This has been understood for a hundred years, but do we change our behavior? No. Because you can't say screw Haiti, the place is a basket case, so we're going to block efforts to bring them food because it's against their better interest. Our tendency in a critical situation is to provide food. That's what we do."

The notion of husbanding the human race as though we were game or livestock horrifies on multiple levels—moral, religious, and philosophical, not to mention legal. To suggest applying principles of wildlife management to our own species conjures abominations such as humans being culled like deer. Although we famously aren't good at remembering history, attempts at thinning our ranks—otherwise known as genocide—are among our most indelible historical memories.

Yet although we strive for the heavens, as Pascal noted, we are still mammals who, like all other Earthly creatures, require food and water—resources that we are now outstripping. Our seafood is down to dregs scraped from the ocean floor; our soils on chemical life support; our rivers fouled and drained. We squeeze and shatter rocks, mine frigid seas, and split atoms in risky places because easily harvested fuels are nearly gone. Like Kaibab deer, every species in the history of biology that outgrows its resource base suffers a population crash—a crash sometimes fatal to the entire species. In a world now stretched to the brink, today we all live in a parkland, not a boundless wilderness. To survive and continue the legacy of our species, we must adjust accordingly.

Inevitably—and, we must hope, humanely and nonviolently—that means gradually bringing our numbers down. The alternative is letting nature—the new nature we've inadvertently created in our own image—do that for us.

How might nature do so? Probably in a number of cascading ways, as one loss ignites another. The fish we eat are no longer threatened simply because we crave them to the point of disappearance: Because we've dug up and burned millions of years' worth of excess carbon buried by nature in less than three centuries, the waters they dwell in now grow warmer than some of them may be able to bear. Decreased oxygen levels and increased metabolic rates in warming waters are already decreasing body sizes of North Atlantic cod and haddock faster than models had predicted.

As oceans absorb our excess carbon dioxide, they become less alkaline. And although our seawater is not yet so acidic that it's turned into salty Perrier, higher levels of dissolved CO_2 corrode developing shells of young mollusks and crustaceans. Warm waters expand, melting ice adds more volume, and the specter of rising seas becomes a certainty as it grows likely that Earth's average surface temperature is headed beyond the 2°C (3.6°F) increase over preindustrial levels proposed as the threshold we dare not pass.[1]

At our present rising rate of greenhouse gas emissions, however, we will eclipse a 2°C increase in the next two to three decades. With two-thirds of the

---

1. The goal of not exceeding an increase of 2°C, used at the 2009 Copenhagen Climate Change Conference, has become an oft-repeated threshold figure. Leading climate scientists, however, such as NASA's James Hansen, Stanford's Ken Caldeira, and the University of Southampton's Eelco Rohling, point to prehistoric high sea levels in times of increased CO_2 and conclude that, given weather disruptions, flooding, and Arctic melting already occurring at 0.8°C, a 2°C increase will be disastrous. Yet with carbon emissions still inexorably rising, a growing consensus among scientists suggests that a 2.4°C increase is now unavoidable. The United Nations Environmental Programme currently projects a 3°C increase by 2050. And the World Bank now warns that unless we change our carbon-based behavior, fast, we'll reach 4°C before the end of the century.

world's population living within two hundred miles of a seacoast, and with most of the world's economy concentrated in coastal cities, the potential swamping of civilization as we know it, should these places flood, overwhelms our ability to fathom. Current budgetary traumas will seem trivial next to the prospect of erecting dikes to protect, in order of population, the likes of Tokyo, Shanghai, Guangzhou, Karachi, Mumbai, Manila, Istanbul, Buenos Aires, Kolkata, Rio de Janeiro, Tunis, Jakarta, New York, Los Angeles–Long Beach, London, Lagos, Hong Kong, Ho Chi Minh City, Miami, Singapore, Barcelona, Sydney, Melbourne, Alexandria (and the entire Nile Delta), Athens, Tel Aviv, Lisbon, Naples, Tripoli, Casablanca, Durban, San Juan, Dubai, Havana, Houston, Beirut, Perth, Marseilles, Stockholm, Odessa, Doha, Boston, Vancouver, Oslo, Macau, Copenhagen, Abu Dhabi, and Honolulu, as well as hundreds more cities the size of New Orleans and smaller, but no less precious to those who live and work there.

We were far fewer, and living far less densely and intensely, when the Black Death killed approximately one-fourth of all humans in the mid-fourteenth century, and also when the 1918–20 Spanish influenza knocked our species, then numbering less than 2 billion, back by an estimated 50 million. In today's tightly bound 7-billion-and-growing world, our antibiotic armor is being breached by mutating, resistant strains of infections from gonorrhea to streptococcus. Like every other monoculture that replaces a diverse ecological mix, the one known as *Homo sapiens* is more vulnerable to opportunistic pandemic than ever.

Unintentionally, we have also spawned our own micro-threats, for which neither we nor anything alive have defenses. The crisis in Tel Aviv's biggest sperm bank—just one man in one hundred now qualifies to be a donor—warns that Israel's transformation of deserts into gardens may have depended too heavily on pesticides. The damaged semen may be due to endocrine disruptors found not just in agro-chemistry, but in pharmaceuticals, household cleaners, detergents, plastics, and even cosmetics and sunscreens. Mounting evidence links them to rising rates of breast and prostate cancer, autism, ovarian cysts, attention-deficit disorder, heart disease, autoimmune deficiency, obesity, diabetes, learning disabilities, and—if that weren't alarming enough—scrambled sexuality in fauna, ranging from fish to frogs to alligators, polar bears, and humans. In some cases, this means sex ratios skewed far beyond than those perpetrated by ultrasound in India or China: In the Saskatchewan River basin, up to 90 percent of a common minnow are now female. Many more fish, amphibians, reptiles, and mammals are being born as hermaphrodites, with intersexual mixtures of male and female genitalia that bode darkly for reproduction.

From animals to us, fertility is dropping not by choice, but by exposure to molecules that never existed before. The term we've invented to describe them, *gender-benders,* is precisely accurate, but unfortunately too snappy to be taken as seriously as it truly is. This is a tragedy—and it is also nature rejecting an unnatural act, making life inhospitable for the actors.

ii. The Chemistry Set

It's too early to know how seriously toxic our environment already is, because we are all part of the experiment to find out. Although every embryo on Earth—all species, not just our own—is now exposed to pervasive gender-bending molecules, thus far not every child is born autistic or gonadally challenged. If we stop depending on organochlorides, organochlorines, organophosphates, and the like, with luck we can purge them from our system—although this may be the definitive case of an evil genie escaping the bottle, as many appear indestructible. But there are other, simpler ways that nature will halt our unimpeded growth if we don't take the reins ourselves. The most basic is the world's oldest: cutting off our sustenance. The bottom line of the twenty-first century is that we will have less food — not more as we did, only briefly, during the Green Revolution.

That is what an odds maker would bet on: We will not be able to grow, hunt, or harvest enough for the 7 billion we already are, let alone the 10.9 billion we're racing toward. With weather now nearly impossible to predict, crop disasters are annual events on at least one continent per year. Hopes that a warmer world would actually enhance harvests are dashed by the reality of thresholds — averages of 84°F for corn; 86°F for soybeans — beyond which yields drop, as farmers from the United States to India are learning only too well.

Likewise, cheerful assurances that farming would expand poleward, turning northern Canada and Siberia into breadbaskets, failed to consider that acidic, conifer-covered taiga soils would take many millennia to adapt to the loamy demands of grains. Our remaining topsoils — those not scoured away by winds and floods or turned to dust by drought — are overworked, overfertilized, overfumigated, and no longer yield what they did fifty years ago.

Further predictions that, in lieu of exhausted land, we'll reap limitless tons of algae from the seas, which we'll fashion into acceptable simulacra of foods we favor, smack of extreme technofix fantasies. As anyone who loves sushi knows, seaweed has many tasty, nutritious uses, and doubtless there are more to discover. However, the logistics of growing, harvesting, processing, and distributing enough to provide mainstay nourishment for billions defy reality, beginning with energy costs—let alone retraining 10.9 billion palates to accept seaweed-based food substitutes. And the same acidification dissolving the shells of oyster larvae will disrupt the chemistry that until now has allowed wakame, nori, kelp, agar-agar, et al., to thrive along our shores.

An animal rights group, People for the Ethical Treatment of Animals, once offered a million dollars to whoever could invent and bring artificial meat to market. Although the award was a publicity spoof, scientists at both Oxford and Amsterdam University, among others, are dutifully trying. The idea of in vitro steak may appall some but appeal to others, if no animals are harmed and no forests are felled. But before firing up our barbecues, it's best to recall that lab-grown nutrients won't be conjured from thin air: even synthetic food requires a feedstock. The Oxford group hopes to grow muscle tissue from *Cyanobacteria hydrolysate,* a primitive algae; their Dutch counterparts, with substantial government backing, are trying pig stem cells—and Japanese researchers claim to have alchemized meat from proteins in human waste. Ick factors aside, producing ground beef artificially anytime soon would cost thousands of dollars a pound, and food scientists suspect that commercial production is at least three decades away.

By then, assuming no catastrophes, we'll be well past 9 billion, headed to 10 billion and more. Despite the reassurance of agro-biotechnology giant Monsanto—whose genetic modifications are already being outsmarted by microbes' and insects' evolutionary talents—being able to feed that many *Homo sapiens* is highly unlikely. We can't feed the 7 billion we already are: a billion of us are chronically malnourished, and 16,000 of our children starve to death daily. Whether we could feed everyone if only we distributed food equitably, as Pope Emeritus Benedict XVI and others insist, is moot in a world where food is mostly produced to profit from people, not to nourish them.

Even granting markets their commodities, protest vegetarians, every human would have plenty of food if only the photosynthesis responsible for everything we eat (except salt) were not diverted into wasteful production of meat. Seventy percent of the grain grown in the United States, they claim, and 98 percent of the soy meal, goes to feed livestock,[2] not

---

2. Worldwide, about half of grain production is used for animal feed.

people (as do 80 percent of the antibiotics sold). Nearly one-third of the planet's ice-free landmass is used for either grazing or for growing animal feed. It takes about six pounds of grain (and roughly 2,400 gallons of water) to produce one pound of beef.[3] Pork is a bit better, as pigs have only one stomach chamber versus cattle's inefficient four. Their conversion rate of grain to edible flesh is 4:1; poultry conversion is half that.

Factoring in energy costs and fertilizer, producing animal protein burns about eight times as much fuel as plant protein. But meat's climatic contribution doesn't stop there, or even with bovine belching and farting. An exhaustively comprehensive 2009 study by World Bank environmental specialists Robert Goodland and Jeff Anhang measured feed, flatulence, forest-to-field loss, packaging, cooking temperature, waste production, fluorocarbons used in meat refrigeration, carbon-intensive medical treatment of livestock and of meat eaters who suffer from heart disease, cancers, diabetes, high blood pressure, and strokes, and even the cumulative CO_2 exhaled by the world's

---

3. Source: University of Massachusetts Extension Center for Agriculture. Beef industry estimates of just 4.6:1 conversion claim to take into account an animal's weight before it enters the feedlot; estimates by vegetarian advocacy groups of up to 20:1 claim to calculate how much of a slaughtered carcass is actually edible beef.

19 billion chickens, 1.6 billion cattle and water buf-falo, 1 billion pigs, and 2 billion sheep and goats.

Their conclusion was that livestock and their by-products account for at least 51 percent of annual worldwide greenhouse emissions.

Yet the vexation of vegan crusaders who in one stroke would cut global warming in half and eliminate world hunger by feeding grain directly to people is that most people aren't interested. Beef demand continues to rise even faster than population, because as more people move to cities, they seek the satisfactions of modern life, including the beef-laden Western diet. By a maddening, market-driven paradox, if rich nations did choose to eat less meat, the price of meat will fall and poor nations would probably eat even more.

A 2011 study published in *Environmental Research Letters* concluded that the Brazilian Amazon had 79 million head of cattle. "Fifteen years ago," noted Kansas State University geographer and coauthor Marcellus Caldas, "it had less than 10 million." In the previous five years alone, the portion of Brazil converted to soybean production to feed them nearly equaled the size of Switzerland. The warming of the climate abetted by all that hamburger is dramatically shrinking Andean and African glaciers that water crops in some of the world's most populous regions.

Himalayan glaciers, frozen as solid as the mountains they cover, will take longer to melt, but as global temperatures rise 2°C beyond the twentieth-century average, and keep going toward 5° and 6°C, meltwater flows to the Ganges and the Indus will increase over the next two decades—and then peak. Before 2100, at a time when Pakistan's population is projected to top half a billion, the Indus could be going dry—two facts in stark contradiction with each other. Either millions of Pakistanis will die, or they will be at war with their neighbors India, Afghanistan, and Iran, which will be suffering similar disasters.

Australia has no glaciers, and has fewer than 23 million people in an area roughly the size of the contiguous lower forty-eight of the United States, which hold 315 million. Yet it has grown so desiccated that it is locked in national debate over whether to cap its population by halting immigration. Even the notion of banning beef, practically a national sacrilege, has been broached. In the meantime, Australian coastal cities are investing US$13 billion in desalinization plants that will require enormous amounts of fuel to work around the clock. To economize, Australia almost certainly will use its own plentiful resource, black coal, further exacerbating climbing temperatures and altered climate that Australians no longer doubt.

During the parched Texas summer, the third biggest

U.S. city, Houston, is already mostly drinking effluent from Dallas and Fort Worth, whose wastewater
discharges constitute nearly the entire downstream
flow of the Trinity River, Houston's principal source.
The American West's main artery, the Colorado
River, hasn't reached its delta since 1984. After two
decades of reduced snowpack in the Rocky Mountains, Scripps Institution of Oceanography researchers report, there is an even chance that by 2017 levels
in Lake Mead, the Colorado's main reservoir, will no
longer cover the Hoover Dam's turbines. By 2021,
the lake could essentially be gone, outflows having
fatally exceeded the inflows that replenish it. In 2010,
Lake Mead was already 100 feet lower than in 2000,
nearly down to where one of two intakes supplies
water to Las Vegas. With the second intake not far
below, Las Vegas began racing to dig a 20-foot-high
tunnel three miles under the lake, in order to install
a third intake 140 feet lower, lest it go dry.

But that may only buy the city—America's fastest growing until the 2008 real estate collapse—
another decade or less, especially since Las Vegas is
only one of eight cities over a million that depend on
Colorado River water.[4] If levels get so low that 25

---

4 The others are Denver, Salt Lake City, Los Angeles, San Diego,
Phoenix, Tijuana, and Mexicali—as well as dozens of smaller cities,
such as Albuquerque and Tucson.

million downstream voters in California demand what little Colorado River water remains, "The nation would have to seriously discuss a stair-step exchange," said Pat Mulroy, general manager of the Southern Nevada Water Authority, in 2009. In that scenario, Nevada would take Denver's Colorado River allotment, because Denver, in turn, would take Nebraska and Kansas's share of the Platte River, because those states could recharge their depleted Ogallala Aquifer by siphoning water from the Mississippi, and so on ever eastward.

It should come as no shock that this grand scheme is probably doomed, if not from astronomically prohibitive engineering expenses, then by the fact that states bordering the Great Lakes, also now at historic low levels, have already passed laws forbidding any other drainage basin from trying to stick straws into Lake Superior and Lake Michigan, et al. In 2008, the state of Georgia was so desperate for water that it contemplated resurrecting a 150-year-old survey dispute that would have pushed its northwestern corner a mile farther north, to the banks of the Tennessee River. The state of Tennessee was not amused, nor charitably inclined.

The upshot is that in the twenty-first century, our species will be subjected to global water torture: alternately raising unaffordable dikes to hold it back, then desperately trying to coax it from any possible source. But like topsoil, there is no practical way to create more fresh water. Removing salt from seawater — the result of millions of years of rain and runoff dissolving rocks en route to the sea — is undercut by the cost of the energy required, and defeated by the distance that separates most arable land from the oceans. Desalination may be the most literal example of how the technological species that we've become stands in defiance of nature: As University of California–Santa Cruz Director of Integrated Water Research Brent Haddad told the *Santa Cruz Sentinel* after a seven-year study of the economic and ecological effects of desalination, "We are reversing the water cycle that has flowed in one direction since the beginning of Earth."

———

Among the many tricks we will try to keep fitting ourselves onto this planet, there is one that we already know. The technology is cheaper than all the others by many orders of magnitude. It is reducing the numbers of bodies to feed by managing our reproduction, before nature steps in to do that for us.

It is not perfect technology: for a small percentage of women, the chemistry of contraception causes migraines or depression, although the copper-T IUD is a benign alternative, easily reversible as long as a trained medical practitioner is handy. Those chemical effects are not confined solely to women's bodies, because while nearly half of estrogen is metabolized, the rest is excreted. Flushed away, a portion is removed in sewage treatment, but the rest finds its way into the ecosystem.

Some of the gender-bending estrogens feminizing not just minnows but trout, bass, and perch in lakes and rivers worldwide are identical to the ones in oral contraceptives. In every big river of North America except the Yukon, female egg cells are now common in two-thirds or more of male largemouth and small-mouth bass. In several studies in the United States, Canada, and England, however, research indicates that, compared to industrial and agrochemical sources, female contraceptives are a minuscule part of the artificial hormonal assault on the environment.

That doesn't mean that current technology needn't be improved; however we can minimize chemical exposure to women and to the ecosystem, the better. Among the most promising options is to counter conception through a far simpler pathway: by short-circuiting male sperm delivery.

Two possibilities are male versions of the Pill, which, unlike their female counterparts, don't manipulate hormones. One, already tested at Kansas State

University on rats, rabbits, and monkeys, uses a compound called H2-gamendazole that stops sperm from forming in men's semen without reducing their sex drive, and is reversible within weeks. The other oral treatment uses a compound developed in the Bradner Laboratory at Boston's Dana-Farber Cancer Institute called JQ1, which targets a testis-specific protein to lower sperm numbers and retard their swimming capability. Again, test mice show no lowered libidos, and regain fertility when they stop taking it.

Two of the most imaginative approaches aren't chemical, but mechanical interventions. Risug—reversible inhibition of sperm under guidance—is already offered in several cities in India, and as of 2012 was in FDA trials in the United States. It involves a fifteen-minute outpatient operation using local anesthetic via a tiny incision in the scrotum to reach the vas deferens tube, into which the doctor injects an inexpensive polymer gel. Within three days, the gel forms a lining that allows semen to pass normally, but electrolytically destroys sperm. The spermicidal effect lasts for ten years, but can be reversed by injecting a baking soda solution. The same Indian developer has been testing another method at the University of North Carolina that uses ultrasound to heat testes for fifteen minutes, resulting in six months of sterility in test animals.

Each of these techniques portends to be cheaper and safer both for humans and the environment than female chemical contraception. For a woman in a steady relationship with a willing partner, it could shift the stress of birth control from her uterus, conserving that organ for the sole use that nature intended. Reliance on male contraception would also, however, mean relinquishing control over her own reproduction, inserting a new test of trust into intergender dynamics. For men, it could mean liberation from the interruptive frustration of using condoms—although, outside of monogamy, there would be a loss of protection from sexually transmitted disease. As long as one epidemic that threatens human existence, HIV, is spread through seminal fluids, protection and contraception must remain related but separate issues.

For the world, simple, nontoxic male contraception would mean a powerful form of population restraint, one which would far more equitably share responsibility for planning families. The politicization of contraception, born of gender wars waged by extremist Catholic and evangelical Christians, fundamentalist Muslims, and ultra-Orthodox Jews, may be befuddled should anyone try prohibiting men from choosing whether to use it. Male pills and instantly reversible vasectomies will be interesting, welcome new elements in the complex mix of managing our future, even as we consummate our desires.

iii. Whither Termination

In 1971, Dr. Malcolm Potts traveled from London to California to meet an ex-convict named Harvey Karman. Potts, a Cambridge don, was an obstetrician and a PhD in embryology. Karman was an abortionist.

The *Roe v. Wade* Supreme Court decision that would legalize abortion in the United States as a fundamental right was still two years away, although in some states such as California, abortions were permitted in cases of rape, or if the health of the mother was at stake. Since he was not a medical doctor, Karman could not legally perform those, but he was well known to California doctors who did. In the mid-1950s, while researching emotional aspects of therapeutic abortion as a psychology graduate student at UCLA, Karman learned that a fellow student had died from a botched illegal abortion. Another, finding herself pregnant, committed suicide. He began an underground service, taking women to Mexico for clandestine abortions. Dismayed by unhygienic conditions there and exorbitant fees, he began performing them himself in motel rooms, for which he eventually spent two and a half years in state prison.

Undaunted, he became a repeat offender and advocate, openly campaigning for abortion rights. He also invented something revolutionary: a manual syringe to conduct abortions by vacuum aspiration. Although machine-powered vacuum aspiration was already becoming preferred to scraping a woman's uterine lining, Karman's invention had prominent advantages. Being manual, it was so silent that a woman often wasn't even aware that the procedure was taking place. Also, it required no costly electric pump, just a cheap reusable fifty-milliliter vacuum syringe. Most important, Karman had designed an attachment made of soft plastic tubing that replaced the conventional rigid metal curette. This flexible cannula, so thin that it avoided the need for dilation, was far more comfortable and far less traumatic, and minimized the chance of a perforated uterus.

By the time *Roe v. Wade* passed, Karman had trained doctors from throughout America in its use, as well as international physicians such as Malcolm Potts. Like Karman, Dr. Potts had become interested in abortion as a grad student during the 1950s. While doing twenty-four-hour obstetric duty at a Cambridge hospital, nearly every night he would be roused to perform a D&C. He wondered how many were spontaneous miscarriages, and how many were bungled induced abortions.

"Nearly all are intentionally induced," an anesthetist told him.

"How do you know?"

Curious himself, the anesthetist had been asking women patients during the dreamy moments before they fell unconscious. Potts was impressed that this colleague refused to publish his findings on the grounds that he had obtained compromising information from defenseless subjects—and because it would implicate several colleagues in illegal moonlighting. But he was even more impressed by the apparent scope of the need.

In 1966, Malcolm Potts visited Eastern Europe, where abortion had been legal and safe for over a decade, and where fertility rates were quite low, even though the most available contraceptive was coitus interruptus. Eventually he advised Parliament on what became the 1967 Abortion Act that legalized the procedure in the UK. He became the first male physician at London's Marie Stopes Clinic. In 1968, he was named medical director of the International Planned Parenthood Federation.

It was in that capacity that he went to meet Harvey Karman. Immediately, he saw how important

Karman's invention would be in undeveloped countries, where death from mud-hut abortions was a principal cause of female mortality. To assure that it could be available in the poorest places on Earth, Karman agreed to coauthor a paper on the device so no one would be able to patent it. Even before their article was published in the British medical journal *The Lancet,* Potts took Karman and three other specialists at the invitation of Bangladesh's government to aid girls and women raped during the 1971 war of liberation from Pakistan. Many of their fifteen hundred patients had been banished by their husbands and families; many more victims had committed suicide. To circumvent Bangladesh's ban on abortion, they called the Karman cannula procedure "menstrual extraction"—a method of regulating a woman's cycle, which, technically, it was. In every village they visited, they taught doctors, nurses, and midwives the simple, painless technique, which is still used there today.

"Like so much else we do as physicians, abortion is a healing process," says Malcolm Potts, who today holds a chair at the University of California, Berkeley, where he directs the Bixby Center for Population, Health and Sustainability, and is married to international reproductive rights advocate Martha Campbell. "A five-minute operation on an unintentionally pregnant seventeen-year-old woman can change the trajectory of the next half-century of her life. Few other procedures in medicine have that power."

As late as 1869, Potts says, the Vatican refused to comment on the subject of when life begins. Pope John Paul II's 1983 assertion that it begins at conception has no medical basis, he adds, as many fertilized eggs never survive to advance from zygote to embryo to fetus to child.

"Religious assertions about when life begins are analogous to religious beliefs about life after death. They are both strongly held, but beyond the realm of science to prove or disprove. As an embryologist, I can no more tell you when life begins by looking down my microscope than an astronomer can tell you if heaven exists by scanning the constellations for the Pearly Gates."

What he does know is that by 2025, 3 billion people will be short of water, and that countries with dwindling rivers such as Pakistan that have failed to control human fertility are more dangerous each year. In 1958, when there were fewer than 3 billion people, President Dwight Eisenhower identified population growth as a strategic security matter. The investigator he appointed, Major General William Draper, spent the rest of his life trying to convince world leaders to fund family planning. Half a century and more than double that number later, as Malcolm Potts reminds people, the 9/11 Commission Report warned that "a large, steadily increasing population of young men [is] a sure prescription for social turbulence."

Over half the world's 7 billion are under twenty-seven years old; over half of those are males; and over half of them are now jostling each other in cities, unmoored from the land-based traditions that defined most of human culture until only recently. Except for volcanic eruptions, every emergency on Earth is now either related to or aggravated by the presence of more people than conditions can bear. Malcolm Potts, who has worked worldwide—he gave Mechai Viravaidya his initial family-planning grant in Thailand—believes that contraception is the indispensible tool for bringing the planet and its people back to health.

He also understands that abortion, fraught as it is with ideology, is the safety net when contraception fails. "No country reaches replacement rate fertility without access to safe abortion," says Potts. "They may be like Ireland, where you have to go to England, or Malta, where you go to Italy. But those two Catholic countries now have replacement fertility."

He recently worked in Addis Ababa, capital of

Muslim Ethiopia, the world's most populous land-locked country, which legalized abortion in 2006. "Seventy percent of the hospital beds — orthopedics, neurology, everything — were occupied by botched abortions. In less than a year, we emptied them. The fertility rate there is now 1.8, because they're offering responsible access to contraception and safe abortion. In fact," he adds, "the most consistent users of contraception are women who've had an abortion."

But outside Ethiopia's capital, there are few trained abortion providers, and only 14 percent of women have any chance to get contraceptives, similar to Niger and other destitute countries. Estimates by the United Nations Population Fund and by the Guttmacher Institute, a premier source for reproductive health and population policy analysis,5 suggest that nearly a quarter of a billion women who would like to delay or stop having babies have no access to modern birth control.

What would it take to get it to them?

5. Founder Alan Guttmacher, 1898–1974, was an obstetrician-gynecologist who taught at the Johns Hopkins, Mount Sinai, and Albert Einstein medical schools. During the 1960s, he was president of the Planned Parenthood Federation of America.

CHAPTER 17

The World With Fewer of Us

i. The Bottom Line

The good news, if the Guttmacher Institute and UNFPA are correct, is that we're three-quarters of the way there. According to their figures, as of mid-2012, 75 percent of the sexually active women in the developing world who aren't trying to get pregnant over the next two years (meaning they're either spacing pregnancies or avoiding them altogether) are already using contraceptives. They calculate that 218 million unintended pregnancies are thus prevented annually, averting 138 million abortions, 25 million miscarriages, and 118,000 mothers dead of complications from childbirth or backroom abortions.

Subtracting the avoided abortions and miscarriages, family planning in developing countries prevents

55 million unintended births. Since we currently add 80 million people annually—a million more of us every 4½ days—without contraception reaching those women, our ranks would expand by a million more hungry humans every 2½ days. That's seven more Beijings a year, instead of the four we're currently adding.

Such big numbers are awfully hard to grasp. "That's because we evolved in small groups," says Malcolm Potts. "Until modern times, none of us ever saw more than maybe a thousand people. So most people's minds go blank after a hundred thousand. Darwin said that we can understand some parts of nature and the universe, but we can't *comprehend* them. A billion seconds equal 31.7 years. In the next twelve years, we're going to add another billion people. So at the rate they're arriving, we couldn't even count them."

Suppose, in the interest of avoiding another billion in the next dozen years, that the quarter-billion[1] women who currently don't or can't plan their childbearing were able to, and did so. According to Guttmacher and UNFPA estimates, such women annually

---

1. The actual 2012 Guttmacher/UNFPA estimate was 222 million women in the developing world whose contraceptive needs are unmet. A 2013 UN Population Division study upped the figure to 233 million by 2015 for all women worldwide *currently married or in a union.* The estimate here of a quarter-billion, or 250 million, reflects an additional unknown number of sexually active girls and women not in unions without ready access to modern contraception.

have 80 million unintended pregnancies. Half—40 million—get abortions, and more than half of those are the unsafe, frightening kind. Another 10 million miscarry. Thirty million have babies, 6 million of whom die before their first birthday.

If all the contraceptive needs in the developing world were met, not all those 30 million unplanned births would be avoided: contraceptives are sometimes forgotten, and sometimes fail. Some women stop using them, fearing side effects, and get pregnant before finding an alternative. Some mistakenly believe that breast-feeding provides total protection. But at minimum there would be 21 million fewer births. Subtract one Beijing per year.

The number of abortions would also drop, from 40 million to around 14 million. For anyone who opposes abortion, that is a powerful pair of numbers. They mean that right now, half the poor women of the world who get pregnant when they can't afford to do something dangerous, and emotionally and physically painful—and often, by their own or someone else's reckoning, sinful. They do this whether or not it's legal, and regardless of what their (invariably male) religious authority permits. Access to contraception for them would prevent an additional 26 million abortions per year worldwide, on top of the 138 million abortions already averted by available birth control—numbers far exceeding any total achieved by pro-life movements. As an added humanitarian bonus, since more than half the abortions that poor women get—22 million—are unsafe, that number would drop to 7 million or less, and some 50,000 women's lives would be saved.

There are barriers to this happening, such as getting birth control to unmarried women where premarital sex is stigmatized, or to married women who traditionally don't get to decide when they're ready to give birth. Some of them will contrive to get an IUD or long-lasting injections without a husband's knowledge, and some single women will find ways to meet their needs—if those ways are locally available.

Whether they are depends on a surprisingly small amount of money to cover the contraceptive needs of every woman on Earth.

Currently, $4 billion each year is spent on contraceptive care in the developing world. UNFPA and Guttmacher estimate that about double that amount, $8.1 billion per year, could fully meet the needs for modern contraception in the developing world.

Between 2001 and 2011, the United States frequently spent more than that per month in Iraq and Afghanistan.

Nearly a billion of the current amount comes from countries such as the UK, the Netherlands, and Germany. The United States is the biggest donor, but since 1984 the amount depends on who happens to be president. Although the United States helped to create the United Nations Population Fund, UNFPA, in 1969 under Richard Nixon, by 1973 the Helms Amendment prohibited using foreign aid to pay for abortion as a method of family planning. In 1984, the Reagan administration proclaimed by executive order what is still known as the Mexico City Policy (or the "Global Gag Rule") requiring foreign NGOs to pledge not to "perform *or promote* [emphasis added] abortion as a method of family planning" — meaning that the option of abortion couldn't even be mentioned — as a condition for receiving U.S. funding, no matter whose money actually funded the abortion counseling or services.

This policy was rescinded by President Clinton, reinstated by President George W. Bush, and rescinded again by President Obama. Bush II also pulled all U.S. funding from UNFPA, claiming that UNFPA's activities in China violated the Kemp-Kasten Amendment, which prohibits funding any program that supports coercive abortion or involuntary sterilization. In 2009, Obama reinstated it with a $50 million contribution, a number chopped steadily by Congress in succeeding years.

Most U.S. donations for population programs,

however, are not sluiced through the United Nations but go directly through USAID, the world's biggest supporter of family planning and reproductive health. The rest of the funding comes from private foundations, local governments, and from consumers buying pills and condoms over the counter.

In 2009, 98 percent of UNFPA's foundation funding came from four American foundations—and 81 percent of that was from just one: the Bill and Melinda Gates Foundation.[2] That the fate of the world's women depends so much on American largesse underscores the fragility of global family planning—especially in the polarized new millennium, as a brutal partisan divide over not just abortion but even contraception has ignited what one side touts as a return to moral values, and the other calls a war on women.

By any name, it would have shocked Republican presidents Eisenhower, Nixon, and even George Bush Senior, who all supported population control.

During the years of Bush the younger, money that would have otherwise gone to international family planning was directed into HIV-AIDS programs. Worldwide, those programs today receive ten times

---

2. The others were the William and Flora Hewlett Foundation, the David and Lucile Packard Foundation, and the John D. and Catherine T. MacArthur Foundation.

more funding than family planning, a fact that greatly worries Malcolm Potts.

"HIV accounts for 5 percent of the global burden of disease, and it's taking 20 percent of the money going from rich to poor countries for international health," says Potts, who was one of the first doctors to bring attention to the threat of AIDS. As frightening as it is, the population crisis scares him more. "In the first five months of this year," Potts and Martha Campbell wrote in 2011, "world population grew by enough to equal all the AIDS deaths since the epidemic began 30 years ago."

Most conversations about population growth, Potts says, use the UN's medium estimate of 9.2 billion people, which was where population was supposed to level off by 2050.

"Now, in a dramatic shift, they say it will exceed 10 billion by 2100. But the UN's high and low estimates for 2100 are equally possible, depending on how serious the world gets about family planning. The difference between them is just half a child per woman. Half a child less, you get a far more sustainable figure of 6.2 billion. Half a child more, you get 15.8 billion. That last possibility would be utter disaster. So what we do in the next ten to fifteen years will make all the difference in the world."

ii. Jasper Ridge

Paul Ehrlich, in an old blue sweater and a floppy canvas hat, armed with a pair of trekking poles, punches his way across the Jasper Ridge meadow that he has studied for more than half a century. It is a brilliant, sunny March afternoon, with a breeze masking the growl of Silicon Valley below. At eighty, Ehrlich still has a stride that makes friends quicken their pace to keep up. "Coming up here makes life worthwhile," he says, gazing happily around the golden grassland, even though the Bay checkerspot butterfly populations he first came to observe in 1959 disappeared here by 1998.

Jasper Ridge, which rises alongside the San Andreas Fault, was part of the original farm that became the Stanford University campus. Ehrlich often says that his one substantial contribution as an ecologist was saving this uplift from the development that devoured surrounding farms and woodlands. For a decade, the maneuvers to create this two-square-mile experimental biological reserve occupied nearly a quarter of his time, as Stanford's finance division considered it ideal for a large, profitable subdivision.

The ridge today looks much as it did then — even better, because the invention of catalytic converters cleared away much of the smog. The lichen-draped valley oaks that Ehrlich sees are just starting to leaf out. The ridge's dry western slope is covered with spiny chaparral; growing on its wetter, north side are smooth-barked red madrones and Douglas firs; and following the streambeds are redwoods — this is the southern extreme of their range. The golden grasses are mainly invasives like wild oats that came on ships and in imported mission bricks: smog-borne, human-generated nitrogen has favored the growth of these invasive annuals. Part of the current research is to determine what it would it take to restore the perennial grasses that covered California before Europeans

Paul Ehrlich on Jasper Ridge

arrived—one of some fifty research projects under way here at any given time.

A downy woodpecker roller coasters between two evergreen oak glades as Ehrlich passes through. During the 1970s, a student project discovered that Jasper Ridge, situated on the Pacific flyway, had the highest density of breeding land birds anywhere in the United States. More than a hundred fifty migratory and resident bird species are found here, as well as bobcat, red and gray fox, weasels, raccoons, mule deer, and mountain lions. A research center here archives fifty years of student projects; a habitat map of two tarantula species by one of Ehrlich's undergrads, Stewart Brand, who would later publish *The Whole Earth Catalog*, is still used.

Years before *The Population Bomb* appeared, Paul Ehrlich had already gained renown among ecologists for the paper he coauthored with Peter Raven, the future director of Missouri Botanical Gardens. It was the first to describe coevolution: how two interacting species, such as butterflies and the plants their larvae eat, each influence the other's development. Although coevolution is often understood as an ever-escalating biological arms race—in which plants evolve chemicals to repel insects, which in turn evolve immunities—their career-making collaboration came from observing that two distinct species of checkerspots, the Bay and the Chalcedon, were feeding on two different related species of flowers.

Across the meadow, Ehrlich can see an undergraduate biology class examining the saffron-colored sticky monkey-flower, the food that coevolved with the Chalcedon checkerspot. Because it typically grows along edges of trails and roads, it's a good species for classes to study without stumbling into one of Jasper Ridge's most abundant botanical species, poison oak, whose little red emerging leaves are everywhere.

It's too early by a couple of weeks for the Chalcedon checkerspot, a mostly black and white butterfly that resembles the now departed Bay, except with far fewer red spots. What extirpated the latter, Ehrlich now knows, were weather extremes characteristic of a changing climate. The Bay checkerspot's cycle depends on its caterpillar entering hibernation before the spring rains end and its host plant dries out. Beginning in the 1990s, years of unusually heavy spring rains that slowed the caterpillars' feeding began alternating with unusually dry years that deprived them of food—either way resulting in mass caterpillar starvation.

Mass starvation was what Ehrlich began to fear back in 1966, after he, Anne, and their daughter, Lisa, found themselves on a mobbed Delhi street, their taxi marooned in an ocean of humanity. This was before the Green Revolution; as a population biologist, Ehrlich knew the mathematics of doubling times, and when he and Anne compared the human race's spiraling numbers with crop data, they concluded that by the 1970s, famines would kill hundreds of millions of people—unless, as they wrote in the prologue to *The Population Bomb,* dramatic programs to increase food production stretched the Earth's carrying capacity.

"But these programs," they said, "will only provide a stay of execution, unless they are accompanied by determined and successful efforts at population control."

Even as their book was published, Norman Borlaug's miracle hybrids were coming to first harvest in India and Pakistan, and the famines the Ehrlichs predicted for the 1970s were averted. In subsequent decades, pro-growth economists made Paul Ehrlich and his forebear Thomas Robert Malthus their favorite punching bags, never missing a chance to ridicule them. Except, among scientists, no one was laughing. Ehrlich is today one of the world's most esteemed ecologists, winner of the Crafoord Prize of the Royal Swedish Academy of Sciences, given in disciplines where there is no Nobel Prize, as well as a MacArthur Fellowship, a Heinz Prize (with Anne), and the Distinguished Scientist Award of the American Institute of Biological Sciences. He is a member of the

National Academy of Sciences and a Fellow of the British Royal Society, among many others.

Neither was Norman Borlaug among his detractors, issuing the identical warning in his Nobel acceptance speech that Green Revolution crops were only buying the world time, unless population controls were implemented. Yet Ehrlich's name has continually incited derision outside of scientific circles, especially after a famous wager with economist Julian Simon of the Cato Institute, a free market think tank.

Simon, the cornucopian author of *The Ultimate Resource 2* who argued that human ingenuity ensured that resources would never run out, frequently challenged environmental scientists to prove otherwise. In 1980, he bet Ehrlich and Berkeley physicists John Holdren and John Harte $1,000 that the price of five commodity metals of their choosing wouldn't rise due to scarcity over the coming decade. They selected chromium, copper, nickel, tin, and tungsten—and ten years later lost the bet, having failed to anticipate a global recession during the 1980s that suppressed demand for industrial metals.

The outcome became a publicity windfall for free marketeers, and is still widely cited as proof that Ehrlich, Malthus, and the authors of *The Limits to Growth,* the 1972 report to the Club of Rome, were and always will be wrong.

Yet in the new millennium, several economists—and *The Economist* of London—have noted that Ehrlich's mistake was only one of timing: the following decade, he and his friends would have won. Ehrlich also would have won a second bet he proposed to Simon: that fifteen environmental indicators—including global temperature, CO_2 concentration, croplands, forests, and human sperm count—would worsen over a decade. Simon declined to wager.

A few years later, in 1994, Simon would write: "We now have in our hands—in our libraries, really—the technology to feed, clothe, and supply energy to an ever-growing population for the next 7 billion years." With world population then growing by 1.4 percent annually, the Ehrlichs checked his math and responded that this was unlikely, because at current growth rates, within six thousand years the mass of human population would equal the mass of the universe.

Ehrlich's vindication is no surprise to him, although there is no joy in being right about matters so disturbing. The unlikely agriculture miracle that he and Anne hoped for in *The Population Bomb*, which unexpectedly arrived with the Green Revolution, also postponed the timing of what increasingly now looks inevitable. With crop ecologists expecting grain harvests to drop 10 percent for each 1°C rise in average temperatures, and with the world now headed beyond 2°C at present rates of emissions, population will be up, food production down, and dikes may have to protect much of the world's rice production. Even at a 0.8°C increase, China barely missed losing its winter wheat crop in 2011. Thanks to last-minute March rains, the harvest was saved; few dared imagine the chaos had shaky Egypt, the world's largest wheat importer, been forced to bid against China for grain.

And no one can predict what North America's massive 2012 drought portends for future crop disasters. With most of the world's meals dependent on a few critical monocultures of rice, wheat, and corn — once three rare weeds, until we made them the most abundant plants on Earth — humanity may be just one disease away from a catastrophe that could shake civilization's foundations. In the past century in North America alone, it happened to elms and chestnut trees. The chance of an epidemic like Ebola wiping us out is far less likely than pathogens blown around the world collapsing our food supply.

The week before Rio+20 — the June 2012 UN conference held twenty years after the original Earth Summit — the world's 105 science academies, led by the Royal Society of Britain, warned that failure to act on population growth and overconsumption would have "catastrophic implications for human wellbe-ing." It was no shock to Paul Ehrlich that Rio+20, billed as the United Nations Conference on Sustain-able Development, ignored the question of popula-tion, for much the same reasons that the Earth Summit did. As in 1992, the Vatican courted support from human rights and feminist groups, contending that population programs unfairly blame poor women for the world's environmental ills. But as he drives his pickup back into Palo Alto, down six-lane El Camino Real, which formerly passed through orchards, not miles of commerce, Paul Ehrlich has no doubt that the most overpopulated country on Earth is his own.

"There is no condom for consumption," he says, sorrowing at the unabashed displays of Silicon Val-ley purchasing power. How to curb human acquisi-tiveness is more vexing a mystery than finding a unified theory of physics. In the last fifty years, world population more than doubled, but world economic growth increased sevenfold. With luck and contra-ception, world population might stabilize, but con-sumption grows on, almost exponentially, as the more people have, the more they want.

"Yet to separate consumption from population," says Ehrlich, "is like saying the length of a rectangle contributes more to its area than its width." The United States is the world's highest per-capita consumer, and its 315 million people are headed to an estimated 439 million or more by 2050. And a new factor has intensified the Impact in the I=PAT formula that he and John Holdren wrote in the 1970s: Population, Affluence, and Technology are further exacerbated by Time.

"The next 2 billion people we add will do a lot more damage than the last 2 billion," says Ehrlich. Those of us already alive have already plucked the lowest-hanging resources. Like wringing oil from rocks, from now on acquiring things we use will be much harder, involving much more energy and leaving much bigger messes in our wake.

The day after the 2008 U.S. presidential election, Paul and Anne Ehrlich wrote a letter entreating Barack Obama to "put births on a par with deaths." During the past century, they wrote, humans had made great progress raising life expectancy. "But given the frightening potential consequences of the explosion in human numbers that has followed reductions of the death rate, it is essential to pay equivalent attention to reducing high birthrates as well."

The goal, they wrote the president-elect, "must be to halt population increase as soon as humanely possible, and then reduce human numbers until births and deaths balance, at a population size that can be maintained with desired lifestyles without irreparable damage to our natural life-support systems."

They didn't mention the 2 billion figure they'd previously suggested. They proposed a global discussion over the next several decades "to reach a consensus on those lifestyles and thus on the appropriate maximum population size—which we already know must be smaller than the present 6.7 billion. Fortunately," they added, "the target can be tentative, since (if we're lucky) it may well be a half-century or more before a worldwide decline can begin, so there will be decades to consider and evaluate the best level at which to stabilize our numbers."

Their letter also called on Obama to "immediately drop the Reagan administration's 'Mexico City policy' for killing women worldwide by suppressing access to legal abortion"—which, to their satisfaction, he did within days of his inauguration. By then, Obama had also chosen Ehrlich's best friend, John Holdren, as his science advisor. The following year, the president signed a bill to make health care and health insurance available to all, and a year later announced that as of 2013, health insurance in America must cover birth control for women with no co-pay. As a result, millions of women who paid up to $50 a month for birth control suddenly found themselves not having to decide between dinner and Depo-Provera.

In a country where nearly half of all pregnancies are unintended, there was finally some reason to feel hopeful. Like most who supported Obama's candidacy, Paul Ehrlich has had his disappointments with the president, starting with his first-term inattention to climate change. Ehrlich well understands, however, what few Americans who expected Obama to be the new Franklin D. Roosevelt ever stopped to consider:

With more than 300 million Americans, Obama had nearly triple the number of citizens to employ, feed, educate, and medicate as FDR had.

He stops to pick up Anne, and drives across campus to the potluck dinner Gretchen Daily is having for her graduate students. Her Costa Rica team is there, as well as young women who have been doing fieldwork in Hawaii and Colombia, several of the Jasper Ridge staff, and some out-of-town visitors. Paul, a head taller than Anne, leads her solicitously through the airy house into the backyard throng, proudly asking everyone if they've met his first wife.

It's an old joke they've all heard, but it's always sweet to see how much Paul adores her. Anne, the associate director of Stanford's Center for Conservation Biology, still publishes prolifically with her husband, and is the acknowledged custodian of their prose. They fill plates with wild salmon and grilled vegetables, and settle into lawn chairs and rapt discussion with Gretchen's young children, Luke and Carmen, both blond as their mother. Gretchen emerges, arms laden with salad bowls. Her laser scientist husband is in Europe; they intersected briefly as she returned from Minneapolis, where she met with partners in her Natural Capital Project. "I was blown away!" she announces, her wide smile suggesting that this was a good thing.

One of those partners, she explains, is the director of the University of Minnesota's Institute on the Environment, a former astrophysicist named Jon Foley, who started applying higher math to this planet and its atmosphere. "He's compiled this fantastic data set on food production worldwide that goes down to the county level for the entire globe. It vastly exceeds the UN Food and Agriculture Organization's own database."

It is also a key source for the free InVEST program they've designed to help decision makers see how conservation can enhance businesses and protect their communities. To make the program broad and powerful enough to benefit users anywhere on Earth requires phenomenal amounts of information. A few years earlier, Foley had realized that while NASA's global satellite images show what is a forest and what is a field, they don't reveal who owns that land, what they're growing, and how they grow it. If they knew that for everywhere and merged it with the satellites' big picture, he reasoned, they could really understand what was happening on the planet.

He was told that such a huge international project would require thousands of researchers, ten to twenty years, and millions of dollars. But Foley reckoned that every country has a ministry of agriculture with guys with clipboards running around in trucks, asking farmers, "What are you growing this season? How much fertilizer are you using? Who are you selling it to?"

"Bullshit," he told detractors. "It will take about ten smart undergraduates who can speak different languages and a lot of persistence — and maybe tens of thousands of dollars, but not millions." So he cast around for students who read Portuguese, Spanish, Chinese, Russian, Arabic, Swahili, Tagalog, and other languages, who were happy to work for $10 an hour at something more interesting than flipping hamburgers. In two years, using interlibrary loans and writing agriculture ministries all over the world, they'd amassed the world's biggest collection of census data on agriculture, covering every country on Earth.

"The only ones we had trouble with were some whose governments fell apart," he told Gretchen. "And we don't have very good information from North Korea."

But for everywhere else, they had rich data from 1960 to 2010: the fifty-year period that encompassed the entire Green Revolution to the present, which tracked the amount of land, water, fertilizer, and chemicals used to grow 175 different crops. Suddenly they were getting calls from Google, the Gates Foundation, the World Bank, even from hedge fund managers, saying this was a gold mine of data. "Which they make available in the public domain," says Gretchen, "giving it away as fast as they can."

Imbuing graphic landscape overlays with Foley's golden data and housing it on Google with its massive distribution power makes InVest one of the most potent environmental planning tools in existence. Behind its dazzle, however, lurks the scientists' foreboding for their species and their planet: trepidation that hangs over every inspiring encounter with brilliant colleagues and students, and with their families and children, making every new publication and every international prize bittersweet.

They are asking, and trying to answer, the most serious question in history: How can we humans go on?

In 2008, Jonathan Foley and twenty-eight colleagues from three continents who had gathered at a conference in Sweden acknowledged that they all felt like they were staring over a cliff: Push the planet a little farther in any of several ways, and the world would change dramatically from anything known to humanity before. No one was sure exactly how much farther, or even if it could be known. But they agreed it would be important to try.

The paper they published in the journal *Nature*—versions also appeared in *Ecology and Society* and in *Scientific American*—identified nine planetary boundaries, beyond which the world would enter a phase shift that could prove cataclysmic for humanity. They acknowledged that, while based on the best science available, these were "rough, first estimates only, surrounded by large uncertainties and knowledge gaps" that will require major scientific advancements to fill. The nine boundaries were climate change, biodiversity loss, disruption of global nitrogen and phosphorus cycles, ozone depletion, ocean acidification, freshwater use, changes in land use, chemical pollution, and atmospheric particulates.

Behind each of these was the same unspoken cause: cumulative human presence, for which they did not hazard a boundary. A decision to limit one's own species is so emotionally loaded that the very idea is as troubling to scientists as it is to any human. Attempting to do so might have unavoidably distracted from this imaginative study that so starkly lay open the state of the planet.

Two of the categories, atmospheric particulates and chemical pollution, they decided had not yet been studied enough to determine Earth's capacity to absorb them. For three categories, however, the boundaries they proposed had already been surpassed.

One was climate change, for which they concluded that atmospheric CO_2 concentrations should not exceed 350 parts per million. At the time of publication, 2009, levels had risen to 387 ppm.[3]

The second was the amount of nitrogen siphoned from the atmosphere for human use, chiefly through the Haber-Bosch process. The boundary they arrived at was 35 million tons per year, versus the current 121 million. (Phosphorus was still within its proposed boundary of 11 million tons flowing into the oceans, although the current 8.5 to 9.5 million tons of phosphates were already contributing to dead zones at the world's great river deltas. Another worry about phosphorus, however, is that this essential mineral nutrient is scarce in the planet's soils, and deposits in Pacific guano atolls and Florida limestone formations are nearly spent. Only one plentiful source remains, in Morocco and neighboring Western Sahara, a barely

---

3. In 2013: 398 ppm, but already spiking over 400 ppm. Source: Global Monitoring Division of NOAA/Earth System Research Laboratory.

functioning state whose future stability has agronomists everywhere concerned.)

The third was biodiversity loss. Before the Industrial Revolution, the fossil record suggests, 0.1 to 1 species per million went extinct annually. The acceptable limit they proposed was 10. The actual current loss is at least 100 missing species per million, a figure widely feared to rise tenfold this century. Nothing remotely similar has happened since an asteroid did away with the dinosaurs.

Assigning actual numbers to how much damage to nature is allowable for humans to still thrive was bold but potentially meaningless. How does one quantify biodiversity? By counting species, or counting what they do? Foley found himself posing unanswerable questions like: Is it more important to lose a bacterium or a dodo bird? Or: Do we really need five hundred kinds of hummingbirds? Or do we need five hundred kinds of bacteria that eat the forest litter and turn it into organic matter and free nutrients?

In a world where total animal biomass is mostly insects, and where most species are microbial, our perceptions are skewed by having much more data on things we can see, such as birds and mammals, than on bacteria or nematodes. To pinpoint exactly which ones we can't live without turns out to be impossible, in the grand experiment called life on Earth, because there is no control group. We will not know for certain until they're gone, when it will be too late to call them back.

What we *do* know is that life does far better when there is a greater assortment of it. The world's longest-running experiment in biodiversity, directed since 1977 by Foley's University of Minnesota colleague David Tilman, is thirty-two miles north of their campus. On hundreds of experimental plots, prairie grasses grow in various combinations or separated into monocultures. Some receive extra blasts of carbon dioxide, or extra warmth from heat lamps, or varying levels of nitrogen, to test the impacts of all these variables. Most apparent is that primary production—the ability of plants to turn atmospheric carbon into more biomass—is highest where biodiversity is highest. The more kinds of plants, the more efficiently they use different resources in the soil.

It is a temperate-zone analog of what Gretchen Daily and Paul Ehrlich's students find in tropical Costa Rica. In each, a corollary is that the higher the diversity of plants, the fewer plant-eating pests— apparently because in a diverse, more natural landscape, a wider variety of other insects, bats, and birds show up to prey on them.

The reason to preserve the flight of songbirds

between the hemispheres each year is not just for our pleasure at the sound of their voices and sight of their plumage. The reason they migrate at all is to bear their offspring where there is an immense food supply. As they eat the insects out of all the fields and trees, they provide our most important pest control. If we lose those birds, we don't know what will happen.

The northern California March night turns chilly, and the party moves indoors. Gretchen's children sit at the piano, picking out melodies for Paul and Anne. Confronted with deepening ecological data and pernicious politics of denial, they are the ones that Ehrlich worries for.

"I don't say there's no hope. When I think there's just a 10 percent chance that we'll avoid a collapse of civilization, I keep working for Luke and Carmen to make it 11 percent."

"Enough already," says Anne.

"I give it less than 50 percent," says Gretchen. "But higher than 10."

Everyone hugs. Paul is so proud of his former protégée, who has applied principles of population ecology to the challenge of running the world, from governments to businesses to NGOs on whose boards she serves, tasked with speaking for voiceless nature in a future that either will or won't hold us all. Apart from stemming consumption, the most intractable puzzle that Paul Ehrlich has encountered is why health decisions about Mother Nature—the mother that gives us life and breath—are made by politicians, not by scientists who know how critical her condition is.

"It's the immoral equivalent of insurance company accountants making decisions about our personal health."

Even a president astute enough to appoint his friend John Holdren as his scientific counselor seemingly has failed to consult him; granted another term, perhaps that will change. But meanwhile, Gretchen Daily and her Natural Capitalists, with their expanding worldwide web of scientists, moneymakers, policy shakers, and software communicants, and their deepening data on the cost-effectiveness gained by not squandering nature's principal, may yet get the plutocracy's attention. Ehrlich is endlessly grateful to her for trying.

———

In 1995, the head of the Laboratory of Populations at Rockefeller University, mathematician and biologist Joel E. Cohen, published a book titled *How Many People Can the Earth Support?* His exhaustive inquiry offered no single numerical answer to that question, except to say that none exists, because it begs so many other questions. Questions such as: At what level of material well-being, and with what degree of distribution among the world's people? With what technology, in what physical environments, and with what kind of governments? With what risk, robustness, or stability—that is, support people for how long? And with what values?

For the ecologists of the world, who are also sons, daughters, and parents, and whose closest friends are humans like themselves, the answers to all of these are informed in their minds by mounds of data and observation, but truly answered in their hearts. There comes a time when what we do and how many of us do it must be fairly considered, measured, and guided, and that time appears to be this century.

In what has become a parable of our age, traced to an American mathematician and meteorologist, chaos theorist Edward Lorenz, we gather that the beating of a butterfly's wings in Brazil might touch off a tornado in Texas. In 1945, a butterfly spotted at a Vermont summer camp touched the imagination of a thirteen-year-old boy named Paul Ehrlich. One thing led to another, leading him to the University of Kansas to learn from a sage as impassioned with bees as he was with *Lepidoptera*. There he met his first and only wife, an artist, biological illustrator, and clear-eyed writer who could draw flawless butterflies and who helped him articulate that the population dynamics of the frailest insects pertain to our own. It was a short step from there to understanding that we are ultimately as fragile as they are. Poison their nectar, usurp their fields, exhaust their sustenance, or disrupt their climate, and they fail—as do we.

Eventually, their communion would reopen a discussion first broached in the eighteenth century by a much-maligned, but never really refuted, economist and cleric named Thomas Robert Malthus. His argument had been all but crushed by the heavy machinery of growth that for the next two hundred years redefined the world. Then, at the point where growth accelerated toward its greatest expression, a book the Ehrlichs wrote reached millions, but brought the same disparagement upon themselves. Legions of pundits and self-styled economic sages tried to drown their message. But it keeps bobbing to the surface.

It isn't very complex, although an infinite, awesome ecology underlies it:

Keep everything in reasonable balance—chemistry, variety, and numbers—and there is hope for our children, and for the spawn of all the birds and butterflies, to continue, together.

Author's Epilogue

If the human race maintains its current trajectory, by the year 2100 there will be more than 10 billion of us. With slight perturbations to that pace, we may be several billion more.

Let's suppose, however—theoretically, social objections aside—that the entire world adopted a one-child policy tomorrow. By the end of this century, we would be back to 1.6 billion, our population in 1900.

That sounds incredible, but it's true if you think about it: If we stopped reproducing completely, in little more than a hundred years our population would be zero. So holding to just one offspring per family for a few generations would exponentially bring us down to size.

That would reduce our numbers by three-quarters, freeing billions of acres for other species, on whose existence a functioning ecosystem—including our place in it—depends. But the thought of a one-child edict is appalling, even to most Chinese, who've tried it. No one wants to be told what to do about something so private and natural.

Nevertheless, many today do choose to limit their procreation, in their own self-interest. In 2008, during a speaking tour in the U.S. state with the highest fertility, Utah, I posed a question about this to audiences that were largely Mormon. Like early Israelites, early Mormons had multiple wives, and for the same reason: It was a strategy to have many children so the tribe would grow quickly. But by the end of the nineteenth century, Mormons had been forced by the U.S. government to abandon polygamy. Still, they kept having a lot of children, and soon a crisis developed, as many Mormon women began dying in childbirth. In order to keep the birth rate up with only one wife per family, women were getting pregnant too quickly after their last delivery.

In a family-centered culture such as the Mormons, motherless families are not only tragic, but a structural threat to the community. Fortunately, Mormons also emphasize education, and by the early 1900s, a growing generation of Mormon doctors realized they needed to counsel women to space pregnancies, lest the Mormon way of life be threatened.

"So it occurs to me," I said, "that a culture that

already chose once to manage pregnancies for the sake of the mother and your society might best understand the need to do so in order to save Mother Nature. Besides, as people who venerate latter-day saints, you may have an advantage over those of us who are still tied to liturgies thousands of years old. You were flexible enough to form a new Christian church in modern times. Flexibility is exactly what we'll need to respond to the environmental crises we all now face."

In the discussion that followed, there was wide agreement that it was in their interest to do so. Many complained about the traffic-clogged hundred-mile strip city that now ran from north of Ogden to south of Provo and clawed ever higher up scenic mountains, where pollution billowed high enough to obscure ski slopes. And the water situation in their desert state, part of the depleting Colorado River Basin, frightened everybody.

"There is not a single problem on Earth that wouldn't be easier if there were fewer people," said a woman in Salt Lake City, and surprisingly, no one objected.

That made me wonder: Was there something in the histories or holy books of the rest of the world's cultures and religions that might embrace the idea of, so to speak, refraining from embracing as much during the next two or three generations, limiting our progeny to bring us back into balance with the rest of nature—at which point, having reached an optimum number, we could resume averaging two children per family?

But as I began journeying to many different lands to probe that question, another one, universal to our entire species, also arose:

Do we have the will and foresight to make decisions for the sake of descendants we will never know?

Once, humans would begin great cathedrals, understanding that they wouldn't be completed for 250 years. The last of these are the unfinished Cathedral of Saint John the Divine in New York, begun in 1892, and Barcelona's Basílica de la Sagrada Familia that Antoni Gaudí began in 1882, whose latest projected completion is 2026—both novel exceptions to the rule that our societies don't plan much for posterity anymore. Touching appeals to preserve nature for the sake of our grandchildren, featuring kids cuddling threatened koalas, are regrettably ineffective. Our immediate needs ultimately take precedence over theirs.

So the question becomes: Might we benefit *right now* if everyone agreed to bring population down in the twenty-first century, much as the world's nations came together during the last century to sign a protocol to save our flickering ozone layer?

In a coffee shop in London's Liverpool Station, I

posed that to twenty-one-year-old Asma Abdur Rahman.

"You mean would it benefit me to only have one child?"

"One or two." Reaching optimum population would be more gradual if some couples chose to have two, but that option makes the possibility far more realistic. Even Paul Ehrlich assures women friends like Gretchen Daily, and his own daughter, that "two will do."

She sipped her tea, her expression thoughtful beneath her red and gold hijab. Born in the UK to Bangladeshi immigrants, Asma was one of four children; her father was one of seven, and her mother one of nine. She was also an Oxford graduate getting her master's at the London School of Economics in environmental policy. Recently she'd made a presentation in class, arguing that population couldn't be addressed in isolation. "If we don't bring down consumption in tandem with population, it could be futile, because a wealthy few can use as much resources as the many."

There is also a risk that families with fewer children become more affluent and consume more. No one she knew of at the London School of Economics had a solution for overconsumption. Neither did I. So back to the idea of lowering the number of consumers.

She typified, she said, educated second-generation Muslim Britons who will never have families as big as their grandparents'. But neither will her cousins in Bangladesh. Since earning the dubious honor of being the world's most densely populated large country, it has committed to family planning. There are now more girls than boys in Bangladesh's primary and secondary schools. The total fertility rate, 6.9 children per woman when it separated from Pakistan in 1971, is now 2.25: nearly replacement. A 2011 Vienna Institute of Demography study that modeled different educational scenarios concluded that if every country ambitiously invested in schooling girls, by 2050 there could be a billion fewer people than if nothing changes.

"But women's education should be promoted for itself, not for bringing down population," said Asma. "Although," she added, "that's a natural side effect."

No argument here, and I suspect that a study that modeled a world where women have full equal rights would be even more revealing. Tapping wasted female brainpower would be a priceless resource exploitation with no downside. It would also help alleviate feared labor shortages as populations shrink. But I reminded her of my question: Would contributing to that shrinkage benefit her?

"I agree: It's not the environment that needs to be

managed, it's us. Imagine how pleasant England would be with half the people. But I don't think I'd be happy having just one. I've been shaped so much by having siblings."

As had I, the second of two children in my own family and the grateful beneficiary of an older sister's love and guidance. In China, I raised the same question at Guangzhou University. At 13 million, Guangzhou, two hours north of Hong Kong, is now China's third biggest city—if taken just by itself. It is actually part of the world's largest metropolitan industrial complex: 40 million people in the Pearl River Delta, where five other now-contiguous cities top 3 million. Their astonishing growth is due to immigration from poorer parts of China for the promise of work in factories.

I was speaking to four hundred college students who, relieved of shackles that restricted an entire prior generation during the Cultural Revolution, were bursting with opportunities to learn and get interesting jobs and make money. The sky was their limit— figuratively, but also literally, and they knew it. Outside, it was possible to gaze directly at the sun, a pallid disk shrouded by the chronic murk of industrial Guangzhou. These Chinese youth knew that the future was theirs, one way or another. Environmental havoc was the bogeyman standing between them and their dreams, and they were keenly interested in how to avert it.

At one point, a thought struck me. "Is every one of them an only child?" I asked my translator.

"Of course," she replied. "We all are."

"You're one of the most animated and intelligent groups of students I've ever met," I told them. "You don't seem psychologically warped. Don't you miss having brothers and sisters?"

They acknowledged that they did, but they understood why reproductive restraint was necessary, and they'd adjusted. "Our cousins and closest friends have become our siblings," the student moderator explained to me.

"We've kind of reinvented the family," said another young woman.

Again, I was reminded how adaptable *Homo sapiens* are, and how much our flexibility explains how we've survived up until now. And maybe portends how we'll be able to keep surviving.

Our current unprecedented numbers came about quite simply: After remaining nearly constant for roughly two hundred thousand years, during the last 0.1 percent of human history, each year fewer people have died than have been born. That happens only two ways: more births, or fewer deaths—and the two are inextricable. Over the past two centuries, we have become brilliant at beating back diseases or preemptively protecting ourselves from them. We repair damaged bodies. Through much of the world, we've doubled average human lifespans from under forty years to nearly eighty.

Had we not done that and let nature take its usual course, it would periodically roar through our population with pandemics, just as it burns through forests to thin overgrowth, and there would be far fewer of us alive. Most of the 2.3 billion of us over forty would not be around. Almost half of all children would have died before age five, and at least one-fifth of all women would have died of pregnancy or childbirth complications before giving birth to all the ones they did.

How our ancestors bore that pain is unimaginable, and we're not going back, at least not voluntarily. Overuse of our miraculous antibiotics, especially in livestock feed, has rendered many of them useless; like the escalating arms race between coevolving insects and plants, emerging resistant strains of bacteria are now firing back at us. Nevertheless, our medical technology is a benefit we've earned by evolving the intelligence to create it—and it also means that there are more people on the planet, because we hang around longer, consuming more food and more everything else. Since all but a few sociopaths oppose raising death rates, if we are ever to lower population, there is only once choice: lowering birth rates.

Is that what most of us would choose? In Utah, as people lamented the relentless urbanity filling their valleys and mountainsides, I again heard them express something I hear wherever I travel. No matter where people are from, or whatever age or politics or faith, everyone remembers a place where they used to go to escape the clamor and congestion of their lives. A place not too far away, where they could hike, or picnic, or ride a dirt bike. Where they could watch birds — or if they like to hunt, kill birds. Where they could hug trees, or cut them for firewood, or just fall asleep beneath one. But now, that favorite place is gone, vanished beneath strip malls or industrial parks or condominia.

Everyone remembers a world that was better. Less crowded. Lovelier. Where they felt freer.

So did I, as I returned to my birthplace, Minneapolis, to meet the University of Minnesota's Jon Foley, compiler of the vast planetary database of what we humans grow. First, though, I headed north of the Twin Cities to the Cedar Creek Ecosystem Science Reserve, the prairie grassland research station where for three-and-a-half decades evolutionary biologist David Tilman has documented, among other things, how we weaken the web of life whenever we extract another species.

Logically, most of the world's settlements occurred near good farmland, much of which unfortunately has disappeared in the past half-century under pavement. Each time I go back home, I am unprepared for how much farther urbanity has advanced. For forty-five miles, I found that State Highway 65 was now lined with ministorages, real estate offices, copy shops, gas stations, discount tire outlets, pet hospitals, Domino's Pizza, tanning salons, mobile home parks, used car and truck sales, credit unions, Hollywood Video, Auto Zone, Chili's, Office Max, and sales lots hawking faux colonial, vinyl-sided prefab homes. On Minnesota Public Radio, two economists discussed how many new housing starts the state needed to again have a healthy market.

Like flood victims clinging to life preservers, amid all the cloned commerce were scattered vestiges of my boyhood: farm stands selling sweet corn, and live bait shops. After an hour, I turned onto County Road 24, now known as 237th Street Northeast. It led to Tilman's field research station, a compound of green wooden buildings in a field of black-eyed Susans and purple bee balm.

It was mid-July, and the humid air already felt chewable. Two grad students, Jane Cowles and Peter

Wragg, took me to see experimental plots planted in combinations of annuals and perennials—swift grass, couch grass, Arctic brome, big and little bluestem, and blue grama grass—along with forbs and legumes such as yarrow, prairie clover, milkweed, goldenrod, and lupine. Infrared heat lamps were warming each plot 2° to 5°C above the already sweltering morning. In the elevated heat, everything was growing taller and faster. Several plants were already flowering. Did this mean, I asked, that global warming is good for crops?

"Not really," said Cowles. "Unless insects change their life-cycle timing, there will be a mismatch between the pollinators and the flowers."

Even with forced warming, growth was significantly more robust in the most biodiverse plots. Unfortunately, however, the vast majority of our crops are monocultures.

In the elevated CO_2 experiment, three circular fields, each containing fifty plots sown with various combinations of plants and fertilizer applications, were ringed by perforated vertical PVC poles that blew carbon dioxide. A sensor in the middle of each ring, Wragg explained, constantly adjusted the flow to maintain a steady 550 parts per million of CO_2, expected to be the atmospheric concentration in

2050.[1] During the initial years of the experiment, heightened CO_2 had enhanced plant growth, much as increased oxygen invigorates us—until it becomes toxic. Likewise, at a certain point the plants' productivity stopped increasing unless extra nitrogen fertilizer was added—a demand that will keep spiraling, as overuse of nitrogen is itself one of the biggest sources of greenhouse gases.

As in the elevated temperature experiment, plots with the highest biodiversity did the best. We were driving next to see an enhanced nitrogen experiment, but suddenly the heavens darkened as though by an unscheduled eclipse. From the south, a phalanx of black cumulonimbus was slamming the sky shut. As we passed through a wooded copse, a birch tree blew down across the road, cutting short my visit.

Heading back, I heard tornado warning sirens. Gripping the steering wheel against wind gusts, watching the sky for funnels, I wondered, as everyone now does, if the dramatic weather was due to our rejiggered climate. On the one hand, having grown up in this northern stretch of Tornado Alley, this felt

---

1. Pre–Industrial Revolution concentrations of atmospheric CO_2 averaged 280 parts per million. In 2013, CO_2 levels passed 400 ppm for the first time in 3 million years. (Some scientists say 15 million; either way, seas were 80–100 feet higher than today.)

familiar. On the other, the radio reported that although it was only midsummer, the heat wave had already killed a million dollars' worth of cattle in Minnesota.

Only over time, scientists caution, can we know if mounting violent weather events add up to a trend that means the climate has entered a phase shift. But if we wait to act until all the numbers are in, we'll have waited too long, which is why scientists keep jamming every possible variable into models that predict our likely future. Because technically they're speculative, their credibility is attacked by whoever profits from business as usual. But thus far, the main failing in climate change models has been timidity: the worst possible case for an ice-free Arctic summer, predicted for 2050 back in 2008, has now been moved to as early as 2016.

At what point, and with what proof or words, might politicians and industry be convinced that drastic change is already upon us, and will only worsen—perhaps fatally—if we don't respond accordingly? Later that year, I would be asked by a prominent Japanese business magazine if I thought that people were being hysterical to demand an end to nuclear power in the wake of the Fukushima tragedy.

"I wouldn't call it hysteria," I answered, "given that all your nuclear plants are in seismic zones or on seacoasts, exposed to typhoons and tsunamis."

"But people will suffer even more if productivity drops. Isn't it hysterical not to take that into account?" the interviewer countered. Over the next half-hour, he kept rephrasing his question, hoping for a more satisfying response—until, during his fourth try, the coffee shop where we sat shook as a tremor struck central Tokyo, rendering my reply unnecessary.

No twisters had dropped from the roiling black clouds into the Twin Cities, but the university's St. Paul campus, where Jon Foley teaches, was littered with broken tree limbs. In his early forties, Foley has a lean, boyish face that smiles far more than you'd expect from someone who knows as much as he does about what we're up against. He showed me a map of the world, color-coded in green and brown.

"All the world's cropland lumped together," he said, indicating the green splotches, "adds up to about the size of South America. All our pastureland"—the brown—"equals the continent of Africa." My shock over urban sprawl was misplaced, he said. Humans use sixty times the amount of land that's paved to feed ourselves. Everything else is either desert or mountains too dry or craggy to cultivate, or forests that we need to soak up carbon.

"We're already using all the cropland we'll ever have. In the coming years, we have to feed two billion more people, using the same land. Add the affluence of Asia's growing middle class, and it means we have to double the world's food supply by mid-century. We're already failing a billion undernourished people now. By the end of the century, there'll be at least a billion more. We'll need to triple today's yields. How we do that is the biggest challenge humanity's ever faced."

I'd heard this all before, but coming from the man who'd gathered more information than anyone about food we coax from the Earth, this felt like a definitive verdict. So I was surprised when he said, "The good news is that I think it's possible."

How?

"Only if everything works perfectly—and so far, we're not emphasizing the right things. If we stabilize populations, as quickly and humanely as possible. Also, if we rethink the diets that are shifting to more meat. Eight or ten billion people can't all eat hamburgers. If we reduce the waste of at least a third of the world's food. In rich countries, we waste it in restaurants or it spoils in refrigerators, at the consumer end of the supply chain."

We were having lunch in a bright, airy St. Paul eatery named Bread & Chocolate, the kind of place where food is a festive subject. Guiltily, I ate the parsley garnish on my plate. "In poor countries," Foley continued, "it's usually at the farmer's end. They can't store grain without losses to disease or pests. Or they can't get it to market in time. Or it's simply lost somewhere."

He paused for a breath. There were more, and even bigger, *ifs* coming.

"If we—" He stopped and corrected himself. "We *have* to hit the sweet spot of growing the most food with the least water and the least nitrogen. They're both so big it's extraordinary. It requires so much departure from business as usual, it's pretty frightening."

Humans were already fighting over water in Old Testament times. But synthetic nitrogen wasn't in widespread use until the 1960s. Since then, Foley said, "Agriculture has become the single biggest hammer we're smashing the planet with. It's the biggest source of greenhouse gases, emitting more than all the factories and power plants together, and more than all our cars, trains, boats, and airplanes combined."

The culprits are deforestation, methane belched by cattle and rice paddies, fertilizer manufacture, and an insidious by-product of overfertilization: nitrous oxide, a heat-trapping gas three hundred times as potent as CO_2.

"It's a Goldilocks parable," said Foley. "Half the world has too little nitrogen. Half the world has too much. Nobody's just right. Here in the U.S., and especially in China and India, we use way too much. Only a quarter to half is taken up by plants. The rest is pollution. But in a place like Malawi, a small application of fertilizer to maize fields could triple their productivity. Again, it's a matter of hitting the sweet spot, for every place and climate and soil and culture."

The path to a happy future was looking very narrow. Especially from my vantage point, back where I'd started. Minneapolis and St. Paul were prosperous milling and railroad cities whose founders deeply valued and endowed education, arts, and culture. Set in a fertile landscape ribboned with plentiful rivers, blessed with rich soils and clear lakes brimming with fish, these graceful cities were lovely but deceptive places to grow up: Until I left and discovered otherwise, I assumed that this was normal. Back in this comforting womb, I struggled to see the big global picture.

"What if Haber-Bosch were never invented," I asked Foley, "and we never had artificially fixed nitrogen? We'd have a lot fewer people with our food supply limited by the ability of bacteria on legume roots to fix nitrogen. Instead, we're hogging half the planet's photosynthesis and stealing 70 percent of the freshwater for crops. If we'd never invented fertilizer, would we have even needed a Green Revolution?"

He winced. "The twentieth century would have been really ugly—uglier than it was—if we hadn't done that. Admittedly, we now need a second Green Revolution, one that's much greener. But by avoiding catastrophic food shortages and the Malthusian crisis we're now headed towards, the Green Revolution allowed us to humanely go through the demographic transition."

The demographic transition—a country's passage from high birth and death rates to low—is considered both an indicator and a result of becoming developed. "Imagine if we'd had a world armed with nuclear weapons and billions of starving people. That's a powder keg that we avoided."

Yet another University of Minnesota scientist, Green Revolution founder Norman Borlaug, warned that we'd really avoided nothing: we'd merely postponed the inevitable population crush. And now Pakistan, a nuclear power and initial Green Revolution beneficiary, is bursting with people headed toward hunger, unless some miracle restores their diminishing water supplies. Israel and India, also nuclear powers, also have water shortages and burgeoning masses.

By Foley's own amazing compilation of numbers, unless we marshaled all the world's unruly minions into exquisitely disciplined resource management, using fertilizer with pinpoint precision and minimizing the tasty, lucrative, status-affirming overconsumption of meat, we were hell-bent on fulfilling Malthus's prophecy.

Wouldn't trying to manage our numbers be a more realistic target than trying to squeeze three times the food from the same, already exhausted land?

Foley pinched the bridge of his long Irish nose. "We were given this amazing planet," he replied, "with huge resources and incredible endowments of energy, biology, and water. Now all the trajectories are in the wrong direction. We've got too many people wanting too much stuff on a planet whose resource base is getting smaller. Those things will continue unfolding for a long time, and the endgame's going to be something radically different. Sometime in the future, the endgame will be for us to survive as a civilization on a planet with fewer people. I don't know how many. A billion or two. Who knows?"

Outside, it was now a calm July afternoon. "We're caught in a sweep of history with much inertia behind it," Foley said as we shook hands. "We can't solve this problem in our lifetime. It's going to take several generations of work. But that doesn't make me feel hopeless; it actually makes me feel kind of empowered. It's like, great: I've got the next couple of generations to work with. I need to get them the best tools to fight with as possible. Maybe one lever we can push is seeing if we can stop at eight instead of ten billion. Instead of only 30 percent of the world's rainforest left, let's give them 41 percent."

————

Driving across the Mississippi River, I thought about his determination. Like his colleague Gretchen Daily, Jon Foley pulled no punches on what we were facing, yet still managed to inspire hope.

A passage in the landmark ecological boundary paper he coauthored referred to exponential growth of human activities that could destabilize systems and trigger abrupt, irreversible environmental changes that could be catastrophic for human well-being. "This is a profound dilemma," it concluded, "because the predominant paradigm of social and economic development remains largely oblivious to the risk of human induced environmental disasters at continental to planetary scales." Muffled in the neutral scientific tone of that turgid sentence was a scream: *We don't even realize what we're doing!*

As Interstate 94 curved past gleaming downtown Minneapolis, I looked for the parking lot where the original Minneapolis Public Library once stood, a nineteenth-century brownstone where I'd passed much of my boyhood. I would visit the small museum on its top floor and stare at the stuffed remains of a passenger pigeon, once the most abundant bird on Earth. Humans wiped them out by 1914—yet as I later read, even when there were a million left, they were already functionally extinct, because the pattern that doomed their critical habitat and food supply was already set. Was it possible, I now wondered, that my own species might also already be the living dead?

The week before, in Washington, DC, I'd met with Reverend Richard Cizik, a former Washington lobbyist for the National Association of Evangelicals. In 2008 he left them and founded the New Evangelical Partnership for the Common Good, a Christian organization with an environmental mission he calls "Creation Care." For the past three years, he told me, "I've been laying theological groundwork for interpreting how the mandate to be fruitful and multiply applies to today, in light of the current crisis of the planet." A thin, intense man with straight, receding blond hair, he'd just come out publicly in support of family-planning funding a few weeks earlier in a piece for the *Washington Post*'s faith blog.

"Family planning is not only moral: it's what we should be doing. Be fruitful and multiply was superseded by a post-flood mandate to live peacefully with all of God's creatures."

He was undaunted by the pushback from conservative evangelicals, he said, and encouraged by the response of a new generation of concerned young Christians.

"Thy will be done on Earth as it is in heaven, Jesus says in the Lord's Prayer. If that's the case, then we should bring the values of heaven to Earth. In heaven things don't go extinct. Sustainability means you don't make things go extinct. Yet that's what we're doing, to entire species. We just don't realize it, unless we listen to the scientists who help explain what Creation can't say to us, but is speaking to us. That's the value of science — to help us understand what Creation is saying about itself."

In parting, he directed me to Revelation 11:18.

"In his vision of the end times, the apostle John foresees God destroying those who destroy the Earth," he said. "So we have a moral obligation to care for it, and live as if our very lives and futures all depended on it."

As a boy, I learned to fish and to swim in Minneapolis lakes. During college, I lifeguarded them, and canoed and sailed and jogged around them during off-hours. Now I stopped at one of the loveliest, Lake of the Isles. Pairs of mallards and blue-winged teals floated near stands of cattails along the shore. Couples of my own species were also present, along with young mothers pushing strollers on the paths beneath weeping willows. So much of this planet was still as beautiful as I always remembered it, and I hoped that Cizik was right about another thing he'd said: that the Scriptures don't predict a world that burns up and disappears, but a refined, purified Earth.

The demographic transition is a reality: among the fruits of development are longevity and a reduced need for parents to make extra copies of themselves, in hopes that at least some survive. Except in poorest Africa or south Asia, or in enclaves of religious extremism such as in the Philippines, Afghanistan, and *haredi* Israel, the momentum of our increase has declined. The question now, as our species presses against the limits of nature's tolerance, is if it's in the best interest of ourselves and our kindred species on this planet to hasten that process.

In other words: Are we bringing down our numbers fast enough to save us from the irreversible, possibly calamitous change of which our finest scientists are trying to warn us?

"Demography isn't destiny," Rockefeller University population mathematician Joel Cohen told a 2012 gathering at Harvard's Kennedy School. "We can influence the world of our children and grandchildren by what we do right now." Concurring with population specialist Dr. Malcolm Potts, just a half-child-per-woman decrease in the world's fertility rate, Cohen said, could bring us back to 6 billion by the end of the century—or half a child in the other direction could take us to 16 billion.

Not that we would ever get there, because we would collapse over multiple thresholds first, possibly never to crawl back. Or we might lower our numbers even faster, with families around the globe bearing just one or two, until we bring our species back from the brink we hadn't realized we were approaching, until now.

As I slowly walked around Lake of the Isles, I noted that several of the grand houses along the lakeside parkway, once the address of milling families and cereal magnates, were now for sale. Toward the end of the previous decade, the housing market, that sacrosanct standard of economic health, proved to be a delusion akin to chain letters and Ponzi schemes. We all know what happened next: The ripples are still shaking the underpinnings of the European Union and world banking systems.

But say you owned a corporation, and you hired as a consultant one of those economists who failed to see the inevitable mortgage debacle coming. Even though they obsess about growth as the measure of a company's strength—the mantra they never question—you already know what they're going to tell you to do to make your corporation healthy:

"You need to get lean. You've got to cut out the fat."

So when your employees arrive the following week, 25 percent find pink slips waiting for them. Rather brutally, your corporation has just cut itself down to a healthier size. That is, unless you run a humane corporation. Instead of culling a quarter of your personnel as though they were excess deer, you use a gentler method: attrition. Each year, as some employees retire or move on or pass away, you simply recruit fewer to take their places. Those who remain learn new technologies to efficiently accomplish what previously took many more to do, and gradually the company reaches a nice, sustainable size.

Unless you actually are fortunate enough to own a corporation, that's a fantasy, but here's some reality on a planet that's now like a company swollen beyond its means, its cafeteria incapable of feeding all its personnel, who have grown too numerous for all to be properly paid what they deserve:

The Earth can't sustain our current numbers, and inevitably, one way or another, those numbers must come down. Even as I write these words, I recall a jarring 2011 radio interview of Dr. Harold Wanless, chair of the University of Miami's Department of Geological Sciences.

"By the end of this century," Wanless warned, "regions of south Florida will be uninhabitable. Miami–Dade County will be abandoned. Mumbai will be abandoned—15 million people. Atlantic City—you name it. With a four- or five-foot rise in sea level, most of the deltas of the world will be abandoned."

Until recently, that might have been dismissed as a crackpot's ranting. But the Intergovernmental Panel on Climate Change's 2007 worst-case scenario of less than a two-foot rise by the year 2100 is now being grimly reconsidered, as poles melt faster than expected and their dark exposed waters absorb more heat, and as thawing methane deposits bubble forth. The only one I've found disputing Dr. Wanless's extreme predictions is a Florida real estate blogger. Scarcely a year after he made them, after not just Atlantic City's, but New York City's shores succumbed to surging seas, it was growing less likely that many others would challenge him.

I don't want to cull anyone alive today. I wish every human now on the planet a long, healthy life. But either we take control ourselves, and humanely bring our numbers down by recruiting fewer new members of the human race to take our places, or nature is going to hand out a pile of pink slips. When you see survival of the fittest portrayed on the National Geographic Channel, it's entertaining. When it happens to your own species, it's not pretty.

I lingered on the grass by Lake of the Isles until the young mothers with their strollers departed, leaving the early evening joggers. As twilight settled and Jupiter rose in a velvet sky, the path around the lake filled with lovers, young and old. Hand in hand, they represented the grand spectrum that has enriched the city of my birth from its early Scandinavian majority into the splendid swirl that defines our globalized species today: Latino, Caucasian, Asian, African, and Native Americans, joined in the ancient courtship rituals of my fellow humans, doing what comes naturally.

For us to keep doing that, all that's required is that we leave space for our fellow species to do the same. So simple, so reasonable, and in our days to come and on beyond us, still so beautiful.

Acknowledgments

Years ago I lived in rural Mexico, where I saw mule riders arrive in remote villages with polystyrene saddlebags filled with vaccines and birth control. The former, to protect living children, gave women the confidence to use the latter—which they were already eager to try, thanks to a powerful message coming to them via a powerful medium.

That was the television soap opera, among the most beloved forms of entertainment in Latin America. Once, at the bottom of Chihuahua's Copper Canyon, I saw five horseback cowboys watching the evening's *telenovela* through the window of a grocery store, where the townspeople gathered around a thirteen-inch black-and-white TV powered by a diesel generator. Among the most popular shows in the late 1970s was one titled *Acompáñame*—Accompany Me—produced, directed, and cowritten by Miguel Sabido. Imbedded in this family drama of three sisters and their respective struggles with their husbands—including over whether to plan their pregnancies—was the message that smaller families live better.

Acompáñame is widely credited for the 34 percent drop in Mexico's fertility rate during the decade the series aired. Sabido's method inspired the work of the Population Media Center in Burlington, Vermont, which today produces soap operas that promote family planning in twenty-two languages: electronic analogs of the family-planning street theater I witnessed in Pakistan. PMC has been a font of information and news about reproductive health, for which I warmly thank Bill Ryerson, Katie Elmore, and Joe Bish.

Acknowledgments

I'm grateful for the guidance of other population NGOs, each with its own approach to this complex subject. My thanks to Marian Starkey of the Population Connection (originally Zero Population Growth); Jason Bremner of the Population Reference Bureau and his colleague Karen Hardee, formerly of Population Action International; Musimbi Kanyoro, past director of the Packard Foundation's Population and Reproductive Health Program; Geoff Dabelko and Meaghan Parker of the Woodrow Wilson International Center's Population, Health, and Environment program; and John Guillebaud and, especially, Roger Martin of the UK's Population Matters, née Optimum Population Trust.

I am also indebted to the readily available resources of the Guttmacher Institute, the United Nations Population Fund, and the Communication Consortium Media Center's invaluable *PUSH Journal* (Periodic Updates of Sexual and Reproductive Health Issues Around the World), which enlightened me daily while working on this book. Finally, a deep bow to Hania Zlotnick, former director of the UN's Population Division, whose office I walked into in 2009 with a raw idea in mind—and walked out of hours later with piles of essential reading and references, and wise, patient advice that sustained me continually over the next three years.

Heather D'Agnes, past director of USAID's Population, Health, and Environment programs, generously offered me encouragement, vital information, and crucial contacts. I'm also beholden to her *en famille* mentors: her mother, Leona D'Agnes, advisor to reproductive health programs in southeast Asia, who helped me navigate trips to the Philippines and Thailand, and her father, Thomas D'Agnes, author of the fine biography of Mechai Viravaidya, *From Cabbages to Condoms*.

In 2003, I spoke at an international conference in Hannover, Germany, on water as a source of conflict in the twenty-first century. The most compelling moment was a joint presentation by an Israeli coordinator for Friends of the Earth–Middle East and the deputy head of the Palestinian Water Authority. No matter how incandescent the tension between their two peoples, every week they managed to speak, because the urgency to preserve a scarce natural resource transcended nationality. Listening to these brave men, many of us were near tears.

That memory inspired my first trip for this book, to the divided land considered hallowed ground by much of the world. In Israel, I thank Daniel Orenstein and his colleagues at Haifa's Israel Institute of Technology; Gidon Bromberg of EcoPeace/Friends of the Earth–Middle East; Eilon Schwartz and Jeremy Benstein of the Heschel Center for Environmental Learning and Leadership, and past Heschel fellow and landscape architect Rachel Landani; Rabbi Dudi Zilbershlag of *Haredim* for the Environment; Tamar Dayan, Yoran Yom-Tov, Amotz Zahavi, and ornithologist Yossi Leshem of Tel Aviv University's Department of Zoology; Jerusalem deputy mayor Naomi Tsur; director Binyamin Eiben Boim of Mea She'arim's Yeshiva Sha'ri Ha Torah; University of Haifa geographer Arnon Soffer; Hebrew University demographer Sergio DellaPergola; Huleh Valley farmer Ellie Galili; journalists Zafrir Rinat of *Haaretz* and Sylvana Foa of the *Village Voice;* desalination planner Dan Perry; Arava Institute for Environmental Studies' Alon Tal, Elli Groner, David Lehrer, Tamar Norkin, and Tareq Abuhamed; Phil Warburg and Tamar Gindis for many valuable contacts; and Sheik Saed Qrinawy and Ahmad Amrani of the Bedouin city of Rahat.

In Palestine, my deep thanks to demographer Khalil Toufakji of the Arab Studies Society in Jerusalem; Jad Isaac and Abeer Safar of Bethlehem's Applied Research Institute–Jerusalem; Palestinian director Nader Khateb of Friends of the Earth–Middle East; Palestinian Water Authority director Shaddad Attili; attorney and peace talks negotiator Diana Bhutto; Al-Amari refugee camp residents Ruwaidah Um-Said, Ayat Um-Said, and her children, Rheem and Zacariah; their neighbors Abed, Jabert, Hayat, and Ahmad Fatah; the family of Firyal, Nisreen, and Ala'a———; Mahmoud and Nidal———; geographer Khaldoun Rishmawi; and especially my guide and translator in both Arabic and Hebrew, Nidal Rafa.

That trip ended in Aqaba, Jordan. My next was to the United Kingdom, where, in addition to Optimum Population Trust/Population Matters, I thank painter Gregor Harvie; Shropshire ornithologist

John Tucker; British National Party deputy chairman Simon Darby; Dr. Mohammad Naseem of the Birmingham Central Mosque; Fazlun Khalid of the Islamic Foundation for Ecology and Environmental Science; economists Sir Partha Dasgupta of St. John's College, Cambridge, and Pavan Sukhdev of Deutsche Bank; director Abdulkarim Khalil, deputy director Yusef Noden, board vice chair Farrid Shamsuddin, and Imam Samer Darwish of London's Al-Manaar Muslim Cultural Heritage Centre; London School of Economics master's candidate Asma Abdur Rahman; and Sara Parkin of the Forum for the Future.

In San José, Costa Rica, director Hilda Picado of the Asociación Demográfica Costarricense and demographer Luis Rosero Bixby of the Universidad de Costa Rica's Centro Centroamericano de Población kindly spared time for me. I then joined conservation biologist Gretchen Daily; Stanford graduate students Chase Mendenhall, Danny Karp, and Melinda Belisle; naturalist Jeisson Figueroa Sandi; and ornithologist Jim Zook at the Organization for Tropical Studies' Las Cruces Biological Station. Like all great field scientists, they seem to work harder and have more fun than anyone, and I'm ever grateful they included me.

Next came Uganda, where I traveled with two dedicated reproductive health specialists, epidemiologist Lynne Gaffikin and Dr. Amy Voedisch, to the Bwindi Impenetrable Forest. Thanks to them, I met the inspiring veterinarian Gladys Kalema-Zikusoka; her husband, Lawrence; and their associates at Conservation Through Public Health, including David Matsiko, Joseph Byonanebye, Alex Ngabirano, Dr. Abdulhameed Kateregga, Melinda Hershey, Samuel Rugaba, and CTPH co-founder Stephen Rubanga: my gratitude and admiration to them all. In Bwindi Community Hospital, I thank Dr. Mutahunga Birungi, Isaac Kahinda, and family- planning director Florence Ninsiima. At the Batwa Development Programme, Richard Magezi, the late Blackie Gonsalves, and the Batwa Pygmy families of Mukongoro settlement. At the Uganda Wildlife Authority, I thank Chief Warden Charles Tumwesigye, who approved my permit to track mountain gorillas, and forest guides Gard Kanuangyeyo and Fred Tugarurirwe.

ACKNOWLEDGMENTS

In Uganda's capital, Kampala, I am grateful to Dr. Peter Ibembe of Reproductive Health Uganda; Susan Mukasa of Population Services International; radio journalist Pius Sawa; Patricia Wamala of Family Health International–Uganda; Dorothy Balaba and Denis Mubiru of the Programme for Accessible Health Communication and Education; Jan Broekhuis of Wildlife Conservation Society–Uganda; and especially to Anne Fiedler of Pathfinder International and Joy Naiga of the Uganda Population Secretariat.

Gretchen Daily kindly invited me to join her again as, with colleagues Chris Colvin, Driss Ennaanay, and Luis Solórzano from the Natural Capital Project, she toured western China with their counterparts from the Chinese Academy of Sciences — who, to my great gratitude, hosted me as well: ecologists Ouyang Zhiyun, Wang Yukuan, and Zheng Hua; and economists Li Jie and Zeng Weihong. Thanks to them, my research for this book also benefited from conversations with residents in the towns of Feng Qian and Ling'guan, in the Tibetan village of Qiaoqi, and on Hainan Island. Throughout our travels in Sichuan, I enjoyed the expert help of translator Yan Jing.

In Xi'an, my great thanks to demographer Li Shuzhou, founder of Care for Girls — and, in Beijing, to his mentor, former missile scientist and demographic planner Jiang Zhenghua. In China's always boggling capital city, I also thank obstetrics nurse Wang Ming Li of the Beijing Aobei Hospital; *Guardian* correspondent Jonathan Watts, author of a gem of environmental journalism, *When a Billion Chinese Jump*; and Beijing journalists Chen Ou, Yan Kai, Fu Hui, and especially Cui Zheng, who was also my able translator. Last, my warm thanks to "Lin Xia" and her parents, who kindly shared their story, and to my perspicacious Chinese literary agent, Jackie Huang.

My trip to the Philippines owed hugely to the help of Dr. Joan Castro of the PATH Foundation and her colleague Dr. Ron Quintana. I was further enlightened by Ramon San Pascual of the Philippines Legislators' Center for Population and Development, Ben De Leon of the Forum for Family Planning and Development, and Dr. Junice Melgar of the community reproductive health NGO known as Likhaan: I am grateful to many women in Likhaan clinics throughout Greater Manila for their time and willingness to talk to me. Thanks also to nurse "Roland" and the unnamed health facility where he works, for his frankness about the struggle between his faith and his profession.

The PATH Foundation also coordinated my travels to Isla Verde, where I was hosted by Jemalyn Rayos, and to Bohol, where another excellent guide, Geri Miasco, introduced me to Dr. Frank Lobo in Talibon, midwife Mercy Butawan in Humay-Humay, and, in Ubay, Mayor Eutiquio Bernales and coastal resource manager Alpios Delima. Geri also accompanied me to the island of Guindacpan, where nutritionist Perla Pañares, nurse Estrella Torrevillas, and numerous fisherfolk took time to show me how the sea is reclaiming their village.

Iris Dimaano-Bugayong arranged my visit to the International Rice Research Institute on Luzon, where director Robert Ziegler kindly granted me his time and access to IRRI's staff. My great thanks to him and to crop scientist Roland Buresh, evolutionary ecologist Ruaraidh Sackville Hamilton, and Paul Quick, coordinator of the C4 Rice Project.

At the International Maize and Wheat Improvement Center (Centro Internacional de Mejoramiento de Maíz y Trigo) in Texcoco, Mexico, I was graciously received by CIMMYT Director Thomas Lumpkin; maize breeder Félix San Vicente; Global Wheat Program director Hans-Joachim Braun; wheat physiologist Matthew Reynolds; deputy director general for research Marianne Bänziger; Genetic Resources Center head Tom Payne; socioeconomists Pedro Aquino-Mercado and Dagoberto Flores; and Peter Wenzl, head of the Crop Research Informatics Laboratory. My thanks to them and to Caritina Venado, who organized my visit. In Mexico City, I thank demographers Silvia Elena Giorguli Saucedo, Manuel Ordorica Mellado, and José Luis Lezama at Colegio de México; poet Homero Aridjis and Betty Ferber of Grupo de los Cien; María Luisa Sánchez Fuentes of GIRE—El Grupo de Información en Reproducción Elegida; Nick Wright of Casa de los Amigos; Areli Carreón of Sin Maíz No Hay País; architect Eduardo Farah; Juan Carlos Arjona of the Mexican Environmental Law Center (Centro Mexicano de Derecho Ambiental); community activist Eduardo Farah; and Carlos Anzado of the Consejo Nacional de Población.

In the state of Morelos, I thank reproductive rights advocate Dr. Estela Kempis and her husband, filmmaker Gregory Berger. And at the Nuestros Pequeños Hermanos orphanage, *mil gracias* to Dr. Luis Moreno, Father Phil Cleary, Paco Manzanares, Elvi Clara Jaramillo, Marisol Aguilar Castillo, Erika Klotz—and with fond remembrance, the late Father William Wasson, whose humanity and legacy lives on in thousands of children he saved.

Early in my career, I wrote about Father Wasson's work, and over the years he became a friend and mentor. Our discussions of Catholicism proved invaluable preparation for my research in the world's smallest country—albeit among the most influential. I thank Monsignor Marcelo Sánchez Sorondo of the Vatican's Pontifical Academy of Sciences and Cardinal Peter Kodwo Appiah Turkson of the Pontifical Council for Justice and Peace for their willingness to discuss sensitive issues I raised with them. For helpful advice on Vatican coverage, thanks also to *National Catholic Reporter*'s John Allen and NPR correspondent Sylvia Poggioli.

Outside the Vatican's walls, I am grateful to demographers Antonio Golini and Massimo Livi-Bacci; political scientist Giovanni Sartori; Italian Senate vice president and now foreign affairs minister Emma Bonino; parliamentarian Claudio D'amico of the Lega Nord; economists Leonardo Becchetti and Tito Boeri; Legambiente president Vittorio Cogliati Dezza; OB-GYN Dr. Carlo Flamigni; male fertility specialist Dr. Giuseppe La Pera; Prof.ssa Lucia Ercoli of Medicina Solidale e delle Migrazioni; the students and faculties of Rome's Scuola Media Pubblica Salvo D'acquisto, Scuola Media Daniele Manin, and St. George's British International School; Gianfranco Bologna of WWF-Italy; immigrant-rap musician Amir Issa; Jacopo Romoli and Claudia Ribet of the Rome Science Festival; corporate manager Ornella Vitale; park guide Licia Capparella; Dr. Vincenzo Pipitone and biologist-nutritionist Claudia Giafaglione; software designer Emilio Vaca and, for all her help and guidance, journalist Sabrina Provenzani. Thanks also to translator Livia Borghese, and to

Acknowledgments

University of Massachusetts–Amherst anthropologist Betsy Krause, who generously shared her insights into Italy's declining fertility. That same topic in another traditionally Catholic European country, Spain, was kindly explained to me by demographer Margarita Delgado in a visit to Madrid's Consejo Superior de Investigaciones Científicas.

En route to Niger, I was hosted in Tripoli, Libya, by journalist Yusra Tekbali, and further enlightened about her country in conversations with her brother, Salam Tekbali, and friends Zubaida Bentaher, Moha Bensofia, Adam Hassan, and Sideq Qabaj. At the time, events that ultimately led to the overthrow of dictator Muammar Gaddafi were in their embryonic stage, and the hopes of these bright young people for a Libyan awakening were inspiring. Within weeks, all were either fleeing, fighting, protecting their families, or reporting on what became the tragic birth of a Libyan future still to be determined. I regret that just after I left, Jamal Said Fteis of Arkno Tours, who facilitated my visa, was gunned down by Gaddafi's soldiers as he left a mosque. I hope that his last act in this world—praying—comforted his final moments.

My guide in the West African Sahel nation of Niger was Nigerien journalist Baraou Idy, a friend I intend to keep: warm gratitude to him and his wife Mariana Hassane Idy. Thanks also to demographer Mounkaila Haruna of the Université Abdou Moumouni Dioffo de Niamey; Bako Bagassa, director of Foula, the condom-distribution program of the Association Nigerienne de Marketing Social (Animas-Sutura); Dr. Galy Kadir Abdelkader of the Educational Research Network for West and Central Africa; Drs. Koli Lamine, Maidaji Oumarou, and Sayadi Sani of Bien Eire el la Femme et de l'Enfant au Niger; Thierry Allafort-Duverger, director of the Alliance for International Medical Action (ALIMA); Col. Abdoulkarim Goukoye, head of Niger's Haute Autorité à la Sécurité Alimentaire; UNFPA's Mme. Martine Camacho at the Multi-sector Demographic Program (PRO-DEM); and Sahidou Abdoussalam, Navid Djewakh, and Agathe Diama at ICRISAT-Niger, the International Crops Research Institute for the Semi-Arid Tropics.

Acknowledgments

Following a trip west of the capital, Niamey, where I was kindly received by the Fulani tribal village of Bongoum, David Boureima drove us east to the Maradi region. My thanks to Maradi Sultan Al-Haji Ali Zaki for his frankness and hospitality; the villagers of Bargaja, especially chief Al-Haji Rabo Mamane; his wives Hassana and Jaimila, and his son Inoussa; chief Noura Bako and the villagers of Souraman; chief Haji Iro Dan Dadi and the villagers of Madarounfa; Maradi mayoral candidate Moktar Kassoum; and Imam Raidoune Issaka and his brother Imam Chafiou Issaka. In the district of Dakoro, thanks to Secretary General Insa Adamon, who approved my entry and offered us an armed escort; nurse Halima Dahaya of the Korahan Health Center; Mahmoud Dou Maliki and Omar Mamane Sani of Contribution a l'Education de Base; the people of the village of Mailafia—and special thanks to the schoolchildren of Dan Dawaye village. Finally, I wish to thank Tahoua region Sultan Al-Haji Manirou Magaji Rogo, and Mayor Abdoulaye Altine of Madaoua for welcoming me to his inaugural town council.

I am grateful to Nadeem Ahmad Niazi at Pakistan's Mission to the United Nations, who helped me secure a journalist visa to his country, and I am indebted to veteran Karachi journalist Shahid Husain for his companionship there. I also thank the University of Karachi's Pakistani studies director Syd Jaffar Ahmed and sociologist Fateh Muhammad Burfat; Tanveer Arif and Naeem Munwar Shah of the Society for Conservation and Protection of Environment; demographer Methab Karim of the Pew Research Center; Dr. Nikhat Saeed Khan of Pakistan's National Committee for Maternal Health; the ——— family in Lyari Town; Jalil Abdul Ibrahim and Nazreen Chandio of the Lyari Resource Center; Lyari Lady Health Workers Asma Tabassum and Nazaqat Chandio; Shaikh Tanveer Ahmed of the Health and Nutrition Development Society; Dr. Sonia Poshni, Dr. Hamid Ali, and Dr. Capt. Liaquat Ali Shaikh of the Civil Hospital–Karachi; and Moach Goth Cemetery caretakers Khair and Nadeem Mohammad.

Heartfelt thanks and condolences to the families of slain leaders Abdul Ghani and Haji Abu Bakar of Karachi's Fisherfolk Development

Organisation, who asked me into their homes amidst their mourning. Thanks also to NPR correspondent Julie McCarthy; to the villagers of Haji Qasim, Mahar, Ahmed Jat, and Ahmed Khan Zour in the Indus Valley; to Shaikh Tanveer Ahmed of the Health and Nutrition Development Society; and to Imam Qari Abdul Basid of Thatta's Shah Gehan Mosque. Finally, my deepest respect and gratitude to Principal Afshan Tabassum, her staff, and students at The Citizens Foundation's Vohra School, and to vice-president Ahson Rabbini for TCF's extraordinarily hopeful work. In one of the most difficult places, they are an example to everyone of how much of the world's ills education can solve.

Judy Oglethorpe and Lee Poston of World Wildlife Fund kindly arranged for me to meet, in Kathmandu, Shubash Lohani and Bunu Vaidya of WWF's Eastern Himalaya Ecoregion Program, who took me to Nepal's Terai region. Many thanks to them and to their colleague Tilak Dhakal; to Moti Adhikiri of the wonderfully named Old Age Home for Livestock and Vulture Conservation Centre; to Bardia National Park ranger Barbadia Echar and ornithologist Gautam Paudyl; and to the many people I spoke to in the Terai villages of Lalmatiya, Madhuwan, Dhallapur, and the Khata Corridor. Thanks also to Dr. Navin Thapa, director of the Family Planning Association of Nepal.

In India, I am grateful to hydrologist Kanwar Jit Singh of the Punjab Agriculture Department; botanist R. K. Kohli of Punjabi University; Dr. G. S. Kalkat of the Punjab State Farm Commission; farm leaders Balbir Singh Rajewal, Biku Singh, and Labh Singh; and widows Gurdial and Sheela Kaur. Thanks to many anonymous women in Kaithal and Ambala districts in Haryana state who spoke to me about illegal ultrasounds and sex-selective abortions. My guide in both Punjab and Haryana was award-winning *Tribune* correspondent Geetanjali Gayatri of Chandigarh, whom I cannot thank enough.

In Kerala, I am equally grateful for the skilled assistance of Ernakulam-based freelancer Anna Mathews. My thanks, too, to former Kerala finance minister Thomas Isaac; economist TK Sundari Ravindran of the Achutha Menon Centre for Health Science Studies; forester James Zacariah; demographer Irudaya Radan; Dr. Theresa

ACKNOWLEDGMENTS

Susan of the University of Kerala's Department of Education; Dr. C. Nirmala, OB-GYN at SAT Hospital and Medical College; Swami Amitavhananda of the Ramakrishna Order; and, especially, the great Malayalam poet Sugathakumari, founder of Abhaya, an institution for distressed women.

I was shown Mumbai and Pune by Prachi Bari, veteran fixer for the BBC and PBS. Deep thanks to her and to journalists Nandini Rajwade and Kalpana Sharma; to Pune environmental activist Ashish Kothari and to Dr. S. B. Mujumdar, president of Symbiosis University; to Mumbai artists Jayanta and Varsha Pandit; to Krishna Pujari of Reality Tours & Travel and the people of Dharavi; to Dr. Faujdar Ram, Dr. Laishram Ladusingh, and Dr. P. Arokiasamy of the International Institute for Population Sciences; to Swami Atmanandaji of the Prema Devi Ashram; to Mumbai's Nagpada police precinct and to Madam "Rukmini" of Siddharthnagar; and to head priest Gajanan Modak and trustee Nitin Kadam of Mumbai's Siddhivinayak Temple.

My final trip for this book began in Japan with Akihiko Matsutani, an economist who, refreshingly in his profession, finds big opportunities in readjusting to a smaller reality. Thanks to him and to finance economist Masaru Kaneko; Tokyo architect Kengo Kuma; Senator Kuniko Inoguchi; samurai descendant Shuhei Nishimura of the anti-immigration Group to Recover Sovereignty; former nuclear engineer Tetsunari Iida, director of Japan's Institute for Sustainable Energy Policies; anti-nuclear advocate Hiroaki Koide of the Research Reactor Institute at Kyoto University; rector Atsushi Seike of Keio University; Kazuhiko Takemoto of the Ministry of the Environment's Satoyama Initiative; Toyooka agronomists Narita Toshimichi and Kawagoe Ynusube and rice farmer Itsuyoshi Nawate; wasabi farmers Yoshimi Kashitani and Yoshio Takeya and trout hatchery manager Osamu Nakatani in Nosegawa, Nara; and robotics engineers Shijie Guo, Susumu Sato, and Takahisa Shiraoke of the Tokai Rubber-RIKEN Riba II project.

Very special thanks to University of Yokohama anthropologist and Sloth Club founder Keibo Oiwa, and to Mari Tokuhisa and Michiko Takizawa of the village of Shiga in Nagano Prefecture.

ACKNOWLEDGMENTS

Finally, *un abrazo caluroso* to my deft trilingual translator and fixer, Junko Takahashi, and her friends Yoko Nishi and Keiko———.

In Thailand, I had audiences with three Buddhist monks: Abbot Athikarn Somnukatti Panyo of the drowning Wat Khun Samut Trawat temple; Ajaan Boonku of the Theravāda forest monastery, Wat Asokaram; and renowned Thai social humanitarian Sulak Sivaraksa. Thanks to them and to American Theravāda monk Ajaan Geoff for help contacting them and to my excellent translator and fixer, Khemmapat Rojwanichkun.

At Condoms & Cabbages in Bangkok I enjoyed the delightful company of Thailand's own Captain Condom, Mechai Viravaidya, and his staff at the Population & Community Development Association and at the Mechai Pattana School in Buriram. Because they've shown that family planning can be not just a responsibility but a source of great fun, Thailand is a far safer, healthier, and happier place. Special thanks to Mechai, his assistant Paul Salvette, school principal Amornrassamee Loipami and deputy principal Kaensri Chaikot, teachers Manapt Meechumnan and Paveena Mettaisong, and project coordinator Isadore Reaud.

Because my own country, the USA, won't issue visas to Iranian journalists, conversely I couldn't get a journalist visa for my last country, Iran, although I thank Dr. Vahid Karimi of the Permanent Mission of the Islamic Republic of Iran to the United Nations for his efforts. However, I found a travel agency that specializes in the Middle East, whose agents had recently scouted Iran. My great thanks to Matthew LaPolice of Absolute Travel, who expertly arranged my trip. Because I wasn't sure how much I'd be able to interview in Iran, I invited along my wife, Beckie Kravetz, to have another pair of eyes. As it happened, we were able to talk to anyone we wanted, and the guide Absolute Travel found for us, the encyclopedic Alireza Firouzi, became my fixer, translator, and a bottomless well of knowledge of his country's past and present. I can never adequately thank him and our driver, poet Ahmad Mojalal.

I am deeply indebted to demographer Mohammad Jalal Abbasi-Shavazi of the University of Tehran, Dr. Hourieh Shamshiri Milani of

Acknowledgments

Shahid Beheshti University of Medical Science, and Dr. Esmail Kahrom of Islamic Azad University for their tremendous cooperation. I am also most grateful to Iranian American author Hooman Majd, who prepped me for my travels and met us in Tehran; to Australian Demographic and Social Research Institute director Peter McDonald, who put me in touch with Iranian demographers; and to Karan Vafadari and Afarin Neyssari of Tehran's Aun Iranian Art Foundation. More thanks to Jafar Imani at the Parvar Protected Area; ranger Jabad Selvari and superintendent Mohammad Reza Mullah Abbasi of Golestan National Park; director Ali Abutalibi at the Miankaleh Wildlife Refuge; Bamou National Park's Hussein Nikham and Rohalah Mohamadi; Mehdi Basiri, Ahmad Khatoonabadi, and Aghafakhr Mirlohi of Esfahan University of Technology and Green Message; and especially the valiant members of the Esfahan chapter of Women's Society Against Environmental Pollution.

Many thanks, too, to Taghi Farvar of Tehran's Centre for Sustainable Development and his CENESTA companions, who requested their full names be withheld, for their wisdom, work, and hospitality. Throughout Iran, from Ramsar and Rasht to Shiraz and Qom, strangers embraced us, invited us to tea and meals, and thanked us for visiting their country. We, in turn, thank them all for the warmth, music, poetry, artwork, history, and stories they willingly shared. We hope that the mistrust between our governments will soon finally be behind us.

In my own country, president Robert Engelman of the Worldwatch Institute was continually helpful and encouraging. An early conversation with Eric Sanderson of the Wildlife Conservation Society helped shape my ideas. I thank them and Lesley Blackner, Alan Farago, and Maggy Hurchalla for explaining their efforts to save southern Florida from human excess, and Duke University ecologist Stuart Pimm for showing me the Everglades. Many thanks also to Rev. Richard Cizik of the New Evangelical Partnership for the Common Good; to University of Colorado emeritus physicist Albert Bartlett; to population specialists Malcolm Potts and Martha Madison Campbell of the University of California–Berkeley; Aijaz Hussain of University Islamic

Acknowledgments

Financial; University of Georgia ecologist Ron Pulliam; and Arizona State University wildlife biologist David Brown.

At the University of Arizona, early in my research I benefited greatly from discussions with geographer Diana Liverman, ethnobotanist Gary Paul Nabhan, and physicist Bill Wing, and from the constant support of School of Journalism director Jacqueline Sharkey and correspondent extraordinaire Mort Rosenblum. Thanks also to UA classics scholar Marissa Gurtler for kindly correcting my Latin.

At Arizona's Prescott College, my thanks to ecologists Mark Riegner, Tom Fleischner, Doug Hulmes, Carl Tomoff, and sustainability director James Pittman. At Tucson's Center for Biological Diversity, I thank Sarah Bergman, Randy Serraglio, and founder Kierán Suckling.

At Cornell University, I'm grateful to agricultural scientists Rebecca Nelson, Peter Hobbs, Norman Uphoff, and David Pimentel—and at the University of Vermont's Gund Institute for Ecological Economics, to Jon Erickson and Joshua Farley.

At the University of Minnesota, thanks to evolutionary biologist David Tilman, grad students Jane Cowles and Peter Wragg, economist Stephen Polasky, and especially to Institute on the Environment director Jonathan Foley.

Stanford University was a remarkable font of generous and helpful sources. Dr. Paul Blumenthal, head of the Stanford Program for International Reproductive Education and Services, gave me invaluable advice before I joined his wife, Lynne Gaffikin, and SPIRES fellow Dr. Amy Voedisch in Uganda. Economists Larry Goulder and Ken Arrow shared helpful insights on how we might achieve sustainable prosperity that would leave room for other living things. My thanks also to neurobiologist Robert Sapolsky; anthropologist Jamie Jones; population biologists Shripad Tuljapurkar and Marcus Feldman; David Lobell of Stanford's Center on Food Security and the Environment; bio-geochemist Peter Vitousek; Chris Field of the Stanford-based Carnegie Institution's Department of Global Ecology; research coordinator Nona Chiariello of the Jasper Ridge Biological Preserve; and lead scientist Heather Tallis of the Natural Capital Project.

Acknowledgments

Special appreciation, once more, to that project's founder, ecologist and Center for Conservation Biology director Gretchen Daily, whom I had the pleasure of accompanying for many discussion-, inspiration-, and chocolate-filled miles. And finally, for their cooperation, humor, indefatigable scholarship, and great prescience, my warm gratitude to the Center's associate director, ecologist Anne Ehrlich, and to its president, population biologist Paul Ehrlich.

I could not have written this book without the research assistance and logistic support of journalist Claudine LoMonaco—who, to my good fortune, took maternity leave from her radio work just as my travels began, making her services available to me. I am ever grateful to her and to her husband, astrophysicist Sydney Barnes, who was always there to do the math.

My thanks to Eileen Clinton of Crowley Travel, who never failed to match air connections to my byzantine itineraries; to Susan Ware and Meeghan Ziolkowski for transcribing hundreds of hours of recorded interviews; to LK James, who compiled this volume's lengthy bibliography; and to copyeditor Joan Matthews.

Much gratitude—for help with this book, and for what they do—also goes to executive director Joel Simon of the Committee to Protect Journalists, and to Mohamed Abdel Dayem, Carlos Lauria, and Bob Dietz, coordinators respectively of CPJ's Middle East and North Africa, Latin America, and Asia programs.

Many colleagues, friends, and relations gave me wise advice, moral support, reassurance, sustenance, and shelter during the research and writing of this book. Thanks for all that, and for constant inspiration, to my partners at Homelands Productions: Jon Miller, Sandy Tolan, and Cecilia Vaisman, and to guest producer Sam Eaton. Deep appreciation also to Alison Hawthorne Deming, Bill McKibben, Katherine Ellison, Stephen Philbrick, Connie Talbot, Alice Cozzolino, Amy Pulley, Roz Driscoll, Alton Wasson, Karen and Benigno Sánchez-Eppler, Jim and Deb Hills, Mary and Alain Provost, Rochelle Hoffman, Peter and Zeynep Hoffman, Brian and Pahoua Hoffman, Joan

Kravetz, Cindy Kalland, Jonathan and Cynthia Lunine, Clark Strand, Perdita Finn, Barry Lopez, Debra Gwartney, Tom Miller, Diana Papoulias, Francie Rich, Bill Posnick, Lynn Davis, Rudy Wurlitzer, Constanza Vieira, Mary McNamara, Richard Stayton, Nubar Alexanian, Rebecca Koch, Jeff Jacobson, Marnie Andrews, Jon Hipps, Liz Story, Ronn Spencer, Blake Hines, Dick Kamp, Barbara Ferry, Diana Hadley, and the late beloved and visionary biological anthropologist Peter Warshall.

My thanks to Richard Norris, Jennie Howland, Maria Gallo, Beth Coates, Laleh Sotoodeh, Dan Stiefl, Fernando Pérez, Shahin Tabatabaei, and Joa Agnello-Traista, for, at various times, patching me up and keeping me going.

My agent Nick Ellison, his foreign rights director Chelsea Lindman, and editorial assistant Chloe Walker of the Nicholas Ellison Agency have always believed in this book and in me, despite my own frequent doubts. I am forever grateful to them, and also for the unwavering support I've received at Little, Brown and Company from David Young, Michael Pietsch, Malin von Euler-Hogan, Carolyn O'Keefe, Amanda Brown, Heather Fain, Peggy Freudenthal, and my superb editor—now for two books and counting—John Parsley. Thank you, all.

And finally, to my wife, sculptor, mask-maker, and theatrical artist Beckie Kravetz, thank you for seeing me through this: yet again, a vast understatement. Thank you for contributing to humanity's collective body of fine art, which is among the greatest justifications for the continuance of our species.

Another is our capacity for love. Thank you for yours.

—Alan Weisman

Bibliography

Selected General Book Citations

Brown, Lester R. *Plan B: Rescuing a Planet Under Stress and a Civilization in Trouble.* New York: W. W. Norton & Company, 2003.

———. *World on the Edge: How to Prevent Environmental and Economic Collapse.* London: Earthscan Publications, 2011.

Brown, Lester R., et al. *Beyond Malthus.* New York: W. W. Norton & Company, 1999.

Catton, William R. *Bottleneck: Humanity's Impending Impasse.* Bloomington, IN: Xlibris Corporation, 2009.

———. *Overshoot: The Ecological Basis of Revolutionary Change.* Champaign-Urbana: University of Illinois Press, 1982.

Cohen, Joel E. *How Many People Can the Earth Support?* New York: W. W. Norton & Company, 1995.

Connelly, Matthew. *Fatal Misconception: The Struggle to Control World Population.* Cambridge, MA: Harvard University Press, 2008.

Daily, Gretchen C., ed. *Nature's Services: Societal Dependence on Natural Ecosystems.* Washington, DC: Island Press, 1997.

Department of Economic and Social Affairs, Population Division. *World Population Prospects: The 2010 Revision.* New York: United Nations, 2010 (Updated: April 15, 2011).

Ehrlich, Anne H., and Paul R. Ehrlich. *The Dominant Animal: Human Evolution and the Environment.* Washington, DC: Island Press, 2008.

———. *The Population Explosion.* New York: Simon & Schuster, 1990.

Ehrlich, Paul R. *The Population Bomb.* Cutchogue, NY: Buccaneer Books 1997.

Engelman, Robert. *More: Population, Nature, and What Women Want.* Washington, DC: Island Press, 2008.

Foreman, Dave. *Man Swarm and the Killing of Wildlife.* Durango, CO: Raven's Eye Press LLC, 2011.

Gilding, Paul. *The Great Disruption: Why the Climate Crisis Will Bring On the End of Shopping and the Birth of a New World.* New York: Bloomsbury Press, 2011.

Livi-Bacci, Massimo. *A Concise History of World Population.* Hoboken, NJ: John Wiley & Sons, 2012.

Longman, Phillip. *The Empty Cradle: How Falling Birthrates Threaten World Prosperity, and What to Do About It.* New York: Basic Books, 2004.

Lovelock, James. *The Vanishing Face of Gaia: A Final Warning.* New York: Basic Books, 2009.

Malthus, Thomas R. *An Essay on the Principle of Population: Text, Sources and Background, Criticism,* edited by Philip Appelman. New York: W. W. Norton & Company, 1976.

———. *Population: The First Essay.* Ann Arbor: University of Michigan Press, 1959.

Mazur, Laurie, ed. *A Pivotal Moment: Population, Justice, and the Environmental Challenge.* Washington, DC: Island Press, 2009.

McKee, Jeffrey K. *Sparing Nature: The Conflict Between Human Population Growth and Earth's Biodiversity.* Piscataway, NJ: Rutgers University Press, 2003.

Pearce, Fred. *The Coming Population Crash: And Our Planet's Surprising Future.* Boston: Beacon Press, 2010.

Pimm, Stuart L. *A Scientist Audits the Earth.* Piscataway, NJ: Rutgers University Press, 2001.

Randers, Jørgen. *2052: A Global Forecast for the Next Forty Years.* White River Junction, VT: Chelsea Green Publishing, 2012.

Rees, W., and M. Wackernagel. *Our Ecological Footprint: Reducing Human Impact on the Earth.* Gabriola Island, BC: New Society Publishers, 1996.

Wilson, Edward O. *The Diversity of Life.* New York: W. W. Norton & Company, 1999.

———. *The Future of Life.* New York: Alfred A. Knopf, 2002.

Worldwatch Institute. *Vital Signs 2012: The Trends That Are Shaping Our Future.* Washington, DC: Island Press, 2012.

Chapter One: A Weary Land of Four Questions

Books

Benstein, Jeremy. *The Way Into Judaism and the Environment.* Woodstock, VT: Jewish Lights Publishing, 2006.

Bernstein, Ellen. *Splendor of Creation: A Biblical Ecology.* Berea, OH: The Pilgrim Press, 2005.

Colborn, Theo, et al. *Our Stolen Future: Are We Threatening Our Fertility, Intelligence, and Survival?—A Scientific Detective Story.* New York: Penguin Books, 1997.

DellaPergola, Sergio. "Jewish Demography & Peoplehood: 2008," in *Facing Tomorrow: Background Policy Documents.* Jerusalem: The Jewish People Policy Planning Institute, 2008, pp. 231–50.

Hillel, Daniel. *The Natural History of the Bible: An Environmental Exploration of the Hebrew Scriptures.* New York: Columbia University Press, 2006.

Leshem, Y., Y. Yom-Tov, D. Alon, and J. Shamoun-Baranes. "Bird Migration as an Interdicipinary Tool for Global Cooperation," in *Aviation Migration,* edited by Peter Berthold, Eberhad Gwinner, and Edith Sonnenschein. Heidelberg and Berlin: Springer-Verlag, 2003, pp. 585–99.

Orenstein, Daniel E. "Zionist and Israeli Perspectives on Population Growth and Environmental Impact in Palestine and Israel," in *Between Ruin and Restoration: An Environmental History of Israel,* edited by Daniel E. Orenstein, Alon Tal, and Char Miller. Pittsburgh: University of Pittsburgh Press, 2013, pp. 82–105.

Status of the Environment in the Occupied Palestinian Territory. Bethlehem, Palestine: Applied Research Institute–Jerusalem (ARIJ), 2007.

BIBLIOGRAPHY

Tal, Alon. *Pollution in a Promised Land: An Environmental History of Israel.* Berkeley: University of California Press, 2009.

Tolan, Sandy. *The Lemon Tree: An Arab, a Jew, and the Heart of the Middle East.* New York: Bloomsbury, 2007.

Vogel, Carole G., and Yossi Leshem. *The Man Who Flies With Birds.* Minneapolis: Kar-Ben Publishing, 2009.

Yom-Tov, Yoram, and Heinrich Mendelssohm. "Changes in the Distribution and Abundance of Vertebrates in Israel During the 20th Century," in *The Zoogeography of Israel,* Yoram Yom-Tov and E. Tchernov, editors. The Hague, Holland: Dr. W. Junk Publishers, 1988, pp. 515–48.

ARTICLES

"After 1,000 Years, Israel Is Largest Jewish Center." Arutz Sheva7, May 1, 2005.

Allen, Lori, Vincent A. Brown, and Ajantha Subramanian. "Condemning Kramer." *Harvard Crimson,* April 19, 2010.

Beit Sourik Village Council v. The Government of Israel. HCJ 2056/04, Israel: Supreme Court, May 30, 2004. http://domino.un.org/unispal.nsf.

Bystrov, Evgenia, and Arnon Soffer. "Israel: Demography and Density 2007–2020." Chaikin Chair in Geostrategy, University of Haifa. May 2008.

Cairncross, Frances. "Connecting Flights." *Conservation in Practice,* vol. 7, no. 1 (2006): 14–21.

Cunningham, Erin. *"Fertility Prospects in Israel: Ever Below Replacement Level?"* UN Population Expert Group Meeting on Recent and Future Trends in Fertility. November 17, 2009.

———. "World Water Day: Thirsty Gaza Residents Battle Salt, Sewage." *Christian Science Monitor,* March 22, 2010.

Finkelstein, Yoram, Yael Dubowski, et al. "Organophosphates in Hula Basin: Atmospheric Levels, Transport, Degradation, Products and Neurotoxic Hazards in Children Following Low-Level Long Term Exposure." *Environment and Health Fund,* http://www.ehf.org.il/en/node/243.

Greenwood, Phoebe. "Israel Threatens to Cut Water and Power to Gaza in Tel Aviv." *Telegraph* (UK), November 27, 2011.

"Israel Tops Western World in Pesticide Use." Argo News, November 1, 2012. http://news.agropages.com/News.

Jeffay, Nathan. "Sand for Sale: An Unusual Solution to Theft in the Negev." *Jewish Daily Forward*, November 26, 2008.

Kaplan, M. M., Y. Goor, and E. S. Tiekel. "A Field Demonstration of Rabies Control Using Chicken Embryo Vaccine in Dogs." *Bulletin of the World Health Organization*, vol. 10, no. 5 (1954): 743–52.

Kennedy, Marie. "7th Generation: Israel's War for Water." *Progressive Planning Magazine*, no. 196 (Fall 2006): 2–6.

Klein, Jeff. "Martin Kramer, Harvard and the Eugenics of Zion." *Counterpunch*, April 12, 2010.

Levy, Gideon. "The Threat of the 'Demographic Threat.'" Haaretz, July 25, 2007.

Orenstein, Daniel. "Population Growth and Environmental Impact: Ideology and Academic Discourse in Israel." *Population and Environment*, vol. 26, no. 1 (2004): 41–60.

"Palestine Denied Water." BBC News, October 27, 2009.

Philosophical Transactions of the Royal Society, vol. 364, no. 1532 (October 2009): 2969–3124.

Prime Minister of Israel's Office. "Cabinet Approves Emergency Plan to Increase the Production of Desalinated Water." Press release, January 30, 2011.

Rinat, Zafrir. "Panel Says Pesticides Are Harming People, Killing Birds." Haaretz, October 20, 2009. http://www.haaretz.com/print-edition/news.

———. "When Coverage of a Water Crisis Vanishes." *Nieman Report*, 2005.

Rozenman, Eric. "Israeli Arabs and the Future of the Jewish State." *Middle East Quarterly*, vol. 6, no. 3 (September 1999): 15–23. http://www.meforum.org/478.

Sanders, Edmund. "Israel Sperm Banks Find Quality Is Plummeting." *Los Angeles Times*, August 15, 2012.

"The Separation Barrier in the West Bank." B'Tselem — The Israeli Information Center for Human Rights in the Occupied Territories (map), February 2008.

Siegel-Itzkovich, Judy. "Birds on His Brain." Science section, *Jerusalem Post,* November 6, 2005, p. 7.

Sontag, Debora. "Cramped Gaza Multiplies at Unrivaled Rates." *New York Times,* February 24, 2000.

Tolan, Sandy. "It's the Occupation, Stupid." *Le Monde Diplomatique,* English edition, September 26, 2011. http://mondediplo.com/openpage/it-s-the-occupation-stupid.

Turner, Michael, Nader Kahteeb, and Kalhed Nassar. *Crossing the Jordan: Concept Document to Rehabilitate, Promote Prosperity and Help Bring Peace to the Lower Jordan River Valley.* Amman, Bethlehem, and Tel Aviv: Eco Peace/Friends of the Earth Middle East, March 2005.

Udasin, Sharon. "Israel Uses More Pesticides Than Any OECD Country." *Jerusalem Post,* November 1, 2012.

Wulfsohn, Aubrey. "What Retreat from the Territories Means for Israel's Water Supply." *Think-Israel* (website), March–April 2005. http://www.think-israel.org/wulfsohn .water.html.

Yom-Tov, Yoram, et al. "Cattle Predation by the Golden Jackal (*Canis avreus*) in the Golan Heights Israel." *Biological Conservation,* vol. 73 (1995): 19–22.

Yuval-Davis, Nira. "Bearers of the Collective: Women and Religious Legislation in Israel." *Feminist Review,* vol. 4 (1980): 15–27.

Zureik, Elia. "Demography and Transfer: Israel's Road to Nowhere." *Third World Quarterly,* vol. 24, no. 4 (2003): 619–30.

Chapter Two: A World Bursting Its Seams

BOOKS

Baird, Vanessa. *The No-Nonsense Guide to World Population.* Oxford: New Internationalist Guide Publication, 2011.

Bartlett, Albert A., Robert G. Fuller, and Vicki L. Plano Clark. *The Essential Exponential! For the Future of Our Planet.* Lincoln, NE: Center for Science, Mathematics & Computer Education, 2008.

BIBLIOGRAPHY

Brown, Lester R. *Plan B: Rescuing a Planet Under Stress and a Civilization in Trouble*. New York: W. W. Norton & Company, 2003.
———. *World on the Edge: How to Prevent Environmental and Economic Collapse*. London: Earthscan Publications, 2011.

Connelly, Matthew. *Fatal Misconception: The Struggle to Control World Population*. Cambridge, MA: Harvard University Press, 2008.

Hartmann, Betsy. *Reproductive Rights and Wrongs: The Global Politics of Population Control*. Boston: South End Press, 1995.

Lovelock, James. *The Vanishing Face of Gaia: A Final Warning*. New York: Basic Books, 2009.

Mazur, Laurie, ed. *A Pivotal Moment: Population, Justice, and the Environmental Challenge*. Washington, DC: Island Press, 2009.

Pimm, Stuart L. *A Scientist Audits the Earth*. Piscataway, NJ: Rutgers University Press, 2001.

Randers, Jørgen. *2052: A Global Forecast for the Next Forty Years*. White River Junction, VT: Chelsea Green Publishing, 2012.

Rees, W., and M. Wackernagel. *Our Ecological Footprint: Reducing Human Impact on the Earth*. Gabriola Island, BC: New Society Publishers, 1996.

Rosenzweig, Michael L. *Win-Win Ecology: How the Earth's Species Can Survive in the Midst of Human Enterprise*. New York: Oxford University Press, 2003.

Shankar Singh, Jyoti. *Creating a New Consensus on Population*. London: Earthscan Publications, 1998.

Simon, Julian. *The Ultimate Resource 2*. Princeton, NJ: Princeton University Press, 1998.

Worldwatch Institute. *Vital Signs 2012: The Trends That Are Shaping Our Future*. Washington, DC: Island Press, 2012.

ARTICLES

Angus, Ian, and Simon Butler. "Panic Over 7 Billion: Letting the 1% Off the Hook." *Different Takes,* no. 73 (Fall 2011).

Bartlett, Albert A. "Arithmetic, Population and Energy." Lecture, Global Public Media, August 29, 2004. http://old.globalpublic media.com/lectures/461.

———. "Democracy Cannot Survive Overpopulation." *Population and Environment: A Journal of Interdisciplinary Studies,* vol. 22, no. 1 (September 2000): 63–71.

———, and Edward P. Lytwak. "Rejoinder to Daily, Ehrlich, and Ehrlich: Immigration and Population Policy in the United States." *Population and Environment: A Journal of Interdisciplinary Studies,* vol. 16, no. 6 (July 1995): 527–37.

———. "Zero Growth of the Population of the United States." *Population and Environment: A Journal of Interdisciplinary Studies,* vol. 16, no. 5 (May 1995): 415–28.

Blackner, Lesley. "Existing Residents Should Guide Community Growth." *St. Petersburg Times,* guest column, May 3, 2004.

Brill, Richard. "Earth's Carrying Capacity Is an Inescapable Fact." *Honolulu Star-Advertiser,* November 5, 2012.

Carter, Jimmy. "Address to the Nation on Energy," April 18, 1977. Transcript and video. Miller Institute of Public Affairs, University of Virginia, http://millercenter.org/president/speeches/detail/3398.

Cave, Damien. "Florida Voters Enter Battle on Growth." *New York Times,* September 27, 2010. http://www.nytimes.com/2010/09/28.

Daily, Gretchen C., Anne H. Ehrlich, and Paul R. Ehrlich. "Response to Bartlett and Lytwak (1995): Population and Immigration Policy in the United States." *Population and Environment: A Journal of Interdisciplinary Studies,* vol. 16, no. 6 (July 1995): 521–27.

Fanelli, Daniele. "Meat Is Murder on the Environment." *New Scientist,* no. 2613, July 18, 2007.

Hartmann, Betsy. "10 Reasons Why Population Control Is Not the Solution to Global Warming." *Different Takes,* no. 57 (Winter 2009).

———. "Rebuttal to Chris Hedges: Stop the Tired Overpopulation Hysteria." AlterNet, March 13, 2009. http://www.alternet.org/authors/betsy-hartmann.

———. "The Return of Population Control: Incentives, Targets, and the Backlash Against Cairo." *Different Takes,* no. 70 (Spring 2011).

Bibliography

Howard, Peter E. "Report Warns of State Growth to 101 Million." National/World section, *Tampa Tribune,* final edition, April 2, 1999, p. 1.

Jansen, Michael. "Palestinian Population Fast Approaching That of Israeli Jews." *Irish Times,* January 8, 2011.

Kennedy, Marie. "7th Generation Israel's War for Water." *Progressive Planning Magazine,* Fall 2006. http://www.plannersnetwork.org/publications/2006_Fall/kennedy.html.

Lori, Aviva. "Grounds for Disbelief." Haaretz, May 8, 2003.

Murtaugh, Paul A., and Michael G. Schlax. "Reproduction and the Carbon Legacies of Individuals." *Global Environmental Change,* vol. 19 (2009): 14–20.

Oldham, James. "Rethinking the Link: A Critical Review of Population-Environment Programs." A joint publication of the Population and Development Program at Hampshire College and the Political Economy Research Institute at the University of Massachusetts, Amherst, February 2006.

Owen, James. "Farming Claims Almost Half Earth's Land, New Maps Show." *National Geographic News,* December 9, 2005.

Pearce, Fred. "The Overpopulation Myth." *Prospect Magazine,* March 8, 2010.

Population and Development Program at Hampshire College. "10 Reasons to Rethink 'Overpopulation.'" *Different Takes,* no. 40, Fall 2006.

Price of Sprawl Calculator website, http://www.priceofsprawl.com.

Rees, William. "Are Humans Unsustainable by Nature?" Trudeau Lecture at the Memorial University of Newfoundland, January 28, 2009.

Tripati, A. K., C. D. Roberts, and R. A. Eagle. "Coupling of CO_2 and Ice Sheet Stability Over Major Climate Transitions of the Last 20 Million Years." *Science,* vol. 326, no. 5958 (December 2009): 1394–97. doi: 10.1126/science.1178296.

Weisman, Alan. "Harnessing the Big H." *Los Angeles Times Magazine,* September 25, 1994.

Whitty, Julia. "The Last Taboo." *Mother Jones,* May/June 2010.

BIBLIOGRAPHY

Chapter Three: Body Counts and the Paradox of Food

BOOKS

Catton, William R. *Bottleneck: Humanity's Impending Impasse.* Bloomington, IN: Xlibris Corporation, 2009.

———. *Overshoot: The Ecological Basis of Revolutionary Change.* Champaign-Urbana: University of Illinois Press, 1982.

Coffey, Patrick. *Cathedrals of Science: The Personalities and Rivalries That Made Modern Science.* Oxford: Oxford University Press, 2008.

Engelman, Robert. *More: Population, Nature, and What Women Want.* Washington, DC: Island Press, 2010.

Malthus, Thomas R. *An Essay on the Principle of Population: Text, Sources and Background, Criticism,* edited by Philip Appelman. New York: W. W. Norton & Company, 1976.

———. *Population: The First Essay.* Ann Arbor: University of Michigan Press, 1959.

McCullough, David. *The Path Between the Seas: The Creation of the Panama Canal, 1870–1914,* reprint edition. New York: Simon & Schuster, 1978.

Nicholson, Nick. *I Was a Stranger.* New York: Sheed & Ward, 1972.

Pimentel, David, and Marcia Pimentel. *Food, Energy, and Society.* Boca Raton, FL: CRC Press, 2008.

Smil, Vaclav. *Enriching the Earth: Fritz Haber, Carl Bosch, and the Transformation of World Food Production.* Cambridge, MA: Massachusetts Institute of Technology Press, 2001.

Vallero, Daniel A. *Biomedical Ethics for Engineers: Ethics and Decision Making in Biomedical and Biosystem Engineering.* The Biomedical Engineering Series. Burlington, MA: Academic Press/Elsevier, 2007.

ARTICLES

Ambrose, Stanley H. "Late Pleistocene Human Population Bottlenecks, Volcanic Winter, and Differentiation of Modern Humans." *Journal of Human Evolution,* vol. 34, no. 4 (1998): 623–51. doi: 10.1006/jhev.1998.0219.

Bibliography

Best, M., and D. Neuhauser. "Heroes and Martyrs of Quality and Safety: Ignaz Semmelweis and the Birth of Infection Control." *Quality Safe Health Care,* vol. 13 (2004): 233–34. doi:10.1136/qshc.2004.010918.

Bodnar, Anastasia. "Stress Tolerant Maize for the Developing World—Challenges and Prospects." Biology Fortified, Inc., website, The Biofortified Blog, March 20, 2010.

Borlaug, Norman. "Billions Served: An Interview with Norman Borlaug." Interviewed by Ronald Bailey. *Reason Magazine,* April 2000.

———. Nobel Peace Prize Acceptance Speech. Oslo, December 10, 1970. http://www .nobelprize.org/nobel_prizes/peace/laureates/1970/borlaug-acceptance.html.

Brown, Lester R. "Rising Temperatures Melting Away Global Food Security." Earth Policy Release, July 6, 2011. Adapted from *World on the Edge.* www.earthpolicy .org/book_bytes/2011/wotech4_ss3.

Canfield, Donald, Alexander Glazer, and Paul G. Falkowski. "The Evolution and Future of Earth's Nitrogen Cycle." *Science,* vol. 330, no. 6001 (October 2010): 192–96. doi: 10.1126/science.1186120.

Dighe, N. S., D. Shukla, R. S. Kalkotwar, R. B. Laware, S. B. Bhawar, and R. W. Gaikwad. "Nitrogenase Enzymes: A Review." *Der Pharmacia Sinica,* vol. 1, no. 2 (2010): 77–84.

Easterbrook, Gregg. "Forgotten Benefactor of Humanity." *Atlantic Monthly,* January 1997.

———. "The Man Who Defused the 'Population Bomb.'" *Wall Street Journal,* September 16, 2009.

Ehrlich, Paul R. "Homage to Norman Borlaug." *International Journal of Environmental Studies* (Stanford University), vol. 66, no. 6 (February 2009): 673–77.

Erisman, Jan Willem, Mark A. Sutton, James Galloway, Zbigniew Klimont, and Wilfried Winiwarter. "How a Century of Ammonia Synthesis Changed the World." *Nature Geoscience,* vol. 1 (October 2008): 636–39.

Fedoroff, N. V., et al. "Radically Rethinking Agriculture for the 21st Century." *Science,* vol. 327, no. 833 (2010): 833–34. doi: 10.1126/science.1186834.

BIBLIOGRAPHY

Floros, John D., Rosetta Newsome, William Fisher, et al. "Feeding the World Today and Tomorrow: The Importance of Food Science and Technology." *Comprehensive Reviews in Food Science and Safety,* vol. 9, issue 5 (2010): 1–28. doi: 10.1111/j.1541-4337.2010 .00127.x.

Fryzuk, Michael D. "Ammonia Transformed." *Nature,* vol. 427 (February 2004): 498–99.

Godfray, H. C., et al. "Food Security: The Challenge of Feeding 9 Billion People." *Science,* vol. 327, no. 5867 (2010): 812–18.

Goran, Morris. "The Present-Day Significance of Fritz Haber." *American Scientist,* vol. 35, no. 3 (July 1947): 400–03.

Haber, Fritz. "The Synthesis of Ammonia from Its Elements." Lecture given June 2, 1920. From *Nobel Lectures, Chemistry 1901–1921.* Amsterdam: Elsevier Publishing Company, 1966.

Hanninen, O., M. Farago, and E. Monos. "Ignaz Philipp Semmelweis: The Prophet of Bacteriology." *Infection Control,* vol. 4, no. 5 (September/October 1983): 367–70.

Harpending, Henry C., et al. "Genetic Traces of Ancient Demography." *Proceedings of the National Academy of Science,* vol. 95, no. 4 (February 17, 1998): 1961–67.

Hawley, Chris. "Mexico's Capital Is a Sinking Metropolis." *Arizona Republic,* April 9, 2010.

Hopfenburg, Russell. "Human Carrying Capacity Is Determined by Food Availability." *Population and Environment,* vol. 25, no. 2 (November 2003): 109–17.

———, and David Pimentel. "Human Population Numbers as a Function of Food Supply." Minnesotans for Sustainability, March 6, 2001. http://www.oilcrash.com/population.htm.

Lobell, David B., Wolfram Schlenker, and Justin Costa-Roberts. "Climate Trends and Global Crop Production Since 1980." *Science,* vol. 333, no. 6042 (July 2011): 616–20. doi: 10.1126/science .1204531.

Madrigal, Alexis. "How to Make Fertilizer Appear out of Thin Air, Part I." *Wired,* May 7, 2008. http://www.wired.com/ wiredscience/2008/05/how-to-make-nit.

Mandaro, Laura. "Better Living Through Chemistry; Innovate: Bullion Cubes, Fertilizer and Aspirin? Credit Justus von Liebig." *Investors,* June 3, 2005. http://news.investors .com/ 06/03/2005.

Matchett, Karin. "Scientific Agriculture Across Borders: The Rockefeller Foundation and Collaboration Between Mexico and the U.S. in Corn Breeding." PhD diss., University of Minnesota, 2001.

McNeily, A. S. "Neuroendocrine Changes and Fertility in Breast-Feeding Women." *Progress in Brain Research,* vol. 133, (2001): 207–14.

Morishima, Hiroko. "Evolution and Domestication of Rice," in *Rice Genetics IV,* proceedings of the Fourth International Rice Genetics Symposium, October 2000, edited by G. S. Khush et al. Enfield, NH: Science Publishers, 2001, pp. 22–27.

Nolan, Tanya. "Population Boom Increasing Global Food Crisis." ABC (Australia), May 4, 2011.

Ortiz, Rodomiro, et al. "Dedication: Norman E. Borlaug, the Humanitarian Plant Scientist Who Changed the World." *Plant Breeding Reviews,* vol. 28 (2007).

Reynolds, Matthew P. "Wheat Warriors: The Struggle to Break the Yield Barrier." *CIMMYT E-News,* vol. 6, no. 6 (October 2009).

———, ed. "Climate Change and Crop Production." International Maize and Wheat Improvement Center, 1996.

———, and N. E. Borlaug. "Centenary Review: Impacts of Breeding on International Collaborative Wheat Improvement." *Journal of Agricultural Science* (Cambridge University Press), vol. 144 (2006): 3–17.

Reynolds, Matthew P., et al. "Raising Yield Potential of Wheat. I. Overview of a Consortium Approach and Breeding Strategies." *Journal of Experimental Botany,* October 15, 2010: 1–14. doi:10.1093/jxb/erq311.

Ritter, Steven K. "The Haber-Bosch Reaction: An Early Chemical Impact on Sustainability." *Chemical & Engineering News,* vol. 86, no. 33 (August 18, 2008).

Ronald, Bailey. "Norman Borlaug: The Greatest Humanitarian." *Forbes,* September, 14, 2009. http://www.forbes.com/2009/09/14/

norman-borlaug-green-revolution-opinions -contributors-ronald-bailey.html.

Singh, Salil. "Norman Borlaug: A Billion Lives Saved, a World Connected." *AgBioWorld.* http://www.agbioworld.org/biotech-info/topics/borlaug/special.html.

Skorup, Jarrett. "Norman Borlaug: An American Hero." *Men's News Daily,* December, 30, 2009. http://mensnewsdaily.com/2009/12/30/norman-borlaug-an-american-hero.

Smil, Vaclav. "Detonator of the Population Explosion." *Nature,* vol. 400 (July 1999): 415.

Smith, Barry E. "Nitrogenase Reveals Its Inner Secrets." *Science,* vol. 297, no. 5587 (September 2002): 1654–55.

Stevens, Emily E., Thelma E. Patrick, and Rita Pickler. "A History of Infant Feeding." *Journal of Perinatal Education,* vol. 18, no. 2 (Spring 2009): 32–39.

U.S. Census Bureau, Current Population Reports. "Longevity and Health Characteristics," in *65+ in the United States: 2005.* Washington, DC: U.S. Government Printing Office, 2005. www.census.gov/prod/1/pop/p23-190/p23190-g.pdf.

Vidal, John. "UN Warns of Looming Worldwide Food Crisis in 2013." *Observer* (UK), October 13, 2012.

Wall, J. D., and M. Przeworski. "When Did the Human Population Size Start Increasing?" *Genetics,* vol. 155, no. 4 (2000): 1865–74.

Wigle, Donald T. "Safe Drinking Water: A Public Health Challenge." *Chronic Diseases in Canada,* vol. 19, no. 3 (1998): 103–7.

World Economic and Social Survey 2011: The Great Green Technological Transformation. New York: United Nations, 2011.

World Health Organization. *Malaria, Fact sheet N° 94,* January 2013. http://www.who .int/mediacentre/factsheets/fs094/en.

Chapter Four: Carrying Capacity and the Cradle

BOOKS

Asbell, Bernard. *The Pill: A Biography of the Drug That Changed the World.* New York: Random House, 1995.

Bibliography

Belton, Tom. "Eugenics Board," in *Encyclopedia of North Carolina*, edited by William S. Powell and Jay Mazzocchi. Chapel Hill: University of North Carolina Press, 2006.

Brandt, Allan M. *No Magic Bullet: A Social History of Venereal Disease in the United States Since 1880*. Oxford: Oxford University Press, 1985.

Brown, Lester R., et al. *Beyond Malthus*. New York: W. W. Norton & Company, 1999.

Buchmann, Stephen L., and Gary Paul Nabhan. *The Forgotten Pollinators*. Washington, DC: Island Press, 1996.

Connors, R. J. *The Coming Extinction of Humanity: Six Converging Crises That Threaten Our Survival*. CreateSpace, 2010.

Ehrlich, Anne H., and Paul R. Ehrlich. *The Dominant Animal: Human Evolution and the Environment*. Washington, DC: Island Press, 2008.

———. *The Population Explosion*. New York: Simon & Schuster, 1990.

Ehrlich, Paul R. *The Population Bomb*. New York: Sierra Club/Ballantine, 1968.

———, and Anne H. Ehrlich. *Extinction: The Causes and Consequences of the Disappearance of Species*. New York: Random House, 1981.

Ehrlich, Paul R., John P. Holdren, and Anne H. Ehrlich. *Ecoscience: Population, Resources, Environment*. San Francisco: W. H. Freeman & Co., 1977.

Foreman, Dave. *Man Swarm and the Killing of Wildlife*. Durango, CO: Raven's Eye Press, 2011.

Gordon, Linda. *The Moral Property of Women: A History of Birth Control Politics in America*. Champaign-Urbana: University of Illinois, 2007.

López, Iris. *Matters of Choice: Puerto Rican Women's Struggle for Reproductive Freedom*. Piscataway, NJ: Rutgers University Press, 2008.

McClory, Robert. *Turning Point: The Inside Story of the Papal Birth Control Commission, & How* Humanae Vitae *Changed the Life of Patty Crowley and the Future of the Church*. New York: Crossroad, 1995.

BIBLIOGRAPHY

McKee, Jeffrey K. *Sparing Nature: The Conflict Between Human Population Growth and Earth's Biodiversity.* Piscataway, NJ: Rutgers University Press, 2003.

Myers, Norman. *A Wealth of Wild Species: Storehouse for Human Welfare.* Boulder, CO: Westview Press, 1983.

Stern, Alexandra. *Eugenic Nation: Faults and Frontiers of Better Breeding in Modern America.* Berkeley: University of California Press, 2005.

ARTICLES

Back, Kurt W., Reuben Hill, and J. Mayone Stycos. "The Puerto Rican Field Experiment in Population Control." *Human Relations,* vol. 10 (November 1957): 315–34.

Camp, S., and S. Conly. "Population Policy and the 'Earth Summit': The Passages of History." *Imbonezamuryango,* no. 25 (December 1992): 29–31.

Campbell Madison, Martha. "Schools of Thought: An Analysis of Interest Groups Influential in Population Policy." *Population and Environment,* vol. 19, no. 6 (November 1998): 487–512.

Cardinale, Bradley J., Kristin L. Matulich, David U. Hooper, et al. "The Functional Role of Producer Diversity in Ecosystems." *American Journal of Botany,* vol. 98, no. 3 (2011): 572–92. doi:10.3732/ajb.1000364.

Carranza, María. "A Brief Account of the History of Family Planning in Costa Rica," in *Demographic Transformations and Inequalities in Latin America: Historical Trends and Recent Patterns,* edited by Suzana Cavenaghi. Rio de Janeiro: Latin American Population Association, 2009, pp. 307–14.

Committee for Puerto Rican Decolonization. "35% of Puerto Rican Women Sterilized." Chicago Women's Liberation Union, Herstory Archive, ca. 1970.

Daily, Gretchen C., Anne H. Ehrlich, and Paul R. Ehrlich. "Optimum Human Population Size." *Population and Environment: A Journal of Interdisciplinary Studies,* vol. 15, no. 6 (July 1994): 469–75.

BIBLIOGRAPHY

Daily, Gretchen C., Gerardo Ceballos, Jesús Pacheco, Gerardo Suzán, and Arturo Sánchez-Azofeifa. "Countryside Biogeography of Neotropical Mammals: Conservation Opportunities in Agricultural Landscapes of Costa Rica." *Conservation Biology*, vol. 17, no. 6 (December 2003): 1814–26.

Ehrlich, Paul R., and Gretchen C. Daily. "Red-Naped Sapsuckers Feeding at Willows: Possible Keystone Herbivores." *American Birds*, vol. 42, no. 3 (Fall 1988): 357–65.

———. "Sapsuckers at Work." *Whole Earth*, no. 93 (Summer 1998): 24–26.

Ehrlich, Paul R., and John P. Holdren. "Hidden Effects of Overpopulation." *Saturday Review*, August 1, 1970: 52.

———. "The People Problem." *Saturday Review*, July 4, 1970: 42–43.

———. "Population and Panaceas: A Technological Perspective." *BioScience*, vol. 19, no. 12 (December 1969): 1065–71.

Ehrlich, Paul R., and Brian Walker. "Rivets and Redundancy." *BioScience*, vol. 48, no. 5 (May 1998): 1–2.

Fox, James W. "Real Progress: Fifty Years of USAID in Costa Rica." Center for Development Information and Evaluation, U.S. Agency for International Development, November 1998.

———. "U.S. Aid to Costa Rica: An Overview." Center for Development Information and Evaluation, U.S. Agency for International Development, March 1996. pdf.usaid.gov/pdf_docs/PDACK960. pdfSimilar 1996.

Fuentes, Annette. "They Call It La Operación." *New Internationalist*, vol. 176 (October 1987). http://www.newint.org/features/1987/10/05/call.

Goldberg, Michelle. "Holdren's Controversial Population Control Past." *American Prospect*, July 21, 2009. http://prospect.org/article/holdrens-controversial-population-control-past.

Gunson, Phil. "Obituary of Jose Figueres: The Wealthy 'Farmer-Socialist' Who Turned Costa Rica into a Welfare State." *Guardian* (UK), June 13, 1990.

Hertsgaard, Mark. P. "Still Ticking." *Mother Jones*, vol. 18, no. 2 (March/April 1993): 20.

BIBLIOGRAPHY

Holdren, John P. "Population and the Energy Problem." *Population and Environment*, vol. 12, no. 3 (Spring 1991): 231–55.

"John Holdren, Obama's Science Czar, says: Forced Abortions and Mass Sterilization Needed to Save the Planet." Zombie Time website. http://zombietime.com/john_holdren.

Kenny, Charles. "An Aging Population May Be What the World Needs." *Bloomberg Businessweek*, February 7, 2013.

Krase, Katherine. "Sterilization Abuse." Newsletter of the National Women's Health Network, January/February 1996. http://www.ourbodiesourselves.org/book/ companion.asp?id=18&compID=55.

La Federación Alianza Evangélica Costarricense. "Lista de Afiliados." http://www.alianzaevangelica.org/index_6.html.

Lakshmanan, Indira A. R. "Evangelism Is Luring Latin America's Catholics: Charismatic Sects Focus on Earthly Rewards." *Boston Globe*, May 8, 2005.

Marks, Lara. "Human Guinea Pigs? The History of the Early Oral Contraceptive Clinical Trials." *History and Technology: An International Journal*, vol. 15, no. 4 (1999): 263–88.

McCormick, Katharine. Katharine McCormick to Margaret Sanger, June 19, 1954. In *Women's Letters: America from the Revolutionary War to the Present*, edited by Lisa Grunwald and Stephen J. Adler. New York: Dial Press, 2005.

Mears, Eleanor, and Ellen C. G. Grant. " 'Anovlar' as an Oral Contraceptive." *British Medical Journal*, vol. 2, no. 5297 (July 1962): 75–79.

Mendelsohn, Everett. "The Eugenic Temptation: When Ethics Lag Behind Technology." *Harvard Magazine*, March–April 2000.

Moenne, María Elena Acuña. "Embodying Memory: Women and the Legacy of the Military Government in Chile." *Feminist Review* (London), no. 79 (March 2005): 150.

"Obama's Science Czar Does Not Support Coercive Population Control." Catholic News Agency, July 15, 2009.

Pacheco, Jesús, Gerardo Ceballos, Gretchen C. Daily, Paul R. Ehrlich, Gerardo Suzán, Bernal Rodríguez-Herrera1, and Erika Marcé. "Diversidad, Historia Natural y Conservación de los Mamíferos de San Vito de Coto Brus, Costa Rica." *Revista de Biología Tropical* (San José), vol. 54, no. 1 (March 2006): 219–40.

Paul VI. "Humanae Vitae." Encyclical letter on the regulations of birth control, May 1, 1968.

"The Pill." *The American Experience,* February 24, 2003. http://www.pbs.org/wgbh/amex/pill/peopleevents/e_puertorico.html.

Planned Parenthood Federation of America. *A History of Birth Control Methods.* Report published by Katharine Dexter McCormick Library, November 2006.

Rodis, Rodel. "Papal Infallibility." *Inquirer Global Nation,* June 25, 2011.

Samuel, Anand A. "FDA Regulation of Condoms: Minimal Scientific Uncertainty Fuels the Moral Conservative Plea to Rip a Large Hole in the Public's Perception of Contraception." Third-Year Paper. Harvard Law School, May 2005.

Sanger, Margaret. "A Question of Privilege." *Women United,* October 1949: 6–8.

———. *Family Limitations.* New York: s.n., 1917, available online at http://archive .lib.msu.edu/DMC/AmRad/familylimitations.pdf.

Shaw, Russell. "Church Birth Control Commission Docs Unveiled." *Our Sunday Visitor Newsweekly,* February 27, 2011.

Smail, J. Kenneth. "Beyond Population Stabilization: The Case for Dramatically Reducing Global Human Numbers." *Politics and the Life Sciences,* vol. 16, no. 2 (September 1997), 183–192.

———. "Confronting a Surfeit of People: Reducing Global Human Numbers to Sustainable Levels," *Environment, Development and Sustainability,* vol. 4, no. 1 (2002): 21–50.

Strong, Maurice. Earth Summit address to the United Nations Conference on Environment and Development (UNCED), Rio de Janeiro, June 1992.

Swomley, John M. "The Pope and the Pill." *Christian Social Action,* February 1998: 12.

Vázquez Calzada, José L., and Zoraida Morales del Valle. "Female Sterilization in Puerto Rico and Its Demographic Effectiveness." *Puerto Rico Health Sciences Journal,* vol. 1, no. 2 (June 1982): 68–79.

Vidal, John. "Rio+20: Earth Summit Dawns with Stormier Clouds than in 1992." *Guardian* (UK), June 19, 2012.

Virgo, Paul. "Biodiversity: Not Just About Tigers and Pandas." Inter Press Service, May 23, 2010.

Zucchino, David. "Forced Sterilization Worth $50,000, North Carolina Panel Says." *Los Angeles Times,* January 10, 2012.

Chapter Five: Island World

BOOKS

Ali, A. Yusuf. *An English Interpretation of the Holy Koran.* Bensenville, IL: Lushena Books, 2007.

Coale, Ansley J., and Susan Cotts Watson, eds. *The Decline of Fertility in Europe.* Princeton, NJ: Princeton University Press, 1986.

Longman, Phillip. *The Empty Cradle: How Falling Birthrates Threaten World Prosperity and What to Do About It.* New York: Basic Books, 2004.

Pearce, Fred. *The Coming Population Crash: And Our Planet's Surprising Future.* Boston: Beacon Press, 2010.

ARTICLES

Allen, Jr., John L. "Synod Notebook: Video on Islam Rocks the House." *National Catholic Reporter,* October 15, 2012.

Anastasaki, Erasmia. *Running Up a Down Escalator.* MSc diss., commissioned by Population Matters, September 2010. http://popula tionmatters.org/documents/escalator_summary.pdf.

Attenborough, David. "People and Planet." RSA President's Lecture 2011. Royal Society for the Encouragement of Arts, Manufactures and Commerce, March 11, 2011.

Beckford, Martin. "Foreigners and Older Mothers Drive Biggest Baby Boom Since 1972." *Daily Telegraph* (UK), July 14, 2011.

"BNP Leader Charged with Race Hate." BBC News, April 6, 2005.

Borland, Sophie. "Schoolgirls of 13 Given Contraceptive Implants." *Daily Mail* (UK), February 8, 2012.

BIBLIOGRAPHY

Davey, E., acting chair: Optimum Population Trust. "Think-Tank Urges Population Inquiry by Government." News release, January 5, 2009. http://populationmatters.org/2009/press/thinktank-urges -population-inquiry-government.

DeParle, Jason. "The Anti-Immigration Crusader." *New York Times,* April 17, 2011.

Desvaux, Martin. "The Sustainability of Human Populations: How Many People Can Live on Earth." *Significance,* vol. 4, no. 3 (September 2007): 102–7. http://population matters.org/documents/ sustainable_populations.pdf. Accessed: June 2009.

———. "Towards Sustainable and Optimum Populations." Optimum Population Trust, April 8, 2008. http://www.population matters.org/documents.

Doughty, Steve. "One in Three Babies Born Today 'Will Live for at Least 100 Years.'" *Daily Mail* (UK), March 27, 2012.

Doward, Jamie. "British Farming in Crisis as Crop Losses from 'Relentless' Floods Pile Up Woes." *Observer* (UK), February 23, 2013.

Fairlie, Simon. "Can Britain Feed Itself?" *The Land Magazine,* no. 4 (Winter 2007–2008): 18–26.

Ferguson, Andrew, ed. "2nd Footprint Forum, Part II: Ethics of Carrying Capacity." *Optimum Population Trust Journal,* vol. 3, no. 2 (October 2003).

Forum for the Future. *Growing Pains: Population and Sustainability in the UK.* June 2010.

Gillis, Justin, and Celia W. Dugger. "U.N. Forecasts 10.1 Billion People by Century's End." *New York Times,* May 3, 2011.

Griffin, Nick. "A Right Menace." *Independent,* May 23, 2009.

Guillebaud, J. "Youthquake: Population, Fertility and Environment in the 21st Century." Optimum Population Trust, 2007.

———, and Hayes P. "Editorial: Population Growth and Climate Change." *British Medical Journal,* vol. 337 (2008): 247–48.

"Inside Out/West Midlands: Report on Sharia Law." *BBC Home,* January 20, 2009.

Islamic Foundation for Ecology and Environmental Sciences. *EcoIslam,* no. 8, June 2011.

Johnson, Wesley. "UK Population 'Largest in Western Europe by 2050.'" *Independent* (UK), July 30, 2010.

Kaiser, Jocelyn. "10 Billion Plus: Why World Population Projections Were Too Low." *Science/ScienceInsider,* May 4, 2011. http://news. sciencemag.org/scienceinsider/2011/ 05/10-billion-plus-why-world-population.html.

Khalid, Fazlun M. "Guardians of the Natural Order." *One Planet Magazine,* August 1996.

———. "Islam and the Environment," in *Social and Economic Dimensions of Global Environmental Change.* Vol. 5 of *Encyclopedia of Global Environmental Change.* Chichester, UK: John Wiley & Sons, 2002, pp. 332–39.

———. "The Copenhagen Syndrome." *Globalia Magazine,* December 1, 2010.

Knight, Richard. "Debunking a YouTube Hit." BBC News, August 7, 2009.

Levitt, Tom. "Chief Scientist Refutes Fred Pearce's Bad Logic About Population and Environment." *Ecologist,* February 14, 2012. http:// www.theecologist.org/News.

Martin, Roger. "Population, Environment and Conflict." Population Matters, paper presented at the African Population Conference in Ougadougou, organized by the Union for African Population Studies (UAPS). UAPS, 2011.

McDougall, Rosamund. "The UK's Population Problem." Optimum Population Trust, 2003, updated 2010.

Morris, Steven, and Martin Wainwright. "BNP Leader Held by Police over Racist Remarks." *Guardian* (UK), December 14, 2004.

Murray, Douglas. "It's Official: Muslim Population of Britain Doubles." Gatestone Institute website, December 21, 2012. http:// www.gatestoneinstitute.org/3511.

"Muslim Demographics." YouTube video. Posted by friendofmuslim, March 30, 2009. http://www.youtube.com/watch?v=6-3X5hIFXYU.

Myhrvold, N. P., and K. Caldeira. "Greenhouse Gases, Climate Change and the Transition from Coal to Low-Carbon Electricity." *Environmental Research Letters,* vol. 7 (2012): 1–8.

Nicholson-Lord, David. "The Fewer the Better." *New Statesman,* November 8, 2004.

Optimum Population Trust. "Britain Overpopulated by 70 Percent." Press release, February 18, 2008.

————. "Population Projections," June 3, 2009.

"People and the Planet." Report for the Royal Society Science Policy Centre, London. Final report, April 26, 2012.

Pipes, Daniel. "Predicting a Majority-Muslim Russia." Lion's Den (blog), *Daniel Pipes: Middle East Forum,* August 6, 2005. http://www.danielpipes.org/blog/2005/08.

"School Children Offered Contraceptive Implants." BBC News, Health, February 8, 2012. http://www.bbc.co.uk/news/health-16951331.

Snopes.com. "Muslim Demographics." Uban Legends Reference Pages, last updated April 2009. http://www.snopes.com/politics/religion/demographics.asp.

Swinford, Steven. "Contraceptive Implants and Injections for Schoolgirls Treble." *Telegraph* (UK), October 30, 2012.

————. "Girls of 13 Given Birth Control Jab at School Without Parents' Knowledge." *Telegraph* (UK), October 28, 2012.

"UK Muslim Population Doubled in a Decade." PressTV, December 22, 2012.

United Kingdom Office for National Statistics, "What Are the Chances of Surviving to Age 100?" Historic and Projected Mortality Data (1951–2060) from the UK Life Tables, 2010-based, March 26, 2012.

Vaïsse, Justin. "Eurabian Follies." *Foreign Policy,* January/February 2010.

Vaughan, Adam. "UK's Year of Drought and Flooding Unprecedented, Experts Say." *Guardian* (UK), October 18, 2012.

Ware, John. "What Happens If Britain's Population Hits 70m?" *BBC Panorama,* April 19, 2010.

Whitehead, Tom. "Immigration Drives UK's Population Boom." *Telegraph* (UK), July 1, 2011.

————. "Women Wait Until 29 and Settle for Fewer Children." *Telegraph* (UK), September 24, 2010.

Wiley, David. "Letter: Optimum Population." *New Scientist,* no. 1944, September 24, 1994.

Wire, Thomas. *Fewer Emitters, Lower Emissions, Less Cost: Reducing Future Carbon Emissions by Investing in Family Planning: A Cost/ Benefit Analysis.* London School of Economics, Operational Research. Sponsored by Optimum Population Trust, August 2009.

Chapter Six: Holy See

BOOKS

Department of Economic and Social Affairs, Population Division. *World Population Prospects: The 2010 Revision.* New York: United Nations, 2010 (Updated: April 15, 2011)

Hasler, August. *How the Pope Became Infallible: Pius IX and the Politics of Persuasion.* New York: Doubleday, 1981.

Keilis-Borok, V. I., and M. Sánchez Sorondo, eds. *Science for Survival and Sustainable Development: Proceedings of Study Week 12–16 March 1999.* Vatican City: Scripta Varia 98, 2000.

Krause, Elizabeth L. *A Crisis of Births: Population Politics and Family-Making in Italy (Case Studies on Contemporary Social Issues).* Belmont, CA: Thomson/Wadsworth, 2005.

———. *Unraveled: A Weaver's Tale of Life Gone Modern.* Berkeley: University of California Press, 2009.

Livi-Bacci, Massimo. *A Concise History of World Population.* Hoboken, NJ: John Wiley & Sons, 2012.

Losito, Maria. *The Casina Pio IV in the Vatican: Historical and Iconographic Guide.* Vatican City: Pontifical Academy of Sciences, 2010.

Maguire, Daniel C. *Sacred Choices: The Right to Contraception and Abortion in Ten World Religions.* Minneapolis: Fortress Press, 2001.

McClory, Robert. *Turning Point: The Inside Story of the Papal Birth Control Commission.* New York: Crossroad, 1995.

Mumford, Stephen. *American Democracy and the Vatican: Population Growth and National Security.* Washington, DC: American Humanist Association, 1984.

BIBLIOGRAPHY

Pontifical Academy of Sciences. *Popolazione e Risorse* [*Population and Resources*]. Vatican City: Vita e Pensiero, 1994.

Seewald, Peter, and Pope Benedict XVI. *Light of the World: The Pope, the Church and the Signs of Times.* Translated by Michael J. Miller and Adrian J. Walker. San Francisco: Ignatius Press, 2010.

Tanner, Norman, and Guiseppe Albergio, eds. *Decrees of the Ecumenical Councils.* Washington, DC: Georgetown University Press, 1990.

ARTICLES

Allen Jr., John L. "Vatican Studies Genetically Modified Crops." *National Catholic Reporter,* May 18, 2009.

Benedict XVI. *Caritas in Veritate:* Encyclical Letter on Integral Human Development in Charity and Truth. June 29, 2009.

"Berlusconi Investigated in Teen Dancer Case." Associated Press, January 14, 2011.

"Berlusconi's 'Party Girls' Driven by Ambitious Parents." Agence France-Presse, January 20, 2011.

Bruni, F. "Persistent Drop in Fertility Reshapes Europe's Future." *New York Times,* December 26, 2002.

Capparella v. E.N.P.A, Civil Court of Rome, February 11, 2009. Conciliation Report, p. 392.

Carr, David. "The Bible Is Pro-Birth Control." *Reader Supported News,* March 8, 2012. http://readersupportednews.org/opinion2/295-164/10356-the-bible-Is-pro-birth -control.

Catholics for Choice. "Truth and Consequence: A Look Behind the Vatican's Ban on Contraception," 2008.

Colonnello, Paolo. "Gli Amici Serpenti del Cavaliere." LaStampa.it, January 19, 2011. http://www.lastampa.it/2011/01/19/italia/politica/gli-amici-serpenti-del-cavaliere-XTm7TjZWlU8f1vvGr32FaN/pagina.html.

Cowell, Alan. "Scientists Linked to the Vatican Call for Population Curbs." *New York Times,* June 16, 1994.

Delaney, Sarah. "Genetically Modified Crops Call for Caution, Bishop Tells Synod." Catholic News Service, October 8, 2009.

BIBLIOGRAPHY

Donadio, Rachel. "Europe's Young Grow Agitated over Future Prospects." *New York Times,* January 1, 2011.

———. "Surreal: A Soap Opera Starring Berlusconi." *New York Times,* January 22, 2011.

Ehrlich, Paul R., and Peter H. Raven. "Butterflies and Plants: A Study in Coevolution." *Evolution,* vol. 18, no. 4 (December 1964): 586–608.

Engelman, Robert. "The Pope's Scientists." *Conscience,* vol. 31, no. 2 (2010).

Flanders, Laura. "Giving the Vatican the Boot." *Ms. Magazine,* October/November 1999.

Fox, Thomas C. "New Birth Control Commission Papers Reveal Vatican's Hand." *National Catholic Reporter,* March 23, 2011. http://ncronline.org.

"Il fratello di Roberta. 'Brava, hai lavorato bene.'" Repubblica TV, September 21, 2010. http://video.repubblica.it/le-inchieste/il-fratello-di-roberta-brava-hai-lavorato-bene /95230/93612.

Glatz, Carol. "Synod Working Document Seeks Ways to Promote Justice, Peace in Africa." Catholic News Service, March 19, 2009.

Grandoni, Dino. "98% of Catholic Women Have Used Contraception the Church Opposes." Atlantic Wire, February 10, 2012.

Gumbel, Andrew. "Italian Men Cling to Mamma; Unemployment and a Housing Crisis Force Males to Live at Home in Their Thirties." The World section, *Independent* (UK), December 15, 1996.

Hebblethwaite, Peter. "Science, Magisterium at Odds: Pontifical Academy Emphasizes Need for Global Population Control — Pontifical Academy of Sciences." *National Catholic Reporter,* July 15, 1994.

ISTAT. *Demographic Indicators: Year 2010.* January 24, 2011. http://demo.istat.it/index_e.html.

Kertzer, David I., Alessandra Gribaldo, and Maya Judd. "An Imperfect Contraceptive Society: Fertility and Contraception in Italy." *Population and Development Review,* vol. 35, no. 3 (September 2009): 551–84.

Kessler, Glenn. "The Claim That 98 Percent of Catholic Women Use Contraception: A Media Foul." The Fact Checker (blog), *Washington Post,* February 17, 2012.

Kington, Tom. "Silvio Berlusconi Gave Me €7,000, Says 17-Year-Old Belly Dancer." *Observer* (UK), October 30, 2010.

————. "Silvio Berlusconi Wiretaps Reveal Boast of Spending Night with Eight Women." *Observer* (UK), September 17, 2011.

Kissling, Frances. "The Vatican and Reproductive Freedom: A Human Rights Perspective on the Importance of Supporting Reproductive Choices." Testimony given by Frances Kissling before the All-Party Parliamentary Group on Population, Development and Reproductive Health at a hearing in the UK Parliament on Monday, July 3, 2006. http://www.catholicsforchoice.org/conscience/current/.

Krause, Elizabeth L. "'Empty Cradles' and the Quiet Revolution: Demographic Discourse and Cultural Struggles of Gender, Race, and Class in Italy." *Cultural Anthropology,* vol. 16, no. 4 (2001): 576–611.

————. "Dangerous Demographies and the Scientific Manufacture of Fear," in *Selected Publications of EFS Faculty, Students, and Alumni.* Paper 4, July 2006.

————. "'Toys and Perfumes': Imploding Italy's Population Paradox and Motherly Myths," in *Barren States: The Population "Implosion" in Europe,* edited by Carrie B. Douglass. London: Berg, 2005, pp. 159–82.

Krause, Elizabeth L., and Milena Marchesi. "Fertility Politics as 'Social Viagra': Reproducing Boundaries, Social Cohesion, and Modernity in Italy." *American Anthropologist,* vol. 109, no. 2 (June 2007): 350–62. doi: 10.1525/AA.2007.109.2.350.

Lavanga, Claudio. "Berlusconi Tells Businessman to Bring Girls, But Not Tall Ones, Wiretaps Reveal." NBC News, September 17, 2011.

Ludwig, Mike. "New WikiLeaks Cables Show US Diplomats Promote Genetically Engineered Crops Worldwide." Truthout, August 25, 2011. http://www.truth-out.org/new-wikileaks-cables-show-us-diplomats-promote-genetically-engineered-crops-worldwide/1314303978.

————. "US to Vatican: Genetically Modified Food Is a 'Moral Imperative.'" Truthout, December 29, 2010.

Meldolesi, Anna. "Vatican Panel Backs GMOs." *Nature Biotechnology*, vol. 29, no. 11 (2011). doi:10.1038/nbt0111-11.

Mumford, Stephen D. "Why the Church Can't Change." *Council for Secular Humanism Free Inquiry*, vol. 21, no 1 (Winter 2000/2001).

———. "Why the Pope Can't Change the Church's Position on Birth Control: Implications for Americans." Presentation to Vatican Influence on Public Policy Symposium, at the Center for Research on Population and Security: St. Louis, Missouri. January 27, 1999.

O'Brien, Jon, and Sara Morello. "Catholics for Choice and Abortion: Prochoice Catholicism 101." *Conscience*, Spring 2008: 24–26.

Partridge, Loren W. Review of *The Casino of Pius IV*, by Graham Smith. *The Art Bulletin*, vol. 60, no. 2 (June 1978): 369–72. http://www.jstor.org/stable/3049799. Accessed: 30/03/2012.

Paul VI. *Humanae Vitae:* Encyclical letter on the regulations of birth control. May 1, 1968.

Pontifical Council for the Family. "Ethical and Pastoral Dimensions of Population Trends." March 25, 1994.

Potrykus, Ingo, and Klaus Ammann, eds. "Transgenic Plants for Food Security in the Context of Development: Proceedings of a Study Week of the Pontifical Academy of Sciences." *New Biotechnology*, vol. 27, no. 5 (November 2010): 445–718.

Raven, Peter H. "Does the Use of Transgenic Plants Diminish or Promote Biodiversity?" *New Biotechnology*, vol. 27, no. 5 (2010): 528–53.

Ravenholt, R. T. "Poorest Peasant Couple in Remotest Village Will Seize Opportunity to Control Family Size." Paper presented to the First USAID World Population Conference, Washington, DC, December 1976.

———. "World Fertility Survey: Origin and Development of the WFS." Paper presented to the Conference at the National Press Club on 30 Years of USAID Efforts in Population and Health Data Collection. Washington, DC, June 3, 2002.

Sarzanini, Fiorenza. "Fede, Mora e le Feste: 'Lui Stasera è Pimpante, Chiama le Nostre Vallette.'" *Corriere della Sera*, January 19, 2011.

BIBLIOGRAPHY

Schnieder, Jane, and Peter Schneider. "Sex and Respectability in an Age of Fertility Decline: A Sicilian Case Study." *Social Science & Medicine,* vol. 33, no. 8 (1991): 885–95.

Shiva, Vandana. "The 'Golden Rice' Hoax: When Public Relations Replaces Science." Accessed at http://online.sfsu.edu/rone/GEessays/goldenricehoax.html.

Swomley, John M. "The Pope and the Pill." *Christian Social Action,* February 1998.

Urquhart, Gordon. "The Vatican and Family Politics." For Conservative Catholic Influence in Europe: An Investigative Series. Washington, DC: Catholics for a Free Choice, 1997.

"Vatican Calls for 'More Solid Morality' in Wake of Berlusconi Sex Scandal." France24 International News 24/7, January 21, 2011. http://www.france24.com/en/20110120-berlusconi-political -persecution-scandal-vows-prostitution-minor-law.

Chapter Seven: Gorillas in Our Midst

BOOKS

Hall, Ruth. *The Life of Marie Stopes.* New York: W. W. Norton & Company, 1978.

Hanson, Thor. *The Impenetrable Forest: My Gorilla Years in Uganda,* revised edition. Warwick, NY: 1500 Books, 2008.

Turner, Pamela. *Gorilla Doctors: Saving Endangered Great Apes.* Boston: Houghton Mifflin Harcourt, 2008.

ARTICLES

Anderson, Curt. "U.S. Arrests 3 in Uganda Tourist Slayings." Associated Press, March 3, 2003.

"Bwindi Impenetrable Forest," Tropical Ecology Assessment and Monitoring Network website. http://www.teamnetwork.org/network/sites/bwindi-national-park-0.

Caccone, Adalgisa. "DNA Divergence Among Hominoids." *Evolution,* vol. 43, no. 5 (1989): 925–41.

Bibliography

Clarke, Jody. "Tullow Accused of Acts of Bribery in Uganda." *Irish Times,* October 14, 2011. http://www.irishtimes.com/newspaper/world/2011/1014/1224305758151.html.

Cohen, Tamara. "What Separates Man from the Apes?" *Daily Mail* (UK), March 8, 2012.

Craig, Allison Layne. " 'Quality Is Everything': Rhetoric of the Transatlantic Birth Control Movement in Interwar Women's Literature of England, Ireland and the United States." PhD diss., University of Texas at Austin, December 2009.

Gaffikin, Lynne. "Population Growth, Ecosystem Services, and Human Well-Being," in *A Pivotal Moment: Population, Justice, and the Environmental Challenge,* edited by Laurie Mazur. Washington, DC: Island Press, 2009.

———, and Kalema-Zikusoka, G. *Integrating Human and Animal Health for Conservation and Development: Findings from a Program Evaluation in Southwest Uganda.* Conservation Through Public Health, Evaluation and Research Technologies for Health, and John Snow, 2010.

Gatsiounis, Ioannis. "Uganda's Soaring Population a Factor in Poverty, Deadly Riots." *Washington Times,* June 14, 2011.

Kanyeheyo, Ivan Mafigiri. "Nation's Population Growth a Self-Laid Economic Trap." *Monitor* (Kampala), June 23, 2011.

Klein, Alice. "Uganda's Fledgling Oil Industry Could Undermine Development Progress." *Guardian* (UK), December 12, 2011.

Lirri, Evelyn. "The Tragedy of the Nation's Many Unwanted Pregnancies." *Monitor* (Uganda), May 28, 2011.

Loconte, Joseph. "The White House Initiative to Combat AIDS: Learning from Uganda." *Heritage Foundation Backgrounder,* no. 1692 (September 29, 2003).

Maykuth, Andrew. "Uncertain Times in the Impenetrable Forest." *Philadelphia Inquirer,* Sunday Magazine, April 23, 2000.

Nanteza, Winnie. "Will Mother Nature Survive Population Pressure?" *New Vision* (Uganda), July 7, 2010.

Nordland, Rod. "Death March." *Newsweek,* March 14, 1999.

Palacios, G., L. J. Lowenstine, M. R. Cranfield, K. V. K. Gilardi, L. Spelman, M. Lukasik-Braum, et al. "Human Metapneumovirus Infection in Wild Mountain Gorillas, Rwanda." *Emerging Infectious Diseases,* vol. 17, no. 4 (April 2011).

Plumptre, A. J., A. Kayitare, H. Rainer, M. Gray, I. Munanura, N. Barakabuye, S. Asuma, M. Sivha, and A. Namara. "The Socio-economic Status of People Living Near Protected Areas in the Central Albertine Rift." *Albertine Rift Technical Reports,* vol. 4 (2004): 127.

Songa, Martha. "Stop Talking and Take Action on Reproductive Health." *New Vision,* July 5, 2011.

"3 Rebels Charged in U.S. Tourist Killings." *Chicago Tribune,* March 4, 2003.

Tumusha, Joseph. "The Politics of HIV/AIDS in Uganda." Social Policy and Development Programme, Paper Number 28. United Nations Research Institute for Social Development, August 2006.

"Uganda Biodiversity and Tropical Forest Assessment." U.S. Agency for International Development. Final report, July 2006.

Wambi, Michael. "When Women Go Without Needed Contraceptives." InterPress Service-Uganda, June 28, 2011.

Wax, Emily. "Ugandans Say Facts, Not Abstinence, Will Win AIDS War." *Washington Post,* July 9, 2003.

Chapter Eight: The Great Wall of People

BOOKS

Fong, Vanessa L. *Only Hope: Coming of Age Under China's One-Child Policy.* Palo Alto, CA: Stanford University Press, 2004.

Greenhalgh, Susan. *Just One Child: Science and Policy in Deng's China.* Berkeley: University of California Press, 2008.

Hvistendahl, Mara. *Unnatural Selection: Choosing Boys Over Girls, and the Consequences of a World Full of Men.* New York: Public Affairs, 2011.

Meadows, Donella, Dennis Meadows, Jørgen Randers, and W. W. Behrens III. *The Limits to Growth.* New York: Universe Books, 1972.

Shapiro, Judith. *Mao's War Against Nature: Politics and the Environment in Revolutionary China (Studies in Environment and History)*. New York: Cambridge University Press, 2001.

Watts, Jonathan. *When a Billion Chinese Jump: How China Will Save Mankind—Or Destroy It*. London: Faber & Faber, 2010.

Articles

Bethune, Brian. "The Women Shortage: Interview with Mara Hvistendahl, Beijing Correspondent for *Science* Magazine." *Maclean's*, June 14, 2011.

Brinkley, Joel. "Abortion Opponents Play Chinese Dissident Card." *San Francisco Chronicle*, June 30, 2012.

Brown, Lester R. "Can the United States Feed China?" Plan B Updates, Earth Policy Release, March 23, 2011.

Burkitt, Laurie. "Agency Move Hints at Shift in China's One-Child Policy." *Wall Street Journal*, Eastern edition (New York), March 11, 2013.

"Buying Farmland Abroad: Outsourcing's Third Wave." *The Economist*, May 21, 2009.

"China to Maintain Family Planning Policy: Official." Xinhua News Agency (China), March 11, 2013. http://english.peopledaily.com.cn/90785/8162924.html.

Collins, Gabe, and Andrew Erickson. "The 10 Biggest Cities in China That You've Probably Never Heard of." *China SignPost*, no. 37, June 1, 2011.

Cruz, Anthony dela. "Chinese Investments in the Philippines." *China Business*, June, 2008.

Daily, Gretchen C. "Conservation and Development for the 21st Century: Harmonizing with Nature." PowerPoint presentation to the Chinese Academy of Sciences, September 24, 2010.

Earle, Christopher J., ed. "Gymnosperms of Sichuan." *The Gymnosperm Database*, November 11, 2011. http://www.conifers.org/topics/sichuan.php.

Ehrlich, Paul R., Peter M. Kareiva, and Gretchen C. Daily. "Securing Natural Capital and Expanding Equity to Rescale Civilization." *Nature*, vol. 486 (June 2012): 68–73.

BIBLIOGRAPHY

Ennaanay, Driss. "InVEST: A Tool for Mapping and Valuing Hydrological Ecosystem Services." PowerPoint presentation to the Chinese Academy of Sciences, September 24, 2010.

Gittings, John. "Growing Sex Imbalance Shocks China." *Guardian* (UK), May 12, 2002.

Goodkind, Daniel. "Child Underreporting, Fertility, and Sex Ratio Imbalance in China." *Demography*, vol. 48, no. 1 (February 2011): 291–316.

Greenhalgh, Susan. "Fresh Winds in Beijing: Chinese Feminists Speak Out on the One-Child Policy and Women's Lives." *Signs* (University of Chicago Press), vol. 26, no. 3 (Spring 2001): 847–86.

———. "Science, Modernity, and the Making of China's One-Child Policy." *Population and Development Review*, vol. 29, no. 2 (June 2003): 163–96.

"Growing Urban Population Strains Chinese Cities." Agence France-Presse. June 26, 2011.

Gupta, Monica Das. "Explaining Asia's 'Missing Women': A New Look at the Data." *Population and Development Review*, vol. 31, no. 3 (September 2005): 529–35.

"Hope in Reforming China's One-Child Rule?" *The Economist*, July 25, 2011.

Huang, Shu-tse. "China's Views on Major Issues of World Population." Speech to the 1974 United Nations World Population Conference, *Peking Review*, no. 35, August 30, 1974.

Hvistendahl, Mara. "Has China Outgrown the One-Child Policy?" *Science*, vol. 329, no. 5998 (September 2010): 1458–61.

———. "Of Population Projections and Projectiles." *Science*, vol. 329, no. 5998 (September 2010): 1460.

Jiang, Steven. "Forced Abortion Sparks Outrage, Debate in China." CNN, June 15, 2012.

Jihong, Liu, Ulla Larsen, and Grace Wyshak. "Factors Affecting Adoption in China, 1950–87." *Population Studies*, vol. 58, no. 1 (March 2004): 21–36.

Johansson, Sten, and Ola Nygren. "The Missing Girls of China: A New Demographic Account." *Population and Development Review*, vol. 17, no. 1 (March 1991): 35–51.

Jones, David. "The Baby Panda Factory." *Daily Mail* (UK), July 30, 2010.

Kim, Hyung-Jin, and Yu Bing. "South Korea Finds Smuggled Capsules Contain Human Flesh." Associated Press, May 8, 2012.

Larsen, Janet. "Meat Consumption in China Now Double That in the United States." Plan B Updates, Earth Policy Institute, April 24, 2012.

"Learning Chinese: Budget Brides from Vietnam." Globaltimes.cn, April 23, 2012. http://www.globaltimes.cn/DesktopModules/Dnn Forge%20-%20NewsArticles/Print.aspx?tabid=99&tabmoduleid =94&articleId=706219&moduleId=405& PortalID=0.

Li, Jie, Marcus W. Feldman, Shuzhuo Li, and Gretchen C. Daily. "Rural Household Income and Inequality Under the Sloping Land Conversion Program in Western China." *Proceedings of the National Academy of Sciences,* May 10, 2011.

Li, Laifang, Xu Xiaoqing, and Xu Yang. "Population Policy to Be Improved." Xinhua News Agency (China), March 5, 2013. http://www.xinhuanet.com.

"The Loneliness of the Chinese Birdwatcher." *The Economist,* December 18, 2008.

Merli, M. Giovanna. "Underreporting of Births and Infant Deaths in Rural China: Evidence from Field Research in One County of Northern China." *China Quarterly,* no. 155 (September 1998): 637–55.

Moore, Malcolm. "China's Mega City: The Country's Existing Mega Cities." *Telegraph* (UK), January 24, 2011.

Myers, Norman, Russell A. Mittermeier, Cristina G. Mittermeier, Gustavo A. B. da Fonseca, and Jennifer Kent. "Biodiversity Hotspots for Conservation Priorities." *Nature,* vol. 403 (February 2000): 853–58.

Oster, Shai. "China: New Dam Builder for the World." *Wall Street Journal,* December 28, 2007.

———. "China Traffic Jam Could Last Weeks." *Asia News,* August 24, 2010.

Bibliography

Ouyang, Zhiyun. "Ecosystem Services Valuation and Its Applications." PowerPoint presentation to the Chinese Academy of Sciences, September 24, 2010.

Patranobis, Sutirtho. "China Softens Its One-Child Policy." *Hindustan Times* (Beijing), March 7, 2013.

Peng, Xizhe. "China's Demographic History and Future Challenges." *Science,* vol. 333, no. 6042 (2011): 581–87.

Pinghui, Zhuang. "Officials Suspended After Forced Late-Term Abortion." *South China Morning Post,* June 15, 2012.

Roberts, Dexter. "China Prepares for Urban Revolution." *Bloomberg Businessweek,* November 13, 2008.

Rosenthal, Elisabeth. "China's Widely Flouted One-Child Policy Undercuts Its Census." *New York Times,* April 14, 2000.

"Second Probe into Capsules 'Made from Dead Babies.'" *Shanghai Daily,* May 9, 2012.

"South-to-North Water Diversion Project, China." Water-technology.net. Net Resources International, 2012. http://www.water-technology.net/projects/south_north/.

Springer, Kate. "Soaring to Sinking: How Building Up Is Bringing Shanghai Down." *Time,* May 21, 2012.

Sudworth, John. "Chinese Officials Apologize to Woman in Forced Abortion." BBC News, June 15, 2012.

Thayer Lodging Group. "What Is the Opportunity in China?" PowerPoint Presentation, October 2, 2011. http://www.hotelschool.cornell.edu/about/dean/documents/.

Wang, Yukuan. "Ecosystem Service Assessment and Management." PowerPoint Presentation, Chinese Academy of Sciences, September 24, 2010.

Webel, Sebastian. "Sustainability Boom." *Pictures of the Future Magazine* (Siemens), Spring 2012: 90–94. http://www.siemens.com/pof.

Webster, Paul, and Jason Burke. "How the Rise of the Megacity Is Changing the Way We Live." *Observer* (UK), January 21, 2012.

Weiss, Kenneth R. "Beyond 7 Billion: The China Effect." *Los Angeles Times,* July 22, 2012.

Wines, Michael. "Qian Xuesen, Father of China's Space Program, Dies at 98." *New York Times,* November 3, 2009.

Wong, Edward. "Reports of Forced Abortions Fuel Push to End Chinese Law." *New York Times,* July 22, 2012.

"The Worldwide War on Baby Girls." *Economist,* March 4, 2010.

Yi, Zeng, Tu Ping, Gu Baochang, Xu Yi, Li Bohua, and Li Yongping. "Causes and Implications of the Recent Increase in the Reported Sex Ratio at Birth in China." *Population and Development Review,* vol. 19, no. 2 (June 1993): 283–302.

Yin, Runsheng, Jintao Xu, Zhou Li, and Can Liu. "China's Ecological Rehabilitation: The Unprecedented Efforts and Dramatic Impacts of Reforestation and Slope Protection in Western China." *China Environment Series* (Wilson Center), no. 7 (2005): 17–32.

Zhao, Xing. "Chinese Men Head to Vietnam for the Perfect Wife." CNN-Go, February 19, 2010. http://www.cnngo.com/shanghai/.

Chapter Nine: The Sea

BOOKS

Aliño, Porfirio M. *Atlas of Philippine Coral Reefs.* Quezon City, Philippines: Goodwill Trading Co., 2002.

Bain, David Haward. *Sitting in Darkness: Americans in the Philippines.* New York: Houghton Mifflin, 1984.

Coastal Resource Management Project/Fisheries Resource Management Project/Department of Agriculture. *Coastal Resource Management for Food Security.* Makati City, Philippines: The Bookmark, Inc., 1999.

Concepcion, Mercedes B., ed. *Population of the Philippines.* Manila: Population Institute, University of the Philippines, 1977.

Goldoftas, Barbara. *The Green Tiger: The Costs of Ecological Decline in the Philippines.* Oxford: Oxford University Press, 2006.

Kiple, Kenneth F., and Kriemhild Coneè Ornelas, eds. *The Cambridge World History of Food.* Cambridge: Cambridge University Press, 2000.

Bibliography

Articles

Alave, Kristine L. "Contraception Is Corruption." *Philippine Daily Inquirer,* August 5, 2012.

Anderson, Maren C. "History and Future of Population-Health-Environment Programs: Evolution of Funding and Programming." MPP Professional Paper, University of Minnesota, 2010.

Annual Report 2010, PATH Foundation Philippines.

Aragon-Choudhury, Perla. "11 Filipinas Die in Childbirth Daily— What About Their Rights to Prenatal Care?" *Womens Feature Service,* September 9, 2010.

Barclay, Adam. "Hybridizing the World." *Rice Today,* October/December 2010: 32–35.

Barlaan, Karl Allan, and Christian Cardiente. "So We Would All Be Informed: Dissecting the Flood Problem in Metro Manilan." *Manila Standard Today,* August 8, 2011. http://www.manilastandardtoday.com/insideOpinion.htm?f=2011/.

"Birth Control Proponents Retreat on 2 Key Fronts." *Manila Standard,* March 26, 2011.

"Bishop Open to Plebiscite on RH Bill." GMA News, November 17, 2010. http:// www.gmanews.tv/story/206151/bishop-open-to-plebiscite-on-rh-billLBG/VVP/RSJ, GMANews.TV.

Boncocan, Karen. "RH Bill Finally Signed into Law." *Philippine Daily Inquirer,* December 28, 2012.

"Budget for Condoms from P880M to Zero." *Philippine Daily Inquirer,* December 18, 2010.

Bugna-Barrer, Sahlee. "Increasing Population and Growing Demand Push Biodiversity to Its Limits." *Business Mirror,* July 8, 2012.

Cabacungan, Gil. "UN to Stop Funding Philippine Population Plan." *Philippine Daily Inquirer,* September 1, 2011. http://www.mb.com.ph/articles/351065/unity-earth-population-devt-last-two-parts.

Calonzo, Andreo. "Pacquiao Says Marquez KO Strengthened His Opposition to RH Bill." GMA News Online, December 13, 2012. http://www.gmanetwork.com/news/story/286164/news/nation/.

BIBLIOGRAPHY

Carpenter, Kent E., and Victor G. Springer. "The Center of the Center of Marine Shore Fish Biodiversity: The Philippine Islands." *Environmental Biology of Fishes,* vol. 72 (2005): 467–80.

Castro, Joan R., and Leona A. D'Agnes. "Fishing for Families: Reproductive Health and Integrated Coastal Management in the Philippines." *Focus on Population, Environment, and Security,* no. 15 (April 2008).

———, and Carmina Angel Aquino. "Mainstreaming Reproductive Health and Integrated Coastal Management in Local Governance: The Philippines Experience." Prepared for the CZAP conference: Cebu, Philippines, 2004. PATH Foundation Philippines.

"Catholics Criticize, Praise Aquino over Family Planning." *Sun Star Davao,* September 30, 2010. http://www.sunstar.com.ph/davao/local-news/catholics-criticize-praise -aquino-over-family-planning.

"Catholics Launch 'Anti-RH with a Smile' Campaign." GMA News, July 22, 2011.

"China Sets Up Yuan Longping Institute of Science and Technology." *People's Daily,* August 7, 2000.

"Church OKs Info Drive on Family Planning." *Philippine Daily Inquirer,* December 20, 2010.

D'Agnes, Leona A. *Overview Integrated Population and Coastal Resource Management (IPOPCORM) Approach.* PATH Foundation Philippines, January 2009.

———, Heather D'Agnes, J. Brad Schwartz, Maria Lourdes Amarillo, and Joan Castro. "Integrated Management of Coastal Resources and Human Health Yields Added Value: A Comparative Study in Palawan (Philippines)." *Environmental Conservation,* vol. 37, no. 4 (2010): 1–12.

"Demographic Trends in Philippines Marine Biodiversity Conservation Priority Areas." PATH Foundation Philippines, November 2009.

Diokno, Benjamin E. "RH Bill over the Hump." *BusinessWorld,* December 19, 2012.

Domingo, Ronnel. "Large Population May Boost Economic Growth, Says BSP: But Raising Purchasing Power Is Crucial." *Philippine Daily Inquirer,* October 24, 2010.

BIBLIOGRAPHY

Eaton, Sam. "Food for 9 Billion: Turning the Population Tide in the Philippines." *PBS NewsHour,* January 23, 2012.

Esguerra, Christian V. "Why Pacquiao Voted No Even if He's No Longer a Catholic." *Philippine Daily Inquirer,* December 14, 2012.

"EU to Infuse 35M to Support PHLs Health System Reforms." GMA News, April 15, 2011.

"Facts on Barriers to Contraceptive Use in the Philippines." Guttmacher Institute, In Brief Series, May 2010.

"Forsaken Lives: The Harmful Impact of the Philippine Criminal Abortion Ban." Center for Reproductive Rights, 2010.

Gutierrez, Jason. "Fewer Bites for Philippine Fishermen." Agence France-Presse, July 8, 2011.

Hamilton, Ruaraidh Sackville. "Agricultural Biodiversity: The Lasting Legacy of Early Farmers." *Rice Today,* October–December 2010.

Herdt, R. W., and C. Capule. *Adoption, Spread, and Production Impact of Modern Rice Varieties in Asia.* International Rice Research Institute, Los Banos, Laguna, Philippines: 1983.

IPOPCORM Monograph. "Overview, Key Lessons & Challenges." PATH Foundation Philippines, September 2007.

Javier, Luzi Ann. "Philippines May Lose 600,000 Tons Rice from Typhoon." *Bloomberg,* October 18, 2010.

Jimenez-David, Rina. "At Large: The Shadow of the A Word." *Philippine Daily Inquirer,* August 10, 2010.

Khan, Natasha, and Norman P. Aquino. "Condom Queues Incite Church Tensions in Philippines." *Bloomberg,* March 27, 2012.

Li, Jiming, Xin Yeyun, and Yuan Longping. "Hybrid Rice Technology Development: IFPRI Discussion Paper 00918." *International Food Policy Research Institute,* November 2009.

Lynch, Wyeth. "General Studies on Hybrid Rice." China National Hybrid Rice Research and Development Center, 2004.

Manson, Jamie L. "Church's Ban on Contraception Starves Families and Damages Ecosystem." *National Catholic Review,* Grace Margins (blog), February 6, 2012. http://ncronline.org/blogs.

Manthorpe, Jonathan. "Lawmakers Back Away from Family Planning Bill." *Vancouver Sun,* November 19, 2012.

Maramag, Sarah Katrina. "Overseas Filipino Nurses, Ailing Healers." *Philippine Online Chronicles,* July 10, 2010.

McDonald, Mark. "In Philippines, a Turning Point on Contraception." *New York Times,* December 18, 2012.

"Meeting Women's Contraceptive Needs in the Philippines." Guttmacher Institute, In Brief Series, no. 1, 2009.

Michael, Christopher. "C4 Rice and Hoping the Sun Can End Hunger: Tales of Plants, Evolution, Transgenics and Crisis." PhD diss., University of California, Davis, 2012. ProQuest (UMI 3540557).

"'Miracle Rice' Finding Proves We Can Never Stop Rice Breeding." International Rice Research Institute, *E! Science News, Earth & Climate,* October 8, 2010. http://esciencenews.com/articles/2010/10/08/miracle.rice.finding.proves.we.can.never .stop.rice.breeding.

Mora C., O. Aburto-Oropeza, A. Ayala Bocos, P. M. Ayotte, S. Banks, et al. "Global Human Footprint on the Linkage Between Biodiversity and Ecosystem Functioning in Reef Fishes." *PLoS Biol,* vol. 9, no. 4 (2011).

Overview Integrated Population and Coastal Resource Management (IPOPCORM) Initiative, Overview, Key Lessons and Challenges. PATH Foundation Philippines, September 2007.

"Philippine Business Supports Birth Control Despite Church." Agence France-Presse, October 26, 2010.

"Philippine Church Hits President on Contraception." Associated Press, September 29, 2010.

"The Philippine Marine Biodiversity: A Unique World Treasure." *One Ocean Information,* OneOcean.org. http://www.oneocean.org/flash/philippine_biodiversity.html.

"Philippine President Vows to Push for Enactment of Pro-Family Planning Bill." Xinhua News Agency (China), April 17, 2011.

"Philippines Says Likely to Miss UN Millennium Goals." Agence France-Presse, September 8, 2010.

"Philippines Women's Groups Call for Legalized Abortions." Channel News Asia. August 17, 2010.

"PHS Vatican Shows Force Against RH Bill." *Philippine Daily Inquirer,* September 19, 2011.

Ramos, Fidel V. "Empowering the Filipino People." Unity of Earth, Population, Dev't (Last of Two Parts). *Manila Bulletin*, February 11, 2012.

Rauhala, Emily. "More Catholic than the Pope? Manila Suburb Cracks Down on Condoms." Global Spin (blog), *Time*, April 4, 2011. http://globalspin.blogs.time.com/2011/04/04/more-catholic-than-the-pope-manila-suburb-cracks-down-on-condoms/#ixzz1n7C TbMkj.

————. "When a Country Cracks Down on Contraception: Grim Lessons from the Philippines." Global Spin (blog), *Time*, February 21, 2012. http://globalspin.blogs.time.com/2012/02/21/when-a-country-cracks-down-on-contraception-grim-lessons-from-the-philippines/#ixzz1n7DMQusS.

"Research Report: Is Emergency Obstetric Care Within the Reach of Malabon's Poor Women?" Likhaan Center for Women's Health, Inc., n.d.

Robles, Raissa. "Bishops Swim Against the Tide on Family Planning." *South China Morning Post*, August 19, 2012.

" 'Rolling Back' the Process of Overfishing: IPOPCORM Approach." Monograph Series No. 2, PATH Foundation Philippines, 2007.

Sandique-Carlos, Rhea. "Philippines Adopts Contraception Law." *Wall Street Journal*, December 29, 2012.

Singh, Susheela, et al. *Abortion Worldwide: A Decade of Uneven Progress*. New York: Guttmacher Institute, 2009.

————. *Unintended Pregnancy and Induced Abortion in the Philippines*. New York: Guttmacher Institute, 2006.

Tan, Michael, L. "Abortion: Realities and Responsibilities." Health Alert, 211. *Health Action Information Network* (Manila), January 2000.

Tulali, Carlos. "Bishops in Our Bedrooom." Philippine Legislators' Committee on Population and Development, Inc., Policy Brief, November 2009.

Walden, Bello. "Rwanda in the Pacific? Population Pressure, Development, and Conflict in the Philippines." *Philippine Daily Inquirer*, August 27, 2011.

Weiss, Kenneth R., and Sol Vanzi. "Philippine Contraceptive Bill Wins Passage." *Los Angeles Times,* December 18, 2012.

Whately, Floyd. "Bill to Expand Birth Control Is Approved in Philippines." *New York Times,* December 17, 2012.

———. "Church Officials Call on Filipinos to Campaign Against Birth Control Law." *New York Times,* December 18, 2012.

Zeigler, Dr. Robert S. "Leading Crop Scientist Warns of Potential Rice Crisis." Interview with Mike Billington and Marcia Merry Baker, *Executive Intelligence Review,* March 2, 2007: 54–63.

Chapter Ten: The Bottom

BOOKS

Murakami, Masahiro. *Managing Water for Peace in the Middle East: Alternative Strategies.* New York: United Nations University Press, 1996.

ARTICLES

Abu, Festus. "Nigeria Population to Hit 367 Million in 2050—UN." *Punch,* April 6, 2012.

Bilger, Burkhard. "The Great Oasis: Can a Wall of Trees Stop the Sahara from Spreading?" *New Yorker,* December 19, 2011.

Bongaarts, John. "Can Family Planning Programs Reduce High Desired Family Size in Sub-Saharan Africa?" *International Perspectives on Sexual and Reproductive Health,* Guttmacher Institute, vol. 37, no. 4 (December 2011).

Cleland, J., S. Bernstein, A. Ezeh, A. Faundes, A. Glasier, and J. Innis. "Family Planning: The Unfinished Agenda." Sexual and Reproductive Health Series, *Lancet,* vol. 368 (2006): 1810–27.

de Sam Lazaro, Fred. "Niger Famine and Re-greening." PBS Religion & Ethics, *NewsWeekly,* June 29, 2012.

Margulis, Jennifer. "Backstory: Are Niger's Giraffes a Fading Spot on the Horizon?" *Christian Science Monitor,* January 11, 2007.

"Niger: Experts Explain Why Malnutrition Is Recurrent." IRIN, March 15, 2010.

BIBLIOGRAPHY

"Niger: Southern Villages Emptying as Drought Bites." IRIN, March 10, 2010.

"Niger Appeals for Emergency Food Aid." Agence France-Presse, March 10, 2010.

"Niger Farmland Threatened by Locusts: Official." Agence France-Presse, June 13, 2012.

"Niger—Food Insecurity." Fact Sheet #1, Fiscal Year 2010. U.S. Agency of International Development and the Office of U.S. Foreign Disaster Assistance, March 16, 2010.

Pitman, Todd. "Niger: Once-Taboo Topic of Hunger Spoken Again." Associated Press, February 26, 2010.

————. "President's Ouster in Coup Praised in Niger." *Guardian* (UK), February 23, 2010.

Polgreen, Lydia. "In Niger, Trees and Crops Turn Back the Desert." *New York Times,* February 11, 2007.

Potts, Malcolm, Virginia Gidi, Martha Campbell, and Sarah Zureick. "Niger: Too Little, Too Late." *International Perspectives on Sexual and Reproductive Health, Guttmacher Institute,* vol. 37, no. 2 (June 2011).

Reij, Chris. "Regreening the Sahel." *Our Planet,* United Nations Environmental Programme, September 2011.

————, Gray Tappan, and Melinda Smale. "Agroenvironmental Transformation in the Sahel: Another Kind of 'Green Revolution.'" Paper prepared for the project Millions Fed: Proven Success in Agricultural Development, International Food Policy Research Institute, November 2009.

Roberts, Leslie. "9 Billion?" *Science,* vol. 333 (July 29, 2011): 540–43.

Rosenthal, Elisabeth. "Nigeria Tested by Rapid Rise in Population." *New York Times,* April 14, 2012.

Russeau, Simba. "Libya: Water Emerges as Hidden Weapon." Inter Press Service, May 27, 2011.

Werner, Louis, and Kevin Bubriski. "Seas Beneath the Sands." *Saudi Aramco World,* vol. 58, no. 1 (January/February 2007): 34–39.

World Food Programme. "Torrential Rains in Niger Lead to Prolonged Flooding and Devastated Cropland." October 2, 2012. http://www.wfp.org/node/3540/3391/ 317705.

BIBLIOGRAPHY

Chapter Eleven: The World Unraveling

BOOKS

Brown, Lester R. *World on the Edge: How to Prevent Environmental and Economic Collapse.* New York: W. W. Norton & Company, 2011.

ARTICLES

Anjum, Aliya. "Education Emergency in Pakistan." *Pakistan Observer,* April 7, 2011.

"As Pakistan's Population Soars, Contraceptives Remain a Hard Sell." December 17, 2011.

"Average Number of Children per Woman in Pakistan Declines from 6.7 to 4.1." OnePakistan News, October 21, 2011. http://pakistan .onepakistan.com/news/city/karachi/.

Baig, Khurram. "Still One of the Worst Places in the World to Be a Woman." *Express Tribune* (Pakistan), July 1, 2012.

Bano, Farida. "A Study of Physical and Major Chemical Constituents of Malir River (Within Karachi) to Determine the Extent of Pollution." Doctoral thesis, Department of Zoology, University of Karachi, 1999.

Bhatti, M. Waqar. "WWF-Pakistan Honours Nature Conservationists with Awards." *News* (Pakistan), January 11, 2013.

Brulliard, Karin. "In Pakistan, Family Planning a Hard Sell." *Washington Post,* December 15, 2011.

"Call for Greater Awareness About Contraception." *Pakistan Today,* September 27, 2011.

Constable, Pamela. "Pakistani Case Shows Limits of Women's Rights." *Washington Post,* April 25, 2011.

Cronin, Richard P. "90149: Pakistan Aid Cutoff: U.S. Nonproliferation and Foreign Policy Considerations." Foreign Affairs and National Defense Division, Congressional Research Service Reports. Updated December 6, 1996.

Daly, Herman E. "Economics in a Full World." *Scientific American,* vol. 293, no. 3 (September 2005).

Bibliography

Datta, Anil. "Population Planning Made More Acceptable Socially." *News* (Pakistan), January 20, 2012.

"Doctors in Rural Areas to Educate People on Population Control." *Pakistan Today,* January 16, 2012.

Dugger, Celia W. "Very Young Populations Contribute to Strife, Study Concludes." *New York Times,* April 4, 2007.

Ebrahim, Zofeen. "Lack of Access to Contraception, Abortion Persist." Inter Press Service, April 30, 2010.

———. "Pakistan: Controversial 'Abortion' Drug Worries Some Experts." Inter Press Service, August 10, 2010.

"Education Emergency Pakistan." The Pakistan Education Task Force. March for Education Campaign, 2011. http://www.educatione mergency.com.pk.

Fatima, Unbreen. "Baby Hatches Are Helping to Save Lives in Pakistan." *Deutsche Welle World,* April 11, 2012.

Giosana, Liviu, et al. "Fluvial Landscapes of the Harappan Civilization." *Proceedings NAS,* vol. 109, no. 26 (June 26, 2012).

Guttmacher Institute. "Abortion in Pakistan." In Brief Series, no. 2 (2009).

Hafeez, A., B. K. Mohamud, M. R. Shiekh, S. A. Shah, and R. Jooma. "Lady Health Workers Programme in Pakistan: Challenges, Achievements and the Way Forward." *Journal of the Pakistan Medical Association,* vol. 61, no. 3 (March 2011): 210–15.

Hardee, Karen. "Where's Family Planning on Climate Change Radar?" Interview by Zofeen Ebrahim. *IPS News,* May 19, 2010.

"High Population Growth Rate Affecting Economy." *Daily Times* (Pakistan), July 12, 2011.

Husain, Shahid. "Malaria Cases Have Risen by 30–35 Percent in Sindh." *News* (Pakistan), April 26, 2012. http://www.thenews .com.pk/Todays-News-4-104990-Malaria-cases-have-risen-by-30 -35-percent-in-Sindh.

———. "Salt in Wounds: Damage to the Water Flow of the Once-Mighty Indus Is Forcing Major Changes in Pakistan—and Could Lead to Conflict." *Guardian* (UK), January 14, 2003.

BIBLIOGRAPHY

Joshua, Anita. "Karachi Violence Leaves 95 Dead." *Hindu,* July 8, 2011. http://www.thehindu.com/news/international/article2211601.ece.

Khambatta, Nargish. "Agents of Change." *Gulf News,* August 21, 2009.

Khan, Faisal Raza. "Mangroves Martyrs." *Islamabad Pulse,* June 1, 2012. http://www.weeklypulse.org/details.aspx?contentID=2369 &storylist=2.

Kristof, Nicholas. "A Girl, a School, and Hope." *New York Times,* November 10, 2010.

Lall, Marie. "Creating Agents of Positive Change — The Citizens Foundation in Pakistan." The Citizens Foundation, Karachi, January 2009. http://www.tcf.org.pk/ePanel/Resources/Download Files/Publications/Category/8/36/Marie%20Lall%20Report .pdf.

"Letter: The Ticking Population Bomb." *Nation* (Pakistan), June 19, 2011.

"90,000 LHWs Working Across Country." Associated Press (Pakistan), May 25, 2010.

"Pakistan: Experts Warn of Desertification." *Right Vision News* (Pakistan), June 18, 2011.

"Pakistan: UNDP and the Youth." From the website of the United Nations Development Programme, Pakistan. http://undp.org.pk/ undp-and-the-youth.html.

"Pakistan: Urgent Need to Fill the Funding Gap for 6,000 Pregnant Women in Sindh." *Right Vision News* (Pakistan), October 12, 2011.

"Pakistan's Rape Laws Amended." *Human Rights Defender,* February/ March 2007.

"Population Explosion in Pakistan." *Business Recorder* (Pakistan), August 9, 2010.

Rauf, Saleha. "Child Protection: 'Islam Has Clear Teachings on Rights.'" *Express Tribune* (Pakistan), April 28, 2011.

Schoof, Renee. "Food Crisis Looms After Floods in Pakistan." McClatchy Newspapers, August 30, 2010.

Shah, Saeed. "U.S. Considers Funding Pakistani Dam Project, Angering India." McClatchy Newspapers, August 16, 2011. http://

www.mcclatchydc.com/2011/08/16/120878/us-considers-funding
-pakistani.html#ixzz1VF0ZkQQA.

"30% Marriages in Pakistan Fall into Child Marriage Category." *Baluchistan Times* (Pakistan), January 19, 2012.

Tran, Mark, et al. "Pakistan Flood Victims Flee Thatta After Another Levee Is Breached." *Guardian* (UK), August 27, 2010.

"UN: Pakistan's Population to Double Within 40 Years." Daily Clarity website, n.d. http://mydailyclarity.com/2009/07/un-pakistan-population-to-double-within-40 -years/.

"UNFPA Rushes Reproductive Health Supplies to Sindh as Floods Worsen." *Pakistan Press International,* September 16, 2011.

"Victims Include 115,000 Pregnant Women." *Statesman* (Pakistan), September 18, 2011.

"World Population Day: South Asia Carries 20% of World Population Burden." *Pakistan Newswire,* July 10, 2010.

Zia, Amir. "Karachi Least Environment Friendly City in Asia: Report." *News* (Pakistan), February 15, 2011. http://www.thenews.com.pk/ TodaysPrintDetail.aspx?ID=4020 &Cat=13.

Chapter Twelve: The Ayatollah Giveth and Taketh Away

BOOKS

Abbasi-Shavazi, Mohammad Jalal, Peter McDonald, and Meimanat Hosseini-Chavoshi. *The Fertility Transition in Iran: Revolution and Reproduction.* London: Springer, 2009.

Cordesman, Anthony H. *Iraq and the War of Sanctions: Conventional Threats and Weapons of Mass Destruction.* Westport, CT: Praeger, 1999.

Dunn, Eliza. *Rugs in Their Native Land.* New York: Dodd, Mead and Company, 1916.

Hiro, Dilip. *The Longest War: The Iran-Iraq Military Conflict.* New York: Routledge, 1989.

Humphreys, P. N., and E. Kahrom, *The Lion and the Gazelle: The Mammals and Birds of Iran.* Gwent, UK: Comma International Biological Systems, 1995.

BIBLIOGRAPHY

Majd, Hooman. *The Ayatollah Begs to Differ: The Paradox of Modern Iran.* New York: Anchor, 2009.

———. *The Ayatollahs' Democracy: An Iranian Challenge.* New York: W. W. Norton & Company, 2010.

ARTICLES

Abbasi-Shavazi, Mohammad Jalal. "The Fertility Revolution in Iran." *Population & Sociétés,* no. 373 (November 2001): 1–4.

———, Amir Mehryar, Gavin Jones, and Peter McDonald. "Revolution, War and Modernization: Population Policy and Fertility Change in Iran." *Journal of Population Research,* vol. 19, no. 1 (2002): 25–46.

———, Meimanat Hosseini-Chavoshi, and Peter McDonald. "The Path to Below Replacement Fertility in the Islamic Republic of Iran." *Asia-Pacific Population Journal,* vol. 22, no. 2 (August 2007): 91–112.

———, S. Philip Morgan, Meimanat Hossein-Chavoshi, and Peter McDonald. "Family Change and Continuity in the Islamic Republic of Iran: Birth Control Use Before the First Pregnancy." *Journal of Marriage and Family,* vol. 71, no. 5 (December 2009): 1309–24.

"Ahmadinejad to Iran's Rulers: Keep Coed Colleges." *New York Times,* July 10, 2011.

Amjadi, Maryam Ala. "Iranian Women Shoulder to Shoulder with Men." *Tehran Times,* August 18, 2011.

Austin, Greg. "IAEA Confusion on Iran Is Not Helpful." *News Europe/EastWest Institute,* November 13, 2011.

Barford, Vanessa. "Iran's 'Diagnosed Transsexuals.'" BBC News, February 25, 2008.

Boms, Nir, and Shayan Arya. "Iran's Environmental Ticking Bomb." *Today's Shazam,* September 14, 2011. http://www.todayszaman.com/.

Brown, Lester R. "Smart Family Planning Improves Women's Health and Cuts Poverty." International Press Service, for Guardian Development Network, April 14, 2011.

Camron, Michael Amin. "Propaganda and Remembrance: Gender, Education, and 'The Women's Awakening' of 1936." *Iranian Studies,* vol. 32, no. 3 (1999): 351–86.

Chaulia, Sreeram. "Go Forth and Multiply?" *Financial Express,* July 29, 2010.

Cincotta, Richard. "Iran: Taking Aim at Low Fertility and Women's Mobility." Stimson Center, October 15, 2012. http://www.stimson .org/experts/richard-cincotta.

———. "Prospects for Ahmadinejad's Call for More Rapid Population Growth in Iran." Stimson Center, November 13, 2006. http://www.stimson.org/experts/richard -cincotta.

Dehghanpisheh, Babak. "Smugglers for the State." *Newsweek,* July 10, 2010.

"Dr. Mohammad Mossadegh Biography: Prime Minister of Iran, 1951–1953." The Mossadegh Project website. http://www.moham madmossadegh.com/biography.

Erfani, Amir. "Abortion in Iran: What Do We Know?" *Population Studies Centre Discussion Papers Series,* vol. 22, no. 1, article 1 (January 2, 2008). http://ir.lib.uwo .ca/pscpapers/vol22/iss1/1.

Femia, Francesco, and Caitlin Werrell. "Socio-Environmental Impacts of Iran's Disappearing Lake Urmia." The Center for Climate & Security website, May 18, 2012. http://climateandsecurity.org/ 2012/05/18.

Ferrigno, Jane G. "Glaciers of the Middle East and Africa—Glaciers of Iran," in U.S. Geological Survey, professional paper 1386-G-2: G31-G47, edited by Richard S. Williams Jr. and Jane G. Ferrigno.

Ghasemi, Shapour. "History of Iran: Pahlavi Dynasty." Iran Chamber Society website, History of Iran. http://www.iranchamber.com/ history/pahlavi.

Girgis, Monique. "Veiling" from Women in Pre-Revolutionary, Revolutionary and Post-Revolutionary Iran, 1996. Iran Chamber Society website. http://www.iranchamber .com/society/articles.

Hersh, Seymour M. "Iran and the I.A.E.A." in Daily Comment (blog), *The New Yorker.* November 18, 2011. http://www.newyorker.com/

online/blogs/comment/2011/11/iran-and-the-iaea.html#ixzz2NeT
46sEd.

Higgins, Andrew. "A Feared Force Roils Business in Iran." *Wall Street Journal,* October 14, 2006.

Hoodfar, Homa. "Volunteer Health Workers in Iran as Social Activists: Can 'Governmental Non-Governmental Organisations' Be Agents of Democratisation?" Occasional Paper No. 10, Women Living Under Muslim Laws, December 1998.

Ibrahim Al Isa, Khalil. "Iraqi Scientist Reports on German, Other Help for Iraq Chemical Weapons Program." *Al Zaman* (London), December 1, 2003.

"Implementation of the NPT Safeguards Agreement and Relevant Provisions of Security Council Resolutions in the Islamic Republic of Iran: Report by the Director General." International Atomic Energy Agency, November 8, 2011.

"Iran: The People Take Over." *Time,* August 31, 1953.

"Iran Environment in Grave Danger." Press TV (Tehran), April 30, 2010.

"Iran Experiencing Population Decline, Growing Old." Mehr News Agency (Tehran), July 9, 2011. http://www.mehrnews.com/en.

"Iran Gives Up Birth Control Program to Boost Population." *Al Arabiya,* August 3, 2012.

"The Iranian Parliament Failed to Take an Action to Save Lake Urmia, Which Is Drying Up Rapidly." Lake Urmia Conservation Institute website, August 27, 2011. http://saveurmia.com/main/2011/08/27.

"Iran Revolutionary Guards Officers Nabbed for Child Prostitution." *Iran Focus,* April 11, 2005. http://www.iranfocus.com.

"Iran to Pay for Babies to Boost Population." *Boston Globe,* July 28, 2010.

"Iran/United Nations: Iran Is Blessed with Dynamic Young Population of 17-M—UNFPA." *Thai Press Reports,* August 12, 2010.

Kadivar, H. "Overseas Medical Elective Assessment: Primary Health Care and Family Planning in the Islamic Republic of Iran." Accessed at: http://keck.usc.edu/en/About/Administrative_Offices/ Global_Health_Scholars_Program/~/media/Docs/Offices/ Global%20Health/H_Kadivar_Iran.doc.

Kahrom, Esmail. "Wildlife Conservation in Iran." *Asian Affairs,* vol. 31, no.1 (2000): 49–56.

Karimi, Nasser. "Iran Urges Baby Boom." Associated Press, July 29, 2012.

Katzman, Kenneth. "Iran: U.S. Concerns and Policy Responses." Congressional Research Service CRS Report for Congress, September 5, 2012.

Kerr, Paul K. "Iran's Nuclear Program: Tehran's Compliance with International Obligations." Congressional Research Service CRS Report for Congress, September 18, 2012.

Khalaj, Monavar. "Iranians Resist Call to Boost Population." *Financial Times,* July 23, 2012.

Khosravifard, Sam. "Iran's Wildlife Under Threat." *Iran IRN,* no. 47, Institute for War & Peace Reporting, August 6, 2010. http://iwpr .net/report-news.

Koushafar, Mohammad, Farhad Amini, and Shiva Azadipour. "The Role of Environmental NGOs in Protection Zayanderood River in Isfahan." *International NGO Journal,* vol. 2, no. 2 (February 2007): 27–29. Available online at: http://www .academicjournals .org/INGOJ 27–29.

Lal, Vinay. "Iran's Revolution and the Global Politics of Resistance." *Economic & Political Weekly,* April 5, 2012.

Linzer, Dafna. "U.N. Finds No Nuclear Bomb Program in Iran." *Washington Post,* November 16, 2004.

Lutz, Wolfgang, Jesús Crespo Cuaresma, and Mohammad Jalal Abbasi-Shavazi. "Demography, Education and Democracy: Global Trends and the Case of Iran." Interim Report Paper, International Institute for Applied Systems Analysis, June 24, 2009.

MacFarquahar, Neil. "With Iran Population Boom, Vasectomy Receives Blessing." *New York Times,* September 8, 1996.

Malekafzali, H. "Primary Health Care in the Rural Area of the Islamic Republic of Iran." *Iranian Journal of Public Health,* vol. 38, supplement 1 (2009): 69–70.

Mehr, Arya, and Shahanshah. "Mohammad Reza Shah Pahlavi." Iran Chamber Society website, History of Iran. http://www.iranchamber .com/history/mohammad_rezashah/ mohammad_rezashah.php.

Bibliography

Mehryar, Amir H., Akbar Aghajanian, Shirin Ahmad-Nia, Muhammad Mirzae, and Mohsen Naghavi. "Primary Health Care System, Narrowing of Rural-Urban Gap in Health Indicators, and Rural Poverty Reduction: The Experience of Iran." Paper accepted for presentation at the XXV General Population Conference of the International Union for the Scientific Study of Population, Tours, France. July 2005.

Mirrazavi, Firouzeh, ed. "The Removing of Hijab in Iran." *Iran Review,* February 7, 2013.

Mirzaie, Mohammad. "Swings in Fertility Limitation in Iran." Working Papers in Demography, no. 72. Australian National University, Research School of Social Sciences, 1998.

Namakydoust, Azadeh. "Covered in Messages: The Veil as a Political Tool." *Iranian,* May 8, 2003.

Obermeyer, Carla Makhlouf. "A Cross-Cultural Perspective on Reproductive Rights." *Human Rights Quarterly,* vol. 17, no. 2 (May 1995): 366–81.

"Overpopulation of Tehran Will Cause Ecological Ruin." Social Desk, *Tehran Times,* October 24, 2010.

PARSA Community Foundation. "Women Society Against Environmental Pollution (WSAEP)," in "In the Spotlight: Environmental Activists and NGOs." http://www .parsacf.org/Page/242.

Pengra, Bruce. "The Drying of Iran's Lake Urmia and Its Environmental Consequences." *UNEP Global Environmental Alert Service,* February 2012. www.unep.org/pdf/GEAS_Feb2012.pdf.

Peterson, Scott. "Ahmadinejad Calls on Iranian Girls to Marry at 16; Iranian President Mahmoud Ahmadinejad's Comment Is His Latest Effort to Create a Baby Boom, Reversing Iran's Lauded Model of Family Planning." *Christian Science Monitor* (U.S.), November 22, 2010.

Radio Zamaneh. "Fewer Female Students Admitted to Iranian University." Payvand Iran News, August 9, 2012.

"Rate of Population Decrease in Iran Is Faster Than Other Countries." Mehr News Agency (Tehran), July 29, 2012.

Risen, James. "Secrets of History: The C.I.A. in Iran—A Special Report; How a Plot Convulsed Iran in '53 (and in '79)." *New York Times,* April 16, 2000.

———, and Mark Mazzetti. "U.S. Agencies See No Move by Iran to Build a Bomb." *New York Times,* February 24, 2012.

Roudi, Farzaneh. "A Perspective on Fertility Behavior of Iranian Women." Research paper submitted to IUSSP International Population Conference, Morocco, 2009. iussp2009.princeton.edu/download.aspx?submissionId=93104.

Salehi-Isfahani, Djavad, M. Jalal Abbasi-Shavazi, and Meimanat Hosseini-Chavoshi. "Family Planning and Rural Fertility Decline in Iran: A Study in Program Evaluation." Working paper, Meimanat Hosseini-Chavoshi Ministry of Health and Medical Education Iran, October 2008.

Shamshiri-Milani, Hourieh, Abolghasem Pourreza, and Feizollah Akbari. "Knowledge and Attitudes of a Number of Iranian Policy-Makers Towards Abortion." *Journal of Reproduction and Infertility,* vol. 11, no. 3 (October/December 2010): 189–95.

Sherwell, Philip, and Colin Freeman. "Iran's Revolutionary Guards Cash In After a Year of Suppressing Dissent." *Telegraph* (UK), June 12, 2010.

Slackman, Michael. "Hard-Line Force Extends Grip over a Splintered Iran." *New York Times,* July 20, 2009.

Spindle, Bill. "As Tehran and West Face Off, Iranians Bear Down." *Wall Street Journal,* March 10, 2012.

Tait, Robert. "Iran Scraps Birth Control and Aims for a Baby Boom." *Daily Telegraph* (UK), August 2, 2012.

———. "Iran Scraps State-Sponsored Birth Control Policy." *The Daily Beast,* August 3, 2012. http://www.thedailybeast.com/articles/2012/08/03/iran-scraps-state-sponsored-birth-control-policy.html.

Tarmann, Allison. "Iran Achieves Replacement-Level Fertility." *Population Today,* vol. 30, no. 4 (May/June 2002): 8–9.

Tomlinson, Hugh. "Revolutionary Guard 'Running Iran Drug Trade.'" *Times* (London), November 18, 2011.

Bibliography

"UN Sanctions Against Iranians in Arms Smuggling." *Agence France-Presse*, April 21, 2012.

Warrick, Joby. "IAEA Says Foreign Expertise Has Brought Iran to Threshold of Nuclear Capability." *Washington Post,* November 6, 2011.

Wright, Robin. "Iran's Population-Control Programs Are User-Friendly." *Los Angeles Times,* May 10, 1998.

Zia-Ebrahimi, Reza. "Self-Orientalization and Dislocation: The Uses and Abuses of the 'Aryan' Discourse in Iran." *Iranian Studies,* vol. 44, no. 4 (2011): 445–72.

Chapter Thirteen: Shrink and Prosper

Books

Daily, Gretchen C., and Katherine Ellison. *The New Economy of Nature: The Quest to Make Conservation Profitable.* Washington, DC: Island Press, 2002.

Daly, Herman E. *Beyond Growth: The Economics of Sustainable Development.* Boston: Beacon Press, 1996.

————, and Joshua Farley. *Ecological Economics.* Washington, DC: Island Press, 2010.

Dyson, Tim. *Population and Development: The Demographic Transition.* London: Zed Books, 2006.

Eggleston, Karen, and Shripad Tuljapurkar. *Aging Asia: The Economic and Social Implications of Rapid Demographic Change in China, Japan, and South Korea.* Washington, DC: Brookings Institution Press, 2010.

Heinberg, Richard. *The End of Growth: Adapting to Our New Economic Reality.* Gabriola Island, BC: New Society Publishers, 2011.

Jackson, Tim. *Prosperity Without Growth: Economics for a Finite Planet.* New York: Earthscan Publications, 2009.

Latouche, Serge. *Farewell to Growth.* Cambridge: Polity, 2009.

Matsutani, Akihiko. *Shrinking-Population Economics: Lessons from Japan.* Tokyo: International House of Japan, 2006.

BIBLIOGRAPHY

Pineda, Cecile. *Devil's Tango: How I Learned the Fukushima Step by Step.* San Antonio, TX: Wings Press, 2010.

ARTICLES

Ackerman, Frank, Elizabeth A. Stanton, Stephen J. DeCanio, et al. "The Economics of 350: The Benefits and Costs of Climate Stabilization." Economics for Equity and Environment, October 2009. www.e3network.org.

Alpert, Emily. "Government Incentives Fail to Reverse Japan's Population Decline." *Chicago Tribune,* August 14, 2012.

Alvarez, Robert. "Why Fukushima Is a Greater Disaster than Chernobyl and a Warning Sign for the US." *Institute for Policy Studies,* April 24, 2012.

Arrow, Kenneth J., Maureen L. Cropper, George C. Eads, Robert W. Hahn, Lester B. Lave, Roger G. Noll, Paul R. Portney, Milton Russell, Richard Schmalensee, V. Kerry Smith, and Robert N. Stavins. "Is There a Role for Benefit-Cost Analysis in Environmental, Health, and Safety Regulation?" *Science,* New Series, vol. 272, no. 5259 (April 12, 1996): 221–22.

Arrow, Kenneth J., Alain Bensoussan, Qi Feng, and Suresh P. Sethi. "Optimal Savings and the Value of Population." *Proceedings of the National Academy of Science,* vol. 104, no. 47 (November 20, 2007): 18421–26.

Arrow, Kenneth J., Bert Bolin, Robert Costanza, et al. "Economic Growth, Carrying Capacity, and the Environment." *Science,* New Series, vol. 268, no. 5210 (April 28, 1995): 520–21. http://www.jstor.org/stable/2886637. Accessed: 10/04/2010.

Astor, Maggie. "Goldman Sachs Sets Aside $10 Billion for Bonuses While Hemorrhaging Money." *International Business Times,* October 21, 2011.

"Average Age of New Mothers in Japan Tops 30 for 1st Time." Jiji Press Ticker Service (Japan), June 5, 2012.

Bird, Winifred. "Japan's Creeping Natural Disaster." *Japan Times,* August 23, 2009.

BIBLIOGRAPHY

Botelho, Greg. "Six Months Post-Fukushima, Weighing Costs, Risks Key to Nuclear Debate." CNN, September 10, 2011.

Brown, Lester R. "Learning from China: Why the Existing Economic Model Will Fail." Earth Policy Institute, September 8, 2011. www.earth-policy.org/data_highlights/ 2011/highlights18.

Burch, Thomas K. "Induced Abortion in Japan Under Eugenic Protection Law of 1948." *Biodemography and Social Biology*, vol. 2, no. 3 (1955): 140–51.

Clark, Matthew. "Germany's Angela Merkel: Multiculturalism Has 'Utterly Failed.'" *The Christian Science Monitor*, October 17, 2010.

Connolly, Kate. "Angela Merkel Declares Death of German Multiculturalism." *Guardian* (UK), October 17, 2010. http://www.guardian .co.uk/world/2010/oct/17/angela-merkel-germany-multiculturalism -failures.

"Cuban Population Declines, Numbers of Homes Increases." Fox News Latino, Efe, December 7, 2012.

Daily, Gretchen C., et al. "Ecology: The Value of Nature and the Nature of Value." *Science*, vol. 289, no. 5478 (July 2000): 395–96.

Daly, Herman E. "A Steady-State Economy: A Failed Growth Economy and a Steady-State Economy Are Not the Same Thing; They Are the Very Different Alternatives We Face." Presented to the Sustainable Development Commission, UK, April 24, 2008.

———. "Economics in a Full World." *Scientific American*, vol. 293, no. 3 (September 2005).

———. "Population and Economics: A Bioeconomic Analysis." *Population and Environment: A Journal of Interdisciplinary Studies*, vol. 12, no. 3 (Spring 1991): 257–63.

Das, Satyajit. "A World Without Growth Is a Possibility." *Global Finance Stratagy News*, August 31, 2011. http://www.gfsnews. com/article/2842/1/A_world_without _growth_Is_a_possibility.

Dasgupta, Partha. "Nature in Economics." *Environmental and Resource Economics*, vol. 39 (2008):1–7. doi: 10.1007/s10640-007-9178-4.

———. "Population, Consumption and Resources: Ethical Issues." *Ecological Economics*, vol. 24 (1998): 139–52.

———. "Regarding Optimum Population." *Journal of Political Philosophy,* vol. 13, no. 4 (2005): 414–42.

Da-ye, Kim. "Population Decrease to Stunt Korea's GDP." *Korea Times,* November 3, 2010.

"Doomsday Demographics." *Washington Times,* November 27, 2004.

Dyson, Tim. "On Development, Demography and Climate Change: The End of the World as We Know It?" *Population and Environment,* vol. 27, no. 2 (2005): 117–49.

Eberstadt, Nicholas. "Japan Shrinks: Many Nations Have Aging Populations, but None Can Quite Match Japan." *Wilson Quarterly* (Spring 2012): 30–37.

———. "Russia's Demographic Straightjacket." *SAIS Review,* vol. 24, no. 2 (Summer–Fall 2004): 9–25.

———. "Russia, the Sick Man of Europe." *Public Interest,* no. 158 (Winter 2005): 3–20.

"Economic Growth Cannot Continue." BBC News. January 28, 2010. Access at: http://news.bbc.co.uk/2/hi/science/nature/8478770.stm.

Farmer, James. "The US: Living in a Lower Population Growth Environment." *IFA Magazine,* January 6, 2012. http://www.ifamagazine.com/news.

Farrell, Paul B. "A 20-Rule Manifesto for New No-Growth Economics; Commentary: Classical Economics Is Fatally Flawed." *MarketWatch,* August 30, 2011. http://www.marketwatch.com/story/.

———. "Population Bomb: 9 Billion March to WWIII." *MarketWatch,* June 28, 2011. http://www.marketwatch.com/story/population-bomb-9-billion-march-to-wwiii -2011-06-28.

———. "Why Big-Money Men Ignore World's Biggest Problem." *MarketWatch,* October 11, 2011.

Filipo, Fabrice, and Francois Schneider, eds. Proceedings of the First International Conference on Economic De-growth for Ecological Sustainability and Social Equity, Paris, April 18–19, 2008.

Freeland, Chrystia. "Demographics Putting a Squeeze on the Debt Dilemma." Reuters, August 1, 2011.

Ghimire, Bhumika. "Germany: Population Decline and the Economy." Suite101 .com, February 22, 2011. http://suite101.com/article.

Goulder, Lawrence H., and Robert N. Stavins. "Eye on the Future." *Nature,* vol. 419 (October 17, 2002): 673–74. www.nature.com/nature.

Graham, James. "Japan's Economic Expansion into Manchuria and China in World War Two." Historyorb.com, May 2004. http://www.historyorb.com/asia/japan _economic_expansion.php.

Harrop, Froma. "Birthrates Did Not Doom Japan." *The Leave Chronicle,* March 22, 2012. http://www.theleafchronicle.com/article/20120323.

Hasegawa, Kyoko. "Japan Faces 'Extinction' in 1,000 Years." Agence France-Presse, May 11, 2012.

Hayashi, Yuka. "Quake-Hit Area Was Already Reeling," *Wall Street Journal,* March 11, 2011.

Heinberg, Richard. "Gross National Happiness." *MuseLetter,* no. 232, September 2011.

———. "Welcome to the Post-Growth Economy." *MuseLetter,* no. 232, September 2011.

"HIV/AIDS in Russia & Eurasia." Center for Strategic and International Studies website, Russia and Eurasia Past Projects. http://csis.org/program/hivaids.

"Immigrants Boost German Population." *The Local,* July 2, 2012.

Jackson, Tim. "Prosperity Without Growth? — The Transition to a Sustainable Economy." Sustainable Development Commission, March 2009.

Jacobson, Brad. "The Worst Yet to Come? Why Nuclear Experts Are Calling Fukushima a Ticking Time-Bomb." AlterNet, May 7, 2012.

Jamail, Dahr. "Fukushima: It's Much Worse Than You Think." Al-Jazeera English, June 16, 2011.

James, Kyle. "No Brakes on Germany's Population Freefall." *Deutsche Welle,* August 17, 2006.

"Japan Has 23.3% Aging Population in 2011: Gov't." Xinhua News Agency (China). April 17, 2012.

"Japanese Women Fall Behind Hong Kong in Longevity." BBC News, July 26, 2012.

BIBLIOGRAPHY

"Japan Revises Up Long-Term Fertility Rate Forecast." Jiji Press Ticker Service (Japan). January 30, 2012.

"Japan's Population Declines for the 3rd Straight Year." Xinhua News Agency (China). August 7, 2012.

"Japan's Population to Shrink About 30% to 86.7 Mil. by 2060." Japan Economic Newswire, January 30, 2012.

"Japan to Test-Drill for Seabed 'Burning Ice.'" Agence France-Presse, July 26, 2011.

"Japan Vows to Continue Nuclear Plant Exports." Agence France-Presse, August 5, 2011.

Johnson, Eric. "Kansai Chiefs Accept 'Limited' Reactor Restart: Even Hashimoto Caves Amid Intense Lobbying, Now Faces Public Ire." *Japan Times,* June 1, 2012.

Kayler-Thomson, Wayne, and Darin Ritchie. "OP-ED: Demographic Debate—It's Now or Never." *Age* (Australia), May 20, 2011.

Kenny, Charles. "An Aging Population May Be What the World Needs." *Bloomberg Businessweek,* February 7, 2013.

Krugman, Paul, Krugman & Co. "Japan's Horror Story Not So Scary After All." Op-Ed, *Truthout,* October 1, 2010.

"Love Is in the Air in Singapore." *Destinations of the World News,* August 5, 2012. Accessed at http://www.dotwnews.com/focus/love-Is-in-the-air-in-singapore.

Mann, Donald. "A No-Growth, Steady-State Economy Must Be Our Goal." Position paper for Negative Population Growth Inc., August 2002.

Mauricio, Vicente. "La Población Cubana Decrece Por Tercer Año Consecutivo." *El País,* June 1, 2008.

McCurry, Justin. "Japan: Below-Par Birth Rate from Fewer Marriages Bucks World Trend and Accelerates Decline." *Guardian* (UK), October 26, 2011.

Merkel, Angela. "Multiculturalism Utterly Failed in Germany." YouTube video, Posted by RussiaToday, October 17, 2010. http://www.youtube.com/watch?v=UKG76HF24_k&playnext=1&list=PL50883A09779FEA59&feature=results_video.

BIBLIOGRAPHY

Mohr, Mark, ed. "Japan's Declining Population: Clearly a Problem, but What's the Solution?" Asia Program Special Report No. 141, Woodrow Wilson International Center for Scholars, July 2008.

Moore, Tristana. "Baby Gap: Germany's Birth Rate Hits Historic Low." *Time,* May 23, 2010. http://www.time.com/time/world/article.

Muzuhashi. "Hay Fever." Muzuhashi (blog), August 3, 2012. http://www.muzuhashi.com.

Normile, Dennis. "The Upside of Downsizing." *Science,* vol. 333, no. 6042 (July 2011): 547. doi: 10.1126/science.333.6042.547.

Oiwa, Keibo. "Nuked and X-rayed." Keibo Oiwa (blog), April 8, 2011. http://keibooiwa .sblo.jp/article/44193716.html.

Oltermann, Philip. "Merkel's Own Goal." *Guardian* (UK), October 17, 2010.

Onishi, Norimitsu. "Japanese, in Shortage, Willingly Ration Watts." *New York Times,* July 28, 2011.

Panchaud, Christine, Susheela Singh, Dina Feivelson, and Jacqueline E. Darroch. "Sexually Transmitted Diseases Among Adolescents in Developed Countries." *Family Planning Perspectives,* vol. 32, no. 1 (January/February 2000).

Petersen, Freya. "Population Clock Shows Japanese Face Extinction in 1000 Years." *GlobalPost,* May 13, 2012.

Petrosian, Kristine. "AIDS Explodes in Russia—HIV Rate 'Fastest' in the World." Russiatoday.com. http://www.russiatoday.com/rusjournal.

Piper, David. "Lack of Babies Could Mean the Extinction of the Japanese People." FoxNews.com, May 11, 2012.

Rees, William E. "Toward a Sustainable World Economy." Presented at the Institute for New Economic Thinking Annual Conference, Bretton Woods, NH, April 8–11, 2011.

Retherford, Robert D., and Naohiro Ogawa. "Japan's Baby Bust: Causes, Implications, and Policy Responses." East-West Center Working Papers, Population and Health Series. No. 118, April 2005.

"Reversing the Population Decline." *Japan Times,* June 19, 2012.

Rodriguez, Andrea. "Cuba's Aging Population Will Test Economic Reform." *Associated Press*, August 7, 2012.

Romm, Joe. "Jeremy Grantham Must-Read, 'Time to Wake Up: Days of Abundant Resources and Falling Prices Are Over Forever.'" Thinkprogress.org, May 2, 2011. http://thinkprogress.org/romm/2011/05/02.

Ryall, Julian. "Japan's Population Has Contracted at the Fastest Rate Since at Least 1947." *Telegraph* (UK), January 4, 2012.

————. "Japan's Vanishing Villages; Gradual Depopulation Has Left Rural Districts Teetering on Extinction." *Straits Times* (Singapore), May 21, 2012.

Sharp, Andy. "Japan's Population Declines by Record in Challenge for Growth." *Bloomberg Businessweek,* April 17, 2012. http://www.businessweek.com/news/2012-04-17/japan-s-population-declined-by-largest-ever-0-dot-2-percent-last-year.

Sherman, Janette D., and Josephe Mango. "A 35% Spike in Infant Mortality in Northwest Cities Since Meltdown: Is the Dramatic Increase in Baby Deaths in the US a Result of Fukushima Fallout?" *Counter Punch,* weekend edition, June 10, 2011. Access at: http://www.counterpunch.org/sherman06102011.html.

Singapore government's Baby Bonus Scheme, website: http://www.babybonus.gov.sg/bbss/html/index.html.

Smith, Ron. "Population, Debt Problems So Big, They Defy Solutions." *Baltimore Sun,* July 18, 2011.

Stewart, Heather, and Phillip Inman. "Age of Austerity Set to Last for Decades: Key Factor Is the Rising Cost of Health Care for an Ageing Population." *Guardian* (UK), July 22, 2011.

Sukhdev, Pavan. "The Corporate Climate Overhaul: The Rules of Business Must Be Changed if the Planet Is to Be Saved." *Nature,* vol. 486 (June 7, 2012): 27–28.

Takahashi, Junko. "Abstinencia a la Japonesa: Crisis Sexual en el País del Sol Naciente." *El Mundo,* April 27, 2008.

Takeuchi, Kazuhiko. "Rebuilding the Relationship Between People and Nature: The Satoyama Initiative." *Ecological Research,* vol. 25, no. 5 (2010): 891–97.

BIBLIOGRAPHY

Tavernise, Sabrina. "Dip in Birth Rates Reflects Recession, Report Suggests." *New York Times,* October 13, 2011.

United Nations, Department of Economic and Social Affairs, Population Division. *World Population to 2300.* New York: United Nations, 2004.

Wehner, Mike. "Sushi-Making Robots Can Crank Out Tasty Fish Rolls 24 Hours a Day." Today in Tech (blog), Tecca, Yahoo! News, April 6, 2012.

"Whose Lost Decade?" *Economist* (UK), November 19, 2011. http://www.economist .com/node/21538745.

Yamada, Takao. "Weighing Economic Growth Against Nuclear Risks Makes No Sense." *Mainichi Daily News* (Japan), August 1, 2011.

Yasunari, Teppei J., Andreas Stohl, Ryugo S. Hayano, John F. Burkhart, Sabine Eckhardt, and Tetsuzo Yasunari. "Cesium-137 Deposition and Contamination of Japanese Soils Due to the Fukushima Nuclear Accident." *Proceedings of the National Academy of Sciences,* vol. 108, no. 49 (December 2011): 1530–34. www.pnas.org/cgi/doi/10.1073/pnas.1112058108.

"Young Japanese Losing Sex Drive." Agence France-Presse, January 14, 2011.

Chapter Fourteen: Tomorrow

BOOKS

Boo, Katherine. *Behind the Beautiful Forevers: Life, Death, and Hope in a Mumbai Undercity.* New York: Random House, Inc., 2012.

Brown, Lester R. *Outgrowing the Earth: The Security Challenge in an Age of Falling Water Tables and Rising Temperatures.* Boca Raton, FL: CRC Press, 2012.

Human Development Report 2005: Kerala. Thiruvananthapuram, Kerala, India: Centre for Development Studies, Government of Kerala, 2006.

McKibben, Bill. *Deep Economy.* New York: Times Books, 2007.

Minahan, James B. *Ethnic Groups of South Asia and the Pacific: An Encyclopedia.* Santa Barbara, CA: ABC-CLIO, 2012.

Bibliography

Sharma, Kalpana. *Rediscovering Dharavi: Stories from Asia's Largest Slum.* New York: Penguin Books, 2000.

Articles

Ahuja, Charanjit. "Water Table Dips in Punjab, Haryana." *Financial Express,* September 2, 2012.

"Annual Estimates of Total Fertility Rate by Residence, India and Bigger States, 2005–10." National Family Health Survey, International Institute of Population Sciences, Mumbai. April 10, 2012. Accessed at: planningcommission.nic.in/data/datatable/0904/tab_137.pdf.

"Appeals for Sanjay Dutt, but Should He Go Free?" *Hindustan Times,* March 24, 2013.

Bagchi, Suvojit. "Punjab suicides cast shadow on polls." BBC News, April 12, 2009.

Bedi, Rahul. "Youth Drug Addiction Crisis Ravages Punjab's Heartlands." June 17, 2010. http://www.sikhphilosophy.net/hard-talk.

Central Bureau of Investigation (India). "Bombay Bomb Blast Cases." http://cbi.nic .in/fromarchives/bombayblast/mumblast.php.

Chavan, Shri S. B., Minister of Home Affairs. "Bomb Blast in Bombay." April 21, 1993. http://parliamentofindia.nic.in/ls/lsdeb/ls10/ses6/0521049301.htm.

Chu, Henry, and Mark Magnie. "For Muslims in India, an Uneasy Calm." *Los Angeles Times,* December 14, 2008.

"Dr. Gurcharan Singh Kalkat." Accessed at: pbplanning.gov.in/pdf/Biodata%20GS %20Kalkat.pdf.

"Farmer suicides: NGO points to Punjab reporting fewer numbers." *Times of India,* December 30, 2011.

Ferris, David. "Asia's Megacities Pose a Stark Environmental Challenge." *Forbes,* August 31, 2012.

Goldenberg, Suzanne. "Where a Baby Is Born Every 2 Seconds." *Guardian* (UK), Saturday 14, 1999.

Gupta, Shankar Prasad. "Forest Tenure Issues in Terai of Nepal: Understanding the Present Management Regimes." A Term Paper Report on Forestry and Wildlife. Kathmandu University, 2011.

Bibliography

Gwatkin, Davidson R. "Political Will and Family Planning: The Implications of India's Emergency Experience." *Population and Development Review,* vol. 5, no. 1 (March 1979): 29–59.

"India Postpones Population Stabilization Target by 15 Years." Merinews (India), May 6, 2012.

Jain, R. K., N. B. Gouda, V. K. Sharma, T. N. Dubey, A. Shende, R. Malik, and G. Tiwari. "Esophageal Complications Following Aluminium Phosphide Ingestion: An Emerging Issue Among Survivors of Poisoning." *Dysphagia,* vol. 25, no. 4 (December 2010): 271–76.

John, Mary E. "Feminism, Poverty and Globalization: An Indian View." *Inter-Asia Cultural Studies,* vol. 3, no. 3 (2002).

Kaur, Naunidhi. "Mumbai: A Decade After Riots." *Frontline,* vol. 20, no.14, July 5, 2003.

Kumar, Siddhartha. "Unwanted Daughters." Deutsche Presse-Agentur, April 18, 2012.

Lewis, Clara. "Dharavi in Mumbai Is No Longer Asia's Largest Slum." *Times of India,* July 6, 2011.

Marquand, Robert. "Six Billion People and a Countertrend: Literate Women in India's Kerala Help Hold Population Growth Nearly Flat." *Christian Science Monitor,* October 12, 1999.

Mathew, E. T. "Growth of Literacy in Kerala: State Intervention, Missionary Initiatives and Social Movements." *Economic and Political Weekly,* vol. 34, no. 39 (September 25–October 1, 1999): 2811–20.

"Methane Gas from Cows: The Proof Is in the Feces." ScienceDaily, June 7, 2011. http://www.sciencedaily.com/releases/2011/06/110606112822.htm.

"Mumbai FY09 Tax Revenue May Miss Target." *Economic Times,* December 16, 2008.

Murali, R., Ashish Bhalla, Dalbir Singh, and Surjit Singh. "Acute Pesticide Poisoning: 15 Years Experience of a Large North-West Indian Hospital." *Clinical Toxicology,* vol. 47, no. 1 (2009): 35–38.

Nag, Kingshuk. "Smaller States a Recipe for Disaster." *Times of India,* June 29, 2009.

Naidoo, G. V., R. Cuthbert, R. E. Green, D. J. Pain, et al. "Removing the Threat of Diclofenac to Critically Endangered Asian Vultures."

PLoS Biol, vol. 4, no. 3 (2006). e66. doi:10.1371/journal.pbio .0040066.

Narayan, Shoba. "It's Mumbai, Yaar!" *Condé Nast Traveler,* October 2009.

"Punjab's Killing Fields." *India Today,* April 15, 2010.

"Ruminant Livestock," U.S. Environmental Protection Agency. http:// www.epa.gov/rlep.

Sekar, Rukmini. "Interview with Sugatha Kumari." *New Internationalist Magazine,* January 1996.

Sen, Amartya. "Capitalism Beyond the Crisis." *New York Review of Books,* March 26, 2009.

Shwartz, Mark. "Global Bird Populations Face Dramatic Decline in Coming Decades, Study Predicts." *Proceedings of the National Academy of Sciences,* online early edition, December 7, 2004.

Singh, D., I. Jit, and S. Tyagi. "Changing Trends in Acute Poisoning in Chandigarh Zone: A 25-Year Autopsy Experience from a Tertiary Care Hospital in Northern India." *American Journal of Forensic Medical Pathology,* vol. 20, no. 2 (June 1999): 203–10.

Sinha, Kounteya. "Average Indian's Life Expectancy up 4.6 Years." *Times of India,* October 2, 2012.

"The Situation of Children in India: A Profile." United Nations Children's Fund (UNICEF), May 2011. http://www.unicef.org/sitan/ files/SitAn_India_May_2011.pdf.

Srivastava, Vivek, Mumtaz Ansari, Somprakas Basu, Damayanti Agrawal, T. K. Lahiri, and Anand Kumar. "Colonic Conduit for Esophageal Bypass in Celphos-Induced Tracheoesophageal Fistula: Our Experience of Two Cases." *International Journal of Colorectal Disease,* vol. 24, no. 6 (2009): 727–28.

Stephenson, Wesley. "Indian farmers and suicide: How big is the problem?" BBC News, January 22, 2013.

Sugathakumari. "Marathinu Sthuthi" [Hymn to Trees], in *Ambala Mani* [Temple Bells]. Kottayam, Kerala, India: National Book Stall, 1981, p. 127.

Tait, Malcolm. "Towers of Silence." *Ecologist,* vol. 34, no. 8 (October 2004): 14.

Tharu, Susie, and J. Ke Lalita. "Sugatha Kumari," in *Women Writing in India, Volume II: The Twentieth Century.* New York: Feminist Press at CUNY, 1993, pp. 398–401.

Thomas, Rajaji Mathew. "Kerala's Silent Revolution." Countercurrents.org, March 18, 2005.

Thomas, Shibu, Bharati Dubey, and Dhananjay Mahapatra. "1993 Bombay Bomb Blasts: Sanjay Dutt Has Little Chance of Relief." *Times of India,* March 22, 2013.

Verma, Vijay Kumar, S. K. Gupta, and Ashok Parihar. "Aluminium Phosphide Poisoning: A Challenge for the Physician." *JK Science,* vol. 1, no. 1 (January–March 2001).

Yadav, Priya. "Another Report Says 73.5% Punjab Youth Drug Addicts." *Times of India,* October 14, 2012.

Chapter Fifteen: Safe Sex

BOOKS

D'Agnes, Thomas. *From Condoms to Cabbages: An Authorized Biography of Mechai Viravaidya.* Bangkok: Post Books, 2001.

ARTICLES

Corben, Ron. "Thailand Floods Worst in Five Decades." *Voice of America,* October 2, 2011.

"Could Thailand Withstand Another Flood?" *Asia Sentinel/The Irrawaddy,* August 31, 2012.

Evans, Ben. "U.S. Condom Factory Losing U.S. Contract to Asian Companies." Associated Press, March 25, 2009.

Hunter, Elise. "Transforming Communities Through Humor, Grit and Entrepreneurship: A Conversation with Thailand's 'Mr Condom.'" *Huffington Post,* March 5, 2013. http://www.huffington post.com/student-reporter.

"Mechai Viravaidya: Using Condoms to Fight Poverty," YouTube video. Posted by Gates Foundation, April 14, 2011. http://www .youtube.com/watch?v=kCCJky_SC4U.

"Paticca-samuppada-vibhanga Sutta: Analysis of Dependent Co-arising" (SN 12.2). Translated from the Pali by Thanissaro Bhikkhu. *Access to Insight,* June 17, 2010. http://www.accesstoinsight.org/tipitaka/sn/sn12/sn12.002.than.html.

Simpkins, Dulcey. "Rethinking the Sex Industry: Thailand's Sex Workers, the State, and Changing Cultures of Consumption." *Michigan Feminist Studies,* vol. 12, 1997–1998.

Szuster, Brian W. "Shrimp Farming in Thailand's Chao Phraya River Delta: Boom, Bust and Echo." *International Water Management Institute River Basin Case Study Project,* January 2003.

"The Thai Floods, Rain, and Water Going into the Dams—Part 1." Bangkok Pundit (blog), *Asian Correspondent,* October 24, 2011. http://asiancorrespondent.com/67873/.

"The Thai Floods, Rain, and Water Going into the Dams—Part 2." Bangkok Pundit (blog), *Asian Correspondent,* November 2, 2011. http://asiancorrespondent.com/67987.

Thai Meteorological Department. "Monthly Current Report Rainfall and Accumulative Rainfall." March 2011. http://www.tmd.go.th.

Thielke, Thilo. "Thailand's Heavy Monsoons: Bangkok Evacuates as Floodwaters Rise." *Der Spiegel,* no. 44 (2011).

Viravaidya, Mechai. "The School That Flies." Qi: Global Network of Innovators video, 2010. http://www.qi-global.com/10mv.

Winterwerp, Johan C., William G. Borst, and Mindert B. de Vries. "Pilot Study on the Erosion and Rehabilitation of a Mangrove Mud Coast." *Journal of Coastal Research,* vol. 21, no. 2 (2005): 223–30.

Chapter Sixteen: Parkland Earth

BOOKS

Bongaarts, John, John Cleland, John W. Townsend, Jane T. Bertrand, and Monica Das Gupta. *Family Planning Programs for the 21st Century: Rationale and Design.* New York: The Population Council, 2012.

BIBLIOGRAPHY

Brinkley, Douglas. *The Wilderness Warrior: Theodore Roosevelt and the Crusade for America.* New York: HarperCollins Publishers, 2009.

Brown, Lester R. *Eco-Economy: Building an Economy for the Earth.* London: Earthscan Publications, 2003.

Carson, Rachel. *Silent Spring.* New York: Houghton Mifflin, 1962.

Cincotta, Richard P., Robert Engelman, and Daniele Anastasion. *The Security Demographic: Population and Civil Conflict After the Cold War.* Washington, DC: Population Action International, 2003.

Clancy, Kate. *Greener Pastures: How Grass-Fed Beef and Milk Contribute to Healthy Eating.* Cambridge, MA: Union of Concerned Scientists, 2006.

Coastal Hazards. Highlights of National Academies Reports, Ocean Science Series, Washington, DC: National Academy of Sciences, 2007.

Kean, Thomas H., Chair. *The 9/11 Commission Report: Final Report of the National Commission on Terrorist Attacks upon the United States.* Washington, DC: National Commission on Terrorist Attacks upon the United States, 2004. http://www .9-11commission.gov/ report/911Report.pdf.

Leopold, Aldo. *Game Management.* Madison: University of Wisconsin Press, 1987.

———. *A Sand County Almanac: With Essays on Conservation from Round River.* Oxford, UK: Oxford University Press, 1949.

Lynas, Mark. *Six Degrees: Our Future on a Hotter Planet.* Washington, DC: National Geographic Society, 2008.

Pimentel, David, and Marcia H. Pimentel, eds. *Food, Energy, and Society,* 3d edition. Boca Raton, FL: CRC Press, 2007.

Sanger, Alexander. *Beyond Choice: Reproductive Freedom in the 21st Century.* New York: Public Affairs, 2004.

ARTICLES

"Additional Investments in Family Planning Would Save Developing Countries More Than $11 Billion a Year." Press release, UN Population Fund (UNFPA), November 14, 2012. http://www.unfpa .org/public/home/news/pid/12601.

BIBLIOGRAPHY

"Ag 101: Major Crops Grown in the United States." U.S. Environmental Protection Agency. http://www.epa.gov/agriculture/ag101/cropmajor.html.

Arima, Eugenio Y., Peter Richards, Robert Walker, and Marcellus M. Caldas. "Statistical Confirmation of Indirect Land Use Change in the Brazilian Amazon," *Environmental Research Letters,* vol. 6, no. 2 (May 2011).

Bachelard, Michael. "Some Say Cows Are Killing the Earth. So Do We Need to Ban Beef?" *Sydney Morning Herald,* September 25, 2011.

Bamber, J. L., and W. P. Aspinall. "An Expert Judgment Assessment of Future Sea Level Rise from the Ice Sheets." *Nature Climate Change,* January 6, 2013.

Barnett, T. P., and D. W. Pierce. "When Will Lake Mead Go Dry?" *Water Resources Research,* vol. 44, issue 3 (March 2008).

Barrett, Julia R. "The Science of Soy: What Do We Really Know?" *Environmental Health Perspectives,* vol. 114, no. 6 (June 2006): A352–58.

Barthole, Jeffrey. "When Will Scientists Grow Meat in a Petri Dish?" *Scientific American,* May 17, 2011.

Bavley, Alan. "Researchers Hopeful About Male Partner for 'The Pill.'" McClatchy Newspapers, February 26, 2012.

Belluck, Pam. "Scientific Advances on Contraceptive for Men." *New York Times,* July 23, 2011.

Binkley, Dan, Margaret M. Moore, William H. Romme, and Peter M. Brown. "Was Aldo Leopold Right About the Kaibab Deer Herd?" *Ecosystems,* vol. 9 (2006):227–41.

Brean, Henry. "Concrete Trucks Rev Up for Third Intake Project at Lake Mead." *Las Vegas Review-Journal,* September 25, 2012.

Brown, J. M. "'Fresh-Squeezed Water': Desalination Debate Raises Financial, Environmental and Philosophical Concerns." *Santa Cruz Sentinel,* September 27, 2012.

Chaudhury, K., A. K. Bhattacharyya, and S. K. Guha. "Studies on the Membrane Integrity of Human Sperm Treated with a New Injectable Male Contraceptive." *Human Reproduction,* vol. 19, no. 8 (Spring 2004): 1826–30.

BIBLIOGRAPHY

Clinkenbeard, Jon. "The Best Birth Control in the World Is for Men." Techcitment .com, March 26, 2012. http://techcitement.com/culture.

Cohen, Joel E. "Meat." First Annual Malthus Lecture for Population Reference Bureau and the International Food Policy Research Institute, Washington, DC, March 2010.

Dewan, Shaila. "Georgia Claims a Sliver of the Tennessee River." *New York Times,* February 22, 2008.

Diamanti-Kandarakis, E., et al. "Endocrine-Disrupting Chemicals: An Endocrine Society Scientific Statement." *Endocrine Reviews* (2009) 30(4):293–342.

"Difference Engine: Waste Not, Want Not." *Economist,* January 20, 2012.

Doherty, Leo F., Jason G. Bromer, Yuping Zhou, Tamir S. Aldad, Hugh S. Taylor. "In Utero Exposure to Diethylstilbestrol (DES) or Bisphenol-A (BPA) Increases EZH2 Expression in the Mammary Gland: An Epigenetic Mechanism Linking Endocrine Disruptors to Breast Cancer." *Hormones and Cancer,* June 2010, 1(3):146-55

Draper Jr., William H. "Oral History Interview with General William H. Draper Jr.," by Jerry N. Hess. Harry S. Truman Library, January 11, 1972. http://www.trumanlibrary.org/oralhist/draperw.htm.

Eaton, Sam. "Antarctica Warming Raises Sea Level Rise Risk." *World,* January 28, 2013.

———. "Sea Levels May Rise Faster than Expected." *World,* December 6, 2011.

Edwards, Haley Sweetland. "From Abortion to Contraception." Latitude (blog), *New York Times,* July 20, 2012. http://latitude.blogs.nytimes .com/2012/07/20/from-abortion-to-contraception-in-georgia.

Erb, Karl-Heinz, Andreas Mayer, Thomas Kastner, Kristine-Elena Sallet, and Helmut Haberl. "The Impact of Industrial Grain Fed Livestock Production on Food Security: An Extended Literature Review." Institute of Social Ecology, February 2012. http://www .uni-klu.ac.at/socec.

BIBLIOGRAPHY

Field, Christopher. Testimony to the House Energy and Commerce Committee Climate Science Hearing, Carnegie Institution for Science, March 8, 2011.

"Finally, the Promise of Male Birth Control in a Pill: Compound Makes Mice Reversibly Infertile." ScienceDaily, August 16, 2012. http://www.sciencedaily.com/releases/ 2012/08/120816121950.htm.

Food and Drug Administration, Department of Health and Human Services. "2009 Summary Report on Antimicrobials Sold or Distributed for Use in Food-Producing Animals." Accessed at: http://www.fda.gov/downloads/ForIndustry/UserFees/AnimalDrug UserFeeActADUFA/UCM231851.pdf.

Foster, J. C. "The Deer of Kaibab: Federal-State Conflict in Arizona." *Arizona and the West,* vol. 12, no. 3 (1970): 255–68.

Goodland, Robert, and Jeff Anhang. "Livestock and Climate Change." *World Watch Magazine,* vol. 22, no. 6 (November/December, 2009): 10–19.

Gwynne, S. C. "The Last Drop." *Texas Monthly,* February 2008.

Hallmayer, Joachim, Sue Cleveland, Andrea Torres, et al. "Genetic Heritability and Shared Environmental Factors Among Twin Pairs With Autism." *Archives of General Psychiatry,* vol. 68, no. 11 (2011): 1095–102.

Hansen, James, Ken Caldeira, and Eelco Rohling. "Paleoclimate Record Points Toward Potential Rapid Climate Changes." *American Geophysical Union,* Fall Meeting (slide presentation), San Francisco, December 6, 2011. http://www.nasa.gov/pdf/ 608352ma in_AGU_paleo_final.pdf.

Harvey, Fiona. "Artificial Meat Could Slice Emissions, Say Scientists." *Guardian* (UK), June 20, 2011. http://www.guardian.co.uk/envi ronment/2011/jun/20/artificial-meat -emissions.

Hay, William W. "Could Estimates of the Rate of Future Sea-Level Rise Be Too Low?" Presentation to Geological Society of America Annual Meeting, Session No. 14, November 4, 2012.

Hertel, Thomas W., Marshall B. Burke, and David B. Lobell. "The Poverty Implications of Climate-Induced Crop Yield Changes by 2030." *Global Trade Analysis Project,* Working Paper No. 59, 2010.

Hickman, Leo. "Why I'd Happily Eat Lab-Grown Meat." *Guardian* (UK), November 30, 2009.

Hinck, J. E., V. S. Blazer, C. J. Schmitt, D. M. Papoulias, and D. E. Tillitt. "Widespread Occurrence of Intersex in Black Basses (Micropterus spp.) from U.S. Rivers, 1995–2004." *Aquatic Toxicology,* vol. 95, no. 1 (October 2009): 60–70.

Hinrichson, D., and B. Robey. "Population and Environment: the Global Challenge." *Population Reports,* series M, no. 15. Johns Hopkins University School of Public Health, Population, and Information Program, Fall 2009.

Howden, Daniel. "Toxic Chemicals Blamed for the Disappearance of Arctic Bays." *Independent,* September 12, 2007.

Hungerford, C. R. "Response of Kaibab Mule Deer to Management of Summer Range." *Journal of Wildlife Management,* vol. 34, no. 4 (October 1970): 852–62.

Joshi, Manoj, Ed Hawkins, Rowan Sutton, Jason Lowe, and David Frame. "Projections of When Temperature Change Will Exceed 2 [deg]C Above Pre-industrial Levels." *Nature Climate Change* 1, no. 8 (November 2011): 407–12.

Karman, Harvey, and Malcolm Potts. "Very Early Abortion Using Syringe as Vacuum Source." *Lancet,* vol. 300, no. 7786 (May 1972): 1051–52.

Koneswaran, G., Nierenberg, D. "Global farm animal production and global warming: impacting and mitigating climate change." *Environmental Health Perspectives,* 2008; 116: 578–582.

La Jacono, S. "Establishment and Modification of National Forest Boundaries: A Chronological Record, 1891–1973." U.S. Forest Service, Division of Engineering, 1973.

Lewis, Marlo. "House Energy and Commerce Climate Science Hearing: Is U.S. Corn Doomed?" GlobalWarming.org (blog), March 11, 2011. http://www.globalwarming .org/2011/03/11/house-energy-and -commerce-climate-science-hearing-Is-u-s-corn-doomed.

Lewis, Tanya. "Sea Level Rise Overflowing Estimates: Feedback Mechanisms Are Speeding Up Ice Melt." *Science News,* November 8, 2012.

Lobell, D. B., W. Schlenker, and J. Costa-Roberts. "Climate Trends and Global Crop Production Since 1980." *Science,* vol. 333, no. 6042 (July 2011): 616–20.

Marcott, Shaun A., Jeremy D. Shakun, Peter U. Clark, and Alan C. Mix. "A Reconstruction of Regional and Global Temperature for the Past 11,300 Years." *Science,* vol. 339, no. 6124 (March 2013): 1198–201.

Matzuk, Martin M., et al. "Small-Molecule Inhibition of BRDT for Male Contraception." *Cell,* vol. 150, no. 4 (August 2012): 673–84.

McGrath, Matt. "Climate Change 'May Shrink Fish.'" BBC World Service, September 30, 2012.

McKenna, Maryn. "Update: Farm Animals Get 80 Percent of Antibiotics Sold in U.S." *Wired,* Science Blog, December 24, 2010. http://www.wired.com/wiredscience/2010/12/news-update-farm -animals-get-80-of-antibiotics-sold-in-us.

McKibben, Bill. "Global Warming's Terrifying New Math." *Rolling Stone,* July 19, 2012.

Meinshausen, Malte, et al. "Greenhouse-Gas Emission Targets for Limiting Global Warming to 2°C." *Nature,* vol. 458: 1158–62. April 30, 2009.

Mellon, Margaret, Charles Benbrook, and Karen Lutz Benbrook. "Hogging It: Estimates of Antimicrobial Abuse in Livestock." *Union of Concerned Scientists,* January 2001. http://www.ucsusa .org/food_and_agriculture/our-failing-food-system/industrial -agriculture/hogging-it-estimates-of.html.

Nicholls, R. J., et al. "Ranking Port Cities with High Exposure and Vulnerability to Climate Extremes: Exposure Estimates." *OECD Environment Working Papers,* OECD Publishing, no. 1, November 19, 2008. http://dx.doi.org/10.1787/011766488208.

Onishi, Norimitsu. "Arid Australia Sips Seawater, but at a Cost." *New York Times,* July 10, 2010.

Parry, Wynne. "2 Degrees of Warming a Recipe for Disaster, NASA Scientist Says." *LiveScience,* December 6, 2011. http://www .livescience.com/17340-agu-climate -sensitivity-nasa-hansen.html.

Peters, Glen P., Robbie M. Andrew, Tom Boden, Josep G. Canadell, Philippe Ciais, Corinne Le Quéré, Gregg Marland, Michael R. Raupach, and Charlie Wilson. "The Challenge to Keep Global Warming Below 2 °C." *Nature Climate Change,* vol. 3 (January 2013). www.nature.com/natureclimatechange.

Philpott, Tom. "Attack of the Monsanto Superinsects." *Mother Jones,* August 30, 2011.

———. "The Meat Industry Now Consumes Four-Fifths of All Antibiotics." *Mother Jones,* February 8, 2013.

Potsdam Institute for Climate Impact Research and Climate Analytics. "Turn Down the Heat: Why a 4°C Warmer World Must Be Avoided." A report for the World Bank, November 2012. http://climatechange. worldbank.org/sites/default/files/Turn_Down_the_heat_Why_a_4 _degree_centrigrade_warmer_world_must_be_avoided.pdf.

Potts, Malcolm. "Abortion Perspectives." *The European Journal of Contraception and Reproductive Health Care,* vol. 15 (June 2010): 157–59.

———. "Global Population Growth—Is It Sustainable?" Presented to the Parliamentary and Scientific Committee, October 22, 2007. *Science in Parliament,* vol. 65, no. 1 (Spring 2008): 18–19.

Prins, Gail S. "Endocrine disruptors and prostate cancer risk." *Endocrine-Related Cancer,* vol. 15 (2008) 649–56.

Rettner, Rachael. "Steak Made from Human Excrement: Is It Safe?" MyHealth NewsDaily.com, June 17, 2011. http://www.myhealth newsdaily.com/1400-poop -meat-safety.html.

Richards, Gwendolyn. "Him or Herring? Chemicals Causing 'Gender-Bending' Fish in Alberta." *Calgary Herald,* July 29, 2010.

Roosevelt, Theodore. "A Cougar Hunt on the Rim of the Grand Canyon." *Outlook,* October 4, 1913: 259–65.

Sansoucy, R. "Livestock: A Driving Force for Food Security and Sustainable Development." *World Animal Review Series* (FAO), 1995: 5–17. http://www.fao.org/docrep/V8180T/V8180T00.htm.

Schellnhuber, Hans Joachim. "Global Warming: Stop Worrying, Start Panicking?" *Proceedings of the National Academy of Science,* vol. 105, no. 38 (September 23, 2008): 14239–40.

BIBLIOGRAPHY

Schlenker, Wolfram, and Michael J. Roberts. "Estimating the Impact of Climate Change on Crop Yields: The Importance of Nonlinear Temperature Effects." *National Bureau of Economic Research,* Working Paper No. 13799, February 2008. http://www.nber.org/papers/w13799.

————. "Nonlinear Temperature Effects Indicate Severe Damages to U.S. Crop Yields Under Climate Change." *Proceedings of the National Academy of Science,* vol. 106, no. 37 (2009): 15594–98.

Singh, Susheela, and Jacqueline E. Darroch. "Adding It Up: Costs and Benefits of Contraceptive Services—Estimates for 2012." Guttmacher Institute. http://www.guttmacher.org/pubs/AIU-2012-estimates.pdf.

Sohn, Emily. "More Hermaphrodite Fish in U.S. Rivers." *Discovery News,* September 15, 2009. http://news.discovery.com/animals/whales-dolphins.

"Soybean Demand Continues to Drive Production." Worldwatch Institute, http://www .worldwatch.org/node/5442.

"Soy Facts." Soyatech, http://www.soyatech.com/soy_facts.htm.

Squires, Rosie. "Male Pill a Step Closer to Reality." *Advertiser* (Australia), August 17, 2012.

"The State of World Population 2012." UN Population Fund (UNFPA), November 14, 2012.

Steinfeld, H., et al. "Livestock's long shadow: environmental issues and options." LEAD/FAO publication, Rome, 2006.

Tash, Joseph S., et al. "Gamendazole, an Orally Active Indazole Carboxylic Acid Male Contraceptive Agent, Targets HSP90AB1 (HSP-90BETA) and EEF1A1 (eEF1A), and Stimulates Il1a Transcription in Rat Sertoli Cells." *Biology of Reproduction,* vol. 78, no. 6 (June 2008): 1139–52.

Tavernise, Sabrina. "Farm Use of Antibiotics Defies Scrutiny." *New York Times,* September 3, 2012.

Thornton, Philip K. "Livestock Production: Recent Trends, Future Prospects." *Philosophical Transactions of the Royal Society, Biological Sciences,* vol. 365, no. 1554 (September 27, 2010): 2853–67. http://rstb.royalsocietypublishing.org/content/365/1554/2853.full.

BIBLIOGRAPHY

"The U.S. Government and International Family Planning and Reproductive Health Fact Sheet." Henry J. Kaiser Family Foundation Menlo Park (CA), with Henry J. Kaiser Family Foundation, April 2012.

Vidal, John. "One Quarter of US Grain Crops Fed to Cars—Not People, New Figures Show." *Guardian* (UK), January 22, 2010.

Weisman, Alan. "Endgame." *Dispatches,* August 2009.

———. "Three Planetary Futures." *Vanity Fair,* April 21, 2008. http://www.vanityfair .com/politics/features/2008/04/envirofutu re200804?currentPage=1.

Weiss, Kenneth R. "Tinderbox of Youth: Runaway Population Growth Often Fuels Youth-Driven Uprisings." *Los Angeles Times,* July 22, 2012.

Wilonsky, Robert. "Thanks to Drought, Houston's Drinking More of Dallas's Wastewater Than Ever Before." Unfair Park (blog), *Dallas Observer,* December 21, 2011. http://blogs.dallasobserver.com/ unfairpark/2011/12/thanks_to_drought_houstons _dri.php.

Wise, Amber, Kacie O'Brien, and Tracey Woodruff. "Are Oral Contraceptives a Significant Contributor to the Estrogenicity of Drinking Water?" *Environmental Science & Technology,* vol. 45 (2011): 51–60.

Woo, Elaine. "Creator of Device for Safer Abortions; Harvey Karman, 1924–2008." *Los Angeles Times* (obituary), May 18, 2008.

Young, C. C. "Defining the Range: Carrying Capacity in the History of Wildlife Biology and Ecology." *Journal of the History of Biology,* vol. 31, no. 1 (1998): 61–83.

Chapter Seventeen and Author's Epilogue: The World With Fewer of Us and Epilogue

BOOKS

Cincotta, Richard P., Robert Engelman, and Daniele Anastasion. *The Security Demographic: Population and Civil Conflict After the Cold War.* Washington, DC: Population Action International, 2003.

Bibliography

Cohen, Joel E. *How Many People Can the Earth Support?* New York: W. W. Norton & Company, 1995.

Ehrlich, Paul R., and Ilkka Hanski, eds. *On the Wings of Checkerspots: A Model System for Population Biology.* Oxford: Oxford University Press, 2004.

Gilding, Paul. *The Great Disruption: Why the Climate Crisis Will Bring on the End of Shopping and the Birth of a New World.* New York: Bloomsbury Press, 2011.

Klare, Michael T. *The Race for What's Left: The Global Scramble for the World's Last Resources.* London: Macmillan, 2012.

Myers, N., and J. Simon. *Scarcity or Abundance: A Debate on the Environment.* New York: W. W. Norton & Company, 1994.

Wilson, Edward O. *The Future of Life.* New York: Alfred A. Knopf, 2002.

Articles

"'233 million women' lacking contraception in 2015." Agence France-Presse, March 11, 2013.

Alkema, Leontine, et al. "National, regional, and global rates and trends in contraceptive prevalence and unmet need for family planning between 1990 and 2015: a systematic and comprehensive analysis." *Lancet,* March 12, 2013.

Ashford-Grooms, Meghan. "'Mexico City Policy' or No, U.S. Aid Can't Be Used on Abortion." *Austin American Statesman,* July 1, 2011.

"Bangladesh's Population Stands at 164.4 Million: UNFPA." *Asia Pulse,* October 21, 2010.

Barnosky, Anthony D., Elizabeth A. Hadly, Jordi Bascompte, et al. "Approaching a State Shift in Earth's Biosphere." *Nature,* vol. 486 (June 7, 2012): 52–58.

———, Nicholas Matzke, Susumu Tomiya, et al. "Has the Earth's Sixth Mass Extinction Already Arrived?" *Nature,* vol. 471 (March 2011): 51–57.

Bartoli, Gretta, Bärbel Hönisch, and Richard Zeebe. "Atmospheric CO_2 decline during the Pliocene intensification of Northern

Hemisphere glaciations." *Paleoceanography,* vol. 26, no. 4 (December 2011).

"Bay Checkerspot Butterfly: Euphydryas Editha Bayensis." EPA Endangered Species Facts. Office of Pesticide Programs, February 2010. http://www.epa.gov/espp.

"Biography: George H. W. Bush." PBS American Experience documentary series. http://www.pbs.org/wgbh/americanexperience/features/biography/bush-george.

Bonebrake, Timothy C., et al. "Avian Diversity at Jasper Ridge: Exploring Dynamics Across Habitats and Through the Decades." https://lbreapps.stanford.edu/searsville/Biology%20studies/StateofPreserve-BirdsDraft1a.pdf.

Boyce, Daniel G., Marlon R. Lewis, and Boris Worm."Global Phytoplankton Decline over the Past Century." *Nature,* vol. 466, no. 7306 (July 2010): 591–96.

Bradsher, Keith. "Rain and Snowfall Ease Drought in China." *New York Times,* March 7, 2011.

Brill, Richard. "Earth's Carrying Capacity Is an Inescapable Fact." *Honolulu Star-Advertiser,* November 5, 2010.

Bump, Philip. "The Arctic Could Be Ice-Free by 2016." *Grist,* September 18, 2012.

Cabal, Luisa. "Regressive Contraception Policies 'Failing Women' in EU." *Public Service Europe,* March 23, 2012. http://www.publicserviceeurope.com/article/1694.

Cafaro, Philip. "Climate Ethics and Population Policy." *WIREs Climate Change,* vol. 3 (2012): 45–61. doi: 10.1002/wcc.153.

Campbell, Martha. "Why the Silence on Population?" *Population Environment,* vol. 28 (2007): 237–46.

Carpenter, Stephen R. "Phosphorus: Approaching Fundamental Limits?" *Stockholm Water Front Magazine,* no. 2 (2011): 4.

Childers, Daniel L., Jessica Corman, Mark Edwards, and James J. Elser. "Sustainability Challenges of Phosphorus and Food: Solutions from Closing the Human Phosphorus Cycle." *BioScience,* vol. 61, no. 2 (2011): 117–24.

BIBLIOGRAPHY

Cincotta, Richard P., Jennifer Wisnewski, and Robert Engelman. "Human Population in the Biodiversity Hotspots." *Nature,* vol. 404 (April 27, 2000): 990–92.

Cizik, Rev. Richard, and Rev. Debra W. Haffner. "Shared Commitment to Women and Children," On Faith, *Washington Post,* March 3, 2011. http://onfaith.washingtonpost .com/onfaith/guestvoices.

"Climate Change: Local Governments Should Wait." *South Dade Matters,* February 9, 2012. http://southdadematters.com/tag/sea -level-rise.

Cohen, Susan A. "The United States and the United Nations Population Fund: A Rocky Relationship." *The Guttmacher Report on Public Policy,* vol. 2, no. 1 (February 1999).

Coleman, Les. "Alarming Climate Change Effects on FL." *Public News Service,* November 21, 2011. http://www.publicnewsservice.org/ index.php?/content/article/23338-1.

"Consumption Driving 'Unprecedented' Environment Damage: UN." Agence France-Presse. June 6, 2012.

DeFillipo, Valerie. "House Appropriations Committee Votes to Defund UNFPA." Another Blow Against Women (blog), *Huffington Post,* May 17, 2012.

Dilorenzo, Sarah. "Energy Agency Warns World Must Take Action to Greatly Reduce Emissions by 2017—or Else." Associated Press, September 9, 2011.

Ehrlich, Anne H., and Paul R. Ehrlich. "Can a Collapse of Global Civilization Be Avoided?" *Proceedings of the Royal Society: Biological Sciences,* vol. 280 (2013). http://rspb.royalsocietypublishing .org/content/280/1754/20122845.full.html#ref- list-1.

Ehrlich, Paul R., and Anne H. Ehrlich. "Letter to Barack Obama: What Needs to Be Done." Department of Biology, Stanford University, November 6, 2008.

Ehrlich, Paul R., and Raven, P. H. "Butterflies and Plants: A Study in Coevolution." *Evolution,* vol. 18 (1964): 586–608.

Engelman, Robert. "Population, Climate Change, and Women's Lives." World Watch Report 183, Worldwatch Institute, 2010.

BIBLIOGRAPHY

Financial Resource Flows for Population Activities 2009. New York: United Nations Population Fund, 2009.

Foley, Jonathan A. "Living on a New Earth." *Scientific American,* April 2010: 54–60.

———, et al. "Global Consequences of Land Use." *Science,* vol. 309 (July 22, 2005): 570–74.

———, Navin Ramankutty, Elena M. Bennett, et al. "Solutions for a Cultivated Planet: Addressing Our Global Food Production and Environmental Sustainability Challenges." *Nature,* vol. 478 (October 20, 2011): 337–42.

Food and Agriculture Organization of the United Nations. "Global Information and Early Warning System on Food and Agriculture Country Briefs: Egypt." September 6, 2012. http://www.fao.org/giews/countrybrief/country.jsp?code=EGY.

"Future Agricultural Demands for Phosphorus, a Finite and Dwindling Resource That Is Essential for Plant Growth, May Be Lower than Previously Projected." *Proceedings of the National Academy of Science,* vol. 109, no. 16 (2012). http://www.pnas.org/cgi/doi/10.1073/pnas.1113675109.

Gates, Melinda. "Let's Put Birth Control Back on the Agenda." TED video. April 2012. http://www.ted.com/talks/melinda_gates_let_s_put_birth_control_back_on_the_agenda.html.

Guttmacher Institute. "Costs and Benefits of Investing in Contraceptive Services in the Developing World." UNFPA Fact Sheet, June 2011.

Haq, Naimul. "Bangladesh Scores on Girls' Schooling." Inter Press Service, May 1, 2012.

Hardin, Garrett. "From Shortage to Longage: Forty Years in the Population Vineyards." *Population and Environment: A Journal of Interdisciplinary Studies,* vol. 12, no. 3 (Spring 1991): 339–49.

Heller, Karen. "Some Family-Planning Wisdom from Nixon." *Philadelphia Inquirer,* April 13, 2011.

Hooper, David U., E. Carol Adair, Bradley J. Cardinale, Jarrett E. K. Byrnes, Bruce A. Hungate, et al. "A Global Synthesis Reveals Biodiversity Loss as a Major Driver of Ecosystem Change." *Nature,* vol. 486 (June 2012): 105–8.

Bibliography

Horton, Tom. "Concerns over U.S. Population Growth Date Back to Nixon Era." *Chesapeake Bay Journal,* April 2012.

IAP: The Global Network of Science Academies. Statement on Population and Consumption, June 2012.

Johnson, Robert. "What the Money Spent in Iraq and Afghanistan Could Have Bought at Home in America." *Business Insider,* August 16, 2011. http://articles.businessinsider.com/2011-08-16/news.

Kareiva, Peter, and Michelle Marvier. "Conservation for the People." *Scientific American,* October 2007: 2–9.

———, Robert Lalasz, and Michelle Marvier. "Conservation in the Anthropocene." *Breakthrough Journal,* no. 2 (Fall 2011).

Kennedy, Kelly. "Drugmakers Have Paid $8 Billion in Fraud Fines." *USA Today,* March 6, 2012.

Kiel, Katherine A., Victor A. Matheson, and Kevin Golembiewski. "Luck or Skill? An Examination of the Ehrlich-Simon Bet." Research Series, Paper no. 09-08. College of the Holy Cross, Department of Economics Faculty, July 2009.

LaFranchi, Howard. "Rio+20 Earth Summit: Why Hillary Clinton Won Applause for Statement on Women." *Christian Science Monitor,* June 22, 2012. http://www.csmonitor.com/USA/Foreign-Policy/2012.

Lewis, Leo. "Scientists Warn of Lack of Vital Phosphorus as Biofuels Raise Demand." World Business, *Times* (London), June 23, 2008.

Lutz, Wolfgang, and K. C. Samir. "Global Human Capital: Integrating Education and Population." *Science,* vol. 333, no. 6042 (July 29, 2011): 587–92.

Malter, Jessica. "Trends in US Population Assistance." *Population Action International,* Guttmacher Institute, October 4, 2011. http://populationaction.org/articles.

Martin, Glen. "Taking the Heat: Bay Area Ecosystems in the Age of Climate Change." January 1, 2008. http://baynature.org/articles/taking-the-heat.

Martin, Jack, and Stanley Fogel. "Projecting the U.S. Population to 2050: Four Immigration Scenarios." A report by the Federation of

BIBLIOGRAPHY

American Immigration Reform, March 2006. http://www.fairus .org/site/DocServer/pop_projections.pdf.

"Melinda Gates' New Crusade: Investing Billions in Women's Health." *Daily Beast,* May 7, 2012.

Melnick, Meredith. "Is the Catholic Church's Argument Against IVF a Bit Holey?" Heathland.Times.com, October 8, 2010.

Moore, Malcolm, and Peter Foster. "China to Create Largest Mega City in the World with 42 Million People." *Telegraph* (UK), January 24, 2011.

Mora, Camilo, and Peter F. Sale. "Ongoing Global Biodiversity Loss and the Need to Move Beyond Protected Areas: A Review of the Technical and Practical Shortcomings of Protected Areas on Land and Sea." Marine Ecology Progress Series. doi: 10.3354/meps09214.

Moreland, Scott, Ellen Smith, and Suneeta Sharma. "World Population Prospects and Unmet Need for Family Planning." Washington, DC: Futures Group, April 2010.

Nordhaus, Ted, Michael Shellenberger, and Linus Blomqvist. *The Planetary Boundaries hypothesis: A Review of the Evidence.* Oakland, CA: The Breakthrough Institute, June 11, 2012

"Obama Administration: Health Insurers Must Cover Birth Control with No Copays." *Huffington Post,* August 1, 2011.

O'Neill Brian C., Michael Dalton, Regina Fuchs, Leiwen Jiang, Shonali Pachauri, and Katarina Zigova. "Global Demographic Trends and Future Carbon Emissions." *Proceedings of the National Academy of Sciences,* August 27, 2010.

Oppenheimer, Mark. "An Evolving View of Natural Family Planning." *New York Times,* July 9, 2011.

Oreskes, Naomi, and Conway, Erik M. "The Collapse of Western Civilization: A View from the Future." *Dædalus, the Journal of the American Academy of Arts & Sciences.* The Alternative Energy Future issue, vol. 2 (Winter 2013): 40–58.

Pimm, S. L., and P. H. Raven. "Extinction by Numbers." *Nature,* vol. 403 (February 2000): 843–45.

———, A. Peterson, Ç. H. Sekercioglu, and P. Ehrlich. "Human Impacts on the Rates of Recent, Present and Future Bird Extinctions." *Proceedings of the National Academy of Sciences,* vol. 103, no. 29 (2006): 10941–46.

"Policy Fact Sheet," The Henry J. Kaiser Family Foundation, April 2012. http://www.kff.org/globalhealth/8073.cfm.

Potts, Malcolm. "A Game-Changer Again." *Los Angeles Times,* February 20, 2012.

———. "Global Population Growth—Is It Sustainable?" Presented to the Parliamentary and Scientific Committee, October 22, 2007. *Science in Parliament,* vol. 65, no. 1 (Spring 2008): 18–19.

———, and Martha Campbell. "The Myth of 9 Billion." *Foreign Policy,* May 9, 2011.

———, and Roger Short. "The Impact of Population Growth on Tomorrow's World." *Philosophical Transactions of the Royal Society,* vol. 364, no. 1532 (October 2009): 2969–3124.

Powell, Alvin. "A Close Eye on Population Growth." *Harvard Gazette,* October 6, 2012.

Report to Prohibit Funding to the United Nations Population Fund. U.S. House of Representatives, 112th Congress, 2d session, January 17, 2012, 112–36.

"The Revenge of Malthus: A Famous Bet Recalculated." *Economist,* August 6, 2011.

"Rio+20 Conference Rejects Calls to Support Abortion, Population Control." *Catholic World News,* June 20, 2012. http://www.catholic culture.org/news.

Rockström, J., W. Steffen, K. Noone, Å. Persson, F. S. Chapin, III, E. Lambin, T. M. Lenton, M. Scheffer, C. Folke, H. Schellnhuber, B. Nykvist, C. A. De Wit, T. Hughes, S. van der Leeuw, H. Rodhe, S. Sörlin, P. K. Snyder, R. Costanza, U. Svedin, M. Falkenmark, L. Karlberg, R. W. Corell, V. J. Fabry, J. Hansen, B. Walker, D. Liverman, K. Richardson, P. Crutzen, and J. Foley. "Planetary Boundaries: Exploring the Safe Operating Space for Humanity." *Ecology and Society,* vol. 14, no. 2, Article 32 (2009).

———. "A Safe Operating Space for Humanity." *Nature,* vol. 461 (September 24, 2009): 472–75.

Sample, Ian. "Earth Facing 'Catastrophic' Loss of Species." *Guardian* (UK), July 19, 2006.

Schneider, Keith. "China's Water Crisis Threatens to Leave Economy High and Dry." *Nation* (Thailand), July 15, 2011.

Schol, John R. "The Christian Case for Environmentalism: The Confluence of Good Friday and Earth Day Is a Reminder of Our Duty to Protect God's Creation." *Baltimore Sun,* May 2, 2011. http://www.baltimoresun.com/news/opinion.

Secretariat of the Convention on Biological Diversity. *Global Biodiversity Outlook 3—Executive Summary.* Montréal, 2010.

Sethi, Nitin. "Reproductive Rights Fail to Find Mention in Rio Declaration." *Times of India,* June 22, 2012.

Shahriar, Sharif. "Bangladesh Achieves Equality in Education." *Khabar South Asia,* June 22, 2012. http://khabarsouthasia.com/en_GB/articles/apwi/articles/features/2012/ 06/22/feature-02.

Singh, S., and J. E. Darroch. *Adding It Up: Costs and Benefits of Contraceptive Services—Estimates for 2012.* New York: Guttmacher Institute and United Nations Population Fund (UNFPA), 2012.

Steffen, Will, Paul J. Crutzen, and John R. McNeill. "The Anthropocene: Are Humans Now Overwhelming the Great Forces of Nature?" *Ambio,* vol. 36, no. 8 (December 2007): 614–21.

Suckling, Kieran. "Conservation for the Real World." *Breakthrough Journal,* April 2012.

Sulat, Nate. "Feasibility Study: Reintroduction of the Bay Checkerspot Butterfly to Stanford University Lands." http://woods.stanford.edu/environmental-venture-projects/feasibility-study-reintroduction-bay-checkerspot-butterfly-stanford.

Temmerman, M., D. Van Braeckel, and O. Degomme. "A Call for a Family Planning Surge." *FVV in ObGyn,* vol. 4, no. 1 (2012): 25–29.

Tilman, David, and John A. Downing. "Biodiversity and Sustainability in Grasslands." *Nature,* vol. 367 (January 27, 1994): 363–65.

———, ———, and David A. Wedin. Letter from Scientific Correspondence in *Nature,* vol. 371 (September 8, 1994): 114.

Tilman, David, Kenneth G. Cassman, Pamela A. Matson, Rosamond Naylor, and Stephen Polasky. "Agricultural Sustainability and

Intensive Production Practices." *Nature,* vol. 418 (August 8, 2002): 671–77.

Turner, Tom. "The Vindication of a Public Scholar." *Earth Island Journal,* Summer 2009.

U.S. Environmental Protection Agency. "Nitrous Oxide Emissions," in Greenhouse Gas Emissions. Last updated: June 14, 2012. http://epa.gov/climatechange/ghgemissions.

"The U.S. Government and International Family Planning & Reproductive Health." Fact sheet, U.S. Global Health Policy, The Henry J. Kaiser Family Foundation, April 2012.

United Nations Population Fund (UNFPA) Annual Report: 2010.

United States Census Bureau. "U.S. & World Population Clocks." http://www.census .gov/main/www/popclock.

"Universal Ownership: Why Environmental Externalities Matter to Institutional Investors." Report by United Nations Environment Programme Finance Initiative, and Principles for Responsible Investment, October 2010.

Vitousek, Peter M., Harold A. Mooney, Jane Lubchenco, and Jerry M. Melillo. "Human Domination of Earth's Ecosystems." *Science,* vol. 227 (July 25, 1997): 494–99. doi: 10.1126/science.277 .5325.494.

"Why Biodiversity Matters," in *Ecosystems and Biodiversity.* Population Matters, 2011.

Wile, Rob. "America 2050: Here's How the Country Will Look Three Decades from Now." *Business Insider,* October 19, 2012. http://www.businessinsider.com.

"World Population to Hit 10 Billion, but 15 Billion Possible: UN." Agence France-Presse. October 26, 2011.

Youssef, Nancy A. "True Cost of Wars in Afghanistan, Iraq Is Anyone's Guess." McClatchy Newspapers, *Stars and Stripes,* August 15, 2011.

About the Author

ALAN WEISMAN is the author of several books, including *The World Without Us,* an international bestseller translated in thirty-four languages, a finalist for the National Book Critics Circle Award, and winner of the Wenjin Book Prize of the National Library of China. His work has been selected for many anthologies, including *The Best American Science Writing.* An award-winning journalist, his reports have appeared in *Harper's,* the *New York Times Magazine,* the *Atlantic, Discover, Vanity Fair, Wilson Quarterly, Mother Jones,* and *Orion,* and on NPR. A former contributing editor to the *Los Angeles Times Magazine,* he is a senior producer for Homelands Productions. He lives in western Massachusetts.